Lecture Notes in Computer Science 2982

Edited by G. Goos, J. Hartmanis, and J. van Leeuwen

Springer

Berlin
Heidelberg
New York
Hong Kong
London
Milan
Paris
Tokyo

Naoki Wakamiya   Marcin Solarski
James Sterbenz (Eds.)

Active Networks

IFIP-TC6 5th International Working Conference, IWAN 2003
Kyoto, Japan, December 10-12, 2003
Proceedings

 Springer

Series Editors

Gerhard Goos, Karlsruhe University, Germany
Juris Hartmanis, Cornell University, NY, USA
Jan van Leeuwen, Utrecht University, The Netherlands

Volume Editors

Naoki Wakamiya
Osaka University, Graduate School of Information Science and Technology
1-3 Machikaneyama, Toyonaka, Osaka 560-8531, Japan
E-mail: wakamiya@ist.osaka-u.ac.jp

Marcin Solarski
Fraunhofer Institute FOKUS
Kaiserin-Augusta-Allee 31, 10589 Berlin, Germany
E-mail: solarski@fokus.fraunhofer.de

James Sterbenz
University of Massachusetts, Department of Computer Science
Amherst, MA 01003, USA
E-mail: jpgs@sterbenz.org

Cataloging-in-Publication Data applied for

A catalog record for this book is available from the Library of Congress.

Bibliographic information published by Die Deutsche Bibliothek
Die Deutsche Bibliothek lists this publication in the Deutsche Nationalbibliografie;
detailed bibliographic data is available in the Internet at <http://dnb.ddb.de>.

CR Subject Classification (1998): C.2, D.2, H.3.4-5, K.6, D.4.4, H.4.3

ISSN 0302-9743
ISBN 3-540-21250-7 Springer-Verlag Berlin Heidelberg New York

Springer-Verlag is a part of Springer Science+Business Media

springeronline.com

©2004 IFIP International Federation for Information Processing, Hofstraße 3, 2361 Laxenburg, Austria
Printed in Germany

Typesetting: Camera-ready by author, data conversion by PTP-Berlin, Protago-TeX-Production GmbH
Printed on acid-free paper   SPIN: 10993163   06/3142   5 4 3 2 1 0

Preface

This volume of the LNCS series contains the proceedings of the 5th International Working Conference on Active Networks (IWAN 2003) held in the ancient cultural city of Kyoto, Japan.

This year we received 73 submissions. The increasing number indicates that Active Networks continues to be an attractive field of research. Through careful reviewing and discussion, our program committee decided to fully accept 21 papers. Three papers were conditionally accepted, and were included after shepherding by members of the technical program committee. This volume thus includes these 24 papers which were presented at IWAN 2003. Additional papers were presented in a poster session at the conference.

The best paper award went to Kenneth L. Calvert, James N. Griffioen, Najati Imam, and Jiangbo Li (University of Kentucky) for "Challenges in Implementing an ESP Service," which begins these proceedings and which began the papers in the High Performance & Network Processors session. Papers in these proceedings are organized into seven sessions: High-Level Active Network Applications, Low-Level Active Network Applications, Self-Organization of Active Services, Management in Active Networks, Experiences with Service Engineering for Active Networks, and Selected Topics in Active Networks, ranging from risk management to context-aware handover and peer-to-peer communications.

We would like to thank the technical program committee members for their hard work in reviewing papers within a very tight time schedule. We would like to thank Hiroshi Yasuda, General Chair of IWAN 2003, and other Japanese committee members for their considerable effort and support in conference organization. We also thank Hitachi, Ltd., Casio Science Promotion Foundation, and Nippon Telegraph and Telephone Corp. for their financial sponsorship, and the Special Technical Group on Active Network Technologies and Applications of the IEICE Communications Society, to which most of the Japanese committee members belong, IFIP TC6, and the IEEE ComSoc Japan Chapter for their technical sponsorship. Details on this and previous IWAN conferences are now available at www.activenets.org.

December 2003

Naoki Wakamiya
Marcin Solarski
James P.G. Sterbenz

Organization

IWAN 2003 was organized as follows. We would like to acknowledge the support of IFIP (International Federation for Information Processing), the technical support of the IEEE Communications Society Japan Chapter, and the technical support of the IEICE (Institute of Electronics, Information and Communication Engineers) Communications Society.

General Chair

Hiroshi Yasuda, University of Tokyo

General Co-chairs

Tadanobu Okada, NTT, Japan
Bernhard Plattner, Swiss Federal Institute of Technology (ETH), Zürich, Switzerland

Technical Program Committee Co-chairs

Naoki Wakamiya, Osaka University, Japan
Marcin Solarski, Fraunhofer FOKUS, Germany
James P.G. Sterbenz, University of Massachusetts, USA

Tutorial Chair

James P.G. Sterbenz, University of Massachusetts, USA

Publications Chair

Akira Kurokawa, NTT, Japan

Publicity Chair

Takashi Egawa, NEC, Japan

Local Arrangements Chair

Osamu Takada, Hitachi, Japan

Local Arrangements Committee

Hideki Otsuki, CRL, Japan
Nahoko Arai, CRL, Japan

Treasurer

Junji Fukuzawa, Hitachi, Japan

Steering Committee

Dominique Gaiti, Université de Technologie de Troyes, France
Michitaka Kosaka, Hitachi, Japan
Fumito Kubota, CRL, Japan
Eckhard Moeller, Fraunhofer FOKUS, Germany
Bernhard Plattner, ETH Zürich, Switzerland
Radu Popescu-Zeletin, Technical University Berlin, Germany
Jonathan M. Smith, University of Pennsylvania, USA
James P.G. Sterbenz, University of Massachusetts, USA

Technical Program Committee

Stephane Amarger
Thomas Becker
Samrat Bhattacharjee
Torsten Braun
Marcus Brunner
Ken Calvert
Hermann DeMeer
Andrzej Duda
Takashi Egawa
Ted Faber
Mike Fisher
Michael Fry
Alex Galis
Anastasius Gavras
Robert Haas
Toru Hasegawa

Michael Hicks
Gisli Hjalmtysson
David Hutchison
Alden W. Jackson
Andreas Kind
Yoshiaki Kiriha
Fumito Kubota
Tal Lavian
Laurent Lefèvre
John Lockwood
Thomas Magedanz
Douglas Maughan
Gary J. Minden
Akira Miura
Toshiaki Miyazaki
Sandy Murphy

Scott Nettles
Gian Pietro Picco
Bernhard Plattner
Guy Pujolle
Lukas Ruf
Nadia Shalaby
Yuval Shavitt
Jonathan M. Smith
Rolf Stadler
Christian Tschudin
Tilman Wolf
Miki Yamamoto
Krzysztof Zielinski
Martina Zitterbart

Sponsoring Institutions

Hitachi, Ltd., Tokyo, Japan
Casio Science Promotion Foundation, Tokyo, Japan
Nippon Telegraph and Telephone Corp., Tokyo, Japan

Table of Contents

Introduction

High Performance and Network Processors

High-Level Active Network Applications

Low-Level Active Network Applications

Self-Organization of Active Services

Experiences with Service Engineering for Active Networks

Management in Active Networks

Selected Topics in Active Networks

Introduction

Active Network: The Base for Content Distribution and Network Security in d-Commerce Environment

Hiroshi Yasuda

Director CCR: Center for Collaborative Research, The University of Tokyo
President cIDf: Content ID Forum

Speeding up of mobile internet bit-rate, rapid deploying of fiber accesses, and digitalization of terrestrial TV Broadcasting, by those, broadband-ubiquitous communication environment for d-Commerce (digital commerce) is coming mature very quickly. With this and advanced network function make everyone a broadcaster, namely, "Personal Broadcast". Moreover, metadata is now playing a key role in every social and business activities, thus metadata themselves are now becoming content, namely "Metadata Content". Environment above mentioned forces everyone to make content, thus we foresee that content creation and distribution would be a next carrier for industries in 21st century. Because of this ambient environment for content, particularly moving pictures, new business models of content distribution are appearing now besides conventional "On Demand Model" for entertainment content. They are "Private Distribution Model" and "Commercial Distribution Model". "Private Distribution Model" corresponds to "Personal Broadcast" and "Commercial Distribution Model" corresponds to "Metadata Content" respectively.

Most important technologies for both models are Intelligentflexible Multicast and DRM: Digital Rights Management which includes Network Security Technology as its basic infrastructure. In order to achieve above mentioned IntelligentFlexible Multicast and DRM on Secure Network, followings are the points to be considered;

1. Utilization of more collaborative Networking functions among FTTH, Mobile and Broadcast :
   By this intelligent collaboration, Metadata will become more useful and attractive. Integrated Network should support intelligent numerous multicast of metadata, so that user would be able to get any metadata on demand/push style. Active network is the best scheme to equip such functions to network easily.
2. Plug and Play of any terminal to the network :
   By this easy human-machine interface, everyone would crate and distribute their own metadata freely and efficiently through networks. Active network is again the great scheme to give such a human friendly intelligent interface.
3. Easy high speed Access to any Archive:
   Easy Networking and Plug & Play access to the network seems to give everyone the power to be a broadcaster. However, to make motion picture content from every element is impossible for non professional creator. They want to reuse elements in the archive to save time and effort to avoid struggles of making sophisticated CG elements. In this case, there should be intelligent network which understands creators' desire and connects the suitable archive where they would get the best fitted elements. Active network will give such intelligence to the network.

N. Wakamiya et al. (Eds.): IWAN 2003, LNCS 2982, pp. 1–2, 2004.
© IFIP International Federation for Information Processing 2004

4. Synchronization among ID and DRM-DB:
   To assign world unique ID to every content is said to be a big key to activate content distribution businesses. This world unique ID would point the Data Base which contains Digital Rights Information of the content of that ID. When content created and assigned the ID, the ID of this content would not change forever. On the other hand addresses of Data Bases would change because of the business activities. So how to keep the resolution (synchronization among IDs and DB addresses) is the key for world unique IDs. Active network would easily include this resolution functionality.

5. Authentication using Network Resources:
   In the mobile ubiquitous environment, authentication through the mobile terminal will become the most important matter. Circumstances for authentication through mobile terminal is not always perfect, like noise against voice authentication, humidity against finger print authentication. In such a case, position identifying function of mobile terminal would add further accuracy to authentication. Active network would help to get position, time and action information of the person to be authenticated, thus add new functionality on person authentication area.

As mentioned above, to enjoy content business century, Active network will play a key role as the infrastructure of the social life and industrial activities. We owe many on Active Network.

Challenges in Implementing an ESP Service

Kenneth L. Calvert, James Griffioen, Najati Imam, and Jiangbo Li

Laboratory for Advanced Networking
Department of Computer Science
University of Kentucky
Lexington, KY 40506
{calvert, griff, najati, jiangbo}@netlab.uky.edu

Abstract. Although active network services have been widely studied, the task of mapping these services and algorithms onto actual network hardware presents an additional set of challenges. For example, high-end routers and switches are designed to handle as many interfaces delivering packets at wire speed as possible; in such an environment decentralized processing, pipelining, and efficient synchronization are crucial for good performance. At the low end (e.g. small routers/firewalls for the home), cost and flexibility are paramount; such systems are often structured as a general-purpose processor running modular software. Thus, the two environments are different and have different goals and objectives. We present a case study based on a representative active service called Ephemeral State Processing (ESP) that highlights many of the issues that arise when mapping services to real hardware. We discuss engineering considerations for ESP in both low-end uniprocessor and higher-end network processor scenarios, and present performance measurements from both implementations.

1   Introduction

Generally speaking, the active networking community has tackled research problems that are "forward looking", focusing on the development of a new network architecture that is radically different from the status quo. With a few exceptions, active networking research has mostly been conducted using idealized platforms and environments that tend to downplay or even ignore real world constraints. Reasons for this include the need to first understand active networking technology and applications themselves, and the perceived barriers to deployment in the present Internet. Although high-level designs and frameworks are a necessary first step, active networks will not become a reality until the problem of mapping active network technology onto actual network hardware—capable of meeting real-world requirements [19]—is addressed.

Constraints related to performance, cost, management, and operation dictate that networks be composed of distinct types of routers, in different roles and with different design objectives. Even if an active network architecture were deployed tomorrow, the need for different classes of routers would not disappear.

N. Wakamiya et al. (Eds.): IWAN 2003, LNCS 2982, pp. 3–19, 2004.
© IFIP International Federation for Information Processing 2004

Consider the class of high-end backbone routers. A key design goal for these systems is performance: the ability to handle as many interfaces as possible, each delivering a highly-multiplexed stream of packets at high speed. In such an environment, decentralized parallel (per-port) processing, pipelining, and efficient synchronization of shared state (e.g. routing state) are critical. Despite the important role this router class plays in the Internet, relatively little attention has been given to the problem of mapping active network services onto such performance-oriented platforms. Indeed, many researchers believe active networking can never be viable at the core of the network, where high degrees of multiplexing are the norm, and performance is paramount.

At the other end of the spectrum are low-end routers, designed for use near the edges of the network. Their design objectives include low cost, flexibility, and ease of maintenance. Performance is less of a priority for these systems, because they may support only a handful of interfaces. Consequently, they may be structured around a general-purpose processor, with routing and forwarding functionality implemented in software. Because the actual computational cost of IP forwarding is modest, as are the line speeds supported, such systems typically have fairly meager processing capacity; this introduces new problems related to performance when they are extended to support active network technology. In addition, integration of active networking functionality into an existing modular software architecture can also be a challenge—particularly when it comes to packets creating and accessing shared state.

In this paper we present a case study of implementing an active network service on two different platforms. One platform represents the design considerations of higher-end routers, emphasizing low-level, "close to the hardware" parallel programming. The second platform represents the more cost-conscious end of the spectrum, providing a higher-level software environment that emphasizes flexibility and code re-use. We used Ephemeral State Processing (ESP) [8] as our representative active service. Like other services, it requires state at routers, executes end-system-specified code, and must handle worst-case conditions (minimum-sized packets arriving at wire speed on all interfaces). In addition to highlighting issues and lessons learned while implementing ESP in both environments, we present performance measurements that illustrate the benefits and drawbacks of each.

The remainder of the paper is organized as follows. Section 2 provides a brief overview of the Ephemeral State Processing (ESP) Service. We then describe our experiences mapping ESP onto two classes of routers in Section 3 and Section 4. Section 5 and Section 6 describe related work and offer some concluding remarks.

2   ESP: A Representative Active Network Service

Ephemeral State Processing (ESP) is a new network-level service that allows packets to create and manipulate small, fixed amounts (64 bits) of state at routers. Each piece of state has an associated *tag*, through which it can be accessed. Tags are chosen at random by users, so ephemeral state can be created and used in "one pass"—there is no separate allocation step. By using the same tag, different packets can access each others' state in the network. While other active network services (notably ANTS [18]) have had similar features, the difference with ESP is that the state maintained at routers on behalf of users is *ephemeral*: it persists for a short, fixed amount of time, and then disappears. It cannot be refreshed, so there is no need for a deallocation process. Throughout this paper we assume 10 seconds as the fixed "lifetime" of all ephemeral state.

The key consequence of this approach is that creating a piece of ephemeral state involves a *fixed resource requirement*, namely 640 bit-seconds. Given bounds on the amount of state that can be allocated per packet and on packet arrival rate, this makes it possible to determine a lower bound on the size of *Ephemeral State Store* (ESS) needed to ensure that no attempt to create a new piece of ephemeral state will ever fail. As an example, if any packet can create up to two new pieces of ephemeral state, and if at most 10^5 packets arrive per second, an ESS with capacity at least 2×10^6 pieces of ephemeral state would never overflow.

2.1 Manipulating State

To compute with the state, ESP defines a set of *instructions*, each of which defines a small, fixed-length computation that updates information in the ESS based on information in the packet, or vice versa. Each ESP packet carries exactly one instruction, plus descriptions of its operands. When execution of an instruction finishes, the packet that invoked it is either forwarded or silently dropped, depending on the instruction and the result of the computation.

A simple example of an ESP instruction is the *count-with-threshold* instruction, which increments a counter (a value with a known tag, stored in the ESS), and if the resulting value is below a threshold, the packet that invoked it is forwarded; otherwise it is dropped. This instruction is useful in a number of different computations, and can be used to implement a simple form of duplicate filtering.

2.2 Ways to Use ESP

Unlike "heavyweight" active networking services designed for arbitrary processing of packets in the network, ESP is intended mainly to implement functions of an auxiliary nature. Examples of such functions include (i) modulating packet flow based on ephemeral state (e.g. to implement congestion control in multicast applications [16]); (ii) identifying nodes in the topology with specific characteristics (e.g. branch points in an explicitly-constructed multicast tree [17]); and (iii) processing small amounts of user data to improve scalability (e.g. consolidating receiver feedback in a large multicast application [8]).

Most computations take place in two phases, which we refer to generically as *setup* and *collect*. The setup phase generally distributes some information to the nodes involved in the computation; in the collect phase, some function over that information is computed and delivered to a controlling end system.

2.3 Designing for Wire-Speed Processing

If we want active services like ESP to operate at IP-like processing speeds, it is worth considering the techniques that are used in modern routers to achieve high-speed IP forwarding, namely *parallelism* and *pipelining*.

Modern high-speed routers consist of a collection of interface cards connected by a high-speed switching mechanism. The goal for such routers is to maximize aggregate packet-forwarding capacity, i.e. to interconnect as many high-speed interfaces as possible. The basic technique used to achieve this scaling is parallel processing: The forwarding lookup required for each packet is performed on the interface card at which the packet arrives. The result of this lookup determines the output card to which the packet must be switched, and the packet is then switched to that card. In addition, each port card may have multiple packet-processing engines, so that packets are processed in parallel even within a card.

One of the main challenges in fast IP forwarding is *memory latency*. At 10Gbps rates, a minimum-sized packet arrives about every 10–12 nanoseconds—far less than the time required for a *single* memory access for commodity DRAM. Obviously it is necessary to minimize the number of accesses to DRAM required per packet. Because routing tables are large enough to require the use of such relatively slow RAM technology, high-speed routers also rely on techniques such as *pipelining* to hide latency. Parallelism and pipelining are feasible because each IP datagram is handled independently of others; the only constraint is that processing should *preserve the ordering of packets belonging to the same flow*, where "flow" generally refers to packets traveling between the same pair of hosts. Assigning packets to forwarding engines based on a hash of their source and destination addresses is sufficient to ensure that this constraint is satisfied.

For ESP, the only constraints required for correctness of the service are:

1. Packets belonging to the same computation must access the same state store.
2. Packets belonging to the same computation must not be reordered.
3. Instructions accessing the same state store must appear to be executed atomically with respect to that store.

It follows that packets belonging to different computations may be processed in parallel, and indeed, may access different state stores. Thus, per-port implementations are feasible. In fact, we can use parallel implementations with *separate ESS's* on the same port card, so long as we can ensure that packets belonging to the same computation are processed using the same ESS.

Unlike IP, however, source and destination addresses are neither necessary nor sufficient to determine whether packets belong to the same computation. The ESP wire encoding therefore includes two important fields—the *Computation ID* and the *Processing Location Designator*—which are controlled by the user to ensure that the above constraints can be satisfied if ESP is implemented in a per-port, parallel processing architecture. Packets belonging to the same ESP computation must carry the same *Computation ID* value, and must be processed in the same ESS context.

The *Processing Location Designator* is necessary because a packet passes through two different port cards—input and output—on the way through a router. For some computations, processing needs to occur on the *input* side of the router, so that packets going to different destinations, and thus potentially leaving by different output port cards, can share state. (Identification of multicast branch points is one such case.) In other cases, packets going to the same destination from potentially different sources (input ports) need to be processed together, so the processing should happen on the output port. The application code at the user's host sets the location bits to control the processing location of each ESP packet. As long as these constraints are satisfied, implementors are free to subdivide Ephemeral State Stores as needed to improve efficiency.

In the next section, we describe our implementation, and how the parallelization and latency-hiding techniques that work for IP forwarding can also be used with ESP.

3   Case Study 1: Supporting High-Performance Active Services

A key objective of high-performance (backbone) routers is the ability to *handle packets at wire-speeds on as many interfaces as possible*. To achieve this level of performance, current (non-programmable) high-speed routers perform packet processing in hardware using application-specific integrated circuits (ASICs). This approach has been highly successful, producing routers that can switch millions of packets per second. However, the approach relies on immutable, special-purpose logic circuits to achieve high performance. The goal of active networks, on the other hand, is to allow end systems to define the processing on-the-fly (at runtime).

To address this issue, several vendors [10,2] have introduced *network processors* that can be programmed to perform packet processing, often in parallel. In some cases, the processing elements are general-purpose processors [1,6]. In other cases, the processing elements offer instructions specifically-designed to assist in packet processing [13,2]. However, in both cases, the packet processing is software-driven and can be modified on-the-fly (at least in principle). To achieve high-speed packet processing, many network processors support multiple processing elements executing in parallel.

Our case study uses the Intel IXP 1200 network processor as our development platform [10,13]. The IXP 1200 is designed for high-performance, deep packet processing, and has general characteristics similar to those of other network processors such as programmability, multiple processing engines, and a multi-level memory hierarchy. Consequently, we expect that insights derived from our experience with the IXP 1200 can be applied to other network processor platforms as well.

3.1 The IXP 1200 Network Hardware

The Intel IXP 1200 network processor is designed to facilitate the deployment of
new value-added services simply by changing the software program. To achieve
line-rate routing/switching, the IXP 1200 supports parallel packet processing on
a set of six processors called *micro-engines*. The architecture is shown in Figure 1.

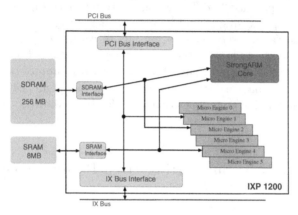

Fig. 1. IXP 1200 architecture

The main processor, called the *core*, is a 233 MHz StrongArm processor. The
StrongArm core is not intended to be involved in normal data packet processing.
It is primarily used for control functions; we do not discuss it further.

The key feature of the architecture for our purposes is the six on-chip micro-
engines each supporting four *hardware threads*. Each of the micro-engines is
individually programmable and supports a set of hardware instructions specifically designed for packet processing. The Intel IXP 1200 "Bridalveil" board we
used supports four 100 Mbps Ethernet ports connected to the IXP 1200 via a
104 MHz IX bus. Like other network processors, the IXP 1200 uses a multi-level
memory hierarchy consisting of registers, SRAM, and SDRAM. Register storage
is the least plentiful (32 registers per thread context), but is the fastest. The
SRAM is next fastest (and smallest), while SDRAM is slowest and most capa-
cious. Our boards were equipped with 8 MB of SRAM accessed via a 32-bit 233
MHz bus, along with 256 MB of SDRAM accessed via a 64-bit 116 MHz bus.

To help hide the memory access latencies of SRAM and SDRAM, each micro-
engine has four hardware threads, each with its own set of context registers.
Memory interfaces are pipelined, and switching contexts among these threads
is almost free; the result is that when one thread issues a RAM read or write
(and thus incurs a long wait), another thread can typically begin executing
immediately. To synchronize between threads, each micro-engine also supports
a set of CAM locks that can be used to ensure mutual exclusion when necessary.
If mutual exclusion or synchronization is needed between micro-engines, it must
be implemented using shared memory (SRAM).

3.2   Mapping ESP to the IXP 1200

To achieve the desired level of performance, we defined a set of design goals for our IXP 1200 implementation:

- **Maximize Parallelism/Minimize Synchronization Overhead.**
- **Minimize Memory Accesses.** Map data structures to storage so that ESS information can be retrieved with as few accesses as possible.
- **Maximize ESS Capacity.** Use memory efficiently.
- **Maintain ESP Semantics.** Maintain the ordering and sharing constraints described above.
- **Continuous Operation.** In order to flush expired values from the ESS, a *cleaner* function is required that examines the ESS, compares the current time against the expiry time, and reclaims the location if the timer expired. This process should not interfere with data packet processing.

Parallelizing ESP. To achieve parallelism, we distribute the ESP processing across the set of IXP micro-engines. Intel's standard micro-engine assignments uses micro-engine 0 for ingress processing (from all interfaces), and micro-engine 5 for egress processing (to all interfaces). Although ingress/egress can, in theory, be done on any micro-engine, Intel discourages this—developing one's own code to read from the IX bus is known to be tricky and error prone. As a result, we only distribute the processing across micro-engines 1-4. Micro-engine 0 serves as the ingress processor and packet dispatcher (based on the computation ID as we will see below). Micro-engine 5 collects all outgoing packets and enqueues them for transmission.

Because we want the ESS to be as large as possible, we store the ESS data itself (tags and values) in SDRAM. Although SDRAM has the highest read/write latency of any of the IXP 1200's storage areas, it is only a bit higher than the latency of the SRAM, and it offers significantly larger capacity. Smaller auxiliary data structures (hash tables) are stored in SRAM for speed.

Related to the issue of where the ESS should be located is the question of "how many ESS's should there be". As described earlier, ESP requires at least one ESS per network interface. This is particuarly helpful when line-cards are independent from one another with no shared memory between them. There are advantages, however, to having more ESS's per interface. First, partitioning computations into different ESS's reduces the number of tags per ESS, thereby reducing the probability of tag collisions. Second, reclamation of expired data requires synchronization between the cleaning thread and the packet-processing threads; on the IXP1200, synchronization across micro-engines is more expensive than between threads on the same micro-engine. Therefore in our design, each micro-engine has its own ESS, used exclusively for packets processed by that micro-engine. To ensure that packets are processed in the correct ESS context, we use a hash of the computation ID to assign packets to ESSs.

Given our choice of SDRAM for the ESS, the next challenge was masking its read/write access latency, given that each instruction requires at least one read/write access to memory. Fortunately the IXP 1200 provides good support for this. As noted above, the micro-engine hardware threads allow pipelining to be implemented transparently: When one thread blocks waiting for a memory access another can immediately begin executing until it too blocks and hands off control to a third thread, etc. Although each individual read or write suffers the standard SDRAM latency, when pipelined in this way, the micro-engine is able to process multiple packets simultaneously.

Concurrent processing by multiple threads raises several interesting issues. First, to ensure that packets from the same computation are not processed concurrently by different threads while allowing parallelism, the packet demultiplexing code dispatches all packets having the same computation id to the same one of four input queues (not just the same micro-engine). Each thread can service any input queue; however, we use local thread synchronization techniques to ensure that no two threads work on the same queue at the same time. Second, given the challenges of synchronizing multiple concurrent threads, it might make sense to further subdivide the ESS into subESS's, with one subESS per thread. The downside of this approach is that memory can become fragmented, wasting valuable ESS space. Although it would simplify synchronization, we decided to stick with a single ESS per micro-engine (shared by all threads).

To support continuous operation of the router, we used one thread on each micro-engine as a *cleaner thread*, reclaiming expired (tag,value) pairs from the ESS. Because the cleaner examines and modifies the state of the ESS, there is potential for interference between it and a normal ESP instruction being executed concurrently by another thread. To address this issue we designed an efficient synchronization method that allows ESS accesses by both the cleaner and instruction-processing threads to be interleaved with minimal synchronization. The basic idea is this: every time a thread starts accessing the ESS, it sets a bit in a global "active threads" register indicating that is is "currently using an entry in the store". When a thread finishes an instruction, it unsets the bit. When the cleaner finds an expired entry, it does not remove it. Instead, it simply makes the entry inaccessible to any *new* ESP instructions, by removing its tag from the list of active tags. ESP instructions that are already in progress can continue to read and write the value until they complete (at which point they unset their bit in the "active threads" register). By monitoring the "active threads" register, the cleaner thread knows when an entry is no longer in use and can be safely deallocated. As a result, the cleaner runs in the background, concurrent with the instruction processing threads.

In order to focus as much of the IXP 1200 board's processing power on ESP as possible, we implemented ESP in the form of an external "pass-through" unit, which sits next to a conventional router, processing packets as they enter/exit on two of the router's ports. The idea is that all packets passing in/out of the router pass through the ESP box (just as they would in a port-card-based implementation in the router). This approach allows us to add ESP transparently to existing infrastructure without modification. Among other advantages, this makes it possible to deploy ESP incrementally. The *Location* field in the ESP packet indicates whether processing should be applied on the input or output side, or both. Because a single micro-engine can support multiple lines running at full-speed, one IXP 1200 board is all that is needed to turn a cisco router with several ports into an ESP-enable router.

3.3   Performance Results

To measure the performance of our ESP implementation, we used the network configuration shown in Figure 2.

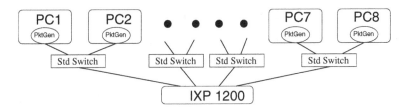

Fig. 2. Test network configuration.

Eight PCs were used to drive the IXP 1200: Two PCs were connected (via a standard switch) to each of the four (full-duplex) Ethernet ports. To generate traffic, we modified the Linux *pktgen* program to send ESP packets at various speeds. The pktgen throughput can be measured both in terms of bandwidth (Mbps) and packets per second. Because we are primarily interested in the number of packets per second that can be handled by the router, we configured pktgen to send minimum-sized packets (64 byte packets) in all our experiments. It should be noted that when using minimum-sized packets, pktgen was not able to saturate a 100 Mbps link to the IXP 1200; 62 Mbps was the maximum attainable rate. Consequently, we used two PCs to drive each IXP line. Even then, we only achieved a maximum rate of 76.25 Mbps per IXP line, because Ethernet cannot run faster than that when using minimum-size packets (due to the interpacket gap and other packet overhead). Thus the total offered load we were able to generate was (76.25 Mbps × 4 lines) = 305 Mbps.

To measure the overhead of ESP processing, we instrumented the IXP 1200 code to record the number of micro-engine clock cycles needed to perform a **count-with-threshold** ESP instruction. As a baseline, we measured the number of cycles it took to complete a single **count-with-threshold** (creating a new tag) using only a single thread (i.e., *no* pipelining of SDRAM reads/writes via multiple threads). The SDRAM read/write time dominated, consuming approximately 750 cyles out of the total of 1100 needed to complete the instruction. When the single thread also had to perform the cleaning, the achievable throughput was roughly 212K **count-with-threshold** instructions per second, or 108 Mbps.

We then measured the throughput with multiple threads. All threads executed on the same micro-engine, so there was no direct increase in parallelism; however, the use of multiple threads resulted in overlapping SDRAM accesses, hiding (at least some of) the latency of reading and writing. To generate enough traffic to keep the threads busy, all eight PCs simultaneously transmitted minimum-sized packets as fast as possible. Each packet carried a **count-with-threshold** instruction; 50% of the packets created a new tag, and 50% simply incremented an existing tag.

Table 1. Throughput of a single micro-engine, with and without cleaner-assist.

No Cleaner-assist	
No. Threads	Throughput
1	234 Kpps = 120 Mbps
2	420 Kpps = 215 Mbps
3	547 Kpps = 280 Mbps

With Cleaner-assist	
No. Threads	Throughput
1	212 Kpps = 108 Mbps
2	410 Kpps = 210 Mbps
3	507 Kpps = 260 Mbps
4	564 Kpps = 290 Mbps

Table 1 shows the throughput, both in packets per second and megabits per second, for 1, 2, and 3 threads. The fourth thread is the cleaner. The "No Cleaner-assist" table shows performance when the cleaner does nothing but clean. The "With Cleaner-assist" table shows performance when the cleaner uses its spare cycles to assist with packet processing. Clearly, at lower loads, the cleaner has more cycles to assist with packet processing than at high loads, and the throughput with one packet-processing thread plus the cleaner assist is comparable to the throughput with two packet-processing threads. Recall that the maximum achievable throughput (with minimum-size packets) is 305 Mbps due to Ethernet limitations. With three threads (plus the cleaner in its spare time) processing packets, the IXP comes within 5% of the full 305 Mbps. In fact, when we changed the mix of instructions so that all packets carry the same tag, the IXP operated at the optimal 305 Mbps rate. Note that this level of performance is achieved with only *a single micro-engine* doing packet processing.

To measure the impact the size of the ESS has on throughput, we measured the rate of successful completion of instructions under various transmission rates and ESS sizes. This experiment also tested the performance of the cleaner thread—if the cleaner thread is unable to free entries in a timely fashion, throughput will be affected. Figure 3 shows the average throughput (number of completed operations per second) over three runs, for increasing ESS sizes. For small ESS sizes, the ESS fills up quickly causing all subsequent ESP packets to be aborted until space can be reclaimed from expiring entries. The result is a limit on throughput that increases linearly with the size of the store. This allows us to pre-compute the store size needed to support any given line rate.

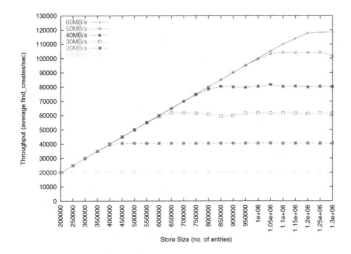

Fig. 3. Avg throughput as a function of store size.

4 Case Study 2: A Modular Software ESP Implementation

Not all routers emphasize performance and scalability as their primary design constraints. Many of the non-core routers in the Internet interconnect only a few networks at modest speeds; for them, wire-speed forwarding is achievable using simpler techniques. The last few years have seen a proliferation of "broadband router/gateway" products that offer bundled functionality in a simple, inexpensive package targetted at homes and small offices [3,5,4]. The design considerations for such routers are quite different from those of the high-end routers; instead of performance and parallelization, these systems focus on robustness, flexibility, and minimizing cost. Moreover, what differentiates these products are their features; the ability to add or change features easily is therefore an important design goal for these systems.

For these routers, a modular software design is of course desirable. By coding the services in software (as opposed to hardware), changes can be made and distributed very easily. Also, designing the software in a modular fashion, with well-defined functional interfaces between components, allows new services to be incorporated quickly, leveraging existing code thereby reducing the size of the code footprint.

In this section we describe an implementation of ESP for *click*, a modular software router.

4.1   The Click Modular Router Platform

Click [11] is a fine-grained modular software approach for implementing routers that need to offer advanced packet-processing features; as such, it is ideal for our purposes.

Click uses the Linux kernel as a base platform, with low-level modifications to handle hardware devices via polling instead of interrupts; this improves click's performance under heavy loads. The basic paradigm of click is to decompose router functionality into small functions that can be performed more or less independently, and encapsulate them in individual modules called *elements*. Elements are organized into a graph according to packet flow; each element consumes packets from *input ports* and emits them on *output ports*. The user controls packet-processing functionality by configuring paths in the graph to include the desired sequences of elements.

Click comes equipped with predefined elements for standard IP processing, including header validation, TTL decrement, packet classification, etc. A standard configuration graph for an IP router with two interfaces is shown (in solid boxes) in Figure 4.

Click does not provide any explicit support for pipelining or parallel processing of packets; the version we used has a single thread and is appropriate for general-purpose uniprocessors (PCs), whose architecture does a reasonable job of hiding memory latency without explicit intervention by the programmer.

4.2   Implementation Considerations for ESP in Click

The first question to be answered in implementing ESP on the click platform is how to modularize it. The click philosophy is for modules to be small and simple; this would suggest separate modules to validate the ESP header, retrieve values from the ESS, execute ESP instructions, and classify packets. This approach has advantages with respect to understandability, maintainability, and reuseability of code. However, a highly-decomposed implementation raises other issues.

Probably the biggest issue is that of support for modules that share state. The usual method of sharing state in click is to *annotate* the packet with the state necessary for its processing; information created by one module travels with the packet. This capability is used, for example, in Click's ICMP implementation to detect and send a redirect message if a packet goes out the same interface it came in on. However, when information needs to be shared among multiple packets *and* multiple modules (as would be the case in a highly-decomposed ESP), additional synchronization mechanisms are needed. Inter-module synchronization can hurt performance, and also complicates the code—thereby offsetting some of the benefits of small modules.

Another possibility is to define an ESS module that exports methods to create, retrieve and update values. However, such methods must be explicitly named in the importing modules; this complicates things when there may be multiple instances of the exporting modules (say, input, output and centralized ESS contexts).

It is worth noting that IP packet processing generally does not require much state-sharing across different functions, and where functions do need to share persistent state, the standard click approach seems to be to encapsulate the functionality in a module (e.g. RoutingLookup and ARPRequest). We took the same approach, and implemented most of the ESP functionality, including instruction execution and state store management, in a single module called *ESPExec*. Some of the benefits of modularity are given up this way, but probably not too many. For example, it is not clear that there is much need for re-use of functional modules within ESP. In addition, the standard composition technique in click has well-known performance costs, and an integrated implementation avoids them.

A second issue is whether and how to implement multiple ephemeral state store contexts per interface. As noted in Section 2, the ESP implementation must ensure that packets with the same computation ID are executed in the same ESS context. To achieve this, it is of course sufficient to implement a single large store and use it for all ESP packets. In a single-threaded uniprocessor implementation with ample memory, there is little performance penalty for doing this, although it slightly increases the probability of tag collision. It avoids any need for synchronization between packets at all.

However, it turns out that separate ESSs *are* necessary for different interfaces. The reason: some global computations associate different semantics with the different processing locations. The best example is when ESP is used to implement *subcasting*, i.e. forwarding packets along a subtree of an existing multicast tree. The idea is that the branches of the tree on which the packets should be forwarded are marked (during the setup phase) with ephemeral state; when a data packet comes along (carrying a *piggybacked* ESP instruction), it checks for the presence of the state, and drops the packet if it is not present. This dropping needs to happen on the *outgoing* interfaces, i.e. after a packet has been duplicated in a router. In a router in which all ESP locations share a single ESS, all branches of the tree leaving that router would get marked if any one of them is marked, and thus subcasting would not be effective.

Thus, we need to implement a separate ESS for each interface on the router. However, there does not seem to be any reason for further subdivision, so our implementation only implements an ESS for each port, plus a "centralized" ESS.

The design of our click ESP implementation is shown in Figure 4.

4.3   Performance Measurements

We report measured performance of our ESP implementation to demonstrate that adding ESP processing to the click path does not result in an unreasonable additional delay. The version we used in our evaluation ran as a Linux Kernel module, executing on a standard Pentium 4 processor with five 10/100 Mbps ethernet ports. (Note that this is a reasonable approximation of the configuration of routers used in low-end home/small business configurations.)

The click authors report the time to process an IP packet is roughly 2900 ns on a PIII running at 700 MHz for a total forwarding rate of 345 Kpps [11]. To baseline our system, a P4 running at 1.8GHz, we reran the same experiment as

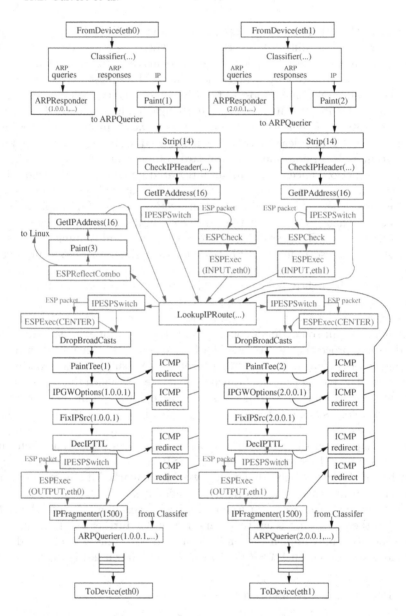

Fig. 4. Router configuration with ESP

the click authors, and found the time to process an IP packet to be roughly 1300 ns for a total forwarding rate of 765 Kpps. Given this base-level performance, we are able to gauge the overhead required by ESP.

The additional ESP processing cost depends on the ESP instruction. The **count-with-threshold** and **compare** instructions are only 55% more costly

Table 2. Added cost of ESP processing.

count	compare	collect	rcollect
660 ns	702 ns	1064 ns	1525 ns

than standard IP processing. The ESP **collect** instuction, on the other hand, involves more tags and thus increases the overhead by 81%. For the more complex **rcollect**, the overhead is about 116%. Although the overhead is substantial, the worst case throughput (with minimum sized packets) is still 354 Kpps or 181 Mbps, which is sufficient to keep all lines on a home router busy.

5   Related Work

Numerous active network platforms have been developed, with varying degrees of (re)programmability. The FPGA-based programmable port card developed at Washington University in St. Louis is an example of a hardware platform whose data-path behavior can be controlled reprogramming the on-board FGPAs [15]. By loading a new bitfile into the FPGA, almost arbitrary processing functions can be defined; the platform includes commonly-used functions and "glue" for connecting modules together. This hardware-based approach provides very high performance for simple functions that need to be applied to packets on the fast path at specific (known) points in the network.

A language-oriented approach that features provably-bounded resource requirements is SNAP [14]. SNAP permits simple, straight-line programs to be carried in packets, allowing users to define the processing applied to their packets. Unlike ESP, SNAP is designed to replace IP as the network layer.

NetBind [9], from the Genesis project at Columbia University, is a tool supporting dynamic construction of datapaths in a network processor. NetBind is based on general ideas and intended to be used on any network processor, though the current design is tailored to the layout of the IXP1200. While NetBind is not an approach to injecting programmability into the network, it addresses one of the most difficult and important parts of programming network processors: dynamic composition of datapaths. By modifying the code store on an IXP1200 microengine at run time, NetBind creates pipelines dynamically according to each packet's needs.

Each of these systems is designed to allow reprogramming on-the-fly, at timescales varying from per-packet (SNAP) to configuration time (DHP). ESP, however, supports a different form of programmability, in which the set of processing options is fixed, but they can be invoked in different orders.

We are aware of few efforts to deploy active network technology on production platforms. The ABone [7], or Active Networks backbone, was a testbed composed of overlay nodes running a software-based active network platform, and supporting a variety of execution environments. Most of the approximately

100 nodes of which the ABone was composed were general-purpose PCs running a variant of the Unix operating system.

Another effort [12] defined an interface on a Nortel router by which processing (e.g. encryption) for particular flows could be configured and turned on and off under user control.

6   Conclusions

We have described two implementations of the Ephemeral State Processing service on real router platforms, together with some of the engineering considerations that went into them.

Our implementation for the Intel IXP1200 was intended to demonstrate that the design goals for ESP were achieved, i.e. that it can be processed at rates comparable to those achievable for IP packets, given suitable hardware support. Our measurements show that store capacity is the limiting factor on throughput of ESP packets when servicing 100 Mbps Ethernet links. Given the modest processing power of the IXP1200, we believe this number can easily scale up to line rates in the gigabits per second for next-generation network processor platforms, which feature both higher-speed engines and greater parallelism. Our results show that ESP can indeed take advantage of additional parallelism to hide memory latency, which decreases much more slowly than processor cycle times.

Our experience with the click software router platform highlights some of the challenges of modularizing active services that involve state-sharing between packets. Our design is well-suited for a uniprocessor router platform. In the future, we will investigate how well it could be mapped onto a multiprocessor architecture. Although the basic click router design seems consistent with the kind of pipelining and parallelism that would be possible on a multiprocessor, as we have noted IP forwarding does not require inter-packet state management. Meanwhile the question of which is better suited for such an environment, a monolithic approach like ours, or a fully-decomposed modular implementation, remains open for now.

It should be noted that measurements of both of our implementations show that achievable throughput rates for ESP processing are comparable to those for IP. This supports our claim that ESP is "IP-like" in terms of its resource requirements. However, because ESP packets are also IP packets, they must undergo *both* types of processing. Thus adding ESP should no more than double the per-packet processing cost. Our click measurements confirm this; it seems a reasonable price to pay for the added flexibility provided by the service.

References

1. BCM4702 airforce wireless network processor, September 2003.
   http://www.broadcom.com/products/4702.html.
2. IBM PowerNP network processor, August 2003.
   http://www.zurich.ibm.com/cs/network%5Fproc%5Fhw/index.html.
3. The Linksys WRT54G Wireless-G broadband router, September 2003.
   http://www.linksys.com/products/product.asp?grid=33&scid=35&prid=508.
4. Linux-based routers and switches, September 2003.
   http://www.linuxdevices.com/articles/AT2005548492.html.
5. US Robotics model 8200 router, September 2003.
   http://www.linuxdevices.com/articles/AT4486854045.html.
6. Vitesse eq 2000 network processor, September 2003.
   http://www.vitesse.com/products/categories.cfm?family%5Fid=5&category%5Fid=16.
7. S. Berson, B. Braden, and S. Dawson. Evolution of an active networks testbed. In
   DARPA Active Network Conference and Exhibition (DANCE) 2002, May 2002.
8. K. Calvert, J. Griffioen, and S. Wen. Lightweight network support for scalable
   end-to-end services. In *ACM SIGCOMM 2002*, August 2002.
9. A. Campbell, S. Chou, M. Kounavis, V. Stachtos, and J. Vicente. Netbind:
   A binding tool for constructing data paths in network processor-based routers.
   http://www.comet.columbia.edu/genesis/netbind/overview/netbind.pdf.
10. Intel Corporation. The IXP1200 Hardware Reference Manual, August 2001.
11. E. Kohler et al. The click modular router. *ACM Transactions on Computer
    Systems*, 18(3):263–297, 2000.
12. T. Lavian et al. Enabling active flow manipulation in silicon-based network for-
    warding engines. In *DARPA Active Network Conference and Exhibition (DANCE)
    2002*, May 2002.
13. Erik J. Johnson and Aaron Kunze. *IXP-1200 Programming*. Intel Press, 2002.
14. Jonathan T. Moore, Michael Hicks, and Scott Nettles. Practical Programmable
    Packets. In *IEEE INFOCOM*, Anchorage, AK, April 2001.
15. D. Taylor, J. Turner, J. Lockwood, and E. Horta. Dynamic hardware plugins (dhp):
    Exploiting reconfigurable hardware for high-performance programmable routers.
    Computer Networks, 38(3):295–310, February 2002.
16. S. Wen, J. Griffioen, and K. Calvert. CALM: Congestion-aware layered multi-
    cast. In *IEEE Conference on Open Architectures and Network Programming (Ope-
    nArch)*, 2002.
17. Su Wen, James Griffioen, and Kenneth Calvert. Building Multicast Services from
    Unicast Forwarding and Ephemeral State. In *IEEE OpenArch 2001*, Anchorage,
    AK, April 2001.
18. David J. Wetherall, John V. Guttag, and David L. Tennenhouse. ANTS: A Toolkit
    for Building and Dynamically Deploying Network Protocols, 1998.
19. Tilman Wolf and Jonathan Turner. Design issues for high performance active
    routers. *IEEE Journal on Selected Areas of Communications*, 19(3), March 2001.

The Role of Network Processors
in Active Networks*

Andreas Kind, Roman Pletka, and Marcel Waldvogel

IBM Zurich Research Laboratory
CH–8803 Rüschlikon, Switzerland
{ank,rap,mwl}@zurich.ibm.com

Abstract. Network processors (NPs) implement a balance between
hardware and software that addresses the demand of performance and
programmability in active networks (AN). We argue that this makes
them an important player in the implementation and deployment of ANs.
Besides a general introduction into the relationship of NPs and ANs, we
describe the power of this combination in a framework for secure and
safe capsule-based active code. We also describe the advantages of of-
floading AN control point functionality into the NP and how to execute
active code in the data path efficiently. Furthermore, the paper reports
on experiences about implementing active networking concepts on the
IBM PowerNP network processor.

1   Introduction

The ongoing convergence of voice, broadcast, and data networks leads to a demand for a novel flexible and high-performance packet-forwarding technology.
Flexibility is needed for short development cycles and for the support of evolving protocols and standards, combined with the shift towards high-performance
packet handling [25] due to the increasing bandwidth demands. Today, packet
handling is performed by application-specific integrated circuits (ASICs), field-
programmable gate arrays (FPGAs), or general-purpose processors (GPPs).
While ASICs have clear advantages in terms of performance, the hardware functions do not provide sufficient flexibility. In contrast, packet forwarding based
on GPPs provides high flexibility, but insufficient performance because GPPs
were not designed with packet forwarding in mind. Finally, FPGAs can be reprogrammed at gate level, combining features from ASICs and GPPs [18]. However,
high-level programmability of FPGAs still is very limited despite improvements
of the level of abstraction [5].

Network processors (NPs) are specifically designed processors for combined
fast *and* flexible packet handling [11]. Typically pairing an embedded processor
complex with application-specific instructions and coprocessor support, NPs can
achieve even higher-layer packet processing at line speeds of several Gb/s. Besides the instruction set, the entire design focuses on high-performance packet

---

* An earlier, shorter version of this paper was presented at ANTA 2002 [15]

N. Wakamiya et al. (Eds.): IWAN 2003, LNCS 2982, pp. 20–31, 2004.
© IFIP International Federation for Information Processing 2004

processing, including memory, hardware accelerators, bus, and I/O architecture. NPs are well suited for most packet-processing tasks, ranging from content switching, load balancing, traffic conditioning, network security, and terminal mobility to active networks [11,4]. This paper focuses on the specific role of NPs in ANs.

Recent work has resulted in secure and manageable AN approaches [20,3,6]. This paper argues that the remaining performance concerns can be addressed with NPs because their balance between hardware and software efficiently addresses the demand for high data-path performance without sacrificing programmability.

The remainder of the paper is structured as follows. The next section introduces NP architectures and their potential applications. The general benefits of NPs for implementing ANs are described in Section 3. The specific advantages of a concrete AN framework are shown in Section 4, and our experience from its implementation is presented in Section 5.

2   Network Processor Architectures

The main goal of NPs is to provide high processing power and fast packet-oriented I/O, the latter being one of the key GPP bottlenecks. As a typical result, on-chip memory is small due to chip area constraints, arithmetic units are much simpler compared to GPPs and high speed is achieved through parallel packet processing by multiple threads in order to hide memory latencies. In addition, common packet-handling functions, such as prefix matching, classification, metering, policing, checksum computation, interrupt and timer handling, bit manipulation, and packet scheduling, are frequently supported by dedicated hardware units. Moreover, NPs are often teamed with an embedded GPP for more complex tasks [4].

Depending on the location in the network (i.e., edge or core), NP architectures differ in terms of hardware design. The bus architecture as well as the size and type of memory units vary considerably. Edge-type NPs are better equipped for intelligent and stateful packet processing, whereas core-type NPs focus on processing aggregated traffic flows rather than individual packets.

A main NP design decision is whether packet processing prefers the *run-to-completion* or the *pipeline* model [8,4,11]. The former dedicates a single thread to packet forwarding from the input interface to the router's packet switch and, likewise, from the switch to the output interface. Threads run on a fixed number of core processors, sharing the memory units, such as lookup trees, instruction memory, and global packet buffers. An alternative to run-to-completion is the pipeline model. Here, the forwarding process is divided into different stages, and each stage is handled by another core processor with its own instruction memory [24].

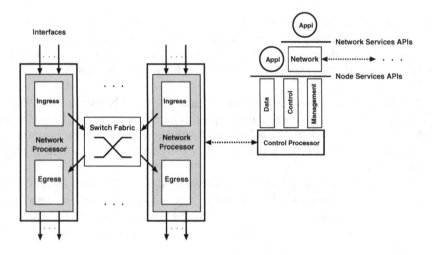

Fig. 1. Network processor programmability.

2.1 Programmability

The NP hardware is typically combined with a horizontally layered software architecture (see Figure 1). On the lowest layer, the NP instruction set provides means for direct packet handling. Many NPs allow access to the instruction memory from a separate control processor, enabling extension or update of the router functionality at runtime.

On the control processor, application programming interfaces (APIs) provide an abstract view of the resources of the network node [1]. The APIs are dedicated to different data-plane, control-plane, and management-plane services of the NP (e.g., initialization, interface configuration, memory and address management, forwarding and address resolution, traffic engineering, classification, diagnostic, event logging, debugging) and can be used for developing portable network applications [9, 4, 11].

2.2 Applications

The use of NPs is beneficial in network applications and services which depend on high data rates as well as rapid development and deployment. In particular, the following application domains have shown benefits from using NPs:

Content switching and load balancing. Information access via HTTP, FTP, or multimedia streaming protocols can result in heavy load on the server. Content switching and load balancing address this problem by transparently distributing client requests across different servers [10, 14].

Traffic differentiation. Quality of service (QoS) and traffic engineering approaches in IP networks require traffic differentiation based on classification, conditioning, and forwarding functions at edge and core routers. These functions increase data-plane processing and are likely to continue evolving in the future, requiring the flexibility provided by NPs.

Network security. With the increase in manual and automated attacks, security functions are needed for protection of systems and network, such as encryption, intrusion detection, and firewalling. This again increases the need for flexible and evolving data-plane processing, a prime opportunity for NPs.

Terminal mobility. The protocols used in mobile/IP convergence networks [2,22] are likely to evolve in the near future. NPs help mobile-equipment manufactures to adjust their products to the latest standards much faster than with dedicated hardware-based solutions. An alternative GPP/software-based solution would not be able to sustain the necessary stateful higher-layer packet processing at wire speed [11].

Active networking. In AN, packets are no longer passively forwarded, but code carried in packets can actively influence the forwarding process at routers. They require not only significantly more data-plane processing, but can only be implemented if routers expose their state of operation and allow the reconfiguration of forwarding functions. Several of the above domains could also benefit from AN-based implementations.

The rest of the paper will focus on the relationship between ANs and NPs.

3   General Advantages of NP-Based ANs

The key idea of ANs [23] is to decouple network services from the networking infrastructure. This is achieved with *active packets* and *active nodes*. The execution environment (EE) on active nodes is typically set up to interpret active programs in byte-code for security and platform independence.

Unfortunately, the interpretation of byte-coded active programs significantly increases the processing overhead per packet. This demand for more performance cannot be addressed with hardware-based forwarding solutions. Routers implemented in ASIC or with FPGAs cannot provide the level of programmability required for active nodes. In the remainder of this section, we discuss how some typical AN concepts can benefit in terms of performance and/or ease of development when implemented on an NP.

Active programs get to the router in two basic forms: as *capsules* and *plugins*. Capsules are self-contained packets including active code that are interpreted or just-in-time compiled [16]. The language used, such as SNAP [19], should be safe with respect to network-resource usage and evaluation isolation. Plugins [13] differ from capsules as the packets contain URL-like pointers, whose contents are then retrieved (if not already cached) and executed by the EE. Both approaches can only gain from NPs: The code can be executed directly on the line card at high speed and direct access to all allowed components.

3.1 Application-Level Multimedia Filtering

In unicast scenarios with peer-to-peer communication between end users, it is possible to negotiate or sense optimum sending rates. However, in multicast scenarios, network resources are difficult to use effectively because the bandwidth up to a congested router may be partially wasted. Positioning application-level packet filters in multicast trees (e.g., preferential dropping of MPEG B-frames) can result in a much better overall link utilization while preserving quality.

It has been proposed that ANs perform application-level multimedia filtering [7], where filters are injected into a network so that an optimum reservation tree is created. The hardware classifiers provided by NPs as well as the corresponding classifier APIs at the control-processor level would make it very easy to implement application-level multimedia filtering.

3.2 Network Management

Active networking for network management [21,17,12,26] results in significantly fewer implementation problems because only few active packets are injected into a network. In general, the forwarding of network-management packets is not time-critical as monitoring and configuration tasks operate on a larger time scale than control- or data-plane tasks. NPs typically provide mechanisms to direct such non-performance-critical packets to the control processor (e.g., using IP header options).

The control processor is equipped with APIs to support typical network-management operations, such as querying and configuring the network nodes. However, active packets sent out for network management-purposes are not used to set and obtain node parameters only, but may include in the code they execute some intelligence for preprocessing and aggregating information from several managed nodes before sending it back to the management station. Such a distributed approach to network management can prevent management stations from becoming overwhelmed with messages, and ensures that the load incurred due to network-management traffic remains low.

4 Advantages of Our NP-Based AN Framework

The advantages of NPs for implementing and deploying ANs have been described in general terms in the previous section. This section introduces a flexible and generic framework for active networking that matches the functionality provided by NPs in order to exemplify the power of the NP/AN relationship.

The goal of this framework is to enable new networking functionality (i.e., focused on QoS support) which can be dynamically deployed while maintaining architecture neutrality. Therefore our framework relies on a capsule-based approach providing flexible and fast execution of active packets in the data path but also allows active code to be stored on active nodes. Most programming languages are unpredictable in terms of resource consumption and therefore inappropriate for safe active networking. A suitable active-networking programming language needs to trade off functionality for flexibility while taking into account security. From the considerable number of security issues entailed by ANs we derive the following requirements such an approach has to comply with.

Safe byte-code language. Architectural neutrality, intrinsic safety properties (intrinsic bounds on CPU, memory, and networking bandwidth), and applicability of the language to current and future application domains are prime criteria when designing or choosing the language.

Resource bound. Resources need to be bounded along two axis: per-node resources and the number of nodes/links the packet will visit.

Safety levels: An appropriate safety hierarchy monitors control-plane and data-plane activities. The handling of active-networking packets is divided into six safety levels as is shown in Table 1. The means for data-plane safety are given through the byte-code language. Safety levels 3–5, called the higher safety levels (HSLs), require admission control at the edge of network domains (i.e., the edge of the domain of trust) using policies depending on the network needs. This also enables easy accounting and charging for active packets. Adding and removing dynamic router services requires a public-key infrastructure for integrity and authentication of active code. Alternatively, higher-level packets can be filtered or, better, disabled for a certain domain only.

Sandbox environment: Any active byte-code is executed in a safe environment called the active networking sandbox (ANSB). Information exchange with the router is protected by so-called router services.

Router services: Router services dynamically enhance router functionality to overcome limitations of the byte-code instructions. They can be static, i.e., defined as opcodes in the byte-code language (e.g., IP address lookup, interface enumeration, flow queue management, or congestion status information), or dynamic (e.g., installation of active code into the ANSB for active queue management (AQM) or scheduling, policy manipulation using a dynamically loaded router service). Dynamic router services are usually tailored to networking tasks with a focus on control-plane functionality, and take significantly more time to execute than normal byte-code instructions do. Therefore, router services belong to the set of instructions with a safety level higher than 1. The installation of new router services is restricted to safety level 5. Such an active packet contains the context for which the new service is applicable, and the code section to be installed is given in the packet's payload.

Routing: Active packets will not interfere with routing protocols. Alternative routes can be proposed by router services as long as the corresponding entries are defined in the local routing table.

In general, we distinguish between safety and security. Safety is given through the definition of the byte-code language itself, the safety hierarchy, and the safe EE for active code. The goal of safety is to reduce risks to the level of traditional IP networks. Security can only be provided by additional network security

Table 1. Safety hierarchy in active networks.

Safety level	Allowed network functionality	Packet and router requirements
5	Dynamic router services (active code): registering new router services	Authentication of active packets needed using a public-key infrastructure.
4	Complex policy insertion and manipulation	Admission control at the edge of network domains; trusted within a domain.
3	Simple policy modification and manipulation	Running in a sandbox environment, limited by predefined rules and installed router services.
2	Creation of new packets and resource-intensive router services (lookups etc.)	Sandbox environment based on the knowledge of the instruction performance.
1	Simple packet byte-code	Safety issues solved by restrictions in the language definition and the use of a sandbox.
0	No active code present in packets	Corresponds to traditional packet-forwarding process.

services including cryptography, authentication, and integrity mechanisms, used to protect the code executed at higher safety levels. This combination achieves both fast packet forwarding in the data path and secure and programmable control-path.

5   Implementation Experience

5.1   Offloading of AN Functionality

The traditional NP control point (NPCP) does not necessarily run on the same GPP as the ANSB and that it even makes sense to separate or dynamically offload AN functionality. For example, the NPCP can run on the external GPP while the higher safety levels of the ANSB are offloaded to the embedded PowerPC (ePPC) available on the PowerNP. The ANSB obtains resources and behavior bounds[1] assigned by the NPCP and administrates them autonomously. Given the distributed layout, which enhances the robustness of the architecture, this is certainly the preferred model. Figure 2 gives an overview of the model based on an IBM PowerNP 4GS3 network processor. In the current implementation, both the NPCP and the ePPC run a Linux 2.4.17 kernel.

In contrast with a standard Linux router without NP, routing and MAC information maintained in the Linux kernel are automatically mirrored to the NP by the NPCP task, enabling the direct use of many standard control-plane applications. NPCP uses the NP APIs provided by the NP device driver (NPDD). These APIs are also used by NP-aware applications, e.g., a resource manager setting up QoS parameters (e.g., Diffserv over MPLS, flow control).

---

[1] The behavior bound consists of a classifier describing to whom the service will be offered, a traffic specification (e.g., sender Tspec), and a resource bound vector that characterizes the maximum resource usage of the router service.

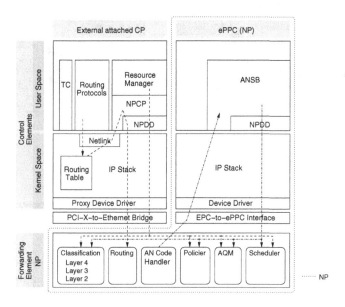

Fig. 2. Architectural overview of the implementation when the ANSB is offloaded to the ePPC.

The AN part is separated from the NPCP as follows. Safety levels 0 and 1 are handled by the active-networking code handler in the data path of the NP. All higher safety levels are offloaded to the ANSB on the ePPC. The ANSB then effectuates NPDD API calls for configuring the NP within the limits of configured policies attributed to the ANSB.

5.2   Packet Definition

Similar to Smart Packets [21] our approach sits directly on top of the networking layer, utilizes the router alert IP header option to indicate active packets, and inserts an active header and code between the IP header and payload. Our approach is a dialect of the SNAP active networking language [19] which allows limited backward loops while still maintaining the safety properties [16]. This approach is downward-compatible, as SNAP-unaware routers will just treat the packet according to safety level 0 and forward them as normal IP packets.

The SNAP header holds information on the safety levels of the active packet in two fields. The first is the initially assigned safety level (IASL) and contains the safety levels in which the packet operates according to the creator of the packet. The second holds the domain-specific safety levels (DSSL) representing the safety levels applicable in the current domain. They are set by packet classification at the ingress of a domain, and remain valid for the entire path through the domain. This mechanism allows a temporary reduction of the safety level within a given domain.

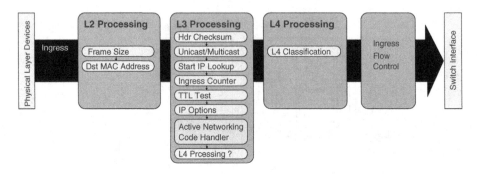

Fig. 3. Ingress data-path processing on a network processor.

The NP-based router architecture, which is no longer centralized as NPs can reside on each blade, divides packet processing into two stages: Ingress processing directs packets from the physical interface to the switch, and egress processing does the reverse. Forwarding and classification decisions are usually taken on the ingress, whereas the egress is mainly involved in packet scheduling. This implies that the processing of an active packet can be performed on the ingress as well as the egress side. Consequently, two entry points have to be maintained.

To minimize data swapping during active packet execution, the memory section of the packet is situated between the packet header and the active-code section. In our case the memory section has a maximum size of 128 bytes. The packet payload delivered to an application remains at the end of the packet and can also be seen like a ROM by the active code. By moving the heap and stack into one memory section that is being fixed when the packet is built, more complex error handling (stack overflow) arises but achieves significant improvements that speed up the execution of active packets in an NP.

For deep packet processing, NPs usually handle packet data in blocks of 64 bytes (pages). Hence, branch decisions in data-path active code encounter an additional penalty if the branch target does not lie in the current page. Forward branches require the chained list of pages to be traversed because the location of pages that have not yet been loaded is unknown. Backward branching can load the correct page immediately, as a page history is maintained.

5.3   Data-Path Elements

This section discusses the integration of the active code into the existing data-path processing. The functional behavior of the forwarding code is shown in Figure 3 for the ingress and in Figure 4 for the egress part.

As soon as active packets have been correctly identified in the layer-3 forwarding code (cf. Figure 3) their processing continues in the active-networking code handler. Depending on their functionality, they still might traverse layer-4 processing later. This is the case for HSL-active packets, which require layer-4

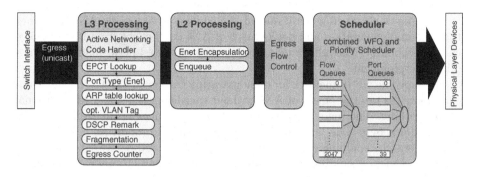

Fig. 4. Egress data-path processing on a network processor.

classification at domain ingress nodes. The egress part is much simpler as there is no layer-4 classification, and active packet processing can immediately start at dispatch time. HSL-active packets have to be classified already on the ingress side (result is kept in the DSSL field) to avoid unnecessary redirection to the ingress. AQM can be provided on the ingress and/or egress by flow control mechanisms which provide congestion feedbacks signals (i.e., packet arrival rates and queue lengths). Note that there is no layer-4 processing at the egress as layer-4 classification has already been performed on the ingress side.

5.4   Control-Path Elements

HSL-active packets can fulfill control-path tasks. These packets require layer-4 classification and verification of the IASL and DSSL done by the active-networking code handler. Matching packets are then redirected to the ANSB on the ePPC. As can be seen in Figure 3, classification takes place only at ingress and redirection is initiated from there. Possible actions are the deposition of active code (safety level 5) and classifier updates (safety levels 3 and 4) within the behavior bounds. Finally, the ANSB translates updated information (e.g., classifier) into NPDD API calls to reconfigure the NP accordingly. Tasks such as routing and interface management are still maintained by the traditional CP as shown in Figure 2.

6   Conclusion

Despite evident advantages of active-networking technology, ANs still lack the support in mainstream networking products. Many vendors fear that the safety and performance of their platforms will be compromised while other vendors using ASICs are prevented from implementing the flexibility required for ANs. Network processors fill the gap by enabling high performance *and* flexibility.

The paper shows in general and in the context of a specific AN framework that the implementation and deployment of ANs can benefit from network processor technology. The advantages are linked to improved performance and simplified development.

The specific NP framework for demonstrating the beneficial AN/NP relationship allows to tap the power of ANs without sacrificing the safety of traditional IP networking. The main security and safety advantages result from the combination of a byte-code language with intrinsic safety properties, a lean 6-level safety hierarchy enabling control-plane functionalities and persistent active code in active nodes, a sandbox environment for code execution, and off-loading of active-networking functionality from the control point to the NP's GPP processor. This isolation provides a physical barrier in our implementation between the packet-processing core of the NP (i.e., the embedded processor complex), the ePPC running the active networking sandbox, and the control and management functions provided by the control point GPP. We believe that this approach will lead to a wider acceptance of AN in networking devices.

References

1. Network Processing Forum. http://www.npforum.org/.
2. The 3rd Generation Partnership Project (3GPP). http://www.3gpp.org.
3. D. S. Alexander, P. B. Menage, A. D. Keromytis, W. A. Arbaugh, K. G. Anagnostakis, and J. M. Smith. The price of safety in an active network. *Journal of Communications and Networks*, 3(1):4–18, Mar. 2001.
4. J. Allen, B. Bass, C. Basso, R. Boivie, J. Calvignac, G. Davis, L. Freléchoux, M. Heddes, A. Herkersdorf, A. Kind, J. Logan, M. Peyravian, M. Rinaldi, R. Sabhikhi, M. Siegel, and M. Waldvogel. IBM PowerNP network processor: Hardware software and applications. *IBM Journal of Research and Development*, 47(2/3):177–194, Mar./May 2003.
5. F. Braun, J. Lockwood, and M. Waldvogel. Protocol wrappers for layered network packet processing in reconfigurable networks. *IEEE Micro*, 22(1):66–74, Jan./Feb. 2002.
6. M. Brunner, B. Plattner, and R. Stadler. Service creation and management in active telecom networks. *Communications of the ACM*, 44(4):55–61, Apr. 2001.
7. I. Busse, S. Covaci, and A. Leichsenring. Autonomy and decentralization in active networks: A case study for mobile agents. In *Proceedings of International Working Conference on Active Networks*, pages 165–179, 1999.
8. P. Crowley, M. E. Fiuczynski, J.-L. Baer, and B. N. Bershad. Characterizing processor architectures for programmable network interfaces. In *Proceedings of the ACM International Conference on Supercomputing*, pages 54–65, May 8–11, 2000.
9. S. Denazis, K. Miki, J. Vicente, and A. Campbell. Designing interfaces for open programmable routers. In *Proceedings of International Working Conference on Active Networks*, pages 13–24, July 1999.
10. Z. Genova and K. Christensen. Challenges in URL switching for implementing globally distributed Web sites. In *Proceedings of the Workshop on Scalable Web Services*, pages 89–94, Aug. 2000.
11. R. Haas, C. Jeffries, L. Kencl, A. Kind, B. Metzler, R. Pletka, M. Waldvogel, L. Freléchoux, and P. Droz. Creating advanced functions on network processors: Experience and perspectives. *IEEE Network*, 17(4), July 2003.

12. A. W. Jackson, J. P. G. Sterbenz, Condell, and R. Hain. Active network monitoring and control: The SENCOMM architecture and implementation. In *Proceedings of DARPA Active Networks Conference and Exposition (DANCE)*, pages 379–393, May 2002.

13. R. Keller, L. Ruf, A. Guindehi, and B. Plattner. PromethOS: A dynamically extensible router architecture supporting explicit routing. In *Proceedings of Int. Working Conf. on Active Networks IWAN*, pages 20–31, Dec. 2002.

14. L. Kencl and J.-Y. L. Boudec. Adaptive load sharing for network processors. In *Proceedings of INFOCOM '02*, June 2002.

15. A. Kind. The role of network processors in active networks. In *Proceedings of the First International Workshop on Active Network Technologies and Applications (ANTA 2002)*, Tokyo, Japan, Mar. 2002.

16. A. Kind, R. Pletka, and B. Stiller. The potential of just-in-time compilation in active networks. *Proceedings of IEEE OPENARCH '02*, June 2002.

17. J. Kornblum, D. Raz, and Y. Shavitt. The active process interaction with its environment. *Computer Networks*, 36(1):21–34, Oct. 2001.

18. J. W. Lockwood, N. Naufel, J. S. Turner, and D. E. Taylor. Reprogrammable network packet processing on the field programmable port extender (FPX). In *ACM International Symposium on Field Programmable Gate Arrays (FPGA '01)*, pages 87–93, Feb. 2001.

19. J. T. Moore, M. Hicks, and S. Nettles. Practical programmable packets. In *Proceedings of INFOCOM '01*, Apr. 2001.

20. S. Murphy, E. Lewis, R. Puga, R. Watson, and R. Yee. Strong security for active networks. *Proceedings of IEEE OPENARCH '01*, pages 63–70, Apr. 2001.

21. B. Schwartz, A. W. Jackson, W. T. Strayer, W. Zhou, R. D. Rockwell, and C. Partridge. Smart Packets: Applying active networks to network management. *ACM Transactions on Computer Systems*, 18(1):67–88, Feb. 2000.

22. R. Stewart, Q. Xie, K. Morneault, C. Sharp, H. Schwarzbauer, T. Taylor, I. Rytina, M. Kalla, L. Zhang, and V. Paxson. Stream Control Transmission Protocol. RFC 2960, IETF, Oct. 2000.

23. D. L. Tennenhouse and D. J. Wetherall. Towards an active network architecture. *ACM Computer Communication Review*, 26(2):5–18, Apr. 1996.

24. M. Venkatachalam, P. Chandra, and R. Yavatkar. A highly flexible, distributed multiprocessor architecture for network processing. *Computer Networks*, 41(5):563–586, Apr. 2003.

25. T. Wolf and J. Turner. Design issues for high-performance active routers. *IEEE Selected Areas in Communications*, 19(3):404–409, Mar. 2001.

26. Y. Yemini, A. V. Konstantinou, and D. Florissi. NESTOR: An architecture for self-management and organization. *IEEE Journal on Selected Areas in Communications*, 18(5), May 2000.

Towards High-Performance Active Networking*

Lukas Ruf[1], Roman Pletka[2], Pascal Erni[3], Patrick Droz[2], and Bernhard Plattner[1]

[1] Computer Engineering and Networks Laboratory
Swiss Federal Institute of Technology (ETH)
CH-8092 Zürich/Switzerland
{ruf,plattner}@tik.ee.ethz.ch
[2] IBM Zurich Research Laboratory
Säumerstrasse 4
CH-8803 Rüschlikon/Switzerland
{rap,dro}@zurich.ibm.com
[3] pascal@promethos.org

Abstract. Network processors have been developed to ease the implementation of new network protocols in high-speed routers. Being embedded in network interface cards, they enable extended packet processing at link speed as is required, for instance, for active network nodes. Active network nodes start using network processors for extended packet processing close to the link. The control and configuration of high-performance active network nodes with network processors such that new services can benefit from the additional processing capacity offered is nontrivial since the complexity to configure a node while providing sufficient level of abstraction is hard to master. In this paper, we present PromethOS NP which is a modular and flexible router architecture that provides a framework for dynamic service extension by plugins with integrated support of network processors, namely the IBM PowerNP 4GS3 network processor. We briefly introduce the PowerNP architecture in order to show how our active networking framework maps onto this network processor and provide results from performance measurements. Owing to architectural similarities of network processors, we believe that our considerations are also valid for other network processors.

1 Introduction and Motivation

Network processors (NPs) have been developed to ease the implementation of new networking functionalities and services in high-speed routers [14]. The programmable environments provided by processor manufacturers remove the burden of creating application-specific integrated circuits (ASICs) or other hardware components needed for extended or new services. Hence, NPs combine the high performance known from ASICs with the capability to adapt networking functionalities in software, while not requiring expensive modifications in hardware. Even though not designed for active networking in the first place, we are convinced NPs provide a perfect processing platform for dynamic service deployment and configuration.

---

* This work is partially sponsored by the Swiss Federal Institute of Technology (ETH) Zürich and the Swiss Federal Office for Education and Science (BBW Grant 99.0533). PromethOS v1 has been developed by ETH as a partner in IST Project FAIN (IST-1999-10561). We would like to acknowledge the great support received from the IBM Zurich Research Laboratory.

N. Wakamiya et al. (Eds.): IWAN 2003, LNCS 2982, pp. 32–43, 2004.

Modern high-performance active network nodes (hANNs) are built by a set of host CPUs and a set of network interface cards (NICs). NICs provide embedded NPs to process packets as close as possible to the network link. Host CPUs and NICs are interconnected by a switching fabric or an node internal bus. A common architecture of NPs is based on a legacy processor core and specialized processing engines on a single chip. Thus, the NPs with these engines and the processor core in conjunction with the host CPUs provide three different processing environments.

Conceptually, hANNs follow a three-level approach to separate management and control plane from packet forwarding [2]. A management plane is required to deploy service specifications and service components as used to setup and configure network-wide services and nodes [1]. In the control plane, service control information is exchanged. For example routing information is distributed. The transport plane provides the functionality to deal with the packets like for example forwarding, content encryption or packet filtering.

A framework that provides a flexible mapping of these three levels to a concrete implementation is essential for the management and control of a hANN. Code portability is important to ease the deployment of service components. At run-time, service components must be installed and interconnected such that the node-local, service-internal communication path can be established easily.

PromethOS NP provides a framework that copes with the complexity of such an hANN. It is based on an extended version of PromethOS [8], a Linux kernel-space-based NodeOS providing the PromethOS EE. The current implementation of PromethOS NP controls an hANN including an Application Reference Board (ARB) that is based on the IBM PowerNP 4GS3 network processor [5].

For the implementation of the PromethOS NP framework it is important how the three levels are mapped to the underlying platform such that the node performance is maximized. Thus, we present the architecture of PromethOS NP and the fundamental design considerations in Section 2. Subsequently, we give a brief introduction to the IBM PowerNP 4GS3 and the ARB in Section 3 and provide further implementation details. Our implementation is then evaluated by performance measurements and the results are presented in Section 4. In Section 5 we review related work, before we summarize and conclude our paper (Section 6).

2 PromethOS NP

The PromethOS NP framework controls an hANN with NICs that provide NPs for extended packet processing. It is composed of management applications and the PromethOS NodeOS as well as the PromethOS EE. Figure 1 provides an overview of the main components of a PromethOS NP node:

- **Management applications:** The management applications control the NodeOS. Further, they initiate component installation and service configuration. They are implemented by the NP Control Daemon (NP CtrlD), the NP Control Client (NP Ctrl).
- **NodeOS:** The PromethOS NodeOS functionality is provided mainly by the PromethOS plugin manager, which is responsible for the creation, configuration and

control of the PromethOS EE. It attaches to the legacy hooks of the IP stack and to the fast-path of the proxy device driver.

- **EE:** The PromethOS EE follows the plugin paradigm, in which plugins are organized as a directed graph of modules.
- **Plugins:** Code components installed in the PromethOS EE are called PromethOS plugins. They provide the service functionality. Every PromethOS plugin is identified by a node unique plugin ID. We make a difference between PromethOS plugins installed on NP cores (specialized processor engines of a NP) and those installed on a general-purpose processor (GPP). PromethOS plugins running on the NP cores are called picoPlugins. In their current implementation, picoPlugins provide packet classification only.

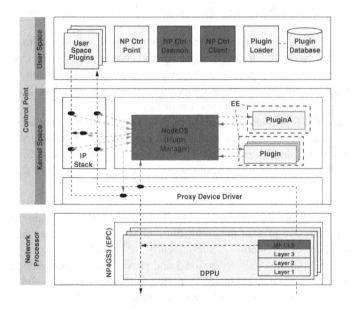

Fig. 1. PromethOS NP: Architectural Overview

A PromethOS NP node spans all processing environments: by design, PromethOS EEs are located on all three levels, thus providing environments for active service components.

PromethOS NP has been extended from traditional PromethOS by the management applications required to control the NP. Further, the fast-path has been introduced that makes benefit of early packet classification: if the picoPlugin is able to demultiplex the packet to the correct service components, packets do not traverse the legacy IP stack of Linux. Like traditional PromethOS, PromethOS NP is registered at the hooks provided by Netfilter [11], too. Thus, it allows for packet reception from the IP stack as well.

The PromethOS EE provides a unified interface to service components irrespective whether PromethOS runs with NP support or not. By the PromethOS NodeOS component, the EE and plugin management is decoupled from the underlying hardware. Thus, source code compatibility is provided for different hardware platforms. With NP support, even program code compatibility is provided for the GPP on the NP and the host CPU if they are based on the same processor architecture.

The PromethOS NodeOS component runs in kernel space while the management applications are located in user space. Conceptually of minor concern, it is important to implement components as close as possible to the network link if they are used frequently: The PromethOS NodeOS component dispatches packets to service components. Thus, it is of major importance to avoid overhead where possible. Management processes are carried out infrequently. So, it is perfectly valid to install the management applications in user space where code development is easier due to extended library and debugging support.

2.1 Design Considerations

There are three different approaches to how PromethOS plugins can be implemented on NPs. First, PromethOS plugins can be added in the embedded processor complex (EPC) and run directly on a NP core. This has the advantage that no additional copying of the packet is required. As actions are taken directly in the data plane, the overhead of sending the packet to a control point processor is avoided. On the other hand, the instruction memory can hold 32k picocode instructions shared among all NP cores, which suffices for traditional packet-forwarding tasks and advanced networking functions [3] but limits the size, and therefore the functionality of PromethOS plugins. Although theoretically feasible, picocode or parts of it cannot be dynamically reloaded with the current version of the network processor application services (NPAS). This would require all plugins to be downloaded during the initialization phase, thereby losing the benefit of dynamic code loading of the plugin approach. Running plugins on NP cores eliminates bottlenecks due to external interfaces but might add new ones on the code-execution level: Additional limits can arise owing to the scaled-down RISC architecture of the NP cores (e.g., there is no floating-point support). Even though a C-compiler for the NP cores exists, efficient code is closely linked to the hardware and therefore often written directly in picocode, which lacks code portability. A just-in-time compiler which translates an architecturally neutral programming language into picocode [9] would then be required. A general question is *where* the code will be executed, i.e., on ingress, egress, or both. Active code placed in the data path and executed on NP cores has been evaluated in [9] for a simple active networking language.

Second, the ePPC (embedded PowerPC) in the EPC can be used to run PromethOS plugins. After classification, PromethOS relevant packets are redirected to the CP residing on the ePPC; all other packets in the data path are handled by the NP cores. The former is done by the general PowerPC handler (GPH), an NP core capable of writing the packet into the ePPC's memory and indicate its arrival to the ePPC by means of an interrupt. The packet then traverses the Linux IP stack before being handed to the plugin manager. The plugin identifier found during classification on the NP allows the plugin manager to select the appropriate plugin. Here the advantages are that only PromethOS-relevant packets will be redirected to the ePPC, while the flexibility of the Linux kernel (e.g., Netfilter support) is retained. No additional processor is needed and

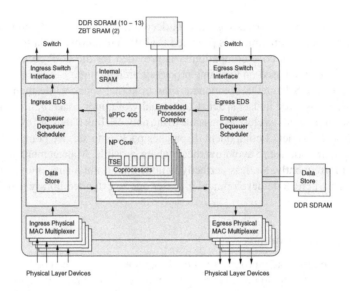

Fig. 2. Main functional blocks of an IBM PowerNP 4GS3.

the approach behaves much like a system-on-a-chip. The approach will eventually en-counter performance limitation due to the interface between NP cores and the ePPC. Moreover, the ePPC is clocked at 133 MHz, which might not be enough for extensive plugin processing.

As a third option, the PromethOS plugin manager can run on an Ethernet-attached external CP, usually a GPP. This approach is similar to the previous one, but uses a physical interface and the GMII Gigabit Ethernet-to-PCI-X bridge to copy packet data into the CP memory. Redirection is done by a guided frame handler (GFH) NP core. Processing of plugins is limited by the clock speed of the attached external GPP CP.

Compared with an approach without NPs the benefits are that packet classification is done by the NP, hence reducing packet handling in the Linux IP stack, while normal data packets are directly forwarded by the NP. In this paper we analyze the latter two approaches, where the plugin manager resides on the ePPC or an external CP. Given its limited functionality, the approach with dynamically (re-)loadable picocode plugins is left for future work.

3   The IBM NP4GS3 Network Processor

3.1   The Power NP4GS3 Architecture

The IBM PowerNP 4GS3 is composed of an embedded processor complex (EPC), the enqueuer dequeuer scheduler (EDS) blocks, the switch interfaces, the physical MAC multiplexers, embedded SRAM memory, and additional memory interfaces for external memories. The EDS is responsible for hardware flow control and scheduling while the MAC multiplexers transfer packets from/to the physical-layer devices. The main functional blocks of a PowerNP are shown in Figure 2.

The EPC consists of 16 packet processor engines called NP cores each supporting two independent threads, a set of eight specialized coprocessors for each NP core, and an embedded PowerPC 405 microprocessor, all running at 133 MHz. The coprocessors perform asynchronous functions such as longest-prefix lookup, full-match lookup, packet classification, hashing (all performed by two tree search engines (TSE) per NP core), data copying, checksum computation, counter management, semaphores, policing, and access to the packet memory. The NP cores are scaled-down RISC processors which execute the so-called picocode. The picocode instruction set is specifically designed for packet processing and forwarding.

Packet processing is divided into two *stages*: Ingress processing directs packets from the physical interface to the switch, egress processing does the reverse. Every NP core can handle both stages, but usually one is associated virtually at dispatch time for convenience. Threads are dispatched upon packet arrival from the physical interface or the switch, or by an interrupt. Each thread has its own independent set of registers, so there is no overhead in switching threads. When a thread stalls (e.g., when waiting for a coprocessor), multi-threading will switch to the other thread if this one is ready for execution. This dynamic thread execution helps to balance the processor load. A thread entirely processes a stage of a packet, which is called run-to-completion mode. Additional context information (e.g., output interface identifier gained from the IP forwarding lookup) can be transferred from ingress to egress along with the packet.

We based our implementation on the Application Reference Board (ARB) from Silicon Software System This board provides a BroadCom PCI-X Ethernet controller (BCM5700) for bridging between the application reference board and the host.

3.2 PromethOS NP Implementation

Figure 3 gives an overview of the architecture for the external CP. In case the CP is internal (running on the ePPC), incoming packets are redirected from the E-EDS to the ePPC directly and outgoing ones vice versa. Administration and configuration of classifier rules are handled by the NP CtrlD and the NP Ctrl. The client allows a user to manage classification rules and plugin IDs similar to tc of the Traffic Control [4] package in Linux. The daemon provides an interface to the client process and talks to the NP using the proxy interface to the NPAS from the NP control point. For this, the daemon performs the necessary translation process and maintains counters of rule hits at the same time. The NP CP uses the Proxy Device Driver to encapsulate control traffic from the CP to the NP.

The implementation of PromethOS on the PowerNP is based on the multi-field classifier from the NPAS which provides a CP API and its corresponding picocode part. Depending on the memory size, up to 5192 multi-field classification rules can be stored. The classifier picocode has been enhanced in order to return the plugin ID (later being used by the plugin manager) if a rule matches. A rule match redirects an incoming packet, including the plugin ID found, to the CP for further processing.

While the redirection *decision* is taken on the ingress (i.e. during packet classification), the redirection *action* occurs at the egress. In the case of an attached external CP,

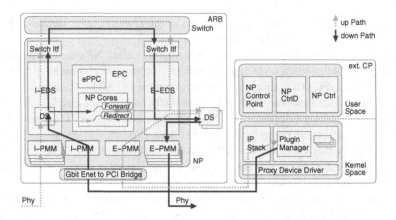

Fig. 3. Data path of packets handled by the external CP.

the packet is sent to the physical interface and then traverses the Ethernet-to-PCI bridge to reach the CP. As the plugin ID is already known, the packet will not traverse the full Linux IP stack, but is handed directly to the plugin manager by the proxy device driver (fast-path). After processing, the plugin manager sends the packet back to the NP. It will again traverse the ingress side of the NP, but this time the forwarding decision is taken. Next it traverses the switch and the egress side of the NP as a normal IP packet does. In the case of an internal CP, the GPH sends the packet directly to the ePPC, where it will be handled, and receives it back afterwards for forwarding on the egress.

3.3 Performance Characteristics

The following list mentions the performance characteristics of the PowerNP that play a major role for all PromethOS NP configurations, as discussed in Section 2.1.

- **Data Mover Units:** The PowerNP provides five data mover units (DMU). Each DMU moves data at 1 gigabit per second (Gbps) in both ingress and egress directions. Four of them can be configured independently (e.g., as an Ethernet medium access control (MAC)). The fifth pair is directly inter-connected to move data from the egress to the ingress side of the NP4GS3.
- **Ethernet:** Three DMUs are configured as 1000Base-T GMII Ethernet ports. The fourth establishes the connection to the attached external GPP by means of a GMII gigabit Ethernet-to-PCI-X bridge.
- **Switch interface:** The switch interface consists of two data-aligned synchronous link (DASL) interfaces in each direction. Each of them provides a transfer rate between 3.25 and 4 Gbps surpassing the accumulated bandwidth of the four gigabit Ethernet interfaces [5]. These interfaces can either connect an NP to a switch fabric, to another network processor, or directly transfer the data from the ingress to the egress interface. Thus, this interface will not cause any performance degradation.

- **Data store coprocessor:** Data are copied into or from the EPC by the data store coprocessor of the NP. The packet throughput depends linearly on the number of bytes copied per packet: Usually only 64 bytes are copied, as this is sufficient for header inspection. The PowerNP achieves 4.80 Gbps of aggregated throughput of Internet-like traffic when doing layer 3 packet forwarding [6]. Depending on the PromethOS configuration, data packets traverse each stage up to two times. Because PromethOS requires additional layer 4 classification we except that the PowerNP can provide up to 1.5 Gbps throughput.
- **PCI bus:** The ARB can be integrated into an hANN using its Ethernet-to-PCI bridge. The BroadCom PCI-X Ethernet Controller BCM5700 permits bridging at 1 Gbps full duplex. The PCI standard v2.3 defines the following bus transfer rates: 1.1 Gbps for an interface with 32 bits width running at 33 MHz (32b/33MHz), 4.3 Gbps (64b/66MHz), and 8.5 Gbps (64b/133MHz PCI-X 1.0). However, the PCI bus does not provide full duplex. So, if the ARB were placed in a 32b/33MHz PCI system, we could expect a throughput of at most 0.55 Gbps (provided the bus is not used by other devices). Thus, at least 2 Gbps are required from the PCI bus bandwidth to satisfy the ARB.
- **General PowerPC Handler:** The ePPC is connected to the general PowerPC handler (GPH), a NP core with extended capabilities, via shared memory for data transmission. The GPH copies data packets into the external DRAM, and signals this to the ePPC by an interrupt. Thus, it provides functionality comparable to a programmable DMA controller. The reverse process is carried out if the ePPC sends a packet. Passing packets to the ePPC has been designed for the control path, hence we cannot expect high throughput for data-path applications. However, it can be extremely valuable to offload complex data-path processing as encountered in active networks in order to prevent packet redirection to an external CP, as long as the rate is bounded to an acceptable value. As it is difficult to estimate the performance of this interface, we provide empirical results in section 4.1.

We conclude from this analysis first that the PowerNP should be powerful enough to carry out packet classification for PromethOS plugins on the one hand, and, on the other hand, to forward packets of other streams at link speed (1 Gbps) simultaneously. Second, the PowerNP has no performance bottlenecks if PromethOS NP is run on an external CP. However, in the case where PromethOS NP and the PromethOS plugins are run on the ePPC directly, we presume performance limitations since the PowerNP was originally not designed for this configuration of transport plane packet handling. This has to be taken into account by the configuration process of PromethOS NP.

4   Evaluation

4.1   Performance Measurements

Following the analysis of all interfaces involved (cf. section 3), we base our evaluation on an hANN with an Intel Xeon 2.4 GHz processor running Linux 2.4.18 in which the ARB is installed. The ARB operates at 64b/66MHz PCI speed.

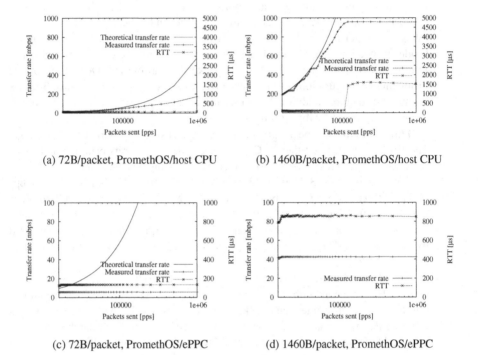

(a) 72B/packet, PromethOS/host CPU   (b) 1460B/packet, PromethOS/host CPU

(c) 72B/packet, PromethOS/ePPC   (d) 1460B/packet, PromethOS/ePPC

Fig. 4. PromethOS NP on the host CPU (a,b) and on the ePPC (c,d) – Transfer Rate and Round Trip Time: (a,c) 72 Bytes per packet; (b,d) 1460 Bytes per packet.

We measured the performance of the hANN without real service functionality of the plugins because otherwise throughput would additionally depend on the service complexity rather than on the efficiency of the framework. Packets were sent by a traffic generator (source) to the plugin manager (sink), whereby the plugin manager acts as source and sink at the same time for convenience. Packets were sent out by one Ethernet interface and received on another via crossed cables. The up and down paths taken by packets traversing a hANN are visualized in Figure 3.

Latency, throughput and packet loss have been measured in two configurations: In the first case PromethOS NP was running on the Ethernet-attached external CP, in the second case it was placed on the CP running on the ePPC. The results are for different packets sizes, namely, 72 and 1460 Bytes. We chose these packet sizes since we assume the former to be the size of signalling control packets approximately while the latter corresponds to usual data packets. In Figure 4 (a) and (b), we plot the results of the first configuration in which the NP cores are only used for packet classification. The measurement results achieved for the second configuration are shown in Figure 4 (c) and (d). The x-axis (number of packets per second) is plotted with a logarithmic scale. The packet size corresponds to the number of bytes sent at the Ethernet interface, omitting the internal header (36 Bytes) added by the Linux proxy device driver for signaling. In Figure 4, the transfer rate (TR) is shown in megabits per second (Mbps), the round trip time (RTT) in units of microseconds (μs), and the packet transfer rate in units of packets per second (pps). For comparison, we also plot the ideal transfer rate, where the number of packets attempted to send corresponds to the number of packets received, assuming all transmission attempts are successful.

Table 1. Comparison of transfer rates and round trip times

PromethOS NP on the host CPU:

72 Bytes per packet			1460 Bytes per packet		
TR (pps)	TR (Mbps)	RTT (μs)	TR (pps)	TR (Mbps)	RTT (μs)
297985	171.639	81.2	81846	955.966	1531.4
20134	11.597	48.7	20110	234.879	96.2

PromethOS NP on the ePPC:

72 Bytes per packet			1460 Bytes per packet		
TR (pps)	TR (Mbps)	RTT (μs)	TR (pps)	TR (Mbps)	RTT (μs)
9807	5.649	135.9	3638	42.497	849.8
9640	5.553	124.3	3574	41.471	786.6

In Table 1, we compare the maximum throughput, the maximum transfer rate, and the minimum round trip time for both configurations. The increase in latency found in Figure 4 (b) corresponds to the default queue-threshold configuration of the PowerNP. We note the difference in performance between the two configurations. We further investigated the second configuration: First, we measured the performance of Linux with regard to its capacity of creating, sending and receiving socket buffers without real transmission, i.e. the socket buffers are not flattened and then sent out at the physical interface, but the receive-function is called directly. We achieved a transfer rate of 697.39 Mbps. Second, we measured the performance of the interface between the NP cores and the ePPC by transferring full-sized packets (1460 Bytes) via the shared memory and interrupt signaling back and forth. We were able to measure a transfer rate of 298.04 Mbps[1].

From the measurement results, we conclude: The first configuration provides sufficient performance to handle at least one gigabit link. Measurements of the PowerNP proved that the PowerNP is still capable of carrying out packet forwarding for an additional, non-active 1 Gbps flow. Measurement results in the second configuration lead to the conclusion that the Linux/PromethOS on the ePPC should not be used for transport plane packet handling. However the extensible platform provides a very useful environment for control plane functionality where less packet processing is expected.

5   Related Work

VERA [7] provides a three-level router architecture to provide a modularized, standards compliant router. It is implemented by a device driver that interfaces to the IXP1200

---

[1] Note that we did not vary the internal socket-buffer limits imposed by Linux which can further improve our results.

and, thus, provides the hardware abstraction. In [13] resource allocation and scheduling issues are analyzed on a three-level processor hierarchy, and evaluates the performance of the Intel IXP 1200 for vanilla IP packets. In [10], an IXP1200-based network interface card offering four 100T ports was evaluated. On the IXP1200 StrongARM core, Linux is run, but used for initialization and debugging purposes only; processing is carried out in the so-called kernels run on the microEngines of the IXP, while the host CPU is used for extended processing. A very interesting approach to datapath packet processing is provided in [12] where the performance of a Click-based NP software architecture is evaluated. The Active Packet Editing (APE) approach [15] is a two-level active networking architecture that consists of an active packet processor in software running on a GPP and a packet editor based on an FPGA with content-addressable memory (CAM) for efficiency. The packet processor configures the packet editor, which performs packet classification and simple packet-modification tasks through active packets. Their packet editor prototype achieves slightly less than 1 Gbps of throughput for simple IP header modifications and the packet processor is capable of handling 10 Mbps of small-sized packets. With the PromethOS NP framework, we focus on run-time extensibility and mapping flexibility of active service components. The unified interface provided by the PromethOS EE allows for the portability of service components. By the PromethOS NodeOS component, the required abstraction is provided such that the service can benefit most from the underlying hardware irrespective whether NP-based or just legacy NICs are available on an hANN. With PromethOS NP running on the ePPC, an active platform for control plane functionality is provided thus allowing for greater scalability of the node since not all control plane traffic must be forwarded to the host CPU.

6   Summary, Conclusion, and Outlook

In this paper, we introduced PromethOS NP, a framework that eases the use of network processors for high-performance active network nodes The framework provides extended NodeOS functionality that supports plugin portability by the PromethOS EE across different node configurations. The presented implementation is based on an hANN supported by network interface cards with an embedded IBM PowerNP 4GS3 network processor. It is run either on the host CPU (Ethernet-attached external control point) or on the embedded general-purpose processor of the network processor. In both configurations, the NP cores provide packet classification for the fast-path to circumvent legacy packet classification by the network stack of the operating system.

Our performance measurements prove the efficiency of our architecture. PromethOS NP supported by the PowerNP was able to handle gigabit link speed ($\sim$956 Mbps); 297,985 packets per second could be processed without any optimization of legacy Linux. In addition, when PromethOS NP was run on the Ethernet-attached external control point (host CPU), the PowerNP provided ample capacity for additional flow-processing. In the configuration with PromethOS NP run on the embedded PowerPC (ePPC), measurement results favour the use of the extensible environment for control plane functionality but not for transport plane packet processing. The PowerNP, whose ePPC is designed for control plane functionalities and exceptional data-plane packet processing, supports, thus, node scalability with regard to control of multiple, concurrent transport plane services.

We are convinced that PromethOS NP in conjunction with the IBM PowerNP 4GS3 provides a flexible and efficient architecture and platform for active services that need to process packets at link-speed. Currently, we are investigating the extended use of the NP cores as well as optimizations of a NodeOS running on the host processor as well as on the PowerNP creating a multiprocessor high-performance active node.

References

[1] M. Bossardt, L. Ruf, R. Stadler, and B. Plattner. A service deployment architecture for heterogeneous active network nodes. In *IFIP International Conference on Intelligence in Networks (SmartNet)*, April 2002.

[2] The FAIN Consortium. *D7: Final Active Network Architecture and Design*, 2003.

[3] R. Haas, C. Jeffries, L. Kencl, A. Kind, B. Metzler, R. Pletka, M. Waldvogel, L. Freléchoux, and P. Droz. Creating advanced functions on network processors: Experience and perspectives. *IEEE Network*, 17(4), July 2003.

[4] B. Hubert et al. Linux Advanced Routing & Traffic Control. `http://lartc.org`, 2003.

[5] IBM Corp. IBM PowerNP NP4GS3 databook. `http://www.ibm.com`, 2002.

[6] IBM Corp. LinleyBench 2002 test results, IBM PowerNP NP4GS3. `http://www.chips.ibm.com/techlib`, 2002.

[7] S. Karlin and L. Peterson. VERA: An extensible router architecture. In *Proceedings of the 4th International Conference on Open Architectures and Network Programming (OPENARCH)*, pages 3–14, April 2001.

[8] R. Keller, L. Ruf, A. Guindehi, and B. Plattner. PromethOS: A dynamically extensible router architecture supporting explicit routing. In *Proceedings of the Fourth Annual International Working Conference on Active Networks IWAN*, December 2002.

[9] A. Kind, R. Pletka, and B. Stiller. The potential of just-in-time compilation in active networks based on network processors. In *Proceedings of IEEE OPENARCH*, pages 79–90, June 2002.

[10] K. Mackenzie, W. Shi, A. McDonald, and I Ganev. An Intel IXP1200-based network interface. In *Proceedings of the Workshop on Novel Uses of System Area Networks at HPCA (SAN-2 2003)*, 2003.

[11] P. R. Russell. The NetFilter Project. http://www.netfilter.org, 2003.

[12] N. Shah, W. Plishker, and K. Keutzer. NP-Click: A programming model for the Intel IXP1200. In *Proceedings of 9th International Symposium on High Performance Computer Architectures (HPCA), 2nd Workshop on Network Processors*, February 2003.

[13] T. Spalink, S. Karlin, L. Peterson, and Y. Gottlieb. Building a robust software-based router using network processors. In *Proceedings of the 18th ACM Symposium on Operating Systems Principles (SOSP)*, pages 216–229, October 2001.

[14] J.P.G. Sterbenz. Intelligence in Future Broadband Networks: Challenges and Opportunities in High-Speed Active Networking. In *Proceedings of IEEE International Zürich Seminar on Broadband Communications (IZS 2002)*, Feb. 2002.

[15] N. Takahashi, T. Miyazaki, and T. Murooka. APE: Fast and secure active networking architecture for active packet editing. In *Proceedings of IEEE OPENARCH '02*, pages 104–113, June 2002.

Application of Hardware Accelerated Extensible Network Nodes for Internet Worm and Virus Protection

John W. Lockwood[1]*, James Moscola[1], David Reddick[2],
Matthew Kulig[2], and Tim Brooks[2]

[1] Applied Research Laboratory
Washington University in Saint Louis
1 Brookings Drive, Campus Box 1045
St. Louis, MO 63130 USA
{lockwood, jmm5}@arl.wustl.edu
www.arl.wustl.edu/arl/projects/fpx/reconfig.htm
[2] Global Velocity
Bandwidth Exchange Building
210 North Tucker Blvd., Suite 315
St. Louis, MO 63101 USA
{dreddick, mkulig, tbrooks}@globalvelocity.info
www.globalvelocity.info/

Abstract. Today's crucial information networks are vulnerable to fast-moving attacks by Internet worms and computer viruses. These attacks have the potential to cripple the Internet and compromise the integrity of the data on the end-user machines. Without new types of protection, the Internet remains susceptible to the assault of increasingly aggressive attacks. A platform has been implemented that actively detects and blocks worms and viruses at multi-Gigabit/second rates. It uses the Field-programmable Port Extender (FPX) to scan for signatures of malicious software (malware) carried in packet payloads. Dynamically reconfigurable Field Programmable Gate Array (FPGA) logic tracks the state of Internet flows and searches for regular expressions and fixed-strings that appear in the content of packets. Protection is achieved by the incremental deployment of systems throughout the Internet.

1 Introduction

Computer virus and Internet worm attacks are pervasive, aggravating, and expensive, both in terms of lost productivity and consumption of network bandwidth. Attacks by Nimba, Code Red, Slammer, SoBig.F, and MSBlast have

---

* This research was supported by a grant from Global Velocity. John Lockwood is a co-founder and consultant for Global Velocity and an Assistant Professor at Washington University in St. Louis. Washington University and John Lockwood may receive income based on a license of related technology by the University to Global Velocity.

N. Wakamiya et al. (Eds.): IWAN 2003, LNCS 2982, pp. 44–57, 2004.
© IFIP International Federation for Information Processing 2004

infected computers globally, clogged large computer networks, and degraded corporate productivity [1]. It can take weeks to months for Information Technology staff to sanitize infected computers throughout a network after an outbreak. The direct cost to recover from just the Code Red Version 2 worm was $2.6 billion.

In much the same way that a human virus spreads between people that come in contact, computer viruses and Internet worms spread when computers communicate electronically. Once a few systems are compromised, they proceed to infect other machines, which in turn quickly spread the infection throughout a network [2]. As is the case with the spread of a contagious disease like SARS, the number of infected computers will grow exponentially unless contained. Computer systems spread contagion much more quickly than humans because they can communicate nearly instantly over large geographical distances. "The Blaster worm infected over 400,000 computers in less than five days. In fact, about one in three Internet users are infected with some type of virus or worm every year. The speed at which worms and viruses can spread is astonishing. What's equally astonishing is the lethargic pace at which people deploy the patches that can prevent infection in the first place", Congressman Adam Putnam said recently when he opened a congressional hearing [3].

Malicious software (malware) can propagate as a computer virus, an Internet worm or a hybrid that contains elements of both. Viruses spread when a computer user downloads unsafe software, opens a malicious attachment, or exchanges infected computer programs over a network. An Internet Worm spreads over the network automatically when malicious software exploits one or more vulnerabilities in an operating system, a web server, a database application, or an email exchange system. Malware can appear as a virus embedded in software that a user has downloaded. It also can take the form of a trojan that is embedded in what appears to be benign freeware. Alternatively, it can spread as content attached to an email message, as content downloadable from a website, or in files transferred over peer-to-peer systems. Modern attacks typically use multiple mechanisms to execute their attacks. Malware can spoof messages to lure users to submit personal financial information to cloaked servers. In the future, malware is likely to spread much faster and do much more damage [4].

1.1 Weakness of End-System Protection

Today, most anti-virus solutions run in software on end systems. To ensure that an entire network is secure from known attacks, some system administrators mandate that every host within the network: (1) run only trusted Operating Systems, system tools, and application software; (2) have a full suite of virus-protection software loaded; (3) have the latest updates and patches installed for all of the programs that might run on the machine; and (4) be carefully configured to guard against running unauthorized software. Should any machine in the network be missed, the security of the overall network can be compromised.

It is difficult for companies, universities, and government agencies to maintain network-wide security. Most Internet worms and viruses go undetected until they cause harm on an end-user's computer. Placing the burden of detection on the end user is neither efficient nor trustworthy because individuals tend to ignore warnings about installing new protection software and the latest security updates. New vulnerabilities are discovered daily, but not all users take the time to download new patches the moment they are posted. It can take weeks for an IT department to eradicate old versions of vulnerable software running on end-system computers.

A recent Gartner study predicts that by the year 2005, 90 percent of cyber attacks will attempt to exploit vulnerabilities for which a patch is available or a solution known. But systems are not always patched immediately, and anti-virus programs are not kept up to date. "System administrators are often times overwhelmed with simply maintaining all the systems they have responsibility for overseeing. Challenges that organizations face in maintaining their systems are significant: with an estimated 4,000 vulnerabilities being discovered each year, it is an enormous challenge for any but the best-resourced organizations to install all of the software patches that are released by the manufacturer. Not only is the sheer quantity of patches overwhelming for administrators to keep up with, but patches can be difficult to apply and also have potentially unexpected side effects on other system components that administrators must then evaluate and address. As a result, after a security patch is released, system administrators often take a long time to fix all their vulnerable computer systems. Obviously, small organizations and home users, who lack the skills of system administrators, are even less likely to be able to keep up with the flow of patches" said the congressman [3].

1.2   A Global Threat

Due to the global expansion of high speed networks and the proliferation of a dominant, monolithic operating system, a large portion of the Internet can be easily and quickly subverted. For SoBig.F, more than 1 million computers were infected within the first 24 hours, 100 million systems within the first five days, and an excess of 200 million computers within a week. The virus accounted for 70 percent of all email traffic on August 20, 2003.

Existing firewalls that examine only the packet headers do little to protect against many types of attack. Many new worms transport their malware over trusted services and cannot be detected without examining the payload. Intrusion Detection Systems (IDSs) that scan the payload can detect malware, but do nothing to impede the attack because they only operate passively. An Intrusion Prevention System (IPS), on the other hand, can intervene and stop malware from spreading. The problem is that current IPS devices cannot keep pace with the volume of traffic that transits high-speed networks. Existing systems that implement IPS functions in software limit the bandwidth of the network and delay the end-to-end connection.

There is a need for devices which can scan data quickly, reconfigure to search for new attack patterns, and take immediate action when attacks occur. By processing the content of Internet traffic in real-time within an extensible network, data containing computer viruses or Internet worms can be detected and prevented from propagating. Inserting a few data scanning and filtering devices at a few key Network Aggregation Points (NAPs) enables Internet worms and computer viruses to be quarantined to the subnetworks where they were introduced. Such a system of intelligent gateway devices recognizes and blocks malware locally to dramatically limit the spread of the worm or virus globally. According to the director of CERT, "It is critical to maintain a long-term view and invest in research toward systems and operational techniques that yield networks capable of surviving attacks while protecting sensitive data. In doing so, it is essential to seek fundamental technological solutions and to seek proactive, preventive approaches, not just reactive, curative approaches" [5].

A complete system has been designed and implemented that scans the full payload of packets to route, block, and track the packets in the flow, based on their content [6]. The result is an intelligent gateway that provides Internet worm and virus protection in both local and wide area networks.

2   Related Work

A common prerequisite for network intrusion detection and prevention systems is the ability to search for predefined signatures in network traffic flows. A virus or Internet worm can be detected by the presence of a string of bytes (for the rest of the paper, a string is synonymous with a signature) in traffic that passes through a network link. Such signatures can be loaded into the system manually by an operator or automatically by a signature detection system.

2.1   Obtaining Signatures

There are many ways to obtain malware signatures. One way to learn about a new Internet worm or computer virus is to participate in group forums that share information about new attacks. When a new virus is encountered, information about it is collected, analyzed, and reported to the group. Agencies like the CERT Coordination Center provide alerts regarding potential threats and provide information about how to avoid, minimize, or recover from the damage [7]. Incident reports on vulnerabilities are collected and distributed once they are found. This data can be used by others to avoid and recover from an attack. New methods of detecting outbreaks can streamline the recognition and analysis of new threats and shorten the time needed to obtain a new signature.

One new way that worms and computer viruses can be automatically detected is with a Honeypot or a Honeynet. Honeynets gather information by monitoring all traffic going to and from a non-production network. All captured activity is assumed to be unauthorized or malicious. Any connection initiated inbound to a Honeynet is most likely a probe, scan, or attack. Data that is captured is analyzed to gain insight into threatening activities. New tools can be discovered, attack patterns determined, and attacker motives studied by monitoring and logging all activities within the Honeynet [8].

Unlike a Honeypot, a Honeynet is an entire network of systems that runs real applications and services. An attacker can interact with operating systems and execute tools on what appears to be a legitimate production network, but is not. It is through this extensive interaction that information on threats is obtained and analyzed. Signatures are obtained from captured traffic that is determined to be malware. These signatures, in turn, can be used to program a data scanning device to block attacks into real systems.

Another automated method for detecting new worms is based on traffic characteristics. The method tracks traffic to detect highly repetitive packet content sent from an increasing population of sources to an increasing number of destinations. The method generates content signatures for the worm without any human intervention. The method can quickly identify the signatures of new worms [9]. As with a Honeynet, these signatures can be used by the system we propose to block worms from attacking other legitimate systems.

2.2 Signature Scanning with Software, Hardware, or FPGAs

Once a signature is found, an IDP can use this signature to block traffic containing infected data from spreading throughout a network. To perform this operation on a high-speed network, the signature scanning and data blocking must operate quickly.

Software-based scanners are not capable of monitoring all traffic passing through fast network links. Due to the sequential nature of code execution, software-based systems can perform only a limited number of operations within the time period of a packet transmission. A comparison of a variety of systems running the Snort [10] rule-based NIDS sensor reveals that most general-purpose computer systems are inadequate as NIDS sensor platforms even for moderate-speed networks. The analysis shows that factors that include the microprocessor, operating system, and main memory bandwidth and latency all limit the performance achievable by a NIDS sensor platform. General-purpose computers, including the Intel Pentium-III and Pentium-4, were found to be inadequate to act as sensors even on a 100 Mbit per second network link. The best-performing system could support only a maximum of 720 header rules without losing packets. For larger numbers of rules, a significant percentage of packets are dropped, thus degrading the NIDS effectiveness in detecting security breaches [11].

Hardware-based systems use parallelism to perform deep packet inspection with high throughput [12]. FortiNet and Intruvert, for example, use Application Specific Integrated Circuits (ASICs) to provide virus protection [13] [14]. TippingPoint also uses hardware for the line of *UnityOne* systems. Its Threat Suppression Engine (TSE) enables intrusion is a blend of ASICs and network processors [15]. Packeteer monitors traffic flows to perform traffic shaping without good hardware acceleration. The maximum throughput of its system is listed as 200 Mbps [16].

FPGAs provide the flexibility and performance to scan for regular expressions within a high-speed network [17] [18]. In previous work, the Field-programmable

Port Extender (FPX) platform was implemented to process Asynchronous Transfer Mode (ATM) cells, Internet Protocol (IP) packets, and Transmission Control Protocol (TCP) flows at OC48 (2.4 Gigabit/second) rates using FPGAs [19] [20] [21] [22]. Several mechanisms were developed to perform exact matching and longest prefix matching for header fields [23] [24] [25]. An automated design flow was created to scan the payload traffic for regular expressions [26] [27]. In addition, a Bloom filter was developed to enable large numbers of fixed-length strings to be scanned in hardware [28]. Web-based tools were developed to enable easy remote monitoring, control, and configuration of the hardware [29].

3   System Architecture

A complete system has been implemented that uses the FPX to protect networks from Internet worm and virus attacks. The system is comprised of three interconnected components: a Data Enabling Device (DED), a Content Matching Server (CMS), and a Regional Transaction Processor (RTP). A diagram of the DED, CMS, and RTP appears at the right side of Figure 1. These systems work together to provide network-wide protection.

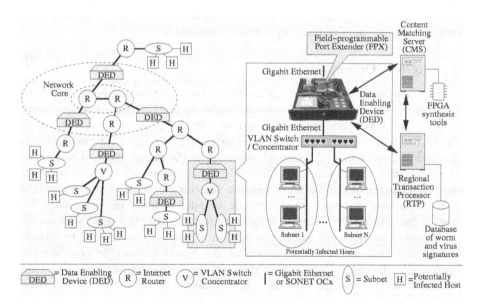

Fig. 1. Example topology of a Network Aggregation Point (NAP) with DEDs added to provide worm and virus protection

Packets in our system are scanned by the **Data Enabling Device (DED)**. At the heart of the DED is the FPX module which scans the content of Internet packets at Gigabit per second rates. DEDs can be installed incrementally at key traffic aggregation points of commercial, academic or governmental networks, as well as on the network core. The more DEDs that are deployed, the better is the granularity of protection between different subnetworks.

In order to reprogram the DEDs to search for new strings, a **Content Matching Server (CMS)** has been implemented. Custom circuits are compiled and synthesized on the CMS by an automated design flow. The CMS reads a table of Internet worm and virus signatures from a database, converts each into an optimized finite automata, instantiates parallel hardware to perform a data scanning function, embeds this hardware into logic that parses Internet protocol messages, synthesizes the entire circuit into logic gates, routes, places the circuit into a FPGA, and reconfigures the hardware.

The **Regional Transaction Processor (RTP)** is contacted by the DED when matching content is found to be passing through the network. The RTP consults the database to provide detailed information about the reason that a certain data flow was blocked. The RTP maintains information about users, agents, properties, owners, and access rights in a MySQL database. Common Gateway Interface (CGI) programs provide a network administrator with an easy-to-use, web-based interface to modify the database tables and to run the scripts that build new hardware. A single RTP can remotely coordinate the activities of up to 100 DEDs. RTPs can be co-located on the same site as the DEDs and be managed by a local site administrator, or they can be located remotely and be administered by a trusted authority.

3.1   System Operation

When a new virus appears, an administrator or an automated process adds the signature of the malware to a database table on the Content Matching Server (CMS). The CMS then synthesizes a new FPGA circuit and reconfigures the FPGA hardware on the Data Enabling Device (DED) to scan Internet traffic for the updated signatures. A targeted signature in the packet payload can appear at any position within the traffic flow. The DED uses parallel hardware circuits to scan all bytes of the traffic. Whenever matching content is found, the DED generates a message that is forward to the intended recipient of the message. The system can also actively block the malware from passing through the network.

To detect an Internet worm, the system would be programmed to look for a signature that contained a portion of the binary executable program that implements the worm. Inadvertent matches can be nearly eliminated by using long and distinct strings that are highly unlikely to appear in normal traffic content. For random data with a signature length of 16 bytes ($16 * 8 = 128$ bits), the odds that a signature will find a match in random traffic is only one in $2^{128} = 3.4 * 10^{38}$. On a 1 Gigabit/second link, this corresponds to finding a match only once in $(3.4 * 10^{38}$ bytes $) * (8$ bits/byte $)/(1 * 10^9$ bits/sec $) = 2.72 * 10^{30}$ seconds . This is equivalent to finding a stray match just once in $2.72 * 10^{30}$ sec $/(60$ sec/min $* 60$ min/hr $* 24$ hr/day $* 365$ day/year $) = 86$ billion billion years, which is an amount of time likely to be far greater than the lifetime of the Internet.

In a typical installation, as shown at the left of Figure 1, Data Enabling Devices (DEDs) are installed at network aggregation points. Traffic flows from end-system hosts attached to subnets are concentrated into high-speed links that are then fed into a router. The DED scans traffic which would otherwise simply be routed back to other subnets or to the Internet. So long as at least one DED is positioned along the path between any two endpoints, the virus signature will be detected. The system allows for the immediate blocking of known viruses and may be rapidly reprogrammed to recognize and block new threats. These upgrades are system-driven, and do not require that actions be taken by end users to assure protection.

Field–programmable Port Extender (FPX)

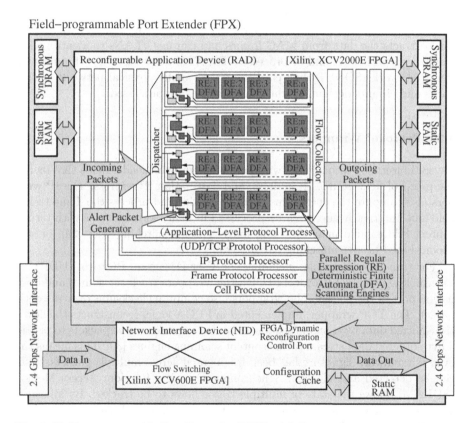

Fig. 2. Field-programmable Port Extender (FPX) with Protocol Wrappers and Regular Expression (RE) Deterministic Finite Automata (DFA) scanning engines

3.2 Field-Programmable Port Extender (FPX) Platform

The Field-programmable Port Extender (FPX) card implements the core functionality of the DED. In order to provide sufficient space to store the state of multiple traffic flows, an FPX can be equipped with up to 1 Gigabyte of SDRAM and 6 Megabytes of pipelined Zero-Bus-Turnaround (ZBT) SRAM. Each FPX contains two FPGAs, five banks of memory and two high-speed (OC-48 rate) network interfaces. On the FPX, one FPGA called the Network Interface Device (NID), is used to route individual traffic flows through the device and process control packets, while the other FPGA, called the Reconfigurable Application Device (RAD), is dynamically reconfigured over the network to perform customized packet processing functions [12]. A diagram of the FPX is shown in Figure 2.

The FPX can process traffic on a wide variety of networks. Line cards have been developed that interface the DED to both Gigabit Ethernet and Asynchronous Transfer Mode (ATM) networks. For Gigabit Ethernet, a GBIC is used to interface with either fiber or copper network ports. The Gigabit Ethernet line card extracts the data from MAC frames and can use VLANs to identify which traffic flows packets should be processed. For ATM networks, a Synchronous Optical NETwork (SONET) line card interfaces to the physical network. Virtual paths and circuits determine which traffic flows are processed.

3.3 Protocol Wrappers

Layered Internet Protocol (IP) wrappers break out the header fields that include the protocol field, source IP address, and destination IP address. The IP wrappers also compute the checksums over the header and process the Time-to-Live field [20]. Internet headers can be processed in many ways, such as with ternary content addressable memories [23], longest-prefix matching tries [24], or with Bloom-based header-matching circuits [25].

For transport protocols, including the User Datagram Protocol (UDP) and Transmission Control Protocol (TCP), the wrappers track the source and destination port of the packet. The wrappers also compute checksums over the entire packet. The TCP wrapper, implemented in FPGA logic, reconstructs the flow of transmitted data by tracking sequence numbers of consecutive packets to provide a byte-ordered data stream to the content scanning engines [30]. This means that even if a malware signature has been fragmented across multiple packets, it still can be detected and blocked. Synchronous Dynamic Random Access Memory (SDRAM) allows the state of multiple traffic flows to be tracked. By allocating 64 bytes of memory for each flow, one 512 Mbyte SDRAM can track 8 million simultaneous TCP/IP flows [22].

Higher-level protocol processing can be implemented above the transport-layer wrappers. For web traffic, a payload processing wrapper could parse HTTP headers to perform filtering on URLs. For email traffic, the payload processing wrapper could parse SMTP headers to block traffic to or from specific email addresses. For peer-to-peer traffic, the payload processing wrapper could scan for signatures of specific content.

3.4   Signature Detection

Many types of Internet traffic can be classified only by deep content inspection [31]. Dynamically reconfigurable hardware can perform content classification functions effectively. Two types of scanning modules have been developed to search for signatures on the FPX: those that use finite automata to scan for regular expressions [26] [27] and those that use Bloom filters to scan for fixed-length strings [28]. With a Bloom filter, a single FPX card can scan for up to 10,000 different, fixed-length strings.

In order to scan packet payloads for regular expressions, a matching circuit was implemented that dynamically generates finite automata. The architecture of the payload scanner with four parallel content scanners searching for n Regular Expressions, $RE:1$-$RE:n$, is illustrated in Figure 2. A match is detected when a sequence of incoming data causes a state machine to reach an accepting state. For example, to detect the presence of the SoBig.F Internet worm as it appears when encapsulated in a Mime64-encoded email, the expression: "**!HEX(683063423739)**" would be specified. In order to achieve high throughput, parallel machines are instantiated. When data arrives, a *flow dispatcher* sends a packet to an available buffer which then streams data though the sequence of regular expression search engines. A *flow collector* combines the traffic into a single outgoing stream. The result of the circuit is the identification of which regular expressions were present in each data flow.

3.5   Performance

Both the finite automata and the Bloom filter scan traffic at speeds of up to 600 Mbps. By implementing four modules in parallel, the FPX can process data at a rate of 2.4 Gigabits per second using a single Xilinx Virtex 2000E FPGA. The parallel hardware enables the FPX to maintain full-speed processing of packets. Data throughput is unaffected by the number of terms that are subject of the search. So long as the working set of signatures fits into the resources on the FPGA and the circuit synthesizes to meet the necessary timing constraints, the throughput remains constant. This is significantly different than software-based solutions, which slow down as the CPU processor becomes fully utilized.

3.6   Web-Based Control Interface and Automated Design Flow

A web-based user interface allows new search strings to be entered remotely. A database tracks the list of search strings, their corresponding description, and a risk value assigned to each virus. When a single 'Build' button is pressed, the design flow is run and the new circuit is deployed on the remote DED [6].

To rapidly generate new hardware that performs the specified searches, a fully automated design flow was developed. The design flow begins when the CMS reads a set of signatures from its database. Finite automaton are dynamically created for each regular expression then optimized to have a minimal number of states. Very-High-Speed Integrated Circuit (VHSIC) Hardware Description

Language (VHDL) code is generated to instantiate parallel automaton that scan the packets passing through the layered Internet protocol wrappers. The VHDL code is synthesized into logic using the Synplicity computer aided design tool. Input and Output (I/O) pins of the circuit are mapped to I/O pins of the RAD. This circuit is then placed and routed with Xilinx tools and a FPGA bitstream is generated. The resulting bitstream is then deployed into a remote FPX platform using the NCHARGE tools [29].

3.7   End-System Applications

The virus protection works for many types of live Internet traffic. Network-wide protection is provided, so long as there is at least one DED in the path from the content sender to the recipient. The DED scans all packets going through the network link and recognizes those that contain a virus signature.

In the passive mode, the DED will detect a virus signature embedded within network traffic and generate a UDP/IP packet that is forwarded to the recipient's computer. An application running on that computer, in turn, is directed to query the RTP to retrieve a full-text description that alerts them to the potential danger that the content represents. This warning message is currently presented to the user via a popup window from a Java application.

In the active mode, the DED not only detects a virus signature, but also blocks the flow of traffic. When a match is found, the DED hardware sends a UDP/IP packet to the intended recipient's network address. The machine that receives that message queries the RTP server using data in that message to retrieve a full-text description that explains why the content was blocked.

An example that shows processing of email traffic is shown in Figure 3. If at least one DED is located along the path between an email server and the intended recipient of the malware, then an infected message can be blocked before it has a chance to reach that end-system. A system protected by a DED will receive an immediate notice whenever a virus-infected message targets the machine. For example, if a DED recognizes that a malware signature is being carried within a POP3 email message, then that inbound data is blocked and a notification is forwarded to the intended recipient's host.

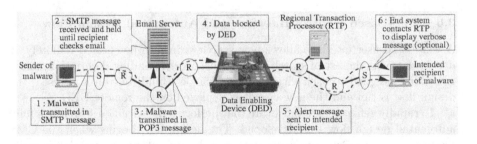

Fig. 3. Example that shows how malware can be blocked by a DED as it attempts to transit from an email server to an end-system

Another example of processing email traffic is shown in Figure 4. If at least one DED is located along the path between the sender and the targeted email server, then an infected message can be blocked before that message even has a chance to reach that email server. Further, the DED can generate a message that alerts the operator on the sending machine that some process on their machine attempted to transmit an infected message.

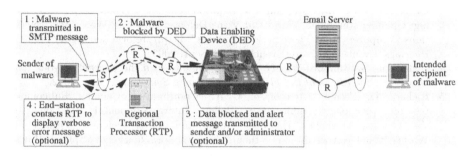

Fig. 4. Example that shows how malware can be blocked by a DED as it attempts to transit from the sender to an email server

The system described here is effective not only against the spread of computer viruses and worms, but also can perform many other functions. Because the system operates at Gigabit speeds and has near-zero latency, it can process live web traffic and scan data sent over peer-to-peer networks. For example, the DED can be configured to detect the unauthorized release of confidential, classified or otherwise sensitive data, and block its distribution. Corporations could scan for proprietary documents passing through a network, and block them before they leave a secure network; and healthcare providers could assure compliance with privacy regulations such as the Health Insurance Portability and Accountability Act. The flexibility of the system to be quickly and remotely reconfigured enables it to meet new needs and perform new tasks. Additional modules can be loaded into the FPX to encrypt and decrypt data, filter packets, and schedule transmission of data over a link to preserve Quality of Service [23].

4   Conclusions

An extensible networking system has been developed that not only blocks the spread of Internet worms and computer viruses, but also can be used to support a wide range of active networking applications. This system uses programmable logic devices to scan Internet traffic for malware at high speeds. Malware is identified by signatures that may consist of either fixed strings or regular expressions. Through the use of layered protocol wrappers, application-level Internet traffic flows can be tracked, with targeted data acted upon before it has an opportunity to damage networks. An automated design flow allows new FPGA circuits to be rapidly deployed to protect the network against new attacks.

References

1. E. Skoudis and L. Ziltser, *Malware: Fighting Malicious Code.* New Jersey: Prentice Hall, first ed., 2003.
2. D. Moore, C. Shannon, G. Voelker, and S. Savage, "Internet quarantine: Requirements for containing self-propagating code," in *IEEE INFOCOM*, (San Francisco, CA), Mar. 2003.
3. US Congressman Adam Putnam, Chairman, Subcommittee on Technology, Information Policy, Intergovernmental Relations and the Census, "Oversight Hearing: Opening statement, Worm and Virus Defense: How Can We Protect the Nations Computers from These Serious Threats." http://reform.house.gov/TIPRC/-Hearings/EventSingle.aspx?EventID=526, Sept. 2003.
4. V. Paxson, S. Staniford, and N. Weaver, "How to 0wn the internet in your spare time," in *Proceedings of the 11th Usenix Security Symposium*, Aug. 2002.
5. Richard D. Pethia, Director of CERT Coordination Center, "Subcommittee on Technology, Information Policy, Intergovernmental Relations and the Census: Oversight Hearing, Worm and Virus Defense: Viruses and Worms: What can we do about them." http://reform.house.gov/UploadedFiles/-Pethia_testimony_Sept2003-v7.pdf, Sept. 2003.
6. J. W. Lockwood, J. Moscola, M. Kulig, D. Reddick, and T. Brooks, "Internet worm and virus protection in dynamically reconfigurable hardware," in *Military and Aerospace Programmable Logic Device (MAPLD)*, (Washington DC), p. E10, Sept. 2003.
7. "CERT coordination center." http://www.cert.org/, 2003.
8. "Know your enemy: Honeynets." http://www.honeynet.org/papers/honeynet, Nov. 2003.
9. S. Singh, C. Estan, G. Varghese, and S. Savage, "The EarlyBird system for real-time detection of unknown worms." UCSD Tech Report CS2003-0761, Aug. 2003.
10. M. Roesch, "SNORT - lightweight intrusion detection for networks," in *LISA '99: USENIX 13th Systems Administration Conference*, (Seattle, Washington), Nov. 1999.
11. L. Schaelicke, T. Slabach, B. Moore, and C. Freeland, "Characterizing the performance of network intrusion detection sensors," in *Proceedings of the Sixth International Symposium on Recent Advances in Intrusion Detection (RAID 2003)*, Lecture Notes in Computer Science, (Berlin–Heidelberg–New York), Springer-Verlag, September 2003.
12. J. W. Lockwood, "Evolvable Internet hardware platforms," in *The Third NASA/DoD Workshop on Evolvable Hardware (EH'2001)*, pp. 271–279, July 2001.
13. FortiNet, "Product overview." http://www.fortinet.com/products/, Nov. 2003.
14. IntruVert, "Press release." http://www.networkassociates.com/us/about/press/corporate/2003/-20030401_173857.htm, Apr. 2003.
15. TippingPoint, "UnityOne 2000." http://www.tippingpoint.com/resource_library/pdfs/2000_Data_Sheet.pdf, Nov. 2003.
16. Packeteer, "Shaping your network for business." http://www.packeteer.com/resources/prod-sol/PacketeerBroFinal2.pdf, Nov. 2003.
17. R. Sidhu and V. Prasanna, "Fast regular expression matching using FPGAs," in *IEEE Symposium on Field-Programmable Custom Computing Machines (FCCM)*, Apr. 2001.

18. R. Franklin, D. Carver, and B. L. Hutchings, "Assisting network intrusion detection with reconfigurable hardware," in *IEEE Symposium on Field-Programmable Custom Computing Machines (FCCM)*, (Napa, CA), Apr. 2002.

19. J. W. Lockwood, N. Naufel, J. S. Turner, and D. E. Taylor, "Reprogrammable Network Packet Processing on the Field Programmable Port Extender (FPX)," in *ACM International Symposium on Field Programmable Gate Arrays (FPGA'2001)*, (Monterey, CA, USA), pp. 87–93, Feb. 2001.

20. F. Braun, J. Lockwood, and M. Waldvogel, "Protocol wrappers for layered network packet processing in reconfigurable hardware," *IEEE Micro*, vol. 22, pp. 66–74, Jan. 2002.

21. D. V. Schuehler and J. Lockwood, "TCP-Splitter: A TCP/IP flow monitor in reconfigurable hardware," in *Hot Interconnects*, (Stanford, CA), pp. 127–131, Aug. 2002.

22. D. V. Schuehler, J. Moscola, and J. W. Lockwood, "Architecture for a hardware based, tcp/ip content scanning system," in *Hot Interconnects*, (Stanford, CA), pp. 89–94, Aug. 2003.

23. J. W. Lockwood, C. Neely, C. Zuver, J. Moscola, S. Dharmapurikar, and D. Lim, "An extensible, system-on-programmable-chip, content-aware Internet firewall," in *Field Programmable Logic and Applications (FPL)*, (Lisbon, Portugal), p. 14B, Sept. 2003.

24. D. E. Taylor, J. S. Turner, J. W. Lockwood, T. S. Sproull, and D. B. Parlour, "Scalable IP lookup for Internet routers," *IEEE Journal on Selected Areas in Communications (JSAC)*, vol. 21, pp. 522–534, May 2003.

25. S. Dharmapurikar, P. Krishnamurthy, and D. E. Taylor, "Longest prefix matching using Bloom filters," in *SIGCOMM*, (Karlsruhe, Germany), Aug. 2003.

26. J. Moscola, J. Lockwood, R. P. Loui, and M. Pachos, "Implementation of a content-scanning module for an Internet firewall," in *FCCM*, (Napa, CA), Apr. 2003.

27. J. Moscola, M. Pachos, J. W. Lockwood, and R. P. Loui, "Implementation of a streaming content search-and-replace module for an Internet firewall," in *Hot Interconnects*, (Stanford, CA, USA), pp. 122–129, Aug. 2003.

28. S. Dharmapurikar, P. Krishnamurthy, T. Sproull, and J. W. Lockwood, "Deep packet inspection using parallel Bloom filters," in *Hot Interconnects*, (Stanford, CA), pp. 44–51, Aug. 2003.

29. T. Sproull, J. W. Lockwood, and D. E. Taylor, "Control and configuration software for a reconfigurable networking hardware platform," in *IEEE Symposium on Field-Programmable Custom Computing Machines, (FCCM)*, (Napa, CA), Apr. 2002.

30. D. V. Schuehler and J. W. Lockwood, "TCP splitter: A TCP/IP flow monitor in reconfigurable hardware," *IEEE Micro*, vol. 23, pp. 54–59, Jan. 2003.

31. Y. Cho, S. Nahab, and W. H. Mangione-Smith, "Specialized hardware for deep network packet filtering," in *Field Programmable Logic and Applications (FPL)*, (Montpellier, France), Sept. 2002.

Active Routing and Forwarding in Active IP Networks*

Jun-Cheol Park

Department of Computer Engineering, Hongik University, 121-791 Seoul, Korea
jcpark@cs.hongik.ac.kr

Abstract. In this paper, we address the problem of active packet routing and forwarding in an active IP network involving both legacy IP routers and active capable routers. We first argue that any traditional routing scheme does not work well in active networks. We then give a formulation of a generalized active routing problem and propose an efficient routing scheme based on the formulation. The scheme is active-destination initiated, and is used for computing paths to a set of active destinations(servers). This selective approach allows the scheme to be seamlessly deployed onto any active IP network. We also present a labeling technique such that a label embedded in a packet can uniquely identify the expected ongoing services on the packet's journey. With a forwarding table indexed by these labels, a simple and quick label lookup is sufficient to resolve any incoming active packet's next hop.

1 Introduction

Routers in the Internet pass any incoming packet without any examination or modification on the packet's payload. They process and modify the packet's header only. A packet in an active network can carry fragments of program code to be executed on the network nodes as well as data to be applied to the code. Thus network users can customize network behavior to suit their requirements and needs by embedding application-specific computation in the packet's code. As a result, it is possible for the users to change the behavior of network nodes on the fly. This ability allows network service providers to develop and deploy new services quickly without going through standardization or vendor-driven consensus.

For a while, results from active network research [1,2,3,4,5,6,7,8,9] will be tested as add-on features onto the existing network infrastructure before active networking is believed to be mature enough to be deployed in a global scale. At any rate, it seems unreasonable to simultaneously convert the whole Internet to a gigantic active network. In the meantime, only some of the routers in the network will support programmability. An active IP network [18], an intermediate step toward pure active networking, involves two different types of network nodes, legacy IP routers and active routers with active processing capability. Both nodes

* This work was supported by 2003 Hongik University Research Fund.

N. Wakamiya et al. (Eds.): IWAN 2003, LNCS 2982, pp. 58–67, 2004.

have been integrated into a single network, and take advantage of the same type of packets and node resources. As a result, users of the traditional IP service do not need to be aware of the existence of active routers. This allows active routers to be deployed seamlessly into an IP network.

In this paper, we address the problem of packet routing and forwarding in an active IP network. In the Internet, each IP packet's next hop is solely based on the packet's destination address. On the other hand, the route of an active packet has to include appropriate intermediate active processing node(s) in between the packet's source and destination. In addition, the current route of an active packet to its destination is subject to change to reflect any further constraint arising later at another intermediate active router. Thus the routing for active packets here is *dynamic* and differs from any Internet routing currently in use. Our goal is to design an efficient active routing scheme and provide a way to deploy the scheme onto active IP networks. The proposed scheme is active destination(server)-initiated: the destination of active application initiates a constrained path computation to itself using dynamic metrics reflecting active processing costs as well as link costs. We also propose a compact labeling technique so that a label embedded in a packet can uniquely identify the expected ongoing services on the packet's journey. The routing scheme constructs a forwarding table arranged by such labels at each active router. Then a simple table lookup suffices for an incoming active packet to determine the next active router to its destination.

The organization of the paper is as follows. Section 2 presents a graph-based formulation of the problem of routing in an active IP network. In section 3, we provide an active destination-initiated routing scheme that constructs a forwarding table indexed with labels at each active node. In section 4, we then show how a simple table lookup with a fixed length label can quickly determine an active packet's next active router. We provide related work of routing in active networks in section 5. In section 6, we conclude the work in the paper and present some future research problems.

2   Routing in Active IP Networks: Problem Formulation

Before we present the problem formulation, we need to resolve a couple of design issues. First, how to address active routers in an active IP network? Since we expect active routers in the network to coexist with other legacy IP routers, we stipulate that each active router is identified by its IP addresses like other IP routers. Second, how to differentiate active packets from ordinary IP packets? We use the Router Alert Option [11] to identify active packets. It allows an active node to process active packets and IP packets differently. An active packet does not cause any alarm when processed by non-active IP nodes and undergoes default IP processing.

The major constraint in active routing is that every active route must include at least one intermediate active node that performs some customized computation within the network. A general form of active routing is to select a sequence of intermediate active nodes through which the active hosts are connected. For example, as observed in [12], an active application for secure data transmission may include both encryption and decryption active processing in that order.

Basically, an active flow can choose its own route on the fly at each intermediate active node in the network. Thus we can't safely assume that the path of an active packet computed at a certain active node remains unchanged throughout the packet's lifetime. For example, if an application can decide whether or not its data be compressed based on the current condition of the network possibly for saving bandwidth of a congested link, the packets of the application may or may not need decompression afterward. Hence this routing problem requires a dynamic routing scheme that should be able to reflect a new constraint, if ever come, on the fly.

We are now ready to formally state a routing problem in an active IP network. The formulation given here is similar to that of the work in [12]. The network is represented by a graph, $G = (V, E)$, in which the nodes correspond to routers and hosts, while the edges correspond to physical links between these nodes. We have a source $s \in V$ and a destination $t \in V$. An edge (u, v) has a non-negative value $cost(u, v)$ representing the "cost" of sending a packet across the corresponding link. Also, for $1 \leq i \leq k$, we let $A_i \subseteq V$ be a subset of the nodes and it contains nodes where the active service i may be performed. We assume that the destination t belongs to A_j for some j. For each node $w \in A_i$, a non-negative value $cost(w)$ representing the cost of performing active service i at the node w is associated. On its journey to the destination, each active packet p processed at an active node $w \in A_i$ has an associated *service list*, denoted $list(p, w)$, which is a sequence $(s_a, \ldots, s_b)$, where $1 \leq s_a, \ldots, s_b \leq k$, representing the active services p need to have from now onward upto the destination. A service list $list(p, w) = (s_a, \ldots, s_b)$ is *dynamic* so that it can be updated to $list(p, w')$ later, where for some $w' \in V_{s'}$, $s' \in \{s_a, \ldots, s_b\}$, $list(p, w')$ is not necessarily a proper suffix of $list(p, w)$.

Throughout this paper, for simplicity, we assume each active node performs only one active service. It is straightforward to extend our work to take care the case when an active node is able to select an arbitrary service among multiple different active services available at the node.

For an active packet, the purpose of our routing algorithm is to find a feasible path that keeps to its current active service constraint at every active node and has "least" cost. The cost of a path is defined as the sum of the costs of its edges and active processing nodes. A least cost path in a legacy IP network is not necessarily the one that our scheme is looking for since the path is obtained with no awareness of service constraint. Given a destination, moreover, the least cost feasible path of a packet at a node is not necessarily a proper suffix of the least cost feasible path of the same packet computed before. Since a packet's processing result in terms of routing is unknown until it is processed, no routing algorithm can always generate global optimum routes in terms of path costs.

A solution was proposed in [12] for finding a least cost feasible path for the special case that the service list constraint is known in advance and remains fixed. We call this routing *static* in the sense that the service list for an active packet remains unchanged along the path to the packet's destination. In the general problem with dynamic nature, it is possible for a "good" route selected at a certain point on the path to be revoked and recomputed at later active nodes in the network.

3   Our Routing Scheme

3.1   Basic Idea

Our routing scheme governs route computation only for the set of active destinations(servers) in an active IP network. For non-active destinations in the network, a popular link state routing algorithm like OSPF2 [16,17] can do the route calculation. Because, in our routing scheme, each initiating active destination(server) takes charge of its route recomputations, the updating of routes to each active destination is uncorrelated. Moreover our active routing is independent of any traditional routing that computes paths for other IP nodes. Hence the scheme can control its routing overhead itself and do not necessarily have to be affected by the dynamic conditions in the active IP network.

A basic assumption in our approach is that each active node has a complete, global knowledge about node connectivity, link costs, and every other active node's information including its identity and providing active service. A modification to the link state protocol OSPF2 can provide the necessary capability. For supporting multicast, OSPF2's link state advertisement packet is marked by a particular bit in its option field. Likewise, an active router may use an unused bit in the option field to indicate its active capability when transmitting its own link state advertisement packets. Non-active nodes would simply ignore the active bit as they are not aware of the meaning of the bit, while active nodes would recognize the active bit and record the identity and location of the packet's sender. In this way, each active node can take active nodes apart from non-active nodes in the network while processing its incoming link state advertisement packets. The scheme can be deployed to any active IP network without modifying OSPF2 software on any legacy IP router.

From an active IP network given as a graph, we generate the *logical* network by extracting only the active nodes and connecting two active nodes with an edge if and when there exists either a direct edge or an indirect path of IP nodes between them. We assume that a link state routing algorithm is used throughout the network for computing paths and generating routing table at each router. A link state routing algorithm like OSPF2 computes the least-cost path between a source and destination using complete, global knowledge about the network. To obtain this information, each node broadcasts the costs of its attached links to all other routers in the network. As the result of the nodes' link state broadcast, all nodes have an identical and complete view of the network, from which each node can then compute the same set of least-cost paths as every other node. Obviously the computation here is for computing paths of IP packets only.

To take care active packet routing, each active node has to exchange information about the current active processing cost of its service with every other active node. The information exchange is done via the imposed logical topology of active nodes overlaying the overall network topology. Thus each active node in the network needs to run the routing algorithm for active packets with service constraints as well as the link state routing algorithm for IP packets. Here we discuss our routing scheme in terms of the logical network of a given active IP network.

3.2   Routing Message Exchange and Forwarding Table Construction

Our routing scheme is destination-initiated, which means each active destination initiates a constrained path computation to itself. The basic mechanism is message flooding in the logical network. An initial routing message is generated at a target destination node periodically. Upon the receipt of a routing message, each node updates its current best path to the destination based on the information carried by the message, modifies the message, and then floods the modified message to all neighbors except the one from which the original message was received.

Each routing message contains a TTL value to prevent it from appearing infinitely and an increasing sequence number to ignore old routing messages generated in the previous rounds. A node may receive more than one routing message with the same sequence number, indicating distinct paths to the destination. A routing message also contains the XOR's over the active services the message has (backward)traversed since its initiation at the destination node. This value becomes a label in the active forwarding table of the arriving node. The forwarding table at a node has a set of entries each represented by a tuple $< label, next\ hop(active\ node), cost, seq\ number >$, where $label$ is the index key value for table lookup, $next\ hop$ is the next hop on the current best route with the corresponding active list, $cost$ is the cost of the route from the node, and $seq\ number$ is used for considering only up-to-date routing messages. Labeling and table lookup methods are discussed in detail in the next section.

Let t be the active destination initiating the computation to its active service s_x. An initial routing message from t at an interval is of the form $[t, s_x, c, seq, ttl]$, where t is the originating node's address, s_x is an advertising service list, c, initially $cost(t)$, is the cost to reach the destination via the services contributed in s_x. Pseudocode is given in Figure 1 for the processing at an arbitrary active node a when it receives a routing message $[b, s_y, c, seq, ttl]$. First, we update the cost c to c' to incorporate the active processing cost at a and the link cost crossing the link (a, b). Then, to insert/update a tuple with the key value s_y, we lookup a's forwarding table. Consider the two cases. Case1: A matching entry is found. We investigate the sequence number seq of the message to see whether it is stale or not. If the message is not stale, then we compare the newly computed cost c' to the one currently stored in the table. In case c' is smaller(i.e., shorter), we replace the stored tuple in the table with the tuple newly having the cost(c'), next hop(b), and sequence number(seq). Then we flood an updated message carrying the new cost, the new label with the active service provided at a is added via XOR, and a decremented TTL. In case the currently stored cost is not greater than c', we simply ignore and discard the message. If the message is stale, we ignore and discard the message as well. Case2: A matching entry is not found. We need to insert the tuple reflecting the message content into the forwarding table, and then flood an updated message similar to the one in Case1.

```
let  c' ← c + cost(a) + cost(a, b);
lookup a's forwarding table entry with the key s_y;
  if matching entry found
      let < l, nh_cur, c_cur, no > be the tuple with the key s_y = l;
    if (no ≤ seq)
      if (c_cur > c')
        replace the tuple < l, nh_cur, c_cur, no > with < l, b, c', seq >;
        forward [a, s_y ⊕ i, c', seq, ttl − 1] to every neighbor of a but b;
        //i is the active service provided at a and
        //⊕ is the XOR operator
      else // c_cur ≤ c' : no better route found
        ignore and discard the message;
    else // no > seq : obsolete message
      ignore and discard the message;
  if matching entry not-found
      insert the tuple < s_y, b, c', seq > to the forwarding table;
      forward [a, s_y ⊕ i, c', seq, ttl − 1] to every neighbor of a but b;
```

Fig. 1. Processing of Routing Message $[b, s_y, c, seq, ttl]$ for Constructing a Forwarding Table at the Node a

As an example, let us consider the propagation of routing messages in the simple logical network shown in Figure 2. In this example, assume that the message forwarded by node X reaches node W before the one forwarded by node Y. Then the forwarding table entry at node W is updated with the new value representing a better route to the destination with the same service list.

3.3   Active Routing Metric

To measure the dynamic active processing cost at an active node, we use the delay measurement for representing node utilization. To do so, each incoming active packet is recorded with its time of arrival at the node and its departure time from the node. Note that the departure time minus the arrival time represents the amount of time the packet was delayed in the node. This number is averaged with the last reported cost to suppress sudden change. The range of value should be carefully adjusted to leverage the processing cost of a plain IP packet.

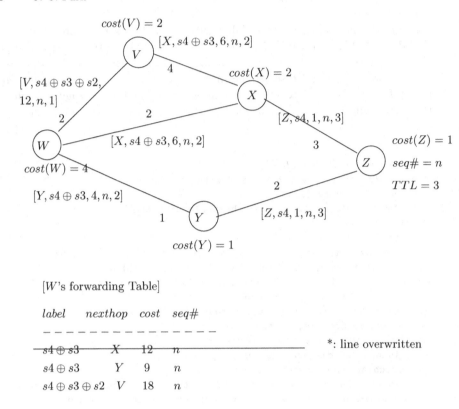

Fig. 2. A Forwarding Table Construction at W when Z initiates the message flooding

4   Labeling and Active Forwarding Table Lookup

The basic idea of labeling is to associate each path with a label computed as the XOR over the services done along the path, and then use this label for each packet of an active application (or flow) to follow that path. Here we assume that each service is uniquely identified among the network with a fixed sized identifier. A path is identified with its service list, say, $(s_1, s_2, \ldots, s_m)$, where s_m is the service available at the destination of a packet following the path. At a certain active node a, where $a \in A_{s_i}$ for some i, the service list $(s_{i+1}, \ldots, s_m)$ is encoded by the label $l = s_{i+1} \oplus \cdots \oplus s_m$. It should be obvious that forwarding tables constructed by the above routing scheme are consistent. The construction ensures that after a packet carrying a label l' generated from its expected service list is processed by service s_i at node a, the forwarding table at a must contain an entry with label $s_i \oplus l'$. Notice that l' should be $s_i \oplus s_{i+1} \oplus \cdots \oplus s_m$ and $s_i \oplus l' = s_i \oplus (s_i \oplus s_{i+1} \oplus \cdots \oplus s_m) = s_{i+1} \oplus \cdots \oplus s_m = l$. It is easy to see that the packet would follow exactly along the path that is linked by the next hop fields of participating nodes.

Active forwarding table lookup is a simple and efficient operation of finding a matching identifier. An active packet carries a short, fixed length label by taking XOR over the service identifiers along the prospect path. To determine the next hop of any incoming active packet, each active node refers its own forwarding table with the packet's label l'. Below we summarize how the forwarding decision is made at an active node a when it receives a packet p with the label l'.

```
the node a processes the packet p with the label l' with its service,
   say s_i;
let (s_{i+1},...,s_m) be the packet p's onward service list revealed at the
   above step;
let l denote s_{i+1} ⊕ ··· ⊕ s_m;
lookup the forwarding table at the node a with the computed label l;
   if matching entry found
      forward the packet p carrying the updated label l to the next hop
         found;
   else // unexpected service list
      compute the packet p's route on the fly;
```

Fig. 3. Forwarding Decision at the Node a for the Packet p with the Label l'

We apply the IP tunneling technique for ensuring active packets sent by an active node to correctly reach to another active node connected to the sending node by intervening IP routers. The receiving side active node, which is the destination of this IP packet, determines that it contains an active packet, and extracts the active packet for customized active processing. In this way, it is certain that the forwarding route of an active packet is always as expected, at least in terms of the correct destination, by the most recently visited active node.

5   Related Work

Maxemchuk and Low [14] discussed how active routing can extend the capabilities and utilization of various routing paradigms such as label switching, QoS routing, mobility, etc. They proposed some implementation techniques including pricing and sandboxes. Their techniques are mainly for enforcing and encouraging economic network resources. Our work has a different goal. We want to provide a way to efficiently deliver active packets with active list constraints in an active IP network. The work in [12] proposed an approach to the problem of configuring application sessions that require intermediate processing. The approach transforms the session configuration problem into a conventional graph theory problem. However, the proposed algorithms assumed that the active service constraint of a packet should remain fixed throughout the packet's lifetime, which limits the applicability. Also, it is unclear how the proposed algorithms can be realized when many of the nodes in the network are non-active. On the contrary, our routing scheme is able to coexist with the popular link state routing algorithm and requires no modification of the behavior of legacy IP routers. The work in [10] might be used as the preprocessing step of our routing scheme in order to discover active neighbors in an active IP network. Unlike our assumption on the fixed locations of services in an active network, a work in [13] proposed a programmable selection and reconfiguration of service location. It would be interesting to see how our scheme could be extended to allow such a dynamic service provisioning. Our routing scheme is partly influenced by the work in [19], which proposes a destination-initiated route computation for a small number of hot destinations. The proposed routing scheme takes advantage of this selective routing idea by taking active routing apart from the traditional IP routing. Using labels for fast packet processing is not new to networking areas [15,20]. For active networks, the work in [15] uses labels for fast demultiplexing of active packets upto their active handlers. The purpose of labels in our scheme is, however, for efficient active path computation and forwarding, which are essential to active routing.

6   Conclusion

The major difference between active routing and traditional IP routing is that routing decision for an active packet depends upon not only the destination address of the packet and the routing table, but other factors including active processing result, policy, etc.

In this work, we addressed the problem of active packet routing in an active IP network, which involves both legacy IP routers and active routers. We formulated a generalized active routing problem in an active IP network and then proposed an efficient active routing scheme based on the formulation. Our scheme is active-destination initiated, and it is used only for the set of active servers without affecting the traditional IP routing for other destinations. This selective approach allows the proposed scheme to be seamlessly deployed onto any active IP network. Also, it reflects dynamic active processing costs metric in addition to link costs when computing routes to active destinations. In order for fast active packet forwarding, we provided a compact labeling technique such that a label embedded in a packet can uniquely identify the expected ongoing services on the packet's journey. With a forwarding table indexed by these labels, it is possible for an incoming active packet to determine its next hop active node by a simple and fast table lookup.

We believe that a large scale experimental study on the proposed scheme is necessary and beneficial to investigate any further questions and problems. As a first step, we are currently working on the extension of OSPF2 protocol and its deployment on a small scale active network testbed. An important problem that must be addressed would be the integration of the proposed routing scheme with existing exterior gateway protocol like BGP4 for a wide area active IP network.

References

1. D. Tennenhouse, and D. Wetherall, "Towards an active network architecture", Computer Communication Review, vol. 26, no. 2, 1996.
2. D. Alexander, W.A. Arbaugh, A.D. Keromytis, and J.M. Smith, "A secure active network environment architecture: realization in SwitchWare", IEEE Network, vol. 12, no. 3, 1998.
3. M. Hicks, P. Kakkar, J. Moore, C.A. Gunter, and S. Nettles , "PLAN: A packet language for active networks", Proc. ACM SIGPLAN Int'l Conf. on Functional Programming(ICFP'98), 1998.
4. B. Schwartz, A. Jackson, T. Strayer, W. Zhou, R. Rockwell, and C. Patridge, "Smart packets for active networks", Proc. IEEE Conf. on Open Architectures and Network Programming(OPENARCH'99), 1999.
5. D. Wetherall, J. Guttag, and D. Tennenhouse, "ANTS: A toolkit for building and dynamically deploying network protocols", Proc. IEEE Conf. on Open Architectures and Network Programming(OPENARCH'99), 1999.
6. S. Bhattacharjee, K. Calvert, and E. Zegura, "An architecture for active networking", Proc. IEEE INFOCOM'97, 1997.
7. Y. Yemini, and S. da Silva, "Towards programmable networks", Proc. IFIP/IEEE Int'l Workshop on Distributed Systems, Operations, and Management, 1996.
8. D. Decasper, and B. Plattner, "DAN: Distributed code caching for active networks", Proc. IEEE INFOCOM'98, 1998.
9. J. Moore, M. Hicks, and S. Nettles, "Practical programmable packets", Proc. IEEE INFOCOM 2001, 2001.
10. S. Martin, and G. Leduc, "RADAR: Ring-based adaptive discovery of active neighbour routers", Proc. IFIP-TC6 4th Int'l Working Conf. on Active Networks(IWAN 2002), 2002.
11. D. Katz, "IP Router Alert Option", Internet Request for Comments 2113, 1997.
12. S. Choi, J. Turner, and T. Wolf, "Configuring sessions in programmable networks", Proc. IEEE INFOCOM 2001, 2001.
13. A.B. Kulkarni, G.J. Minden, V. Frost, and J. Evans, "Survivability of Active Networking Services", Proc. 1st Int'l Working Conf. on Active Networks(IWAN 1999), 1999.
14. N.F. Maxemchuk, and S.H. Low, "Active routing", IEEE Jr. on Selected Areas in Communications, vol. 29, no. 3, 2001.
15. T. Wolf, D. Decasper, and C. Tschudin, "Tags for high performance active networks", Proc. IEEE Conf. on Open Architectures and Network Programming(OPENARCH2000), 2000.
16. J. T. Moy, OSPF Anatomy of an Internet Routing Protocol, Addison-Wesley, 1998.
17. J. T. Moy, OSPF Complete Implementation, Addison-Wesley, 2001.
18. D. Murphy, Building an Active Node on the Internet, M.E. Thesis, MIT, 1997.
19. J. Chen, P. Druschel, and D. Subramanian, "A new approach to routing with dynamic metrics", Proc. IEEE INFOCOM 1999, 1999.
20. I. Stoica, and H. Zhang, "LIRA: An approach for service differentiation in the Internet", Proc. NOSSDAV'98, 1998.

A Sustainable Framework for Multimedia Data Streaming

Alessandro Bassi[2], Jean-Patrick Gelas[1], and Laurent Lefèvre[1]

[1] LIP INRIA RESO, Ecole Normale Supérieure de Lyon
46, allée d'Italie, 69364 Lyon Cedex 07, France
laurent.lefevre@inria.fr, Jean-Patrick.Gelas@ens-lyon.fr
[2] LoCI Laboratory - University of Tennessee
203 Claxton Building - 37996-3450 Knoxville, TN, USA
abassi@cs.utk.edu

Abstract. Streaming is the ability to use multimedia data while they are being sent over networks. We propose a realistic and sustainable approach called Active Logistical Cache as a framework to support an efficient caching of multimedia streaming inside the Internet. The approach is based on active networking support (dynamicity, new services and protocols) merged with logistical storage. The tools proposed are the Tamanoir[1] execution environment combined with the Internet Backplane Protocol middleware. By describing a scenario, we illustrate the realistic potential of this approach.

1 Introduction

It is easily predictable that in a near future multimedia streaming will play a major role in consuming a huge share of Internet resources, as it already does it today; and as it does not seem likely a future limitation of this kind of traffic on the commodity Internet, but instead an exponential growth, solutions beyond a blind faith in the Moore's law might preserve ourselves and younger generations to catastrophic traffic congestions. Unfortunately, we can notice that the remedies we see today proposed by the scientific community are not implemented on the mainstream equipment market, and this picture seems to not likely change in the near future.

Currently, the limiting factors of a scalable growth of multimedia streaming over the Internet are:

- Fixed protocols : streaming applications designers must choose network transport protocols (UDP, TCP, RTP...). This choice often does not fit with local and global configurations, such as firewalls, dropping UDP streams, or being TCP not adapted to high performance networks.

---

[1] This work is supported by the French RNTL Etoile project
(http://www.urec.cnrs.fr/etoile).

N. Wakamiya et al. (Eds.): IWAN 2003, LNCS 2982, pp. 68–79, 2004.
© IFIP International Federation for Information Processing 2004

- Proxy and mirrors : these equipments, commonly used in Web traffic, are not natively adapted to multimedia stream caching.
- Network services : multimedia streams rely on services seldom deployed like multicast. To bypass these limitations, stream applications must implement personalized solutions.

Another factor preventing the wide diffusion of clients for multimedia streaming can be identified in the dominion of proprietary solutions for streaming, from companies such as RealNetworks, Microsoft, and Apple; as their standards are not compatible between each other, consumers are forced to download and run more than one dedicated clients to ensure the capability of receiving any stream.

With this article we would like to introduce a framework, based on a combination of an high-performance active networking environment (Tamanoir [8]), providing the necessary dynamism for the deployment of new services, and the logistical networking storage middleware (Internet Backplane Protocol [2]), allowing data to be temporarily stored in the network and transferred efficiently between endpoints.

The Tamanoir Execution Environment is an active software dedicated to deploy and maintain personalized network services for streams transport in an efficient way. Its main achievement is the ability to deal with some of the historical problems that this kind of approach has to face, such as security and high performance, implementing an efficient multi-streams active transport and dynamic services deployment in the network. Tamanoir has an original and unexplored approach with regards to on-the-fly storage in the network, as it takes advantage of the Internet Backplane Protocol (IBP) suite to manage the ability to store data in the network. IBP is designed to allow applications to use shared storage resources in an exposed way. IBP is the corner stone of Logistical Networking, where the term logistical comes from the similarity with the industrial and military world, in which depots are used to store goods (instead of data) in transit.

This paper is organized as follows: after a brief description of the reasons of the sustainability of this approach in section 2, we provide a definition and the architecture of the Active Logistical Cache and their composing parts in the section 3; section 4 focuses on the basic Multimedia services the Tamanoir-IBP marriage is able to offer to a potential application, section 5 describes a quite common scenario, and how can various problems be addressed with our solution. After briefly talking about related projects in section 6, we present our conclusions and future works.

2   Sustaining the Visions

In the recent years many cache systems, with almost any level of intelligence, activeness, responsiveness, have been studied and proposed to the scientific community. We feel that our role is not to argue about how good or bad any of these approaches are. We actually believe that many, if not most of them, are based on solid theory basis, and their widespread adoption could be very beneficial to the entire community.

Our focus is slightly different. Looking at all this theoretical and practical effort, a reader could ask himself why any of those systems are not adopted widely. This main question is not if those systems are scalable as they should, but instead (and much more pragmatically) if those systems are *sustainable*.

In this context, by *sustainable* we mean a solution that can be deployed and managed world-wide in an easy way.

Why do we feel that the work we are presenting has better chances than any other one, and why do we feel that it is sustainable ? Mainly because what we are proposing is a *framework* to build active and intelligent caches distributed in the network. Logistical (IBP) and Active (Tamanoir) Networking are two independent general-purpose projects, complementing each other perfectly, whose success or failure will not depend solely on multimedia stream treatment. IBP middleware is used already in many different areas, from basic services like check-pointing or data staging, to more complex ones such as overlay routing or massive data transfers. IBP depots have already been deployed in around 300 different sites around the whole world, offering a publicly available storage space of around twenty Terabytes. The IBP traffic monitored by Abilene shows that this protocol is used for everyday operations. Tamanoir is an active networking execution environment, allowing any data stream to receive differentiated treatment according to the service linked to it. While the core team is focused on the development of the execution environment, many on-going projects are developing different services to fit their particular research needs, from reliable multicast to programmable transport protocols for scientific grid projects.

Their deployment follows a different strategy also, as IBP depots tend to be positioned as close as possible to very well-connected nodes in the core network topology, offering storage services in places easy to reach, while Tamanoir Active Nodes lie more on the network periphery, between the core network and the clients, to optimize the transport performance. Both network storage and active services can be, if they are not already, top items in a service (or infrastructure) provider agenda, giving a chance to this particular environments to be widely adopted.

A typical ISP can be interested in deploying this two frameworks in order to offer to his customers additional services, like the capacity of storing huge quantities of data for a certain period of time, or provide opportunistic encryption between two sensitive network points.

In this paper, we are proposing a framework to multimedia streaming application developers, to let them implement new solutions, such as active caches schemes or protocols. ALCs will give them the possibility of using and managing a storage space of several Terabytes distributed worldwide, and to use an high performance execution environment to develop new active services. Or, in other words, a mean for sustaining their visions.

3   The Active Logistical Cache Framework

3.1   Basic Definition

An Active Logistical Cache (ALC) framework is a network element composed by a Tamanoir Active Node and an IBP depot. During streaming transport, any crossed ALC can dynamically store streams on the fly not only on the crossed node, but on any convenient depot, and for any stream size. ALC can cache various kind of streams :

- Stored streams : considered like files with possible missing parts, streams can be dynamically and entirely stored in ALCs;
- Live Internet Television or Radio : to allow new users to join a multicast group and to apply on the fly services on multimedia data, only a temporal part of the stream is stored in the ALC (variable window);
- VoD streams : to allow asynchronous users to join a video broadcast session by sending them earlier part of the data, stream movies can be stored since the beginning of the broadcast.

Multimedia stream services can be efficiently and dynamically transported and deployed thanks to the Tamanoir Active Network infrastructure. Therefore, services such as store and forward, dynamic compression of video streams, multicast, and video transcoding can be easily applied by any ALC.

3.2   The Logistical Networking Infrastructure

IBP has been developed to allow the sharing of distributed storage resources, scaling to any size in all the dimensions involved, which are the aggregate storage space, the number of separate depots, and the community size. IBP gives to any application the possibility of allocating a discrete amount of space for a discrete amount of time, on a specific server. The mechanism and his philosophy have been clearly identified, but the protocol itself has not yet been standardized, although there are plans to submit its specifications in the very near future to the Global Grid Forum and to the Internet Engineering Task Force.

The IBP software has been successfully tested for different OSes and hardware architectures (such as Linux on i686 and ia64, Solaris, Windows 2000, AIX, DEC alpha, OS X), and its current version is 1.3.1.

IBP depots publicly available through the Logistical Backbone are currently around 150, deployed in around 60 different sites in the whole world, with a total aggregate storage space of around 10 Terabytes. IBP has also been adopted by projects such as 6Net, an European IST project and, together with Tamanoir, by e-Toile, a French-scale Grid project.

3.3   Tamanoir : High Performance Active Networking

The integration of new and standard technologies into the shared network infrastructure has become a challenging task, and the growing interest in the active networking field [13] might be seen as a natural consequence. In "active" networking vision, routers or any network equipments (like gateway or proxy) within the network can perform computations on user data in transit, and end users can modify the behavior of the network by supplying programs, called *services*, that perform these computations.

The Tamanoir architecture design does not interphere with the core network, mainly to guarantee higher performance results, and it's deployed only on the network periphery.

The injection of new functionalities, called services, is independent from the data stream: services are deployed on demand when streams reach an active node which does not hold the required service. New services can be downloaded, when required, either from a service repository or, from the last Tamanoir Active Node crossed by the data stream.

For the implementation process of the Tamanoir execution environment we choose the JAVA language, because it provides great flexibility, shipped with standard library and support dynamic class loading. Each new service is inherited from a generic class, called *Service* which is a Java *Thread*. Performances achieved with light services, which do not require a lot of processing power, are adapted to current networks requirements. As an example a Tamanoir Active Node is able to support, over local and wide area Gbits Link, from 450 Mbps to 1.6Gbits (depending on number of processing unit, network technology and number of active data streams).

3.4   Architecture

Both Tamanoir Active Node (TAN) and IBP depot are two independent processes communicating through a socket over a reliable transport protocol (TCP). (see Figure 1). As an ALC generally access a local depot, tools on a higher level of the Logistical Networking stack such as the exNode tools or the full Logistical Run-Time System suite are not necessary, and the active node can communicate directly with the IBP depot using the IBP API.

Each service willing to use logistical storage has to instantiate its own IBP client classes in order to to communicate with an IBP depot. These classes provide constructors and methods to create *Capabilities* (cryptographically secure URLs to IBP allocations) on any IBP depot, capabilities with whom the Tamanoir service can write, read and manage data remotely on the IBP depot.

We also measure the overhead introduced by the caching action in an IBP depot close to the Tamanoir Active Node. For these results we ran an IBP depot on the same node than the TAN.

Our testbed, disconnected from the production network, is set up with one active Tamanoir node which is a PC (Dual-Pentium III, 1 Ghz, 256MB RAM) shipped with several *Ethernet 100Mbits* network interface cards and a standard IDE hard-drive. We link to this PC different other PC who have the role to either feed the network or receive data. These PCs run under GNU/Linux with a 2.4.16 kernel (distribution *Debian 2.2r3*).

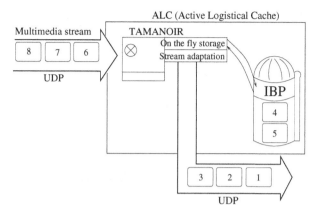

Fig. 1. Inside an Active Logistical Cache : Tamanoir and IBP frameworks for a multimedia stream adaptation service

When an ANEP packet reaches the TAN, its payload is extracted and sent towards the required service. At the beginning, the service copies the payload in the local IBP depot. For the measures we have set up only one client which consumes data as fast as possible. Next, the payload is read in the cache and forwarded to the client immediately. For each packet, we measure the time to cross a TAN (latency) with and without caching action. A chronometer is located as low as possible in the kernel. We use *Netfilter* [12] which is a package for filtering in the Linux kernel. NetFilter allows us to introduce timer code just behind the network interface card. When an ANEP packet reaches the TAN, our NetFilter module analyzes the packet, and the timer is started. When the same ANEP packet leaves the TAN, the timer is stopped.

In figure 2 we present the latency of a TAN by an ANEP packet. In the first case (lower curve) packets are immediately forwarded and not cached in the IBP depot, in the second case packets are cached and next forwarded.

As shown, caching doesn't introduce a very important overhead. For any packet size, overhead remains constant. For small packets size, performances are weak due too the policy of transmission of Linux kernel TCP implementation which tries to aggregate small packets before being transmitted. So, small packets are released just after a timeout.

4   The ALC Service Tool-Box for Data Streaming and Multimedia

Tamanoir offers various network and high level services to multimedia and data streaming applications. These services, dynamically deployed, allow users and operators to manage multimedia streams with active logistical caches efficiently.

ALC active available services can be classified into various categories : transport services (multi-protocols, multicast, QoS. . .), network services (content

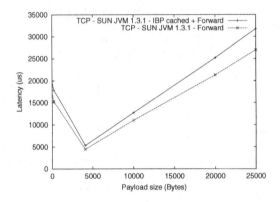

Fig. 2. Overhead introduced by caching data in a local IBP depot

based routing, dynamic network management, monitoring...) and stream services (transcoding, compression on the fly, multi-codes...).

Moreover, users and applications designers can deploy their own personalized services inside an ALC. We focus this section on few services dedicated to active cache and open a discussion about the ones under development.

4.1   Video Adaptation

Todays' networks have to deal with three kind of heterogeneity. The first one is the *data* heterogeneity, which is depending by the applications requirements in terms of throughput, synchronism, jitter, error injected during transport, and so on. The second one can be identified in the *physical transport media* heterogeneity which, having different throughput characteristic, may limit the reliability and therefore introduce asymmetry. The last heterogeneity class comes from different *clients terminals* (PDA, cell phone, desktop, TV, ...), having different processing power and ability to restore informations. Active Networks give us the opportunity to create and/or adapt transport protocols and configure it dynamically for a targeted type of stream or an application. They also give the capacity to process the data stream to adapt it for the client's processing needs, its type of connection and its application requirements (see Fig. 1).

Services must be efficient and must guarantee an high performance to be able to sustain the bandwidth throughput without introducing too much latency. To achieve good results, we must use appropriate data structures for an efficient data processing (using hierarchical coding like MPEG-4 for video transfer) A service embedded in the TAN is able to reduce the quantity of informations just by dropping the surplus of data unused by light terminal at a very light cost (Fig. 1).

4.2   Multi-protocols: UDP – TCP

Using UDP or TCP protocols on a controlled "load free" local area network does not show spectacular differences in term of throughput and latency. But in a long distance context, even if some packets are lost with the UDP protocol, it is pretty difficult to use TCP for time constraint applications. TANs can be used to change the transport protocol during the packet's journey, as they are deployed in the access layer. As an example, an application might choose to use any transport protocol in the first part of the transfer, in a campus or a company for example, until packets cross the TAN which will put the data in a user datagram (UDP) for traveling the long distance part through the network; and, finally, when packets reach the other side of the network, another TAN might change the protocol transport if requested, and send it towards the end nodes. In this context, TANs can be seen as gateway in charge to change the transport protocol in function of the application requirements. In this case TANs should manage the connections. One more time the Active Networking concept gives the opportunity to achieve better performance by injecting code and processing power into the network equipments.

5   A Possible Scenario

5.1   Multicast Today

Nowadays, when applications need to send data to many receivers they are have two possibilities to choose from: repeated transmissions or multicast (see Fig.3). Classic applications like the web or ftp have a client-server approach, which just needs a point-to-point protocol. But applications like audio and video broadcasting, information push or distributed virtual world obviously require point-to-multipoint communications, and this kind of communications does not seem to be well deployed on the current Internet [7] infrastructure.

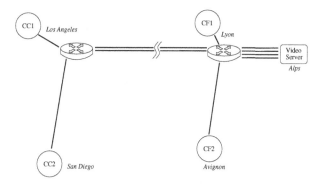

Fig. 3. A current scenario without multicast for multimedia streams

Although born as the same epoch (1990) than the web (which represents today more than 80% of all Internet traffic) and universally perceived as useful, multicast (class D of IP) is still not large-scale deployed and not proposed by a majority of ISP (Internet Service Provider).

Unfortunately, the original IP multicast is based on an *open* service model which was not designed with a robust strategy or in function of clear commercial requirements. For example, there are no restrictions for users to create a multicast group, or to receive from and send data to a multicast group. There is also a lack of simple and scalable mechanisms for supporting: access control (group creation and membership), security (routing, data integrity), address allocation, network management (tools) and finally, multicast datagram are like IP datagram: best-effort and unreliable.

This is why, even though multicast is shipped with most commercial routers, most IP carriers have not yet enabled the service in the networks.

5.2   The Active Logistical Networking Solution

We would like to introduce a scenario to illustrate which services an active logistical caching architecture can provide in multimedia streaming delivery. We have a server producing video stream on the Alps nearby Lyon, France, and connected with a radio connection to a router in our lab, with two clients (CF1 and CF2) located in Lyon (with a ADSL connection to our Active Node) and in Avignon, France (with a 56K modem), and two clients (CC1 and CC2) located respectively in San Diego, Ca, and Los Angeles, Ca., one with an ISDN and the other with a T3 connection (see Fig. 4). For the purpose of this scenario, we will only add an Active Node in Los Angeles, while all the remaining infrastructure is already in place, and therefore we will use their real URL names in this example.

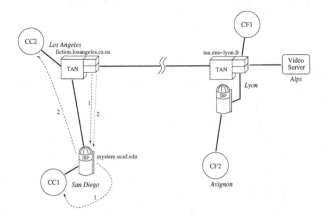

Fig. 4. Active networking and cache scenario

At a first glance, we can observe that, while for performance reasons the optimal solution would be to have the TAN and the IBP depot on the same machine (such as tan.ens-lyon.fr), our architecture works equally as well when the IBP depot is sitting on a remote machine (which is the case of California, where the TAN is installed in Los Angeles, and the IBP depot in San Diego). In other words, the deployment of TANs and of IBP depots can be done (as it is) independently and in parallel, and it is possible to reuse public depots not specifically dedicated to work with a TAN and already deployed in the Internet.

Moreover, if the clients are connecting at a different time, they can get the video stream from the beginning, as it's cached nearby the active node, and the only QoS connection they are depending upon is the one between the TAN and their machine. This is extremely important in case the first connection, as in our scenario, is particularly bad: if a packet is lost a the beginning of its journey, no client would be able to get it. In environments like the one described an application could use the Active Node to switch between TCP and UDP according to the importance of the link in the global architecture, the underlying network connections, real-time traffic considerations, QoS demands and so on.

Using distributed storage servers is also fundamental in relieving the network of having the same packets sent over and over the same wires to satisfy clients asynchronous needs; so, when a client (CC2, for instance) contacts the TAN in Los Angeles for the video stream, the TAN redirects its request to the San Diego depot holding the video; and, in case it's the first client with this particular request, the TAN forwards the request to the TAN running in Lyon, having the stream starting from Lyon, and not from the original source. As the bandwidth between Lyon and Los Angeles might be different from the "last mile one" between the Client and the TAN, as it is in reality, data can be buffered and cached in the nearest IBP depot, the San Diego one, using a classical store-and-forward service; and the IBP built-in fast data mover module and other facilities such as the exNode could be used for handling the data transfer between depots.

6   Related Works

IBP has often been compared with many network storage systems and technologies, such as FreeNet [6], OceanStore [10], AFS [9], even NFS, although with a different storage philosophy, making our research more similar to works carried for Storage Area Network in local networks. IBP can also show some similarity with projects coming from the scientific Grid community, such as GASS [3] and the SDSC Storage Resource Broker [1].

Active networks projects using storage facilities are not intensively addressed. The most related projects are Active Disks [11] or active-network-storage [14] which explore the increasing of intelligence in Network Attached Storage. Our active logistical cache is more related with [4] and [5] by adding logistical and active networks functionalities. The main distinction between ALC presented in this paper and that being undertaken in other areas is that this proposed architecture is low impact, efficient and easily adaptable for each stream or application.

7   Conclusion and Future Works

Although a particular implementation might be sub-optimal, we firmly believe that without explicit control of *computation* and *storage* resources in the network any caching system for multimedia streaming is doomed. Therefore, merging two environments like IBP and Tamanoir allow us to propose an architecture (named Active Logistical Cache Framework) as a central solution for building efficient streaming algorithms over the Internet.

We also believe that, to keep up with the always growing demand, only execution environments developed with a strong attention to performance, like Tamanoir, can show and prove the potential of Active Networking ideas to a wide public.

Active networks equipment usually do not propose storage services. Meanwhile, distributed storage technologies do not rely on dynamic services. ALC frameworks elements can be installed and deployed inside networks by operators, ISP or campus administrators. ALC services can be proposed and deployed by applications designer who want to efficiently broadcast streams.

Concerning future plans, both projects envisage to deploy more Active Nodes and IBP depots in wide area network, Tamanoir is looking upon the development of new services for Multimedia oriented applications, which make use of more layers of the logistical networking framework, such as the ex-Node, the Logistical Runtime System Tools (LoRS) and the Data Mover. Meanwhile, the IBP project aims to deliver new versions of the Data Mover and of Logistical Runtime System Tools.

References

1. C. Baru, R. Moore, A. Rajasekar, and M. Wan. The SDSC Storage Ressource Broker. In *CASCON'98*, Toronto, Canada, 1998.
2. M. Beck, T. Moore, and J. Plank. An end-to-end approach to globally scalable network storage. In *Proceedings of the ACM SIGCOMM 2002 Conference*. SIGCOMM, august 2002.
3. J. Bester, I. Foster, C. Kesselman, J. Tedesco, and S. Tuecke. Gass: A data movement and access service for wide area computing systems. In *Sixth Workshop on I/O in Parallel and Distributed Systems*, may 1999.
4. E. Bommaiaha. Design and implementation of a caching system for streaming media over the internet. In *IEEE Real-Time Technology and Applications Symposium (RTAS)*, Washington D.C., USA, May 2000.
5. P. Cao, J. Zhang, and K. Beach. Active cache: Caching dynamic contents (objects) on the web. In *IFIP International Conference on Distributed Systems Platforms and Open Distributed Processing (Middleware '98)*, pages 373–388, The Lake District, England, sept 1998.

6. Ian Clarke, Oskar Sandberg, Brandon Wiley, and Theodore W. Hong. Freenet: A distributed anonymous information storage and retrieval system. In Hannes Federrath, editor, *Designing Privacy Enhancing Technologies: International Workshop on Design Issues in Anonymity and Unobservability*, LNCS 2009. Springer: New York, 2001.

7. Christoph Diot, Brian Neil Levine, Bryan Lyles, Hassan Kassem, and Doug Balensiefen. Deployment issues for the ip multicast service and architecture. *IEEE Network*, 14(1):78–88, jan 2000.

8. Jean-Patrick Gelas and Laurent Lefèvre. Mixing high performance and portability for the design of active network framework with java. In *3rd International Workshop on Java for Parallel and Distributed Computing, International Parallel and Distributed Processing Symposium (IPDPS 2001)*, San Fransisco, USA, April 2001.

9. J.H. Morris, M. Satyanarayan, M.H. Conner, J.H. Howard, D.S.H. Rosenthal, and F.D. Smith. Andrew: A Distributed Personal Computing Environment. *Communication of the ACM*, 29(3):184–201, 1986.

10. Sean Rhea, Chris Wells, Patrick Eaton, Dennis Geelsand Ben Zhao, Hakim Weatherspoon, and John Kubiatowicz. Maintenance-free global data storage. *IEEE Internet Computing*, 5(5), september 2001.

11. Erik Riedel. Active disks - remote execution for network-attached storage. Technical Report CMU-CS-99-177, Electrical and Computer Engineering Carnegie Mellon University, Pittsburgh, PA 15213, Nov. 1999.

12. Rusty Russell. Linux Filter Hacking HOWTO. july 2000.

13. David Tennenhouse and David Wetherall. Towards an active network architecture. *Computer Communications Review*, 26(2):5–18, April 1996.

14. A. Tomita, Y. Takamoto, S. Inohara, H. Odawara, F. Maciel, M. Sugie, and N. Watanabe. A Scalable, Cost-Effective, and Flexible Disk System Using High-Performance Embedded-Processors. In *IEEE International Conference on Parallel Processing*, 2000.

Deployment of Collaborative Web Caching with Active Networks

Laurent Lefèvre[1], Jean-Marc Pierson[2], and SidAli Guebli[2]

[1] LIP INRIA RESO, Ecole Normale Supérieure de Lyon
46, allée d'Italie, 69364 Lyon Cedex 07, France
laurent.lefevre@inria.fr
[2] LIRIS, INSA de Lyon
7, av. Jean Capelle, 69621 Villeurbanne cedex, FRANCE
jean-marc.pierson@liris.cnrs.fr

Abstract. Deploying "distributed intelligence" inside the network through the help of collaborative caches is a difficult task. This paper focus on the design of new collaborative web caches protocols through the help of active networks. These protocols have been implemented within the high performance Tamanoir[6] execution environment. First experiments on local platform are presented.[1]

1   Introduction

Nowadays, and for almost a decade now, the World Wide Web generates a huge amount of traffic from the heart of the network down to the home end-users. This amount of information have to be tackled efficiently in order to achieve global good response times. We examine in this contribution two tools to increase the potentiality of the current architectures. On one hand, cache techniques have been proved efficient since a long time to reduce the latency of the network as well as its bandwidth consumption. While the basic technique consists in keeping copies in a cache of the web documents closer to their clients, collaborative caches give the opportunity for different caches to share their content, increasing the global efficiency of the system. Efficient collaborative proxy caches have been deployed worldwide (for instance the well known Squid [12]), and any institution, company or ISP have deployed one (or many) today. They often consist in a specialized host either connected to the communication infrastructure (usually with high speed links) or on-board in the routers or gateways traversed by the web queries. Limited possibilities to change the behavior of the interconnection devices make it difficult to propose and deploy new caches inside the network. On the other hand, active networks allows to dynamically deploy new services in the networks, without interfering with the commonly used protocols. Their programming facilities offer new directions for protocol and network designer to apply new technologies without going through heavy standardization process.

---

[1] The authors wish to thank J.P. Gelas for his help with Tamanoir platform.

N. Wakamiya et al. (Eds.): IWAN 2003, LNCS 2982, pp. 80–91, 2004.

Our goal in this work is to link those aspects, that is to create a collaborative cache framework and to embedded it in an active network through adapted and usable services. The idea is to put the management of the collaborative cache schema in the access layer of the network, and to propose non-intrusive collaborative services. Some of the difficulty lays in the limited resources of the active nodes (in terms of CPU, memory and disk). We have thus to propose an adapted solution taking into account these constraints. The goal of our framework is to add some kind of intelligence in the routing of the web traffic and document caches replication in the edges of the network. We clearly benefit from active networks support by transparently deploying active caches through data path without modifying and re-configuring Web clients and servers. Moreover active caches services can communicate in point to point way through control communication channel between active nodes. We propose an implementation of these web caching active services through the help of the Tamanoir[6] execution environment and present first experimental results.

The remaining of this article is organized as follows : We first analyze in section 2 the work done for collaborative caching and we give the characteristics we want to offer. In section 3 we detail some fundamentals of the active networks and we exhibit the constraints we have to tackle for our framework. In section 4, we propose an adapted framework for collaborative caching in the context of active networks. We give in section 5 some implementation issues as well as results of experimentation on a Tamanoir platform. We finally conclude in section 6.

2   Collaborative Caching

Caching techniques have been used in many domains of computer science for several decades, with much work on Web caching [1]. Basically, caches copy data delivered by a server closer to the potential clients to answer data requests later in place of the server. The main expectations are the reduction of the data server load and the improvement of the latency time. A side effect is the reduction of the network load.

In [13], the authors describe the potential impact of the collaborative scheme for the benefit of the hit rate, through real proxy data analysis and an analytic model of web behavior. Several collaboration protocols between caches have been proposed : Hierarchical caches (like Harvest [4] and Squid [12]), Adaptive caches [14,8] and Geographical caches [7]. In this latter technique, the server pushes documents to geographically located proxies that serve groups of users.

Adaptive caching [14,8] explores the idea of creating interleaving meshes with caches. Caches are grouped to answer cooperatively the requests of the users. In this system, the groups dynamically adapt to the changes in the network, and membership of a cache in a group might be revoked if its membership does not give a sufficient benefit.

Hierarchical caching [4,12] proposes to create a hierarchy between the caches of the system. The bottom level is composed of caches close to the clients (for instance the caches incorporated in the web browsers). The next level represents institution caches. The upper level is close to the network backbones, managing several institution caches. Although some intermediary levels can be added, Wolman et al. [13] exhibit that using more than two levels do not give extra performances. In this approach, the basic idea is that a request to a document go up in the hierarchy until it retrieves the document. As explained in [11], some features limit their efficient deployment : (1) To grow up a hierarchy, the caches have to be placed at strategic points of the network, leading to a necessary high coordination between each peer of the system. (2) Each level introduces an additional delay. (3) The upper level of the hierarchy might represent a bottleneck. (4) Multiple copies of the same document might be present in the system.

All the collaboration schemas need a communication protocol between caches. The well known ICP (Internet Cache Protocol) [12] focuses on the efficient inter-cache communication module and mechanisms to create complex hierarchies. When a document is requested and not present in a cache, ICP multicasts a query to its neighbors (this neighboring has to be constructed beforehand). The extensibility of the protocol is a problem, since the number of messages increases with the number of collaborative caches in the system. In [5], Fan et al. show that the network traffic can increase up to 90%.

Other promising techniques for communicating information between caches are based on creating and maintaining summaries of the contents of these caches, communicating those, and performing finally a local decision, based on this knowledge of the distributed contents of the caches. Cache digest [10] and Summary cache [5] are such examples. While in Cache digest the caches exchange periodically their summaries (thus generating network load), a push strategy is used in Summary cache (reducing the traffic). The main problem with these approaches lays in the consistency of the summaries as compared to the actual contents of the caches. Indeed, the content of the summary might be partly false due to the dynamic of the documents in each cache. The challenge is to find the right parameters (how often to exchange summaries) to have a good consistency between the summaries and the actual contents of the cache.

One important point in the behaviors of the caches is the replacement strategy of the documents in the cache. While many exist in the literature [3], we will focus in this paper on the schema of collaboration between caches. Thus we will use in the experiment a simple LRU strategy (Least Recently Used) where the oldest document is removed from the cache first [2]. Note that this replacement strategy does not interfere with the remaining of the proposal.

Based on these related works, our proposal will rely on a mix of :

- hierarchical caching (with a limited two levels hierarchy),
- adaptive caching (the community of caches might be dynamic),
- and an adapted communication protocol using summaries.

---

[2] We also design content-aware strategy[9] where usages and contents of documents are used to determine their time to live in the cache, which is out the scope of this paper.

taking into account the constraints and benefits of using active networks. Thus, we now present briefly the active networks and their key features in the framework of this proposal.

3   Using Active Networks for Collaborative Web Caches

In order to efficiently deploy our Collaborative Web cache architecture we need an open network platform easily manageable and deployable. We based our deployment of Collaborative Web Caching infrastructure on the Tamanoir[6] execution environment developed in RESO - LIP laboratory. Its architecture is designed to be an high performance active router able to be deployed around high performance backbone. This approach concerns both a strategic deployment of active network functionalities around backbone in access layer networks and by providing an high performance dedicated architecture.

Tamanoir Active Nodes (TAN) provide persistent active nodes supporting various active services applied to multiple data streams at the same time. The both main transport protocol (TCP/UDP) are supported by the TAN for carrying data. We rely on the user space level of the 4 layers of the Tamanoir architecture (Programmable NIC, Kernel space, User space and Distributed resources) in order to validate and to deploy our active collaborative cache services.

Some of the difficulty lays in the limited resources we want to deploy on the active nodes (in terms of CPU, memory and disk). But, we clearly benefit from active networks support by transparently deploying active caches through data path without modifying and re-configuring Web clients and servers. Collaborative web caches services have been developed in Java (see Fig.2) inside Tamanoir EE. These active cache services can be dynamically modified (parent, child) and communicate in point to point way through control communication channel between active nodes.

4   Framework for Web Caching Services in Active Networks

The goal of our framework is to add some kind of intelligence in the routing of the web traffic in the edges of the network, that is in the active nodes. We define a communication protocol and a cache management schema that is light-weighted (in terms of CPU consumption and memory usage on the active nodes) and that does not ask for heavy data transfer (not to overload the network bandwidth).

We will address in the following two major points of our proposal : the location of the documents cached in the collaborative system, and the delivery of these documents to the end-user. Two questions will have to find solutions : (1) Where is a document in the collaborative caches system ? and (2) How do we exchange documents between caches ? The section 4.2 will address the first question while the section 4.3 will address the latter.

4.1   Overview of the Collaborative Caches

The caches are organized in a hierarchy of two levels. On the lower level are the so-called *children-caches*, that play the role of proxies for a community of users. On the upper level are the *parent-caches*, that play the roles of coordinators of a set of children-caches. For the sake of simplicity, we will use in the following either child-cache or child and parent-cache or parent. We are interested in this work in the efficient management of the caches in such a cache community, thus composed of one parent and many children, each child serving a community of end-users. In such a context, the parent of a cache-community is thought to handle web requests for a company or an institution, while the children are basically attached to a department in the company. We work in the framework of the access to the network, i.e. between the end-users and the backbone of the network.

We have not investigated in this work the collaboration between parents. Indeed, we believe that such a collaboration won't add to the efficiency of the system because cache parents are to be used in distinct institutions or companies. The actual price to pay to obtain documents from another cache community will be the same price than to obtain it directly from the original server.

The hierarchy of this architecture is used to share the knowledge of the contents of the documents in the caches of the community. We do not intend to cache the documents at the parent level, but only at the children level. Only the summaries of the content will have to be stored at the parent level.

4.2   Summary of the Cache Contents : The Mirror Table

Since we aim at providing the cache service on an active node where memory and disk space might be small, we have to define a compact representation of the contents of the caches. As in [5] and [10], we use the Bloom filter [2] technique to spare space with this representation.

Bloom Filter. This method is due to Burton Bloom in 1970 [2]. This probabilistic algorithm aims at testing membership of elements in a set (URL of documents presents in a cache, in our case) using multiple hash functions and a simple bit array. This algorithm consumes a fix small amount of memory regardless of capacity or usage of a cache.

Its principle follows : We first determine a size m for the bit array F (the filter, initially with 0 values) and a number k of independent h_i ($i \in \{1...k\}$) hash functions (those results vary from 0 to $m - 1$). Adding a new element a to the filter consists in computing k values $\{h_1(a), h_2(a), ...h_k(a)\}$, representing k positions in the F filter. These positions are then set to 1 in the F filter. Note here that one particular bit of the F filter might be set to 1 by more than one element. Note also that whatever number of elements have to be filtered, the size of the bit array does not vary, thus the compact form of representation is assured (and controlled).

To test if an element a is present in the set, we first compute the k values $\{h_1(a), h_2(a), ...h_k(a)\}$. If one of the corresponding bits is set to 0, then a is not in the set (the search is definitely a MISS). If all the positions are set to 1, a is present with a certain probability (this is common when using hash functions). That means the bits might be set to 1 while the element is not in the set. In [5], the authors show that the probability of such an error can be minimized with a value of $k = \frac{m}{n} ln2$, where n is the number of elements in the set.

We use the following four definitions in the rest of the paper :

- True HIT : the filter correctly predicts that an element is in the set.
- False HIT : the filter predicts that an element is in the set, but the element is not actually in the set.
- True MISS : the filter correctly predicts that an element is not in the set.
- False MISS : the filter predicts that an element is not in the set, but the element is actually in the set.

The False MISS should not occur with the Bloom filter technique when the filter and the set are strongly linked (for instance when a new document enters the set, the filter updates its bit array). The False MISS problem occurs when the filter and the set are not updated together, for instance when they are located on different hosts, as we will see later in section 4.4.

The False HIT can occur at any time, even with a strong consistency policy. Thus the problem will be fully addressed in section 4.4 and a specific protocol organized to maintain at best cost the consistency.

Mirror Tables. The information sent from the children caches to the parent is compacted in a bloom filter used by the parent to localize the documents in the collaborative community.

We define a *mirror table* as a compact structure representing (reflecting) the content of a child-cache. It contains the following fields : an identifier of the cache reflected by this mirror table (an IP address for instance), a bit array (for the bloom filter F), the size of the bit array (m), the number of hash functions (k) and the number of false HIT.

A parent keeps one such mirror table for each of its children. While it is easy to add new elements in the filter, to delete an element is impossible. Indeed, one particular bit may have been set to 1 by more than one element. Thus, if we put a bit to 0 when an element is suppressed, we may make the filter inconsistent. Doing nothing is obviously not good : If the element we intend to suppress was the only one to have set the bit to 1, the cache is inconsistent, too. A solution here should be to use a counter telling us how much time a bit has been set to 1, instead of only a meaningless 1. This solution increases the size of the mirror table but decreases the number of false HIT. Our proposal is to handle modified mirror tables at the children caches, where the bit array is replaced by a counter array of the same size m. When a document is added (resp. suppressed), the counters for each position set by the hash functions are increased (resp. decreased) instead of setting a simple 1. From this local table,

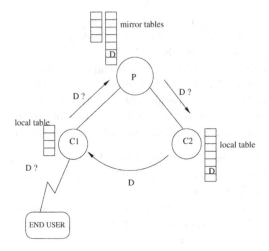

Fig. 1. Inter cache protocol, when the requested document D is in the collaborative system

the child simply constructs the filter when needed : When the counter is 1 or more, the corresponding entry in the filter is set to 1.

The parent has copies of the filters present in its children. From the parent point of view, when the filter becomes inconsistent (the number of false HIT becomes very high), this parent asks the corresponding child for a new version of its filter. Conversely, when a child has made a lot of changes in its filter, it takes the local decision to send it to its parent (see section 4.4). Note here that only the filter (the bit array) is sent from one child to its parent. With this mechanisms, only a small amount of information has to be stored at the parent, and the resulting traffic for update is kept reasonable (the bit array, that means m bits). On a child, the consistency of the filter is kept relevant at any time.

4.3   Location and Delivery of a Document

Figure 1 illustrates the inter-cache protocol we propose. When contacted by an end-user browser for a document D, a child $C1$ examines its own cache. If D is present locally, $C1$ serves directly the end-user. Otherwise, $C1$ forwards the requests to its parent P. This one checks its mirror tables (step 1) to detect if one of its other children has the document D (with a certain probability). Two scenarios can occur :

- if none of the brothers of $C1$ owns the document (from the parent knowledge, extracted from the mirror tables), the request is forwarded to the original server. This one sends D back to P, who forwards it to $C1$. $C1$ caches D, updates its local table and sends D to the end-user;

- if a child $C2$ seems to have D (from P point of view)[3], P sends a control message to $C2$ in order to allow the transfer of D from $C2$ to $C1$. If $C2$ really owns D, a peer to peer communication is set up between $C2$ and $C1$. Otherwise, a false HIT occurred : $C2$ informs P of that false HIT. P increases the corresponding field in its mirror table, and generates a new check of its mirror tables (back to step 1), excluding $C2$ from the search. The peer to peer communication between $C1$ and $C2$ permits to decrease the amount of work and number of messages involved at the parent level.

4.4   Consistency of the Information

The size of caches are limited, so a replacement schema is used to control them and delete documents. This behavior, inherent to the techniques of caching, involves in our case an inconsistency between the mirror tables at the parent and the actual contents of the caches at the child. This will generate some false HIT in the system, leading to unnecessary communications between parents and children.

To minimize this problem, we introduce two mechanisms : at the parent level, we maintain for each child the number of false-HIT generated during the communications with it. When this counter reaches a given validating threshold α, the parent asks the child for a new version of its filter, considering its mirror table as obsolete. This solution is acceptable in the general case, when the parent often communicates with its children.

However, when a child is less contacted by its parent, the content of its cache might evolves locally. In this scenario, the content of the mirror table at the parent is not consistent. The child must anticipate some possible false MISS and false HIT and send a new version of its filter to its parent, when the number of changes in the local table becomes greater than a validating threshold β.

Note also that the problem of the false HIT is inherent to the Bloom filter technique : it is the price to pay to compact the information. Only a good choice in its parameters k and m (see section 4.2) can decrease the number of false HIT.

We propose therefore two protocols (and two parameters α and β) to handle the consistency of the information at the parent level based on both pull and push strategies. When either the parent or the child observes a high probability of dysfunction in the system future, it initiates the refreshing of the filter.

5   Implementation Issues and Experiments

5.1   Functional Architecture of a Collaborative Cache Active Node

Design and implementations of cache techniques have been made trough the implementation of active services All web browser clients are configured to send

---

[3] Note that more than one child-cache might have D; a LRU (Least Frequently Used) algorithm is used to load balance the queries among the candidates

their HTTP requests through a children cache of our system. This cache deploys active HTTPHandlerS service to handle this request.

Collaborative caches services are dynamically deployed on Tamanoir active node depending on cache configuration (parent, child). Figure 2 describes features embedded in active node to support cache collaborations.

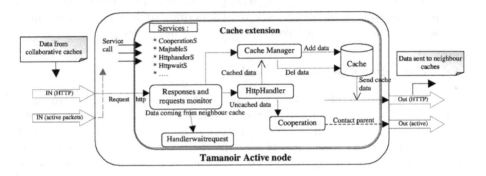

Fig. 2. Active Web cache architecture

5.2   Construction of the Collaborative Community

In this section we address the different methods to create the collaborative cache systems. The active nodes dynamically decide if they run a parent-cache or a child-cache.

In a fully static method, each node in the network willing to join the system must have some information about it. For instance, a node willing to become a new child must know one parent and use its *JoinparentS* service to contact this parent. Additionally, a parent (which is an active node) can ask another node to act as a child dynamically, by sending an active packet (thus sending a *JoinparentS* service this node can use to join the system). This situation can occur if the parent receives/sends some web traffic from/to another active node actually not in the system. This dynamic inscription is made possible by the active networks characteristics.

In our system, at least one node needs to be configured as a parent-cache.A full automatic deployment of this system would require that the parent also might be dynamic or change dynamically in a collaborative community : Indeed, the first parent-cache node deployed (statically or dynamically) may be a poor candidate for such a role and another node (better connectivity, more memory, more CPU) might take this role. This future work will have to be investigated.

5.3   Test Architecture

We experiment our collaborative cache solutions on an active networks platform based on Tamanoir Execution Environment. Our experiments are based on log files extracted from a real proxy server[4]. Different logs are used with different caches.

```
Time    elapsed    remotehost    code/status      bytes
1035849606.566 394 252.183.145.92 TCP_CLIENT_REFRESH_MISS/200 1160

method   Ur    rfc931     peerstatus/peerhost     type
GET http://br.yimg.com/i/br/cat.gif - DIRECT/200.185.15.91 image/gif
```

Fig. 3. Log example

5.4   Results

We define *Quasi Hit* operations in order to evaluate improvement provided by caching collaborative actions. A quasi hit occurs when a cache is able to download requested documents from one of its neighbor.

In our following experimental evaluations, we fix the mirror size for all caches. We choose 4 hash functions for the bloom filter. Filter size is also fixed at the optimal value of 8000 bits (as explained in section 4.2.1, filter size is derived from the number of hash functions and the number of documents in the set (1766 in our experiments)). False hit probability is then 0.11.

We first consider caches with unlimited size (they can cache all data requested during the experiment). Figure 4 shows the impact of validating thresholds (α and β) value on updating table operations and communication. α and β follow the same value. Performances increase with threshold value but consistency between tables is not supported.

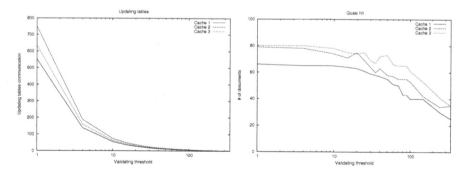

Fig. 4. Updating tables - unlimited cache   **Fig. 5.** Quasi hit with unlimited cache

We illustrate the impact in terms of table coherence through the Quasi Hit effect (Figure 5). When the validating threshold increases, quasi hit rapidly decreases and we lose the benefits of collaborative caches due to a weak consistency of the tables. This experiment is done on 3000 requests on 1766 different documents. Local Hit of each cache is constant (cache1=439, cache2=221,

---
[4] Trace logs available on http://www.ircache.net

cache3=339). Local hit represents the number of requests to document in the cache. Note here that the total number of document in the cache might be larger than this, since some documents might be put once in the cache and never accessed later on.

Within experiments presented in figures 6 and 7, we deploy collaborative caches with limited resources (10% of needed storage). We observe cache replacement effect through a simple LRU policy. Local Hit decreases compared to unlimited caches experiments but remains constant (cache1=355, cache2=149, cache3=291). Quasi hit increases compared to unlimited cache experiment. But we show that quasi hit results remain low compared to the small available amount of cache. Due to the limited size of the cache, the local hit decreases as compared to unlimited caches : Indeed some requested documents , that had been already requested (thus potentially in the cache), might have been replaced by the replacement strategy. The combination of addition and suppression of documents in the cache allows in the limited cache experiment to update more often the mirror table than in the unlimited case, leading to more accurate consistency between parent and children mirror tables.

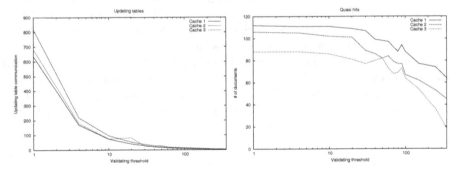

Fig. 6. Updating tables with limited cache   **Fig. 7.** Quasi hit with limited cache

We can note on figure 7 that the amount of quasi hit increases compared to unlimited cache experiments. This result benefits from the updating of mirror tables after document removal (these updating operations are generated through depending on the β threshold).

6   Conclusion

Collaborative web caches allow to quickly find a requested document in a community of distributed caches while avoiding that parent caches keep a copy of documents. This solution greatly improves performance of document localization compared to hierarchical caches. In this paper, we present our first step towards the design of new collaborative web caches protocols. Deploying and maintaining collaborative caches is pretty difficult in IP networks. With the help of active networks approach, these caches can be easily managed and the deployment of cache policy can be dynamically broadcasted.

Caching documents inside a network requires high level and efficient intelligence support inside network equipments with limited resources. Moreover we needed an high performance network execution environment able to support multiple services dealing with web streams based on TCP transport layer. Through the help in terms of dynamicity and easiness of implementing new services, we benefit from the high performance Tamanoir active node framework. This paper presents our first experiments in evaluating our collaborative cache protocols. We are currently more evaluating performance aspects of our cache collaboration.

References

1. G. Barish and K. Obraczka. World wide web caching: Trends and techniques. *IEEE Communications Magazine Internet Technology Series*, 38(5):178–184, May 2000.
2. B. Bloom. Space/time trade-offs in hash coding with allowable errors. *CACM*, 13(7):422–426, July 1970.
3. L. Breslau, P. Cao, L. Fan, G. Phillips, and S. Shenker. Web caching and Zipf-like distributions: Evidence and implications. In *Proceedings of the INFOCOM '99 conference*, March 1999.
4. A. Chankhunthod, P. B. Danzig, C. Neerdaels, M. F. Schwartz, and K. J. Worrell. A hierarchical internet object cache. In *USENIX Annual Technical Conference*, pages 153–164, 1996.
5. L. Fan, P. Cao, J. Almeida, and A. Z. Broder. Summary cache: a scalable wide-area Web cache sharing protocol. *IEEE/ACM Transactions on Networking*, 8(3):281–293, 2000.
6. Jean-Patrick Gelas, Saad El Hadri, and Laurent Lefèvre. Towards the design of an high performance active node. *Parallel Processing Letters*, 13(2), jun 2003.
7. J. S. Gwertzman and M. Seltzer. The case for geographical push-caching. In IEEE, editor, *Proceedings Fifth Workshop on Hot Topics in Operating Systems (HotOS-V)*, pages 51–55, 1109 Spring Street, Suite 300, Silver Spring, MD 20910, USA, 1995. IEEE Computer Society Press.
8. T. Lanmbrecht, P. Backx, B. Duysburgh, L. Peters, B. Dhoedt, and P. Demeester. Adaptive distributed caching on an active network. In *IWAN 01*, Philadelphia, USA, 2001.
9. J.M. Pierson, L. Brunie, and D. Coquil. Semantic collaborative web caching. In *Web Information Systems Engineering 2002 (ACM/IEEE WISE 2002)*, pages 30,39, Singapore, dec 2002. IEEE CS Press.
10. A. Rousskov and D. Wessels. Cache digests. *Computer Networks and ISDN Systems*, 30(22–23):2155–2168, November 1998.
11. J. Wang. A survey of Web caching schemes for the Internet. *ACM Computer Communication Review*, 25(9):36–46, October 1999.
12. D. Wessels and K Claffy. ICP and the Squid Web cache. *IEEE Journal on Selected Areas in Communication*, 16(3):345–357, April 1998.
13. A. Wolman, G. M. Voelker, N. Sharma, N. Cardwell, A. R. Karlin, and H. M. Levy. On the scale and performance of cooperative web proxy caching. In *Symposium on Operating Systems Principles*, pages 16–31, 1999.
14. H. Zhang, H. Qin, and G. Chen. Adaptive control of chaotic systems with uncertainties. *Int. J. of Bifurcation and Chaos*, 8(10):2041–2046, 1998.

A Retransmission Control Algorithm for Low-Latency UDP Stream on StreamCode-Base Active Networks

Hideki Otsuki[1] and Takashi Egawa[2]

[1] Communications Research Laboratory,
4-2-1, Nukui-Kitamachi, Koganei, Tokyo, 184-8795 Japan,
eiji@crl.go.jp,
[2] NEC networking laboratories,
4-1-1 Miyazaki, Miyamae-ku, Kanagawa, 216-8555 Japan,
t-egawa@ct.jp.nec.com

Abstract. We propose an algorithm for real-time data stream that achieves low latency as well as low packet loss rate. In our algorithm a sequence number is included in each packet, and it is renumbered as if there is no packet loss in the upper stream when a packet loss and corresponding packet retransmission occurs. This conceals the packet loss and its recovery from succeeding nodes in the downstream, thus simplifies packet processing in succeeding nodes. This algorithm can easy be implemented on capsule-type active networks, and we evaluated this algorithm on StreamCode based active networks. It is implemented with 1.0k line in-packet programs plus node initialization programs, and the evaluation results show that 27.1% end-to-end packet loss rate is suppressed to around 5.6%.

1 Introduction

Real-time multimedia applications such as video conferencing and live-video distribution are becoming popular on the Internet. Applications of this kind are sensitive to latency as well as packet loss. Packets for these applications must be delivered in 'allowable delay' to replay audio and video data, and if a packet does not arrive in time, the retransmission of the packet do not contribute to the application quality improvement.

Ordinary TCP is not appropriate for these applications. TCP is designed to achieve perfect error recovery [1]. This means that a transmission failure of a packet can block other packet transfer, and can drastically increase latency. Moreover, the retransmission of TCP is processed in an end-to-end manner, which causes long RTT and thus large latency.

There are a few kinds of proposals that aim at satisfying the requirements of these applications. One is to use UDP/IP with Forward Error Correction (FEC). In this method lost packets are recovered from redundant information included in other packets. This enables to avoid retransmission, which shortens latency. However, huge amount of redundant data must be attached to recover bursty packet loss, which is common in the Internet.

The second proposal is to insert TCP/IP bridge in the TCP/IP's end-to-end feedback loop, and to make them an accumulation of multiple shorter TCP/IP loops. This shortens

N. Wakamiya et al. (Eds.): IWAN 2003, LNCS 2982, pp. 92–102, 2004.

retransmission delay and overall latency [2]. However, this method still aims at perfect error recovery, which means that a packet can block other packet transfer.

We therefore have to develop an algorithm that enables partial error recovery that suppresses packet loss to acceptable level.

In designing partial error recovery algorithms, the method to detect packet loss is important. Sequence number is commonly used for the detection, and if we use it in the same manner for partial recovery, a packet loss that is never recovered generates multiple NACK packets in every downward nodes, none of them contributes to application quality improvements.

Similar problem occurs in reliable multicast, and [3] proposed to use broadcast for NACK suppression. [4] proposed to establish an independent session for packet retransmission to distinguish retransmitted packets. However, these methods consume much node resources and bandwidth. We believe we should use more simple method because perfect error recovery is not required. We therefore propose a novel transport protocol algorithm for UDP data that suppress these problems by

- retransmitting lost packets at every intermediate node,
- simplifying the protocol by limiting the message type to NACK (negative acknowledge) only,
- limiting the number of packet retransmission of each packet, and
- renumbering the sequence number to hide retransmission from downstream nodes.

This paper is composed as follows. In chapter 2 we describe the details of this proposed algorithm. We then explain this algorithm is appropriate for capsule-type active networks, and describes the method to implement it on StreamCode-based active networks in chapter 3. The detailed implementation of experimental system and its evaluation results are stated in chapter 4, and in chapter 5 we conclude the paper.

2   Proposed Algorithm

2.1   Application and Network Model

We assume that applications for this algorithm contain a transmitter and a receiver. As shown in figure 1, packets from the transmitter to the receiver contain application level sequence number. The receiver has an application level buffer, and if the sequence of a packet reverses, it corrects the order before using it. The size of the buffer is decided to store packets for a certain amount of time.

As for the network, we assume that it consists of several routers, some of which have buffers for this algorithm. These routers with buffers (we name this relay nodes) implement the algorithm described in this chapter, and if a relay node detects packet loss it tries to recover the loss by requesting retransmission to the previous relay node as shown in figure 2.

The transmitter and the receiver lie at each end of the network. It is not necessary for every router to be a relay node. Since such ordinary routers do not affect to the behavior of this algorithm, we do not discuss this issue in more details in this paper.

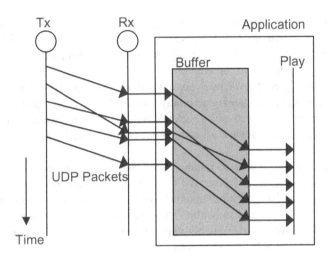

Fig. 1. Target application model

2.2 Algorithm Overview and Its Basic Features

The algorithm described here is a generalized version of [5] by eliminating allowable delay parameter. As stated in Figure 2, packets are buffered at every relay node. Each packet contains a sequence number that is independent of the application level sequence number mentioned in Figure 1.

Figure 3 shows the overview of the retransmission and corresponding sequence number renumbering. When a packet arrives at a relay node, the node checks the sequence number. If it detects packet loss(es) by a jump of the sequence number, it asks the previous relay node to retransmit the lost packet(s). Then the node renumbers the sequence number of the arrival packet so that the next relay node will receive packets whose sequence number do not jump, and transfers it to the next node. Thanks to this renumbering, a packet loss between a relay node pair is hidden from succeeding nodes, which prevents redundant retransmission requests by succeeding nodes.

If the previous node retransmits the lost packet and the packet is recovered successfully, the sequence number of the recovered packet is also renumbered in the same manner. This hides the fact that the packet is a retransmitted one, and the succeeding nodes can process it as an ordinary packet. This simplifies the packet processing in routers, and enables packet processing without waiting lost packets. This shifts the burden of packet renumbering to relay nodes to end hosts, which is compliant to the end-to-end argument.

In this algorithm packets are retransmitted between intermediate routers, which shortens the retransmission delay compared with the delay of end-end retransmission.

This algorithm do not aims at perfect packet loss suppression. If a packet retransmission request fails for some reason (e.g., the packet has already discarded in the previous router or the request packet is lost), the succeeding routers do not do anything. This may seem insufficient, but we believe that this is the right recover policy for real-time applications because even if a packet loss is recovered thanks to several retransmission

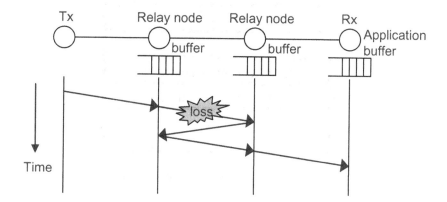

Fig. 2. Network model

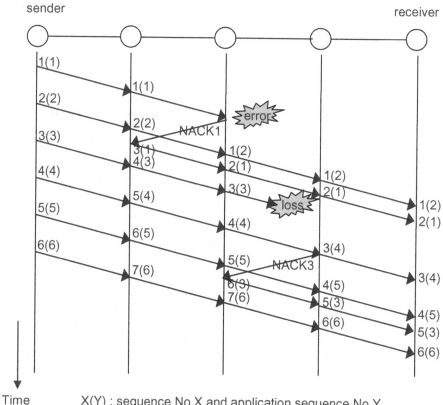

X(Y) : sequence No.X and application sequence No.Y
Relay nodes renumber the sequencd No.X

Fig. 3. Packet sequence renumbering

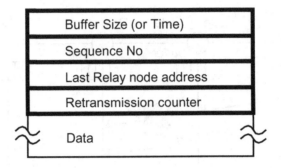

Fig. 4. Required infomations for this algorithm

trials, it is often useless because retransmission trial takes much time and the latency of the packet becomes so large for the application.

This algorithm requires all packets to go through the same route, because the packet loss detection depends on the sequence number. We believe that in active networks it should be done by the routing algorithm of active networks. This problem is out of the scope of this paper.

2.3   Processing on a Node

Figure 4 shows the information required in the packet.

Using this information, each node processes packets as shown in Figure 5.

- If a node receives a data packet, the node (re)writes the sequence number in the packet so that the sequence number does not jump in the next node, changes the node address to request NACK in the packet to itself, and forward it to the next node. Before forwarding the packet, the node makes a copy of the packet and stores it in the buffer with expiration time information. It also checks the sequence number of the received packet to see whether there is a jump in the sequence number, which means that packet(s) is lost.
    - If packet(s) loss is detected, the node sends a NACK to the previous node and returns to an idle state.
    - If there is no packet loss, the node returns to an idle state.
- If the node receives a NACK packet, the node checks the buffer whether the packet is stored. If stored it restores the lost packet, the node creates the sequence number so that the sequence number does not jump in the next node, and sends it out to the next node if retransmission counter is smaller than predetermined threshold. If the packet has already been discarded and is not stored in the node, or retransmission counter is larger than threshold, it just returns to the idle state. The total number of retransmission among links is therefore suppressed by this threshold in end-to-end basis.
- If the time out of a packet stored in the buffer arrives, the node discards the packet from the buffer. In our current implementation this is virtually realized by checking the expiration time of the packet before sending the restored packet out on receiving a NACK packet.

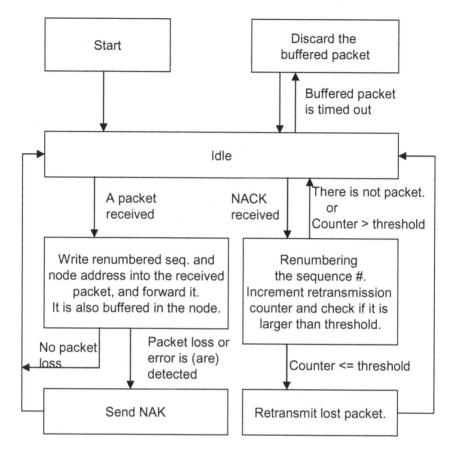

Fig. 5. Node behavior

3 Implementation on StreamCode Based Active Networks

3.1 Merit of Capsule-Based Active Network Implementation

We decided to use StreamCode-based active network [6,7] as the platform for the implementation of the proposed algorithm.

StreamCode is a capsule-type active networks in which packet processing algorithms are defined with in-packet programs that is written in StreamCode instruction set, a set that is defined for secure and high-performance packet processing.

There are two reasons why we used this system for the implementation.

1. Easiness of implementation.
   A new algorithm can easily be implemented on SC-based active networks. The proposed algorithm is implemented in merely 1.0k line in-packet programs except for the node initialization programs.
2. Flexibility against the network condition changes.
   On StreamCode network, we can change the processing algorithm for each packet

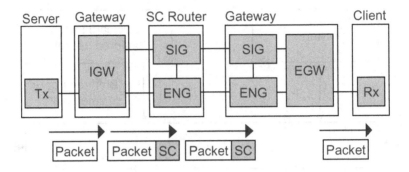

IGW: Ingress gateway proccess
SIG: Signaling process
ENG: Stream code engine
EGW: Egress gateway process
SC: Stream code

Fig. 6. Stream Code architecture

by attaching different programs to each packet. This means that we can choose optimal algorithm considering various network conditions, e.g., congestion, topological
change or the occurrence of failures. For example, if the network is not congested
we can choose no-retransmission algorithm and can enjoy less delay and less buffer
consumption on each node. If the network congestion changes we can switch to
our proposed algorithm without any modification in the network and can suppress
packet losses.

3.2   Detailed Implementation Method on StreamCode Networks

Figure 6 shows the current StreamCode-based network architecture.

The network is composed of a server, a client, two gateways and StreamCode-based
routers. Server sends out UDP/IP packets. StreamCode program is attached to each
UDP/IP packet at the ingress gateway, and removed at the egress gateway. In this figure,
the ingress gateway has Ingress Gateway Process (IGW) only. It is possible to implement
SIGnaling process (SIG) and stream code ENGine (ENG) processes on the gateway, but
we assume they are not implemented because of the simplicity. A StreamCode-based
router has a StreamCode engine that has two functions. One is a function to process
in-packet StreamCode programs, and the other is a function to process signaling that
establishes sessions among StreamCode routers and gateways. By establishing a session
among the related nodes, buffers for this algorithm is allocated and initialized on each
node. Authentication information for each data packet is also distributed during the
session initialization, and it enables the authentication and authorization of each packet
to access the allocated buffer.

Shown in figure 7 is the essence of the algorithm of in-packet StreamCode program
for data packets, and the information stored in the packet.

SC

```
START
  IF (source address !=0) {
    packet loss check;
    IF ( packet is lost ) {
}     send NACK SC;
    }

  Write sequence number from service table
    into this packet;
  Increment sequence number in service table;
  Forward this packet itself;
  Write time to packet table;
  Write this packet into packet table;
END
```

Service table

Service ID
Route ID
Sequence Number
Source address
Max packets
Max packet size
NACK SC size
NACK SC
Packet table (buffer area) ⋮

SC data

Sequence No.
Retransmission counter
Allowable delay
Originate address
Service ID

NACK SC

```
START
  LOOP (The Number of lost packets) {
    Get packet from packet table;
    IF (packet is buffered) {
      Write sequence no of service table
      into the packet;
      Inclement sequence no of service table;
      Decrement retransmission counter in
      the packet;
      IF ( retransmission counter >=0 ) {
        retransmit the packet;
      }
    store the packet into packet table;
    }
  }
END
```

SC data

Destination address
Lost packet sequence (start)
Lost packet sequence (End)

Fig. 7. Stream Code for proposed retransmission control

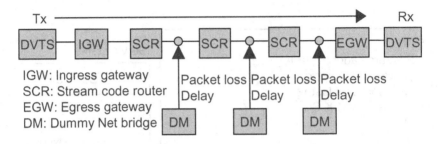

Fig. 8. Test system

A NACK packet also contains a StreamCode program called NACK SC. When it arrives the previous node the program checks the retransmission counter of the packet stored in the buffer, and if the counter is under the limit the program generates retransmission packet(s). In the current implementation one NACK packet can regenerate multiple packets that corresponds to a consecutive packet loss. It suppress the number of NACK packets, but a loss of a NACK packet may cause a consecutive loss. NACK packet should therefore be protected (e.g., duplicate NACK) more if the better packet loss rate is necessary.

4   Experimental System and Its Evaluation Results

4.1   Experimental System

Shown in Figure 8 is the experimental system to evaluate this proposed algorithm. It is composed of the StreamCode-based active network described in chapter 3.2, and two terminals on which Digital Video Transport System (DVTS) [8] is working. DVTS is an application that transmits and receives Digital Video stream on RTP [9]. Between some active routers we inserted dummynet [10] that can emulate packet loss and link delay.

4.2   Evaluation Method and Its Results

DVTS itself has little buffer and cannot adapt to the reversal of packet sequence, thus is not compliant to the application model described in chapter 2.1. We therefore made a program that buffers packets of 500msec stream, and reorders the packet sequence if a reversal occurs. Thanks to this program application-level packet loss does not occur if retransmission completes in 500msec.

Using this system we measured the end-to-end packet loss with our proposed algorithm and compared it with the theoretical packet loss ratio without retransmission, changing the link delay of each link using dummynets. The link delay and the packet loss rate of three dummynets are the same. The results are shown in Table 1.

When the packet loss rate of each link is 10becomes 27.1% if there is no retransmission. This value greatly decreases to around 5.6% if the proposed retransmission algorithm is applied. When the rate of each link is 5% and 1%, the end-to-end packet

Table 1. End-End packet loss

Packet loss rate of each link	Theoretical end-end packet loss	delay of each link (msec)					
		50	60	70	80	90	100
10%	27.10%	5.58%	5.62%	5.65%	5.59%	5.67%	5.68%
5%	14.26%	1.47%	1.50%	1.48%	1.47%	1.49%	1.50%
1%	2.97%	0.08%	0.09%	0.09%	0.11%	0.09%	0.08%

loss rate is suppressed from 14.26% to around 1.5% and from 2.97% to around 0.1%, respectively.

The packet loss should become slightly larger if the link delay of each link increases. However, thanks to the retransmission times limitation the packet loss rate was almost constant against link delay in our evaluation.

Figure 9 shows the pictures of DVTS with and without our proposed algorithms. The picture quality becomes higher in (b), the one with our proposed algorithm.

(a) UDP (packet loss rate=10%)   (b) Using proposing SC
                                        (Packet loss rate=10%)

Fig. 9. Application quality

5 Conclusion

We proposed an algorithm for real-time stream that achieves low latency as well as low packet loss rate. It renumbers the sequence number in each packet if a packet loss and the corresponding packet retransmission occurs, which simplifies the packet processing in succeeding nodes. This algorithm can easy be implemented on capsule-type active networks, and we evaluated this algorithm on StreamCode based active networks. The evaluation results show that 27.1% end-to-end packet loss rate is suppressed to around 5.6%, which proves the effectiveness of our proposed algorithm.

Thanks to the implementation in StreamCode, we can easily change the algorithm if we sense the change of network conditions, e.g., congestion or failure. We therefore are planning to design an algorithm that dynamically changes buffer consumption as well as the latency and packet loss ratio by changing the StreamCode attached to the packet.

References

1. TCP Selecive Acknowledgement Options, RFC2018
2. Kammouane XONSIHAPANYA, Katsunori YAMAOKA, Yoshinori SAKAI: Improvement of Average Delay Performance in Packet Network by Introducing Intermediate Node, Proc. of ICOIN12 (1998) 25–28
3. Sally Floyd, Van Jacobson, Ching-Gung Liu, Steven McCanne, Lixia Zhang: A Reliable Multicast Framework for Light-weight Sessions and Application Level Framing, IEEE/ACM Trans. on Networking Vol.5 No.6 (1997) 784–803
4. Sneha Kumar Kasera, Gisli Hjalmtysson, Donald F. Towsley, James F. Kurose: Scalable Reliable Multicast Using Multiple Multicast Channels, IEEE/ACM Trans. on Networking Vol.8 No.3 (2000)
5. Hideki OTSUKI, Katsunori YAMAOKA, Yoshinori SAKAI: A Realtime Media Stream Transfer Protocol with Finite Retransmission between Relay Nodes, Proc. of IEICE CQR2002(2002) 223–226
6. Takashi Egawa, Koji Hino and Yohei Hasegawa: Fast and secure packet processing environment for per-packet QoS customization, Proc. of IWAN 2001 (2001)
7. Takashi Egawa and Hideki Otsuki: Per-packet authentication for capsule networks; its pros and cons, Proc.of ANTA2003 (2003)
8. Digital Video Transport System, http://www.sfc.wide.ad.jp/DVTS/index.html
9. RTP:A Transport Protocol for Real-Time Applications, RFC1889
10. http://info.iet.unipi.it/ luigi/ip_dummynet/
11. Hideki OTSUKI, Katsunori YAMAOKA, Yoshinori SAKAI: Adaptive Protocol Relay Capability with Allowable Delay of Media Transmission, Proc. of IEEE PACRIM2001 (2001) 627–630

TCP Enhancement Using Active Network Based Proxy Transport Service

Siddharth Patil and Mohan Kumar

Department of Computer Science and Engineering,
The University of Texas at Arlington, Arlington TX 76019, USA,
siddharth@utaengineers.com, kumar@cse.uta.edu

Abstract. TCP performance degrades with increasing round trip time
(*rtt*) due to longer slow start periods and slower rate of increase of the
congestion window. The proposed, PTS (proxy transport service) is an
active network based service, that can improve the end-to-end performance of TCP connections with large *rtt's*. PTS also reduces the response
time of TCP to congestion and can be used by other active services. A
PTS session consists of two separate TCP connections, one between the
source host and a designated intermediate node (the PTS node), and
another between the PTS node and the destination host. PTS complements TCP without compromising reliability. Simulation studies show
the effect of PTS node location, buffer size and node service time on the
performance of PTS. Performance can be significantly improved by deploying an interactive distributed service that allows the host to choose
the proxy node.

1 Introduction

In addition to providing reliable communication, Transmission Control Protocol
(TCP) effects error control, flow control and resequencing of segments received
out of order. TCP uses the arrival rate of acknowledgments to adjust the current size of congestion window (*cwnd*). During bulk data transfer, the TCP
connection frequently alternates between *slow start* and *congestion avoidance*
phases. The rate at which the *cwnd* increases depends upon the round trip time
(*rtt*) of TCP segments. Current variants of TCP give good bulk data transfer
performance over shorter connection paths. However, as the separation between
the source and the destination host increases, *rtt* increases resulting in reduced
TCP throughput. TCP enters *slow start* phase more frequently for longer connection paths. In this paper we propose, proxy transport service (PTS), an active
network based service that improves the TCP bulk data throughput for TCP
connections with large average *rtt*. The *rtt* for TCP packets on a connection
can be large when the connection spans multiple subnets, or when one of the
node en route is congested with no alternate route available to the destination
or when propagation delay for one of the intermediate links is very high (e.g.,
a satellite link or a slow wireless link). PTS service is deployable at various active nodes that can be programmed to perform desirable computations on user

N. Wakamiya et al. (Eds.): IWAN 2003, LNCS 2982, pp. 103–114, 2004.

packets within the network. PTS works by splitting the TCP connection between the sender and the receiver into two separate TCP connections: i) *PTS Connection-1* between the source host and a chosen active node (called the PTS node); and ii) *PTS Connection-2* between the PTS node and the destination host. Ideally, PTS node is an active node located in the path between the source and the destination host such that it is approximately equidistant in terms of delay from each of the hosts. A PTS node acknowledges the source's TCP segments on *PTS Connection-1* and forwards the segments to the destination host on *PTS Connection-2*. PTS node implements all the functionalities of a host TCP sender for *PTS Connection-2* i.e., it retransmits lost segments, performs flow control and responds to congestion. PTS throughput for a session depends on three parameters: location of the PTS node, mean time (T_r) an average packet spends inside the PTS node, and the buffer space available at the PTS node. The location of the PTS node determines the *rtt* for the two PTS connections. Since the PTS node cannot transmit TCP segments as fast as they arrive, large buffer space will be required for this session. Otherwise segments will be dropped at the PTS node leading to poor TCP throughput. As the number of PTS sessions handled by a PTS node increases, T_r increases, leading to reduced PTS throughput. PTS complements TCP to improve performance for long delay connections without compromising TCP's reliability. PTS does not reduce the end-to-end delay for a TCP segment but it improves the rate at which the sender's congestion window increases. Through simulation studies we show that PTS improves the TCP throughput for TCP connections having large average *rtt*. Also we show the effect of PTS node location, PTS service time and buffer space per session on PTS throughput. Current research in the areas of security, active node architectures, active packet formats and active network applications will provide the essential components required to deploy PTS [1,2,3,4].

1.1 Related Work

The concept of using a proxy transport service for improving TCP throughput has been in use in wireless networks and in networks with high delay variations. **Indirect TCP (I-TCP):** In ITCP, the TCP connection between a fixed host (FH) and a mobile host (MH) is broken into two separate TCP connections [5]. The variant of TCP residing in the MH and the base station (BS) masks effects of mobility. The connection between the FH and the BS uses standard TCP. The BS acknowledges the TCP segments from the FH increasing the TCP throughput of the sender, and transmits the TCP segments over the wireless link. The BS also intercepts retransmission requests from the MH and retransmits using a cached copy if available instead of propagating the request all the way to the FH. ITCP can be considered as a specialization of PTS with the BS acting as the PTS node. PTS service can also work over connections spanning heterogeneous networks. An intermediate link can be a satellite link or a wireless last hop. Unlike ITCP, where the location of the proxy is fixed at the BS, PTS provides users with a proxy transport service at a location that can give maximum throughput. In ITCP, the FH is not aware of the proxy service. The nontransparent approach adopted by PTS distributes knowledge among the hosts and provides flexibility in selecting a suitable PTS node according to the host requirements.

Performance Enhancement Proxies (PEP): Performance Enhancement Proxies (PEP) proposed in [6] uses transport proxies to improve TCP throughput. PEP residing on the network edge monitors all TCP flows going in and out of the network and manipulates their TCP ACK packets to improve TCP throughput. PEP is a transparent service that has the same problems as that of ITCP with regards to fixed proxy location and transparent service.

QoS using RSVP: RSVP (Resource reservation protocol) is the signaling protocol used for resource reservation in integrated services framework to provide quality of service [7]. RSVP requires a state to be maintained at each and every node in between the sender and the receiver for every single session in order to provide guarantees of delay, bandwidth or packet loss. RSVP does not scale to multiple users. PTS does not require a state like RSVP to be maintained at each and every node en route.

2 TCP Enhancement

In this section we discuss the flow control mechanism employed by TCP and the PTS enhancement that improves TCP performance. If the two hosts of a TCP transmission are not local, then packets can get queued at an intermediate router. When a new TCP connection is established the sender initializes its *cwnd* to 1, and increases *cwnd* by one whenever an acknowledgement is received. The maximum number of unacknowledged segments that can be sent is equal to the minimum of the advertised window and the *cwnd*. The bulk data throughput of the TCP connection is affected by flow control and slow start algorithm. The theoretical maximum window size which can give maximum TCP throughput is dependent on the bandwidth-delay product of the connection, given by, $capacity(bits) = bandwidth(bits/sec) * rtt(sec)$. A TCP sender can detect a packet drop either when a retransmission timer(rto) expires or when duplicate ACK's are received. A timeout is a better indication of congestion inside the network. A duplicate ACK indicates out-of-order delivery of packets. When a timeout occurs *cwnd* is set to 1 and *slow start* begins. Congestion avoidance is flow control imposed by the sender, while advertised window is flow control imposed by the receiver. Long connection paths result in larger *rtt's*. Larger the *rtt*, slower is the rate at which ACK's are received. During *slow start* the rate at which *cwnd* increases depends on the rate at which ACK's arrive. For higher *rtt's*, it takes much longer for a TCP throughput to reach the network capacity. During congestion avoidance phase, a TCP connection spanning longer paths takes much longer time to increase its throughput. A TCP connection having large number of hops is also quite likely to span across networks under different administrative domains.

In PTS, two separate TCP connections are established, one between the source host and a designated intermediate node (the PTS node), and another between the PTS node and the destination host. All the TCP segments from the sending host are acknowledged (to the source) and forwarded by the PTS node (to the destination) as illustrated in Fig. 1.

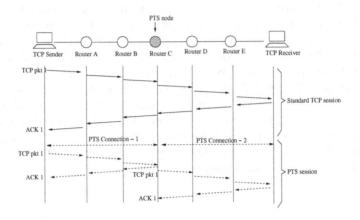

Fig. 1. Proxy Transport Service

During the setup of a PTS session, a requested amount of buffer space is provided for that session inside the PTS node. For every TCP segment received by the PTS node, a copy of the segment is stored in the buffer and an acknowledgment is sent to the source host. PTS node in turn transmits accepted TCP segments to the destination host on *PTS Connection-2*. The copy of the TCP segment is preserved in the buffer until an acknowledgment is received from the destination host. The PTS node also takes care of retransmitting unacknowledged segments on *PTS Connection-2* when a timeout occurs or duplicate ACK's are received.

3   Simulation Results and Analysis

This section compares the TCP throughput of PTS with that of a direct TCP connection and other proxy schemes. Network Simulator 2 [8] was used for the simulation studies. The performance of a proxy service is affected by three parameters namely: PTS node location (X), PTS service time (T_s) and PTS buffer capacity per session (C_{max}). The simulation topology consists of two hosts separated by variable number of hops (N_{hops}). The location of the PTS node is indicated by X, which refers to the number of hops between the PTS node and the source host. All the links between the two hosts have the same capacity (L_C) and propagation delay (L_d). Tahoe TCP agents reside on the two hosts. We simulated ftp application traffic between two hosts. PTS functionality is provided in the form of an agent. Any node in between the sender and the receiver can become a PTS node by executing the PTS agent. PTS node uses a single FIFO queue for every session. To represent a more realistic scenario, the service time of the PTS node is exponentially distributed over mean service time T_s . The ftp application sends unlimited packets from the source host to the destination host.

We use fixed sized packets (1000 bytes) throughout the simulation. A Direct-TCP and a PTS-connection are compared in terms of *cwnd* and *seqno* measured in packets. Also, we use TCP throughput (number of segments received by the destination host per unit time) to measure performance.

3.1   Comparison of PTS and TCP

As can be observed from Fig. 2, the *slow start* period lasts longer for TCP than that for PTS connections due to the reduced *rtt* for each of the PTS connections. Also the rate of increase in *cwnd* during *congestion avoidance* is larger in case of PTS because the ACK's arrive faster. More number of packets are sent in PTS within the same time frame due to reduced *rtt* for each PTS connection.

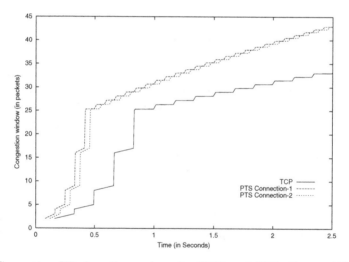

Fig. 2. Congestion Window Comparison for TCP and PTS. $L_C = 10Mb$, $L_d = 10ms$, $T_s = 100\mu s$, $N_{hops} = 8$, $X = 4$

The extra delay that a packet suffers within the PTS node overlaps with the transmission of previously processed packets at the node. For the experimental results in Fig. 2 to 4, $L_C = 10$ Mb, $L_d = 10$ ms, $T_s = 100$ mico sec, $N_{hops} = 4$ and $X = 4$. Figure 3 shows the performance of PTS and TCP sessions when timeout occurs or duplicate ACKS are received. Both TCP and PTS sessions are subjected to the same amount of congestion in the same part of the network, at the same time. In this case, the packet drop occurs in between the source host and the PTS node. As soon as the source host detects a possible packet loss, it sets the *cwnd* to 1 for both TCP and PTS sessions. Because the packet drop

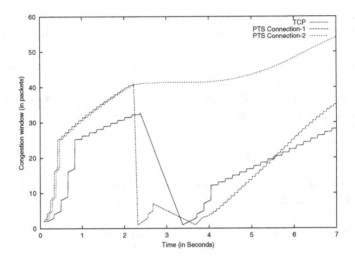

Fig. 3. CWND Comparison of TCP and PTS with Congestion. $L_C = 10Mb$, $L_d = 10ms$, $T_s = 100\mu s$, $N_{hops} = 8$, $X = 4$

occurs in between the source and the PTS node, the *cwnd* of *PTS Connection-2* is not affected. PTS node keeps transmitting to the destination host as long as it has unsent segments in its buffer. Thus the end-to-end TCP throughput will not be affected if the congestion in the first part of the PTS connection is momentary. If the congestion were to be in the second part of the PTS connection then the PTS node will set its *cwnd* to 1 causing the TCP throughput to fall.

If the congestion in the second part of the PTS connection is not momentary then at some point the PTS node is going to run out of buffer space. Due to shorter *rtt* PTS node will recover its steady state transmission rate for this session much faster than a direct TCP connection. Figure 4 compares the *seqno* for PTS and TCP sessions. A dip in the plot signifies that no ACKs have been received for segments starting from that *seqno* and hence TCP is going to re-transmit packets. The first dip for both sessions has been marked. PTS detects congestion almost 1s before a direct TCP connection.

PTS Node Location: Location of the PTS node along the path between the source and destination host determines the end-to-end performance of the PTS session as shown in Fig. 5. $X = 0$ represents a direct TCP session. As the PTS node location moves towards the center of the path we are able to achieve higher end-to-end reception rates. Assuming that the PEP [6] is located at a fixed location of 6 hops from the sender, we can see why the "one fixed proxy serves all" approach will not be able to give the best throughput to each and every host.

PTS Service Time: Every TCP segment will be delayed by a bounded amount of time inside the PTS node. This time consists of the waiting time to get serviced and the service time to modify the TCP header of the segment. The PTS node modifies the TCP header of accepted segments that arrived on *PTS Connection-1* from the source host before forwarding them on *PTS Connection-2*. The packet might be copied within the PTS node more than once before it is queued for

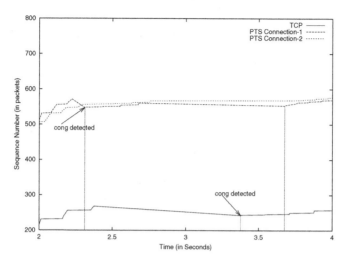

Fig. 4. Seqno Comparison of TCP and PTS with Congestion. $L_C = 10Mb$, $L_d = 10ms$, $T_s = 100\mu s$, $N_{hops} = 8$, $X = 4$

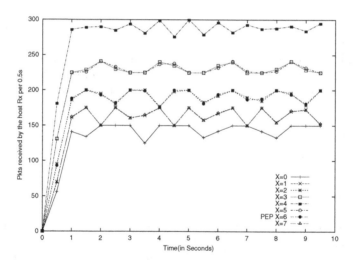

Fig. 5. Effect of PTS Node Location on TCP Throughput. $L_C = 10Mb$, $L_d = 5ms$, $T_s = 100\mu s$, $N_{hops} = 8$, $C_{max} = 1024pkts$

transmission on the outgoing link. Also in presence of multiple sessions competing for the CPU resources on the PTS node, a packet may have to wait longer until it gets serviced. Together this delay significantly affects the end-to-end performance of the PTS session. Figure 6 shows the effect of mean PTS service time on throughput. To represent a more realistic scenario, we used exponential distribution of T_s. When T_s is very much less than rtt on PTS Connection2, PTS session will give better throughput than a direct TCP connection. It is important for PTS nodes to advertise their current estimate of service times so

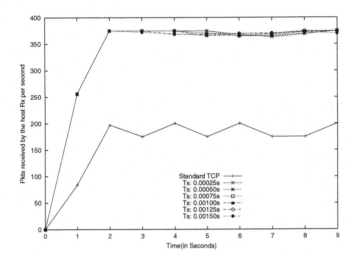

Fig. 6. Effect of PTS Delay on TCP Throughput. $L_C = 10Mb$, $L_d = 8ms$, $N_{hops} = 8$, $X = 4$, $C_{max} = 400pkts$

that a host can choose a less loaded PTS node thereby achieving load sharing.
Multiple PTS Nodes: In Figure 7, the two hosts are separated by distance of
14 hops. PTS node equal to 0 represents the throughput when a direct TCP connection is setup between the two hosts. As observed for one and two PTS nodes
the performance is almost equal. As the number of PTS nodes increases beyond
two, the throughput starts decreasing. Each TCP segment suffers a bounded
amount of delay in every PTS node. This delay adds up to a significant amount
if more than one PTS node is used, thus a single PTS node is adequate for proxy
transport service.

4   Proxy Transport Service (PTS)

PTS complements TCP and is a nontransparent service that employs active
nodes for code execution within the network. In this paper, we are proposing
PTS as one of the predeployed services available to the end user as well as to other
active network services. In PTS, predeployed programs or services can be checked
to have security loop holes and they can be fine-tuned for high performance.
Unlike schemes in [5,6], PTS is an on-demand service i.e., a host must explicitly
make a request for PTS service to the active node. In order for an end host to
use PTS, a PTS clients must reside on the source as well as the destination. The
PTS component inside an active node is referred to as PTS. Figure 8 shows the
interaction between the end systems and the active node components for setting
up a PTS session.

The PTS Client is responsible for initiating a PTS connection setup request,
selecting a PTS node for a session and, establishing and terminating a PTS connection. The PTS Client hides these details from the application. PTS Clients

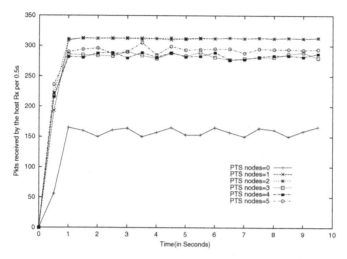

Fig. 7. Multiple PTS Nodes. $L_C = 5Mb$, $L_d = 2ms$, $N_{hops} = 14$, $T_s = 1ms$, $C_{max} = 1024pkts$

communicate with the PTS through active packets using unused IP header bits to identify an active packet [4,9]. When this active packet arrives at a passive node it is routed using information in its IP header via the fast forwarding path. When an active packet arrives at an active node, the IP classifier sends it to the active engine for processing. In addition to rtt, TCP throughput also depends on the bandwidth of the connection. The location of the PTS node determines the end-to-end performance of PTS. Ideally, a PTS node should be located approximately in the middle of the path connecting the two hosts so that, $rtt_{(PTS\ Connection-1)} = rtt_{(PTS\ Connection-2)} = \frac{1}{2}rtt_{total}$. A requesting host may not be able to find an active node or PTS service at a location which can give optimal performance, settling for suboptimal but "better than direct TCP connection" performance. Therefore the PTS node should be chosen in such a way that the difference between the rtt's of *PTS Connection-1* and *PTSConnection-2* is minimal.

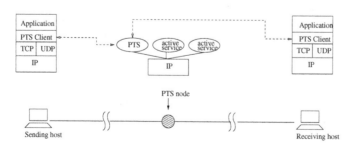

Fig. 8. PTS Architecture

PTS Node Discovery: It is the mechanism by which PTS nodes are discovered and their location and status conveyed to the hosts. Using the knowledge obtained from PTS node discovery, the initiating host evaluates the suitability of a PTS node for its application. This mechanism is called PTS node selection. Since PTS is a host initiated service, a host must contact a PTS node requesting for proxy service. Therefore an initiating host must be aware of all the PTS capable active nodes located in the path (between the sender and the receiver). Also the initiating host needs information about the status of the PTS node, specifically: the location of the PTS node in terms of rtt (rtt_X), current PTS service time estimate (T_s) of the PTS node and, maximum buffer capacity (C_{max}) that can be provided by the PTS node for this session. This information is used to evaluate a *rank* expression for each PTS node. Higher the value of the *rank* expression, better is the suitability of the PTS node in consideration. A basic PTS node discovery mechanism is as follows: 1) The initiating or source host sends an active, PTS probe datagram (including timestamp) to the destination host, 2) A passive node in the path will forward this datagram on the fast forwarding path, whereas an active node, in addition to forwarding the datagram to the destination host, will also send a copy to its active engine. If the PTS service is available, a PTS Available packet is generated which advertises this active node as a PTS node to the initiating host. The timestamp in the PTS probe packet is echoed back in the PTS Available packet so that the initiating host can calculate the rtt between itself and the PTS node. This packet also contains information about the current state (PTS service time per average size packet and maximum buffer space) of the service on this active node. If the PTS service is not available on this node, the active engine ignores this datagram. A PTS node may not send any more PTS Available packets if it is already overloaded with PTS sessions. Finally when the destination host receives a PTS probe packet, it sends back an acknowledgment to the sending host echoing back the timestamp in the PTS probe packet. This helps the host to estimate the total rtt. 3) The initiating host collects all the replies to the PTS probe message. If the only PTS Available message received is from the destination host then it means that there are no active nodes hosting PTS service currently available along the path between the sender and the receiver. In this case, a direct TCP connection is established between the sender and the receiver. If no reply is received from the destination host within a certain period of time, the sender times out and retransmits the PTS probe datagram, discarding all the PTS available messages received if any. **Setup Time Comparison with direct TCP:** The setup time for a direct TCP connection is given by $t_{setup} \approx \frac{3}{2} rtt_{total}$. We can deduce the setup time $t_{setup'}$ for a PTS session as, $t_{setup'} \approx rtt_{total} + \frac{1}{2} rtt_X + t_s + (rtt_{total} - rtt_X) + rtt_X \approx 2rtt_{total} + \frac{1}{2} rtt_X + t_s$ where t_s is the time required by the PTS node to service the connection setup request. If only one PTS available message is received (from the destination host) then a direct TCP connection will have to be setup because there is no PTS node along the path. In this case the setup time is, $t_{setup''} \approx \frac{5}{2} rtt_{total}$. As seen from the above equations, $t_{setup'}$ as well as $t_{setup''}$ are greater than t_{setup}. The PTS node discovery takes about one rtt_{total} more than the time required to setup a direct TCP connection. If any intermediate router drops the PTS probe packet then it will take more than one rtt_{total} to discover PTS nodes. For this reason, use of PTS for short sessions(small data transfer) is not justified if the primitive approach is used to discover PTS nodes. Instead of the host discovering PTS nodes when there is a request for PTS service, a more proactive approach can be adopted in which PTS nodes are probed periodically.

Proactive PTS Node Discovery: In order to discover PTS nodes proactively every host can send PTS probe messages periodically to its prospective destinations and build a table of services available along that path. But there are problems with this naive approach. If every host in the network is going to periodically perform PTS node discovery like this, then the network will be inundated with the 'probe' and 'reply' messages. Also it is difficult to guess in advance the destinations with which the host will be communicating. Another problem lies in the timeliness of the PTS service information being gathered. The services table may not reflect the most up to date status of the PTS node e.g., between the probing interval the loads might change or the routes itself might change making a particular PTS node no longer appear on the route to a destination. There are additional problems if the end point is not a conventional computing element. If the initiating host is a wireless device, PDA or mobile phone for example, then it may not have sufficient memory to store the services table, nor is it advisable to perform PTS node discovery over the already bandwidth constrained and unreliable wireless link. PTS node discovery can be accomplished by deploying an active service offered over active networks.

5   Conclusions

Proxy transport service (PTS) proposed in this paper is an active network based service targeted towards improving the TCP throughput of large rtt connections. PTS results in faster rate of increase of the source host's congestion window leading to higher TCP throughput. The main difference between PTS and other enhancing schemes is the non-transparent nature of PTS service. PTS is not localized to any node and can be deployed on any node within the network. As active nodes proliferate the network, higher is the probability that a host will find a suitable PTS node, leading to better load sharing among the active nodes providing PTS service. We have demonstrated the working of PTS and proved its advantages over a direct TCP connection for large rtt connections. Three major factors affecting the PTS throughput are: PTS node location, PTS service time per packet and PTS buffer size per session. With the availability of high speed processors, efficient active node architectures, and distributed nature of PTS, PTS service can scale to large number of users. PTS node discovery can be accomplished by agents executing on active nodes. A proactive PTS Node discovery scheme can reduce the setup time.

Acknowledgements. This material is based upon work supported by the National Science Foundation under Grant No. 0129682.

References

1. Tennenhouse, D.L., Smith, J.M., Sincoskie, W.D., Wetherall, D.J., Minden, G.J.: A Survey of Active Network Research. IEEE Communications Magazine **35** (1997) 80–86
2. Tennenhouse, D.L., Wetherall, D.J.: Towards an Active Network Architecture. Computer Communication Review **26** (1996)
3. Wetherall, D., Legedza, U., Guttag, J.: Introducing new internet services: Why and how. IEEE Network Magazine, special issue on Active and Programmable Networks (1998)
4. Psounis, K.: Active Networks: Applications, Security, Safety, and Architectures. IEEE Communications Surveys (1999) 1–16
5. Bakre, A., Badrinath, B.R.: I-TCP: Indirect TCP for mobile hosts. 15th International Conference on Distributed Computing Systems (1995)
6. Dutta, D., Zhang, Y.: An Active Proxy Based Architecture for TCP in Heterogenous Variable Bandwidth Networks. IEEE GLOBECOM (2001)
7. Zhang, L.: Resource Reservation Protocol-Version 1 Functional Specification. Network Working Group -RFC 2205 (1997)
8. Breslau, L., Estrin, D., Fall, K., Floyd, S., Heidemann, J., Helmy, A., Huang, P., McCanne, S., Varadhan, K., Xu, Y., Yu, H.: Advances in Network Simulation. IEEE Computer **33** (2000) 59–67
9. Calvert, K.: Directions in Active networks. IEEE Communications Magazine: Special Issue on Programmable Networks (1998)

DataRouter: A Network-Layer Service for Application-Layer Forwarding

Joseph D. Touch and Venkata K. Pingali

USC/Information Sciences Institute, 4676 Admiralty Way
Marina del Rey, CA 90292
{touch,pingali}@isi.edu
www.isi.edu/{touch,pingali}

Abstract. DataRouter forwards network layer packets using application layer tags, without requiring per-hop termination of transport protocols and the consequent reimplementation of transport services in the application. DataRouter provides network delivery based on pattern matching and string replacement. It combines a byte string as a loose source route IP option tag and regular expression routing entries to provide a new network service. DataRouter tags have a variety of forms, including fixed-length with exact matches for distributed hash tables and variable-length with regular expression matches for URL redirection. Tagged IPv6 packets traverse non-DataRouter routers transparently. On a platform forwarding IPv4 packets at 310K packets/sec., an unoptimized FreeBSD IPv4 DataRouter forwards hash-match packets at up to 270K packets/sec. (87% of max.) and pattern-match packets 155K packets/sec. (50% of max.). DataRouter thus provides a viable, higher-performance alternative to application-layer implementation of forwarding, in a generic service more interoperable with existing network and transport protocols.

1 Introduction

DataRouter is an open, generic string match and rewriting facility for Internet packets. It augments the traditional, numeric address in an IPv4 or IPv6 header with an application-provided string used as a variant of loose source routing. The result provides an integrated facility for content delivery networks (CDNs), resource discovery, and advanced overlay network architectures.

The difference between a conventional IP packet and a DataRouter IP packet is shown in Figure 1 (only the relevant fields of the headers are shown). The DataRouter packet includes an option field, akin to the existing loose source route (LSR) option in IPv4 or the router header option in IPv6 [11][18]. The option contains a byte string (or multiple byte strings) with tag information. As with LSR, the packet is forwarded using existing IP routing tables towards the destination IP address; once there, the string is extracted, matched, indexed, and the packet header rewritten to indicate the IP address of the next hop router in the DataRouter topology.

N. Wakamiya et al. (Eds.): IWAN 2003, LNCS 2982, pp. 115–126, 2004.
© IFIP International Federation for Information Processing 2004

1.1 Background

The Internet forwards packets based on fixed endpoint identifiers, i.e., IP addresses. Routing uses these addresses to direct packets toward their destination, using longest-prefix match in forwarding tables, on tables that have been loaded either manually or by a routing protocol. The Internet currently supports a single, global address space, and a single, global set of forwarding tables.

Existing techniques to support additional matching schemes require separate distributed systems. Conventional Internet resource discovery uses an external table, specifically the DNS, to resolve names to IP addresses. As another example, Google is a central database that resolves text phrases to URLs, which include DNS names or IP addresses directly. More recent peer-to-peer architectures forward requests over application-layer tunnels (e.g., TCP connections) and use a distributed application to direct queries to a table [17].

Such services enable interesting and useful content-directed forwarding at the expense of violating the "end-to-end principle" [21]. In the Internet architecture, the network layer forwards packets, the transport layer maintains ordering and reliability (if desired, as well as congestion control), and only the application deals directly with the payload data. In a CDN, data-layer information is used for forwarding, e.g., peeking at the URL inside an HTTP request to route HTML requests over a slow pipe and JPG (image) requests over a fast pipe. CDNs can direct requests for bandwidth, cache aggregation, or policy-based routing.

However, in all cases the TCP connection must be terminated per-hop, in order to reassemble the packets sufficiently to recover the data stream; this necessitates application-layer mechanisms to ensure end-to-end reliability and resequencing. An alternative is to peek into packets and try to recover the data without terminating the connection, which can be challenging when packets take diverse paths or when the data is encrypted. Either case violates (or badly strains) the "end-to-end" principle.

DataRouter replaces CDN's external, application-layer mechanisms with an open, network-layer matching and rewriting service. End host applications can add a byte string to the network (IP) header as a new type of IP option, and that header is looked up and/or rewritten at intermediate hops, using a separate set of loadable tables. The result achieves integrated routing based on application data utilizing a unified network layer service, without requiring per-hop TCP termination or peeking at packet data.

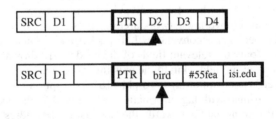

Fig. 1. IPv4 Loose Source Route (top) vs. DataRouter (bottom) options

Current Internet routing supports "loose source routing" in IPv4 and IPv6, in which packets are forwarded to a chain of explicitly-selected routers using an IP header option [11][18]. The packet contains a conventional source IP address, the IP address of a destination where LSR is performed, and the header option with a list of subsequent destination IP addresses. At each intermediate destination, the header IP destination field is exchanged with the address at the option's pointer, which is then incremented (Figure 2, left). The process stops when the pointer exceeds the option length.

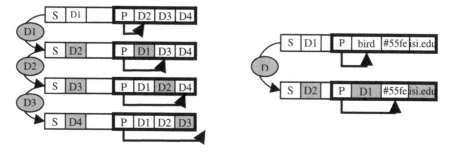

Fig. 2. IPv4 Loose Source Routing (left) and processing step in DataRouter (right)

DataRouter extends LSR so that the chain can contain arbitrary application-configured strings such as DNS names, URLs, etc. DataRouters lookup these strings to entries in a table that indicates the IP address of the next rewriting-router and rules for rewriting the string (if desired) (Figure 2, right).

DataRouter's LSR-like forwarding allows overlay networks to be incorporated in the base Internet architecture. This facilitates multi-overlay paths without the need for inter-overlay gateways. The string labels allow application-layer content-based routing without requiring connection termination at each hop, avoiding complications with end-to-end reliability and further facilitating the integrated use of various content delivery (a.k.a. distribution) systems (CDNs). The key reason for per-hop connection termination is to allow the forwarder to access packet data [17]. DataRouter places that information in the IP packet header, making it accessible to the forwarder and thus avoiding the need for separate, hop-by-hop connections

The result is more consistent with conventional network architectures, where forwarding uses packet header as context, and transport (TCP) connections provide end-to-end reliability. DataRouter thus provides content-based routing without violating the "end-to-end argument," or requiring separate, application-layer reliability mechanisms [21]. It can also be used to integrate DNS resolution and TCP connection establishment (SYN) phases, reducing connection latency and improving performance for short connections or anycast services [13][15].

Although there have been a number of new recent network architectures, both at the peer-to-peer and network overlay levels, incremental deployment and management of these systems has been examined in a limited way. Most systems assume that new capabilities are deployed at specific routers connected by tunnels at the application or network layer. DataRouter provides an alternative deployment environment in which new routing tables are loaded, but no new tunnels need to be created. This provides new opportunity, but also represents a paradigm shift for application-layer network architects; they focus on being routing protocol designers more than tunnel engineers.

Current inter-peer and inter-overlay communication requires gateways, explicitly deployed at key points in the architecture. DataRouter allows composition of inter-overlay paths by concatenating data tags in the IP option, providing new opportunity for more pervasive, flexible, and dynamic creation of heterogeneous routing paths.

Finally, DataRouter also supports both anycast and late-binding TCP [13][15]. Both capabilities merge address lookup with packet delivery. For anycast, the service (e.g., "printer") is the string in the anycast IP packet, and the initial destination is the first lookup node of an anycast database. A type of late-binding TCP can place the DNS name is the string in the SYN packet, and set the base IP destination address to the DNS server. This variant of TCP is related to dispatching HTTP requests within web server farms, as well as to reduce TCP connection establishment over fast links. Other support is required, e.g., to allow late resolution of port numbers, but the DataRouter provides a key component of a solution.

2   DataRouter

DataRouter is a generic string match and rewriting capability at selected routers. It consists of the following components: (1) an IP option structure, (2) forwarding and rewriting tables at selected routers, (3) a fixed set of matching algorithms, (4) an API for applications to write/read the IP option, and (5) an API for routing algorithms to load the tables. The combination of these components provides a string match and string replacement corollary to the current IP forwarding and routing mechanism.

2.1   IP Option Structure

The current IPv4 Loose Source Routing (LSR) option (also called Loose Source Route and Record) consists of a tagged option entry with a pointer and length fields, followed by a sequence of IPv4 addresses; a similar option called a routing header (RH) exists for IPv6 [11][18]. In IPv4, the LSR option uses 3 octets for the LSR tag (0x83), the option length, and an octet pointer used to step through the addresses (Figure 3, left).

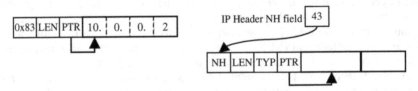

Fig. 3. IPv4 and IPv6 LSR Options

In IPv6 (Figure 3, right), the RH option is indicated by a field in the previous option or base IP header, and the option consists of 4 octets of control information – the type of the next header (NH), the length of the option in 8-octet units (excluding the first 8 octets), the type of routing (e.g., 0 indicates LSR), and a counter indicating the number of unprocessed segments left (effectively a pointer), followed by the address list. Overall, the two options are essentially the same, except that in IPv4 the space for all options is limited to 40 octets, whereas in IPv6 there is no limit per se to option space.

DataRouter uses a chain of labeled strings rather than numeric addresses as the source route. As with LSR, the DataRouter option contains a length and a pointer indicating the string to be manipulated at the next destination hop, in addition to the option tag itself (Figure 3, left). A list of string structures follow, where each string is tagged with a routing class, a matching and lookup algorithm, and the string's length (Figure 4, bold; string shown in shaded area). The routing class indicates which tables are used for matching and translation, enabling concurrent use by multiple routing systems.

The structure shown in Figure 4 is for an IPv4 DataRouter option. In IPv6, the option is a variant of the existing routing header option (Figure 4, where the type (TYP) is DRO (DataRouter option). IP addresses resolved by patterns match the IP version of the base header, a requirement enforced by the routing protocol.

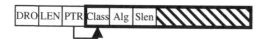

Fig. 4. DataRouter Option

The fixed set of lookup algorithms include (1) longest pattern match (2) exact match, (3) range match, (4) longest prefix/suffix, and (5) "closest" match (fuzzy match).The first three have been implemented and tested, as discussed in Section 3. The addition of a cost function (for (5)) both increases the complexity of the implementation (and thus lowers its performance) and increases the potential for ambiguity. Note that (2) and (3) are special cases of (1), e.g., where all patterns are exact matches, and would be provided as specially-tuned alternatives.

The use of a set of predefined classes enables concise descriptions of various anticipated configurations. The following examples define sample forwarding methods, including a tag string, and a string-based routing class for each method:

- *DNS:*   lookup=#long_sufx class=#DNS   string=*joe.com*
- *URL redirection*:   lookup=#exact   class=#URL   tag=*joe.com/apple*
- *Napster/Chord/CAN:* lookup=#exact   class=#MP3   tag=*hash(song name)*
- *Google*:   lookup=#closest   class=#WEB   string=*"Potter movie"*

The use of different routing classes allows two schemes with the same lookup algorithm to utilize separate tables, even at the same router, e.g., b) and c) above. Lookup algorithms and classes are shown as constants (#), but are represented by numeric indices. Current IPv4 LSR capabilities can be shown in this generic scheme:

- *IPv4 LSR:*   lookup=#long_prfx class=#IPv4   string=*10.0.0.2*

IPv4 has limited capability for such options, with only 37 octets of total DataRouter option payload possible (40 max., less 3 for the option tag), where each string requires an additional 3 octets of overhead. Optimizations may be possible, e.g., merging the string Class and Algorithm fields, to reduce this overhead, but it is clear that IPv4 DataRouting is constrained.

An IPv6 DataRouter option can be much larger. The existing RH option, which can be used for DataRouter (e.g., using Type=1), can be up to 2K octets per instance, and appears to be no limit to the number of RH options in a single packet. The total IPv6 option space can consume as much of the overall packet size as desired (64K conventionally, or 4G using jumbograms) [3].

2.2 Forwarding and Rewriting Tables

All DataRouter-capable routers include a separate set of forwarding/rewriting tables, to be matched by the strings in the DataRouter option. The set of tables for each class used by a particular option is indexed by the class identifier. Each class table entry consists of:

- **match field:** the field against which the string is matched.

- **rewriting rules field:** a set of rules for rewriting this, or perhaps subsequent (but not antecedent) DataRouter option strings. In most of the examples shown above, the rule is "replace with the current router's IP address".

- **IP address:** the address of the next DataRouter in the path for this entry.

This set of rules provides a generic capability; the rewriting rules in particular augment the indexing capability to allow on-the-fly revision of subsequent DataRouter options.

2.3 Lookup Algorithms

DataRouter includes a small set of fixed lookup algorithms. The objective is to provide a flexible and generic capability, not a complete programming environment. Perl-like patterns represent some of the more powerful descriptions, because they can find repeated strings, or context-based matches. More common usage will be dominated by the string structure: (a) exact match for hashes, (b) longest prefix for IP addresses, and (c) longest suffix for DNS names

URLs represent a special case, one where the rewriting rules may be especially useful. Consider http://www.isi.edu/touch/index.html, which benefits from successive DataRouter resolution: longest suffix anchored at the first single "/" – once there, remove http://www.isi.edu/ , and longest prefix thereafter. In this case, DataRouter would rewrite the current option or insert a copy before the next string to be processed. Alternately, component operations may be decomposed by the application.

2.4 IP Option API

Applications need a mechanism by which to set the IP DataRouter option, and a way to read the option contents upon delivery. Unix sockopts provide this capability. For DataRouter, the options can be set per-packet, or per socket (per-association for UDP or per-connection for TCP). There may be further implications on the requirements for Internet hosts, as well as for the routing table values [4].

The DataRouter requires additional transport layer support for late binding [13]. Incrementally resolving strings into IP addresses is consistent with existing IP, but UDP and TCP include the final endpoint address in a loose source route list in the transport protocol processing. For TCP and optionally UDP, this affects the calculation of the transport checksum. For TCP, it also affects connection processing, because TCP expects to match returning SYN/ACKs with the emitted SYNs, based on addresses and ports. Existing solutions that support host mobility can be applied, notably the Host Identity Payload (HIP) protocol, which uses an intermediate header between the IP and transport protocol, providing exactly the decoupling required [16].

2.4 Table Loader API

The tables of a DataRouter-capable router need to be loaded by a routing protocol. This proposal does not address the routing protocol, as there are many to choose from, and it focuses instead on enabling the development of these protocols. The API for loading forwarding tables is a variant of the Unix route command called droute:

```
droute  class class_id add pat dest [alg (long|exact...)]
```

The default algorithm is "longest". "Dest" indicates the IP address of the next hop to use when this pattern matches. The current implementation supports regexp patterns [20]. Further details of the pattern are under development, including how best to indicate the following: (a) match only & delete current string, (b) match & substitute on current string, and (c) if matching current string, then substitute on all subsequent strings.

The table loader API is intended to be used by either static routing commands or a dynamic routing protocol. Such a protocol could support Chord-style forwarding at the network layer, by having a Chord application insert DataRoutes into the forwarding table. The purpose of DataRouter is to support this and other kinds of forwarding in a generic service.

3 Preliminary Results

A preliminary implementation of the DataRouter has already been completed in FreeBSD 5.0, using a new IPv4 option and UDP data packets [14]. It includes a preliminary API for inserting and reading options and configuring tables. It supports exact and longest suffix match, and was tested for the classes of MP3 hashes and DNS names. This implementation consists of ~700 lines of kernel code and ~1,000 lines of application code for testing. This version consists of longest-pattern match lookup only, to indicate the upper-bound performance of an unoptimized system.

The results of preliminary tests indicate the utility of this mechanism. Both conventional DNS and peer-to-peer style MP3 hash lookups are supported using a single interface. The system avoids per-hop transport-layer tunnels and works as an intermediate step in a global Internet path. The data are summarized in Figure 5.

On a dual-processor 2.4 GHz Xeon PC running the existing FreeBSD 5.0, IPv4 packets are forwarded around 310K packets/sec, indicated as "IP/reg" in Figure 5 (leftmost bar). Forwarding the same packets on a kernel with DataRouter extension support (IP/RER), i.e., data routing capability is present but not used, does not affect performance measurably. DataRouted packets forwarded based on an exact match of a 32-bit hash decreases performance to around 270K packets/sec (Hash/RER, striped), and forwarding based on a regular expression (in this case, "*.(isi|usc).edu") results in 155K packets/sec. (dark bar). The graph shows averages of 10 1-minute runs over 64-bit/66 MHz PCI gigabit Ethernet connecting three machines (source, router, sink), with error bars indicating +/- 1 standard deviation. These are simple baseline experiments, in which all packets for a test have the same header, and the forwarding tables have only one entry of each type (regular longest-prefix, hash, and regular expression). The results are promising, and more experimentation is planned to study the performance aspects of the DataRouter and design optimizations.

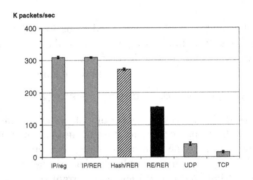

Fig. 5. Comparative IPv4 forwarding performance (in K packets/sec)

Compare these results to application layer forwarding, also shown in Figure 5 (right two bars). Trivial application-layer UDP forwarding, using a single, default output route, runs at 40K packets/sec. on the same PCs. TCP forwarding is limited to the number of new connections per second, 15K connections/sec. when TCP TIME_WAIT states are discarded on close. Moving forwarding into the kernel avoids data copying across kernel-user boundaries, as well as reducing interrupt processing overheads. Although these rates could be increased with tuning, application forwarding still complicates end-to-end semantics for TCP connections.

These tests measured an IPv4 option; the ultimate goal is an IPv6 implementation. IPv6 provides additional option space and provides a safer environment in which to experiment with new options. IPv4 options should be ignored at intermediate hops, notably at routers forwarding DataRouter packets toward their next hop.

IPv4 packets with new, unrecognized options should be ignored (i.e., forward normally) at intermediate routers on paths between DataRouters [2]. Past experience in the Internet community deploying new options suggests caution, however, notably because options not already supported often divert packets from hardware 'fast-path' processing to outboard 'slow-path' software. We suggest a technique to overcome this potential pitfall elsewhere [26].

The code can be transitioned to the core of the Internet if desired, using either PCs as buddy-routers or by integration into native routers. Because DataRouter provides CDN-like redirection, implementation in the Internet core is not necessary, and it may be more convenient to rely on edge-based DataRouter services for directing initial requests, where subsequent data connections can utilize conventional IP packets.

4 Related Work

DataRouter extends the concepts of a number of peer, overlay, and alternative network architectures, unifying the generic capability believed to support many of these systems. It is a very specific capability, and though it could be deployed using programmable (Active) networks, it is more consistent with a static capability with dynamic configuration than a truly programmable system [24]. Further, it is distinct from most of these related architectures in being integrated (and relying upon) the underlying IP forwarding infrastructure. DataRouter augments IP routing with data routing, but does not replace it.

Data routing trades space within the header and slightly increased node complexity to reduce protocol complexity and application participation in network layer forwading. Trading header space for computational complexity has been explored earlier [9]. for improving route lookup performance. DataRouter uses a language similar to Data Manipulation Language [9] to encode routing instructions.

DataRouter is inspired by the use of application data for content-directed routing in peer networks [17]. Whether accessing URLs in an HTTP connection in a TCP stream, or hashes as used in CAN or Chord, these systems forward using packet data, rather than packet headers [19][23]. In some cases the data is extracted en-route, in other cases the hash is performed a-priori to provide a header destination address. The use of data for forwarding distinguishes them from VPN or overlay networks, which rely on conventional endpoint addresses.

The cost of forwarding using packet data is large – either an entire, separate topology must be deployed (CAN/Chord) or each hop must terminate the data (TCP) connection (to access the packet data properly). The former is cumbersome and prohibitive, and the latter violates the end-to-end argument, requiring separate application-layer reliability mechanisms on top of conventional transport protocols [21]. A recent approach uses data expressed as selection predicates [7]. that are constraints over a set of attribute value pairs. DataRouting supports regular expressions that are strictly more general than selection predicates. However, the constrained language of selection predicates allowed for efficient matching algorithms to be designed. DataRouter could be easily extended to incorporate the special case of selection predicates. Further, DataRouter supports string rewriting, which is not included in [7].

There are more recent systems which focus on the naming structure of CDNs (e.g., INS) or use CDNs for rendezvous-based communication (e.g., III, or i3) [1][22]. In both cases, as well as with other CDN systems (hash or string-based), DataRouter can provide a platform in which INS, i3, or other architectures can load the rewriting tables, allowing network-layer processing based on application-layer data, and avoiding the need for each of these (and other emerging) architectures to reimplement a network layer processing capability.

Overlay networks are deployments of virtual infrastructure, using separate endpoint addresses, tunnels, and routes. They too are cumbersome to deploy, and require separate name-to-address mapping mechanisms to be useful. DataRouter builds on virtual networking systems such as the X-Bone [25] to provide an integrated system with overlay-like capabilities using the core Internet, replacing tunnels with data-directed loose source routing. LSR was abandoned as a mechanism to deploy new protocols in the early days of the M-Bone, because LSR-tagged IPv4 packets are processed inefficiently at every router hop [12]. IPv6 removes this impediment, such that LSR-tagged packets are handled differently (from non-tagged packets) only at hops where the LSR header is manipulated [11].

DataRouter allows the deployment of alternate network architectures, notably those that benefit from an index-based forwarding. It thus enables tests and incremental deployment of IPNL, TRIAD, Heaps, and Network Pointer architectures. It is fundamentally based on the Linda [6] system's tuple-style message delivery, integrated with existing IP forwarding and extended with rewriting capability.

IPNL is a multi-level routing hierarchy, utilizing different forwarding tags at various routing levels [13]. DataRouter can be used as a platform for developing IPNL concepts, using sequences of DataRouter strings for the various IPNL forwarding tags. TRIAD similarly uses an alternate tag architecture, preferring DNS names to IP destination addresses; here again DataRouter option strings can be used to provide TRIAD-like service [10]. Similar multilayer forwarding in Network Pointers, and Catanet can be supported [7][23][27].

Catanet first described the use of source routes and addresses having additional structure, albeit using different classes of more conventional IP addresses [8]. This concept is augmented to use pointers (Network Pointers) or heaps in newer proposals [5][27]. DataRouter is a more general variant of the use of multiple addresses, although currently assuming a linear structure. Instead of focusing on the semantics of the addresses (pointers are a form thereof), it focuses on generalizing the indexing and rewriting capability present in various forms in all these earlier or alternate proposals, specifically allowing the indexing to occur in the network on the path.

5   Related Issues

Preliminary implementation of the DataRouter option in IPv4 suggests that string matching can be done at reasonable rates. Ultimately, its use by application and protocol designers will determine its impact. There are a number of open issues in the current DataRouter research which are largely a matter of development. We identify several of them here but discuss only the end-to-end issues in some detail. Discussion on the rest of the issues can be found elsewhere [26].

Major issues include IPv4 transparency, optimization, late binding, and end-to-end issues. DataRouter functions can be transparently added to the network layer via a modified IP option format. Integration of the DataRouter option with existing routing protocols requires similar extensions to those protocols. The current implementation does not include any optimizations, though caching and precomputation of pattern machines may increase throughput substantially. DataRouter can support late binding, given dynamic endpoint identification negotiation, similar to emerging standards, with interesting additional requirements [13][16]. Even given those potential issues, the benefit to application protocol designers, notably avoiding the need to reimplement transport layer services in the application layer, is substantial. Finally, the DataRouter does not require application protocols that reinvent transport services, as would violate the end-to-end principle.

As noted earlier, application layer forwarding has a negative effect on end-to-end protocols [21]. Connectionless (e.g., UDP) fragmented packets must be reassembled at the forwarding routers, and connections (e.g., TCP) must either be terminated at each hop or snooped and spoofed to reconstitute their internal data. Encrypted data connections prohibit application layer forwarding, unless keys are distributed to all intermediate routers, destroying end-to-end security. When connections are terminated at intermediate hops, error detection and correction must be reimplemented at the application layer, to ensure end-to-end reliability. DataRouter avoids this complexity, allowing the application to place forwarding data directly in the network-layer header. That data is then accessible by DataRouters, copied into fragmented packets, and not subject to data encryption.

6 Conclusions

DataRouter provides a generic string matching and rewriting capability, enabling application-directed forwarding with network layer efficiency, yet without requiring extraordinary measures at the application layer. A preliminary IPv4 implementation demonstrates that DataRouting can operate at 50% of IP forwarding rates, 4 times faster than is possible at the application layer.

The DataRouter enables deployment of new forwarding services incrementally, forwarded like loose source routed packets over existing legacy Internet infrastructure. These new capabilities require modest extensions to existing transport protocol processing, akin to those already required for IP mobility and anycast. By providing an integrated, network-layer capability, DataRouter enables application and protocol designers to focus on the specific features of the system, rather than the details of the mechanism that provides it.

References

1. Adjie-Winoto, W., *et al.,* "The Design and Implementation of an Intentional Naming System," Proc. ACM SOSP (OS Review, V34 N5), Dec. 1999, pp. 186-201.
2. Baker, F., "Requirements for IP Version 4 Routers," RFC1812, June 1995.
3. Borman, D., Hinden, R., Deering, S., "IPv6 Jumbograms," RFC 2675, Aug. 1999.
4. Braden, R., ed. "Requirements for Internet Hosts -- Application and Support," RFC 1123, Oct. 1989.
5. Braden, R., Faber, T., Handley, M., "From Protocol Stack to Protocol Heap – Role-Based Architecture," Proc. HotNets-I, Oct. 2002, in ACM CCR, Jan. 2003, pp. 17-22.
6. Carriero, N., Gelernter, D., "The S/Net's Linda Kernel," ACM Transactions on Computer Systems (TOCS), V4 N2, Nov. 1986, pp. 110-129.
7. Carzaniga, A., Wolf, A. L., "Forwarding in a Content-Based Network," Proc. Sigcomm 2003, Aug. 2003, pp. 163-174.
8. Cerf, V., "The Catanet Model for Internetworking," IEN 48, July 1978.
9. Chandranmenon, G. P., Varghese, G., "Trading packet headers for packet processing," Proc.Sigcomm, Aug. 1995, pp. 162-173.
10. Cheriton, D., Gritter, M., "TRIAD: A Scalable Deployable NAT-based Internet Architecture", Stanford Computer Science Technical Report, Jan. 2000.
11. Deering, S., Hinden, R, "Internet Protocol, Version 6 (IPv6)," RFC 2460, Dec. 1998.
12. Eriksson, H., "MBone: The Multicast Backbone," Communications of the ACM, Vol.37, Aug. 1994, pp.54-60.

13. Francis, P., Gummadi, R., "IPNL: A NAT-Extended Internet Architecture," Proc. Sigcomm 2001, Aug. 2001, pp. 69-80.
14. FreeBSD man pages, e.g., http://www.freebsd.org/
15. Johnson, D., Deering, S., "Reserved IPv6 Subnet Anycast Addresses," RFC 2526, March 1999.
16. Moskowitz, R., Nikander, P.,"Host Identity Payload Architecture," (work in progress), April 2003..
17. Oram A., (ed.): Peer-To-Peer: Harnessing the Power of Disruptive Technologies, O'Reilly & Associates, Sebastopol, U.S.A., 2001.
18. Postel, J., (ed.) "Internet Protocol," RFC 971, Sept. 1981.
19. Ratnasamy, S., Karp, R., Francis, P., Handley, M., Shenker, S., "A Scalable Content-Addressable Network," Proc. Sigcomm 2001, Aug. 2001, pp. 161-172.
20. *Regexp* Unix Manual Pages, June 1993.
21. Saltzer, J., Reed, D., Clark, D., "End-To-End Arguments in System Design," ACM Transactions on Computer Systems, V2 N4, Nov. 1984, pp. 277-288.
22. Stoica, I., Adkins, D., Zhuang, S., Shener, S., Surana, S., "Internet Indirection Infrastructure," Proc. Sigcomm, Aug. 2002, pp. 73-86.
23. Stoica, I., *et al.*, "Chord: A Scalable Peer-to-Peer Lookup Service for Internet Applications," Proc. Sigcomm, Aug. 2001, pp. 149-160.
24. Tennenhouse, D., Smith, J., Sincoskie, W., Wetherall, D., Minden, G., "A Survey of Active Network Research," IEEE Comm. Magazine, Vol. 35, No. 1, Jan.1997, pp. 80-86.
25. Touch, J., "Dynamic Internet Overlay Deployment and Management Using the X-Bone," Computer Networks, July 2001, pp. 117-135.
26. Touch, J., Pingali, V., "DataRouter: A Network-Layer Service for Application-Layer Forwarding," ISI Technical Report ISI-TR-2003-578, May 2003.
27. Tschudin, C., Gold, R., "Network Pointers," Proc. ACM HotNets-I, Oct. 2002, in ACM CCR, Jan. 2003, pp. 23-28.

SORD: Self-Organizing Resource Discovery Protocol for ALAN

Ioannis Liabotis, Ognjen Prnjat, and Lionel Sacks

Department of Electronic & EE, University College London,
Torrington Place WC1E 7JE, UK
{iliaboti | oprnjat | lsacks}@ee.ucl.ac.uk

Abstract. We present the design and implementation of the protocol for efficient resource discovery and job allocation in Application Level Active Network environments. The protocol is fully distributed and is based on the neighbour lists and small world topologies. Protocol is in XML for interoperability and extensibility; and was prototyped and first tested in the context of the ANDROID project - thus, this paper also describes the ANDROID management architecture. We present the protocol validation in the ANDROID trial, and also give detailed simulation results.

1 Introduction

Current trend in communications and distributed computing is that of peer-to-peer models, independent of centralised control and management. Examples are active and programmable networks, cluster computing and the Grid. Requirement on the decentralised management of these environments is that of autonomy and self-organisation of components. The points of control in these environments will be multiple, where no actor having the global knowledge. Many large network operators are facing these operational issues.

A key requirement in these environments is the ability to allocate the incoming workload (processes) placed on a cluster of (active) nodes in such a way as to optimally use the distributed resources. A node can be considered to be optimal for a process in terms of availability of resources: CPU; memory; encoding hardware; hard resource allocation; availability of particular software. In active networks, work has to be executed in close to real time as the components tend to be part of interactive applications. Thus, in our developments, the work is not queued: success of workload allocation is considered to be almost immediate execution. The resources in these environments are heterogeneous, dynamically changing, highly distributed, and within different domains. Resource availability is dynamic and conditional on local constraints. In such large dynamic environments, centralised resource information repository or resource broker based solutions for resource discovery and information storage could suffer from scaling and efficiency problems. Thus, a light-weight, adaptive resource discovery algorithm, available at distributed nodes, is a preferred solution.

N. Wakamiya et al. (Eds.): IWAN 2003, LNCS 2982, pp. 127-136, 2004.

Resource management and allocation in active networks is still an under-researched issue. Most systems providing the middleware support for the Grid, such as Globus [1] and Sun Grid Engine [2], rely on the centralised or hierarchical solutions for information repositories and job allocation points. Here we present a decentralised, scalable, adaptive resource discovery protocol initially developed for Application Level Active Network (ALAN) environments, but also applicable to cluster computing and Grid scenarios. Using this protocol, network administrators could effectively distribute the workload so as to maximise resource utilisation and availability, while not relying on a centralised mechanism. Thus, resource location transparency could be achieved and hidden from applications programmer/end user.

Protocol presented here was initially prototyped, and first demonstrated, in the context of the European project ANDROID [3]. The protocol was further developed for cluster computing and the Grid (Self-Organizing Grid Resource Management project [4]), with basic principles and performance assessment presented in [5] [6]. Here we give the details of the protocol, deployment of its prototype in the final ANDROID trial, and new simulation results.

In section 2, we introduce basic principles of ALAN and ANDROID. In section 3, we present the details of our approach. Section 4 gives the protocol specification. Section 5 presents the demonstration of implementation in the context of ANDROID; while section 6 gives simulation results. Section 7 discusses the related work and 8 gives the conclusion.

2   ALAN and ANDROID

ANDROID project (Active Network DistRibuted Open Infrastructure Development) [3][5][7] focused on policy-based management of ALAN-enabled networks. ALAN [8] is the active networks approach where active services (proxylets), engineered by developers/users, are deployed on a group of servers in the existing Internet. Proxylets introduce new service functionality or enhance the level of existing service provided to the user. The active servers provide the execution environment for proxylets, and as such are envisaged to be deployed in large active server farms where various user-specified processes (proxylets) can be dynamically loaded and run. Thus, there is an analogy to cluster computing and Grid paradigms.

The ANDROID management architecture [3] deploys policies as means of control, while events (observations or changes of system state) are used for monitoring and as policy triggers. Policies allow specification of the target behaviour of autonomous components: when an event is received, policies (after conditions based on local information are evaluated) trigger a response. Policies and events are specified in XML and are communicated through the system via the Management Information Distribution system (MID). Persistent storage of policies is provided through the Directory Service (DS), which features a dynamically programmable interface to a range of underlying storage systems.

The core management functionality is policy-controlled security and resource management [3][7]. Security Manager controls the proxylet admission, in terms of deployer and process authentication, and process access control. Resource Manager [9] deals with proxylet admission control from the resource perspective; resource/process monitoring; and process/resource (re)allocation.

The ANDROID architecture has been deployed in 3 trials. In the final trial, the integrated active networking scenario was conducted, where the architecture was deployed for managing VPNs, multicast services and active server resources and security. The resource discovery protocol has been prototyped in the 5-machine active server farm, and the details of this aspect of the trial are given in section 5.

3   Resource Discovery Protocol: Basic Principles

Our resource discovery protocol is fully distributed, and is based on the ideas of peer-to-peer computing [10]. Each node acts autonomously to identify the best possible node that can serve a request. Each node is connected to a number of neighbours. Initially the neighbours are the nearest topological neighbours (based on geographical location and bandwidth availability between nodes), and a few "*far*" ones. We use a 2-level control mechanism: first is query-based; second is advertisement-based. The query-based mechanism is invoked when an incoming request cannot be resolved by the node that received it. Query time to live (QTTL) determines the number of times a query can be forwarded. The advertisement-based mechanism is activated when a new node appears and advertises its resources. It is also initiated when a dynamic resource changes state, *e.g.* when a node becomes underutilised it can advertise resource availability to its neighbours. Advertisement time to live (ATTL) determines the number of hops that the advertisement can to be forwarded.

Information about resource availability in the network is distributed using the queries-replies and advertisements. This information is cached in the nodes that receive replies and advertisements. Nodes use this information to gain experience on resource availability. Using a different cache for each type of resource, different virtual network topologies are created for each resource. Initially the nodes are connected to their nearest neighbours and some random far neighbours creating a small world topology [11]. As requests arrive and query/advertisement protocols are activated the resource availability caches are populated with state information. The list of neighbours is changing giving separate lists for different resources; generating different virtual topologies.

Fig. 1 depicts the resource management and discovery components on a node. Self-organising resource discovery (SORD) implements the distributed discovery algorithm. It retrieves and stores information on the various caches of the system. There are 3 different caches. "*Known Resources Cache*" contains information about the resources known to the node. This includes the known resources available in the neighbour nodes, which in turn are stored in the "*Neighbour List Cache*". "*Server Meta Data Cache*" contains information on resource availability on the node. Caches can be implemented in different ways: Globus Management Distribution System or ANDROID Directory Service [5]. Our implementation uses ANDROID DS.

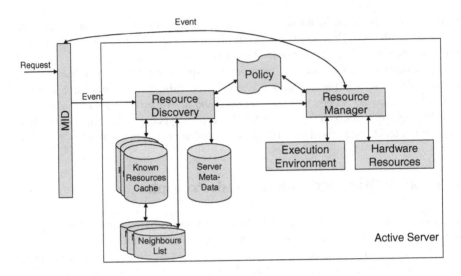

Fig. 1. Resource management and discovery architecture [5]

Typically, user requests the start of the service by sending the relevant events to SORD, which finds the optimal server to run the proxylet, and forwards the event to the resource manager of the hosting machine. Resource manager is responsible for executing a specific request on the local execution environment using the hardware resources available. After performing the resource checks based on policies, the resource manager loads the proxylet(s). Runtime management involves the resource manager monitoring the behaviour of the proxylets, and, in case of unexpected behaviour, applying the relevant policies to preserve the resource integrity and security. Policies can also control modification of service parameters, (initiated by the user or the operator), relating to proxylet reallocation or increase/decrease of resources dedicated to the proxylet. Service termination of is also policy-controlled.

4 SORD Protocol Specification

The protocol allows distributed nodes to communicate, exchange information and locate resources requested by users. The aim is to provide a decentralised mechanism for resource discovery among heterogeneous interconnected resources. Protocol defines the way in which nodes communicate over the network. It consists of a set of messages (Table 1) for communicating information about resources and a set of rules governing the exchange of messages between nodes.

A new node connects itself to the network by keeping in an internal cache the address of at least one other node currently in the network. Using the query/reply and advertisement messages the new node can obtain information about other nodes that participate in the network, and their resources.

Table 1. SORD message description

Message	Description
StartRD	Initiates resource discovery procedure. A node receiving this message is expected to send a "Reply" message to the node that sent the resource discovery request.
Query	The primary mechanism for searching for distributed resources. A node that receives a "Query" message will reply with a "Reply" message with the match found based on the query.
Reply	Response to the "Query". This message provides the recipient with information about resource availability on a node.
Advertise-ment	The advertisement of resource availability on a specific node.

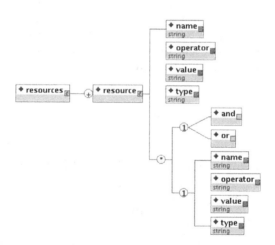

Fig. 2. The resources schema

The protocol uses XML to communicate information between nodes. Messages are exchanged as events sent by the originator to the recipient. Top level event specification follows the ANDROID event specification [3]. The data element of the event contains a *sordmessage*. Every *sordmessage* contains 4 elements: *eventtype* defines the type of the event. (possible values are *StartRD, Query, Reply, Advertisement*); *ttl* specifies the time to live that is associated with each *sordmessage*; *resources* describes a number of resources; *hosturi* is optional and, if used, gives the URI of the host that has those resources. *Resources* element provides description for resources available at a host, or for resources required by user/application. Resources are described using the Globus Resource Specification Language (RSL v1.0) [12]. Each name-value in the description serves as a parameter to control the behaviour of one or more components in the resource management system. Each resource is identified by its *name*, which is an ID known to the management system. The *value* provides either the current or the expected value of the resource. The *operator* determines what values of resource are expected by users/applications. Fig. 2 shows the resources XML schema.

5   Implementation and Demonstration

In the final ANDROID trial, the protocol was used to find an active server suitable for running the proxylet with respect to resource availability and security profile. Our query based mechanism was used to search for the active server that has the required resources. The mechanism is invoked when an incoming request cannot be resolved by the incoming node: a query is sent to the neighbours, which reply about resource availability. The "best" reply reaches the node that initiated the query and the request to run the proxylet is forwarded to the "best" node. Information on resource availability is gathered directly from the active server (*e.g.* Native Library availability). SORD is initiated by the Resource or Security Managers based on the management policies: when a new "run proxylet" event arrives at the Resource Manager and there are not enough CPU resources to run it, the Resource Manager initiates SORD by sending it "eStartRD" event.

Table 2. SORD protocol evaluation

Message Type	Message Sending (ms)	Message parsing, info gathering & evaluation (ms)	Message Size (bytes)
StartRD	40	300	1002
eQuery	36	280	713
eReply	34	210	583

For the trial, we assumed that a user requests to run a proxylet that requires the least loaded active server that also has a CPU load of less than 10%, and the software library. The protocol was evaluated measuring the time that a message needs to be transferred from a machine to another, the time that is needed for parsing, information gathering and evaluation, as well as the size of the messages in bytes. Table 2. shows the values of the evaluated properties for the different types of messages exchanged by SORD. Total time needed for discovery in the scenario that included resource discovery among 5 machines was 1634ms or 1.6 sec. Total traffic generated by was 4890 bytes. Traffic and amount of time required by the protocol depends on the query time to live, the number of neighbours that each node contacts, the available bandwidth and the available processing power. The nodes where connected on a 100Mbit Ethernet LAN, and were powered by Pentium III processors.

6 Simulation

The protocol has been simulated in order to evaluate its performance and fine-tune its properties. Simulation topology was a lattice network of different sizes (number of nodes). The first part of the simulation includes the discovery of one type of resource, (CPU). The request arrival is a random process, and the request duration follows the Gaussian or the Pareto distribution. Metrics used for performance evaluation are: *total network load* (the mean load of all the nodes); *success rate* (number of times SORD returns the best available resource based on the request requirements divided by the total number of requests); and the *number of messages* sent per request. The messages include queries and advertisements. Furthermore we measure the *actual traffic* generated by the messages, defined as the number of hops that a message has to traverse in order to move from source to destination based on the network topology. Note that since we do not consider queuing of jobs/proxylets (since we require immediate execution in case of active network real-time scenarios); the actual job/proxylet loading can fail if there is no resource found.

Each node queries a specified number of neighbours in order to discover the requested resource. We evaluate 2 different types of neighbour selection: random; and selection based on previous replies. Random selection is based on querying random nodes; previous replies selection caches node IDs that previously gave "good replies".

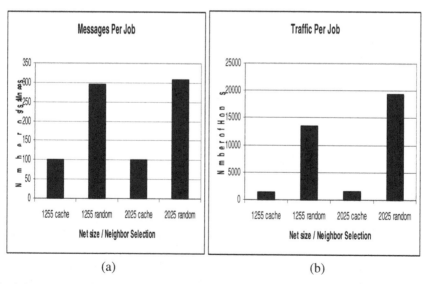

(a)   (b)

Fig. 3. Messages and traffic per job request for different network sizes and different neighbour selection policies

Results shown in Fig. 3. (a)(b) were obtained using Gaussian job duration, while the network load was 94%. The success rate of the protocol was 98%. Fig. 3. (a) presents the number of messages generated by the protocol for two different network sizes (1225 and 2025 nodes) and the two different neighbour selection policies (cache and random). The figure shows that the neighbour selection based on cached information generates 3 times less messages than the random selection. Fig. 3. (a) also shows that the number of messages generated by SORD does not increase as the network size increases from 1255 to 2025 nodes. Fig. 3. (b), presents the actual traffic generated by SORD for 2 different network sizes (1225 and 2025 nodes) and 2 different neighbour selection policies (cache and random). The traffic generated using the neighbours cache is significantly less than the random neighbour selection.

Second set of simulations was conducted assuming that the request duration follows the Pareto distribution. Pareto was chosen since UNIX process lifetimes were shown [13] to follow it. We anticipate that processes running on an ALAN enabled network will also follow Pareto. Fig. 4 shows the success rate of SORD for two networks (1225/2025 nodes). While the utilisation of the network is low the success rate is 100%. For utilisation higher than 95% the success rate drops. For 98% and higher, the success rate drops to 92% giving less guarantees that the optimal node will be found. This is not considered as a drawback since we anticipate that active network operators will run their networks with a target utilisation of 75% to 85%.

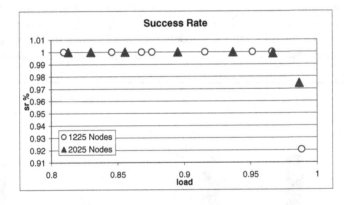

Fig. 4. Success rate of SORD for Pareto request duration

7   Related Work

The details of our work specific to ALAN management in the ANDROID context are presented [3][5][9]: Resource management for the Grid is an active area of research. The Globus management architecture [14] [15] tackles the problem through deploying distinct resource management components: local manager, resource broker and resource co-allocator. The exchange of resource requirements is facilitated via the resource specification language. Resource discovery has been addressed in several application contexts (see [5]). In the context of Grid, different projects have proposed various centralised, hierarchical or distributed algorithms. Globus [1] Nimrod-G [16] and AppLeS [17] use local resource managers (GRAM) to update a directory service with information about availability and capabilities of managed resources. The directory service is based on LDAP. Condor [18] deploys a centralised *collector* that provides a resource information store which tracks the resource availability. The *Data Grid* project [19] uses a decentralised discovery mechanism and hierarchically organised scheduler based on LDAP. Peer-to-peer resource discovery protocols have been applied to file-sharing systems: Gnutella [20] uses aggressive flooding; Freenet [21] request forwarding and file replication. PEERS project uses iterative deepening directed BFS and local indexes [22]. Chord [23] is a protocol for data discovery in a distributed system that uses key association to data items and key mapping to nodes according to hashing algorithm. [24] proposes a fully decentralised resource discovery mechanism for Grid environments, based on a peer-to-peer architecture using request forwarding algorithms.

8 Conclusion

In this paper, we describe a self-organising mechanism that aids the optimal resource discovery in a farm of Application Level Active Network nodes. The protocol is fully distributed and policy controlled. The protocol is defined using XML events for interoperability and extensibility. We also identify a set of rules that construct virtual overlay topologies over the existing IP connectivity. The protocol has been effectively deployed in ANDROID project trial where it was used to find an optimal ALAN active server to run the user-specified proxylet. Moreover, the protocol was also validated through a set of simulations which demonstrate its efficiency.

References

1. The Globus Toolkit. www.globus.org
2. http://wwws.sun.com/software/Gridware/
3. O. Prnjat, I. Liabotis, T. Olukemi, L. Sacks, M. Fisher, P. McKee, K. Carlberg, G. Martinez, "Policy-based Management for ALAN-Enabled Networks"; IEEE 3rd International Workshop on Policies - Policy 2002.
4. The SO-GRM project: Grant GR/S21939 under the UK eScience program, though EPSRC and sponsored by BTExacT
5. L. Sacks, et. al., "Active Robust Resource Management in Cluster Computing Using Policies", JNSM, Special Issue on Policy Based Management of Networks and Services, Vol. 11., No. 3, September 2003.
6. I. Liabotis, O. Prnjat, T. Olukemi, A. L. M. Ching, A. Lazarevic, L. Sacks, M. Fisher, P. McKee, "Self-organising management of Grid environments", International Symposium on Telecommunications IST'2003.
7. T. Olukemi, I. Liabotis, O. Prnjat, L. Sacks, "Security and Resource Policy-based Management Architecture for ALAN Servers", Net-Con'2002 - IFIP and IEEE Conference on Network Control and Engineering for QoS, Security and Mobility, 2002.
8. M. Fry, A. Ghosh, "Application Level Active Networking", Computer Networks, 31 (7) (1999) pp. 655-667.

9.   I. Liabotis, O. Prnjat, L. Sacks, "Policy-Based Resource Management for Application Level Active Networks", Second IEEE Latin American Network Operations and Management Symposium LANOMS 2001.

10. http://www.openp2p.com/

11. D. J. Watts, "Small Worlds", Princeton Univ Pr; ISBN: 0691005419; 1999.

12. The Globus Resource Specification Language RSLv1.0, http://www-fp.globus.org/gram/rsl_spec1.html

13. W. E. Leland and T. J. Ott., "Load-balancing heuristics and process behaviour", in Proc. Joint International Conference on Measurement and Modelling of Computer Systems (ACM SIGMETRICS '86), pages 54--69, Raleigh, NC, May 1986.

14. I. Foster, C. Kesselman, "Globus: A metacomputing infrastructure toolkit", The International Journal of Supercomputer Applications and High Performance Computing, 11(2): 115-128, Summer 1997.

15. K. Czajkowski, I. Foster, N. Karonis, C. Kesselman, S. Martin, W. Smith, S. Tuecke, " A Resource Management Architecture for Metacomputing Systems", Proc. IPPS/SPDP '98 Workshop on Job Scheduling Strategies for Parallel Processing, pp. 62-82, 1998.

16. R. B. David. "Nimrod/g: An architecture for resource management and scheduling system in a global computational Grid", 2000.

17. F. Berman and R. Wolski, "The AppLeS Project: A status report", Proceedings of the 8th NEC Research Symposium, Berlin, Germany, May 1997.

18. M. Litzkow, M. Livny, M. Mutka: "Condor – a hunter of idle workstations", 8th International conference of distributed computing systems (ICDCS 1988)

19. W. Hoschek, F. J. Janez, A. Samar, H. Stockinger, K. Stockinger: "Data management in an international data Grid project." In "Grid", pages 77-90, 2000.

20. Gnutella protocol specification, http://www.clip2.com/

21. I. Clarke, O. Sandberg, B. Wiley, T. W. Hong, "Freenet: A distributed anonymous information storage and retrieval system", in "Designing Privacy Enhancing Technologies", Springer LNCS, New York, 2001.

22. G. Molina, H. Yang, "Efficient search in peer-to-peer networks", technical report http://dbpubs.stanford.edu:8090/pub/2001-47, October 2001.

23. I. Stoica, R. Morris, D. Karger, M. F. Kaashoek, H. Balakrishnan. "A scalable peer-to-peer lookup service of internet applications", Proceedings of the 2001 ACM SIGCOMM Conference.

24. A. Iamnitchi, I. Foster: "On fully decentralized resource discovery in Grid environments" IEEE International workshop on Grid computing, Denver, 2001

Self-Configuring Active Services for Programmable Networks

Ralph Keller and Bernhard Plattner

Computer Engineering and Networks Laboratory
Swiss Federal Institute of Technology, Switzerland
{keller | plattner}@tik.ee.ethz.ch

Abstract. This paper presents a service framework that allows routers to be programmed with user-specific code and coordinated such that the underlying network provides anticipated network services on behalf of applications. We describe how network services can be composed based on a high-level specification defining required and conditional processing steps, how capabilities about processing resources can be disseminated throughout the network by extending the OSPF protocol daemon, how services requirements are mapped onto the underlying network while minimizing both link and processing costs, and how service code is installed on selected nodes and forwarding state established along explicitly routed paths.

Keywords: Active networks, service specification, resource discovery, self-configuration, service deployment.

1 Introduction

During the last decades the original Internet architecture evolved dramatically with new functionality being added to the network layer to support a wide range of emerging applications. Network services such as firewalls, congestion control, media gateways, and traffic engineering all require a network that not only forwards packets based on the destination address, but also performs *packet processing* on nodes interior to the network. As a reaction to such application-specific packet handling requirements, router manufacturers have started to embed programmable elements into routers with the objective of providing network services in a more flexible way. However, deploying new services is usually a manual and time consuming process, requiring the installation of code on multiple routers distributed all over the network. Given the complexity of how services can be composed, the only feasible approach is to automate this process.

In this work we present a services infrastructure that allows router resources to be programmed and coordinated such that the underlying network provides anticipated services on behalf of applications. We have implemented the *active network control software* (ANCS) that offers a generic service abstraction and automates the configuration of processing resources to form network services. Our system accepts processing demands from applications based on a high-level service description,

N. Wakamiya et al. (Eds.): IWAN 2003, LNCS 2982, pp. 137-150, 2004.

discovers available processing capabilities within the network, maps processing requirements onto the network, and configures the appropriate underlying resources such that the network provisions the expected service. In the remainder of this paper, we focus on all the mechanisms involved in the establishment of network services.

2   A Framework for Self-Configuring Services

In the following, we discuss the design rationales of our envisioned service framework that enables applications to coordinate network resources for building network services.

2.1   Overall Network View

To enable flexible services within a programmable network, there is a need for an additional control layer built on top of raw processing capabilities that facilitates the deployment and configuration of user-supplied code. The ANCS can be seen as a distributed system that automates the configuration of network resources to form services that applications use. The system accepts processing demands from applications using a network programming interface (NPI), discovers available processing resources, maps those processing requirements onto network resources, and configures the appropriate state on network nodes. The fact that nodes can perform this mapping autonomously on behalf of applications is a distinct feature of ANCS's design.

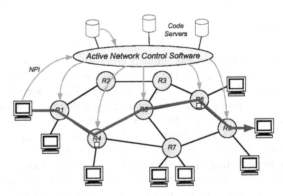

Fig. 1. Distributed network control software for active networks

Figure 1 illustrates our envisioned system where nodes participate in the establishment of application services. Each node continuously monitors the state of its locally available processing resources and distributes information it has on resources to its neighbors. Based on this scheme, each router learns about the location and capabilities of processing resources of other routers and propagates this information throughout the network. To set up network services, applications send a request (using the NPI) to the network control software running on the active nodes.

The router that receives the request then tries to determine the network resources that are needed to satisfy the request. More specifically, the router computes the location for placing processing resources and communication channels connecting the peers with the processing nodes. If a feasible configuration could be computed, a signaling protocol then sets up the service by deploying code on the selected nodes and by establishing communication channels such that packets are routed through the processing functions. Packet processing code comes in form of router plugins [8] that are loaded into the execution environment of the data plane. If processing code has not been loaded previously, it is retrieved from a code server [3].

2.2 Active Node Architecture

Figure 2 illustrates the architecture of an individual active node, with the following components participating in the establishment of network services:

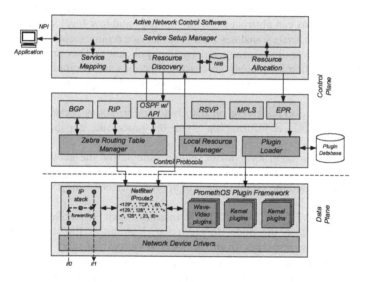

Fig. 2. Architecture of an individual active

- The *active network control software* accepts service establishment requests from applications, gathers information about processing resource capabilities, determines suitable locations for placing the packet processing functions, and initiates the configuration of associated network state.
- The *OSPF protocol daemon* has been extended with an API such that it can provide the ANCS with information about the topology and availability of processing resources.
- The *explicit path routing* (EPR) protocol installs processing code on selected nodes and establishes forwarding state such that traffic gets routed accordingly.
- The *plugin loader* retrieves router plugins from remote code servers when new packet processing code needs to be installed on a node.

- The *PromethOS plugin framework* provides an environment for the dynamic loading of plugin classes, the creation of plugin instances as well as the execution of packet processing code.

In the following, we describe the ANCS in more detail.

3   Active Network Control Software

The ANCS can be seen as a new control layer implementing the functionality needed to set up services, thus freeing applications from knowing about the topology and details of low-level processing elements. Internally, the ANCS provides the following functions (see Figure 2 top):

- The *service setup manager* accepts service requests from applications using the NPI. To simplify the deployment of services, this interface needs to be designed in a way applications can abstract from the topology and low-level system details.
- A *mapping mechanism* translates high-level service requirements onto the network based on the constraints formulated by the application. This process determines the optimal location for placing processing functions and communication channels connecting the intermediate processing steps while guaranteeing application constraints.
- A *resource discovery mechanism* distributes information about the node's own resources and collects information about the processing capabilities from other active routers.
- A *resource deployment mechanism* sets up state across the network as computed by the mapping process. This includes the installation of processing code on selected routers and the establishment of appropriate forwarding state.

As depicted in Figure 2 the ANCS interacts with a number of underlying components present on the node. In particular, it monitors the state of its locally available processing resources from the local resource manager, and disseminates state information using the extended OSPF protocol to its neighbors. This way, each node learns about the topology and availability of resources embedded in the network. For the deployment of code and the establishment of network state across the network, the ANCS uses our proposed EPR signaling protocol. In the following, we describe each of the core functions involved in the establishment of services in more detail.

3.1   Service Specification Using Active Pipes

As a network programming interface between the user and the active network, we propose *active pipes* [7] that allow specification of communication and processing requirements by applications, regardless of the underlying topology and node-specific details. The idea of specifying transmission and processing requirements is to model a connection as a sequence of functions that have to be performed on the data stream. This concept is analogous to pipes in UNIX where data can be sent through a sequence of programs. In the context of active networks, these functions can be distributed on several nodes (unlike UNIX pipes were all processes execute on the same computer). Processing steps correspond to code modules that have to be instantiated along the path of the connection. However, an active pipe is a more general definition of the execution sequence since processing requirements can either be *required* or be *conditional*. That is, we distinguish between the following two types of code modules used in an active pipe:

- A *required* module provides a packet processing function that must be performed exactly once in the network. This functionality is essential for the correct operation of the application and cannot be omitted. Such a processing function typically changes the format of the data stream. An example is encryption, where the data stream must be encrypted exactly once within the network.
- A *conditional* module provides a functionality that is installed on all matching locations whenever a certain condition is satisfied. As a result the code module can be deployed *multiple times* along the path. If the condition is not satisfied at all, then no modules need to be installed. These code modules typically do not change the format of the data stream. A typical example is application-specific congestion control for video. If the data stream transits several congested links, congestion control modules will need to be installed before each of those links. If the data stream is not routed through any congested links, congestion control can be omitted.

Figure 3 depicts an active pipe for a scenario where a connection for sensitive data transmission should be established between two dislocated domains, and congestion control mechanisms desired on parts of the network where the stream is encrypted.

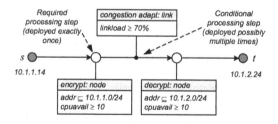

Fig. 3. Secure data transmission modeled using active pipe

The encryption and decryption steps are *required* exactly once within the source and destination domains, congestion control is *optional* (and deployed possibly multiple times) on links between the encryption and decryption steps. From a logical point of view, code modules can be deployed on either a *node* or along a *link*.

- *Deployment on a node* means that processing will be performed when the appropriate node is transited by the data traffic. An example for this type of processing is transcoding, where packets that go through the node need to be processed, regardless of the link from where the packet enters or leaves the node.
- *Deployment on a link* means that processing needs to happen when a given link is traversed. Here, the link that the data traffic enters or leaves a node is crucial for

the application. For example for congestion control, processing needs to be performed when traffic is sent to congested links.

That is, for each processing step the application must specify whether processing should be performed when traffic either goes through a node or when traversing a link.

In addition to defining a sequence of required and conditional modules, the user can define individually for each processing step, *installation conditions* that describe the circumstances under which an active code module should be deployed. Since applications can have stringent requirements on the location of processing modules, each processing step can have *multiple* installation conditions to be considered for the deployment of a given function. Constraints restrict the location where processing can be performed. Each constraint is defined as a tuple *<attr, rel, value>*, expressing that attribute *attr* must fulfill *value* by the relation *rel*. If no constraints are defined for a processing step, all locations are considered to be valuable processing sites. In the example above, encryption and decryption must be placed within the given address ranges on nodes with sufficient processing cycles available, and congestion adaptation on the encrypted stream will be installed along all links where a certain congestion level is exceeded.

3.2   Mapping Active Pipe onto Network

Using active pipes, applications can now describe their processing requirements using a formalism that *abstracts* from the underlying physical network topology. However, this requires a mechanism that maps an active pipe onto the network, preferentially while minimizing network costs. In the following, we first explain how this mapping can be done in the case of a single required or conditional processing step, deployed on nodes or links. Then we look at how the mapping works for a combination of processing steps as in an active pipe. The main idea is to transform all the cases into specific shortest path problems and use the methods incrementally to generate a shortest path problem for the complete active pipe (see [4] and [7] for more details).

To state the mapping problems more formally, we use the following notation. We are given a directed graph, $G = (V, E)$, with a transmission cost $c(e)$, for each link $e \in E$, and a processing cost unit $c(v)$, for each node $v \in V$. Let the source be defined by s and the destination by t. In graphs, we denote transmission costs on the links and the unit for processing costs within the node. For now we assume that all modules require a cost of 1, that is, the cost for processing a module corresponds to $c(v)$. In addition, we assume that processing costs are scaled to match link cost metric. This convenience will allow us to express the mapping problem as a shortest-path problem.

3.2.1   Required Processing

For a single required processing step, we need to determine the location for placing the processing function and a path from the sources s to the destination t that transits the processing module (which can be placed only on one the candidate nodes). The mapping algorithm's objective is to minimize the sum of all transmission costs on links plus the processing cost for the module.

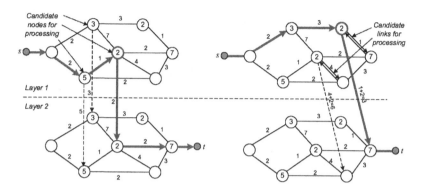

Fig. 4. Routing for required processing steps on a node (left) or on a link (right)

When processing should happen on a node (as for the encryption module), given the candidate set of nodes $N \subseteq V$ (defined by attribute constraints such as it must be placed within 10.1.1/24 and sufficient CPU cycles available), we need to determine the optimal node $n \in N$, where processing is performed. We can solve this problem by transforming it to a generic shortest path problem. As illustrated in Figure 4 (left), we modify the graph G by making two copies which we identify as layer 1 and layer 2. For each vertex v in the initial graph, let v_1 denote the vertex in layer 1 of the target graph while v_2 denotes the vertex copy in layer 2. To model the processing of modules, we add edges *between* the two layers. For every node $n \in N$, where processing may occur, we add an edge (n_1, n_2) in the target graph and let the link cost of (n_1, n_2) be the processing cost on node n, $c(n)$. The source node in layer 1, s_1, is the source for this new graph and the destination node in layer 2, t_2, is the new destination node. This transformation ensures that the path from the source to the destination is *forced* to go through exactly one processing site. Now, to solve the routing problem with one mandatory processing site, we find a least-cost path in the target graph using a shortest path algorithm. The path can then be mapped back to the original graph by *projecting* the two layers onto a single layer and the processing is optimally performed where the path crosses the two layers.

In the case of processing on a link, the procedure of determining the optimal location is similar to the previous case, except for one small variation. Given the candidate set of links, $L \subseteq E$, the application wants the processing to be done on exactly one link among the set that needs to be traversed. Again, we transform the graph G by making two copies as illustrated in Figure 4 (right). Now for every edge $e \in L$, which connects nodes i and j, we add a new *diagonal edge* (i_1, j_2) in the target graph *between* the two layers. The weight of this new edge is the sum of the processing cost at the node and the transmission cost of the link. This is given by the expression $c(k) + c(e)$, with $k = i$ when processing should be done at the node preceding the link (as assumed in the figure), or $k = j$ for processing at the succeeding node, respectively. The shortest path from s_1 to t_2 gives us an optimal path that transits one of the candidate links, with the node with the outgoing layer-crossing link denoting the optimal location for processing.

3.2.2 Conditional Processing

In the conditional processing case, active modules should be installed along the path at locations that satisfy a given condition. In the following, we look at the cases for conditional processing on nodes and links and describe how the locations for placing these modules can be determined.

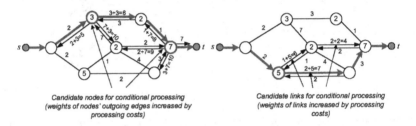

Candidate nodes for conditional processing
(weights of nodes' outgoing edges increased by
processing costs)

Candidate links for conditional processing
(weights of links increased by processing
costs)

Fig. 5. Routing for conditional processing steps on nodes (left) and links (right)

In the case of conditional processing on nodes, we are given a candidate set of nodes, $N \subseteq V$, and we need to determine the set of nodes where the active module should be installed such that the path cost is optimal. More formally, suppose there exists a path $<s, v_1, v_2,...., t>$ from the source s to the destination t, and if $v_i \in N$, then an active module should be installed on that node v_i. This can be solved as follows. For every node $v \in N$, let $\{e_1, e_2, e_3,....e_n\}$ be the set of outgoing edges. As shown in Figure 5 (left), the graph transformation is to *increase* the edge weights of the outgoing links by the processing cost of the node, that is, $c_{new}(e_i) = c(e_i) + c(v)$, while source and destination remain the same.

In case of conditional processing on links, the application wants modules at all links in the path given a candidate set of links, $L \subseteq E$. An example for this scenario is congestion control, where congestion control modules need to be installed whenever a congested link is traversed. Similar to the conditional node case, all links belonging to the candidate set where processing could happen are marked with the processing step. The transformation on the graph is, as illustrated in Figure 5 (right), for every edge $e \in L$ to increase the edge weight by the processing cost of the node adjacent to that link. That is, $c_{new}(e) = c(e) + c(v)$, where v is either the node preceding or succeeding the link e.

3.2.3 Combination of Required and Conditional Processing

The mapping for the processing steps in an *active pipe* includes a combination of required and conditional steps. Our approach is to combine the transformations described above and produce a target graph that represents the solution for the complete active pipe.

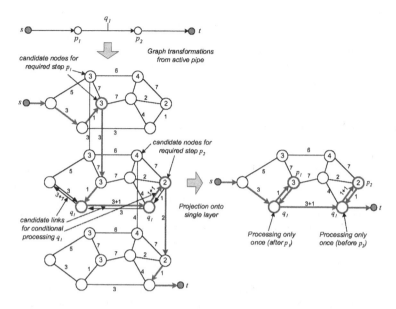

Fig. 6. Transformations for two required and one conditional processing steps

More formally, an active pipe includes of a source s, destination t, a set P of required processing steps, and set Q of conditional processing steps. For each *required step* $p_i \in P$ we extend the graph by adding a *new layer* according to the transformations defined previously. With k the number of required processing steps, the target graph G has $k + 1$ layers, each layer representing a copy of the original graph. Between layers, we add edges in the target graph when a node is suitable for that processing step. Each *conditional step* $q_j \in Q$ results in modification of links weights of the current layer c. Initially, $c = 1$, and whenever a new layer is being added, c is incremented by 1 to reflect the most recently added layer. Each conditional processing step performs modifications of the current layer only. A number of *conditional processing steps* can be installed together *on the same layer* using a superposition of transformations, resulting in modifying link weights for each of the modules.

Figure 6 describes the graph transformations for the secure data transmission example presented in Figure 3. This active pipe contains the required encryption step p_1 and decryption step p_2, and a conditional processing step q_1 for congestion control on the encrypted stream. The target graph includes three layers. The candidate nodes suitable for a processing step on a given layer are indicated with arrows. The inter-layer edges represent the required steps p_1 and p_2, and changes of the link weights on the middle layer represent conditional processing q_1. The resulting graph satisfies all processing requirements given by the active pipe because for each step a corresponding graph transformation has been performed. Solving the shortest path for the resulting graph returns the optimal place for p_1, p_2, and in addition all the locations for q_1.

Note that to compute a path for $k + 1$ layers, the running time for a solution of the layered graph is essentially $k + 1$ times the cost of computing a shortest path in the original graph, thus the total computational complexity remains polynomial and therefore scales to large networks. As shown in Figure 6, the solution can produce *non-simple paths* where a given node can be visited *multiple times* and a node can potentially be used more than once as a processing site. This fact must be taken into account by the signaling protocol.

3.3   Resource Discovery Based on Extending OSPF

Since the objective of our service framework is to facilitate the deployment of active services while hiding the topology and network-specific details from users, the service frameworks needs to be able to discover the underlying network topology needed for the mapping process. Thus, the framework requires a protocol that can distribute information about the (1) topology of the network and (2) the locations, capabilities, and availability of network-embedded processing resources.

First, to obtain information about the network topology, our approach is to directly access the link-state database of underlying routing protocols. Routing protocols such as OSPF John Moy, "OSPF Version 2," , IS-IS ISO DP 10589, "Intermediate System to Intermediate System Intra-Domain Routing Ex, and PNNI ATM Forum Technical Committee, "Private Network-Network Interface Specification Ve build an internal topological database describing the connectivity between routers. Each individual piece of this database represents a particular router's local state. Based on this link-state database, we can compute a graph representing the network topology.

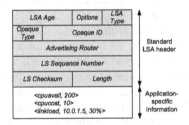

Fig. 7. Processing capabilities encoded as OSPF opaque LSAs

Second, to obtain information about processing resources embedded within the network we propose to use *OSPF opaque link-state advertisements* (LSA) [5]. Information within opaque LSAs is completely transparent for the routing protocol but can be interpreted by other instances such as the ANCS to identify processing resources.

An opaque LSA includes arbitrary information, typically encoded as a collection of *type-length-value* (TLV) objects, where each object carries information related to a particular network attribute (Figure 7). As shown in Figure 2, we have extended the OSPF protocol daemon with an API such that our ANCS can *retrieve* the link-state database as well as can *originate* opaque LSAs representing network attributes. The OSPF protocol then transparently distributes opaque LSAs to other routers. Since the link-state database built by the routing protocol provides complete connectivity information from which the topology graph including processing attributes can be generated quite easily.

3.4 Resource Allocation Protocol

The final phase in deploying a network service is the installation and configuration of processing modules on selected nodes (as computed by the mapping algorithm) and the establishment of associated state across the network. In the context of active networks, conventional destination-based routing schemes are not sufficient since traffic needs to *transit* processing sites in a given order which is generally not the IP default path. Our proposed *explicit path routing* protocol [8] supports flow-based explicit path establishment for one-way, unicast flows routed through a predefined list of hops and the installation of plugin modules along such paths.

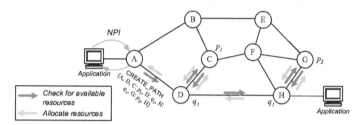

Fig. 8. Explicit Path Setup Protocol

Figure 8 illustrates the configuration of network state for the secure data example as computed by the mapping process (see Figure 6). The establishment of path state is based on *two phases*: In the first phase, the protocol verifies whether sufficient resources are available along the downstream path. Beginning at the source access router, each router checks whether the required resources are locally available and if true, reserves (but does not allocate yet) resources, and forwards the reservation request to the next node along the downstream path. This process is repeated until the destination access router is reached. Once the first phase of the setup process has been completed, it is assured that sufficient resources are available. In the second phase, the actual allocation of network resources takes place. This happens along the reverse path, that is, on all routers from the destination access router towards the source access router. This step includes the installation of flow-specific filters in the format <srcaddr/len, destaddr/len, sport, dport, proto, incoming interface> such that packets matching the filter are explicitly forwarded on the corresponding outgoing interface, and the installation and configuration of plugins and binding them to the filter. The incoming interface in the filter is used to discriminate when a non-simple path enters the same node several times. Once all state has been established along the path, the application is informed and can begin transmitting traffic.

If during the first phase a request is refused due to limited resources, the path setup process cannot continue and is aborted. The node then sends a reservation release message along the reverse path so that nodes that have already reserved resources can free them. When the establishment fails, the application is notified that the path could not be set up.

The EPR protocol uses TCP as the transport mechanism between EPR peers (hop-by-hop) for sending control messages to establish paths, deploy plugins, and release resources. This guarantees *reliable* control messages distribution. However, for both path forwarding and plugin state stored on nodes, EPR uses *soft-state* to take into account that nodes and links are inherently unreliable and can fail. For that reason, an application that sets up a path is required to refresh the path (by sending the path establishment request periodically), otherwise nodes will purge path and plugin state once the time-out expires.

4 Demonstration of Security Gateway Scenario

We have implemented a fully functional prototype of our service framework, consisting of PromethOS [8] for loading and executing code, an extended OSPF daemon for resource discovery [9], the EPR [8] protocol for configuring network state, and the ANCS daemon to establish network services. All our code is free available [1].

To give the reader a feel for the simplicity of how services can be specified and deployed, we illustrate the commands necessary to configure a security gateway scenario.

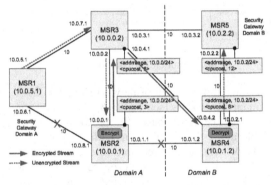

Fig. 9. Security gateway scenario

Figure 9 illustrates our test network. Nodes MSR1 and MSR5 are assumed to be security gateways that interconnect domain A and B and provide transparent encryption. We assume that the links MSR1 to MSR2 and MSR2 to MSR4 have failed and cannot be used. We require encryption to be placed on either MSR2 or MSR3 (MSR1 does not offer processing), and decryption on MSR4. To simplify the scenario somewhat, the congestion control steps mentioned earlier have been omitted. We assume that node MSR2 has faster CPU capabilities and therefore set the processing costs on MSR2 to 3 units while on MSR3 to 5 units, meaning that processing on MSR2 is favored if possible. Now to set up this scenario, we configure appropriate network state using the following statements (the CRYPT router plugin performing AES [11] encryption and decryption is assumed to have a cost of 10 processing units):

```
# acm create --src 10.1.0.0/16 --dest 10.2.0.0/16 --from 10.0.5.1 --to 10.0.2.2
    --plugin required node CRYPT E/mykey 10
        --constraint addrrange subset 10.0.0/24
        --constraint cpucost lt 10
    --plugin required node CRYPT D/mykey 10
        --constraint addrrange subset 10.0.2/24
        --constraint cpucost lt 10
```

Both processing steps are mandatory on nodes, but they have distinct installation conditions. The established service path for this scenario then looks as follows:

```
# acm status
active pipe from: 10.0.5.1 to: 10.0.2.2
flowspec src: 10.1.0.0/16 dest: 10.2.0.0/16 sport: 0 dport: 0 proto: 0 if: 0
Established path:
        10.0.5.1 (msr1) in: 0.0.0.0 out: 10.0.5.1 distance: 0
        10.0.0.2 (msr3) in: 10.0.7.1 out: 10.0.0.2 distance: 10
        10.0.0.1 (msr2) in: 10.0.0.1 out: 10.0.0.1 distance: 20
            plugin: CRYPT init: E/mykey cost: 10
        10.0.0.2 (msr3) in: 10.0.0.2 out: 10.0.4.1 distance: 60
        10.0.1.2 (msr4) in: 10.0.4.2 out: 10.0.2.1 distance: 70
            plugin: CRYPT init: D/mykey cost: 10
        10.0.2.2 (msr5) in: 10.0.2.2 out: 0.0.0.0 distance: 150
```

It is visible from the computation that the selected path is non-simple since MSR3 is being visited twice. Because processing on MSR2 is less expensive than on MSR3, the selected path is still better even when considering the additional link costs of the detour (twice the link cost between MSR2 and MSR3).

5 Conclusions

In this paper we have presented our active network control software that offers a generic service abstraction and automates the configuration of processing resources. Our system uses active pipes as a high-level programming abstraction to the active network, freeing applications from knowing about the underlying topology, location, and properties of processing nodes. Our system automatically discovers available processing capabilities within the network, maps processing demands onto available network resources based on an algorithm with polynomial complexity, and configures the network nodes such that traffic gets routed appropriately, thus significantly simplifies the use of active networks on behalf of applications.

References

[1]   Active Network Control Software, Project Website,
       http://www.tik.ee.ethz.ch/~keller/ancs/
[2]   ATM Forum Technical Committee, "Private Network-Network Interface Specification
       Version 1.0," March 1996.
[3]   Sumi Choi, "Plugin Management," Washington University in St. Louis, *Technical
       Report WUCS-00-04*.
[4]   Sumi Choi, Jonathan Turner, Tilman Wolf, "Configuring Sessions in Programmable
       Networks," In *Proceedings of INFOCOM 2001*, March 2001.
[5]   Rob Coltun, "The OSPF Opaque LSA Option," *RFC 2370*, July 1998.
[6]   ISO DP 10589, "Intermediate System to Intermediate System Intra-Domain Routing
       Exchange Protocol for use in Conjunction with the Protocol for Providing the
       Connectionless-mode Network Service (ISO 8473)," February 1990.

[7]   Ralph Keller, Jeyashankher Ramamirtham, Tilman Wolf, Bernhard Plattner, "Active Pipes: Service Composition for Programmable Networks", *Milcom 2001*, Lean VA, October 2001.

[8]   Ralph Keller, Lukas Ruf, Amir Guindehi, Bernhard Plattner, "PromethOS: A Dynamically Extensible Router Architecture Supporting Explicit Routing," *IWAN 2002*, December 4-6, 2002 ETH Zürich, Switzerland.

[9]   Ralph Keller, "Dissemination of Application-Specific Information using the OSPF Protocol", *Technical Report Nr. 181*, TIK, ETH Zurich, November 2003.

[10] John Moy, "OSPF Version 2," *RFC 2328*, April 1998.

[11] National Institute of Standards and Technology (NIST), "Advanced Encryption Standard (AES)," *FIPS PUBS 197*, November 2001.

[12] Quagga/Zebra Project, Project Website, http://www.quagga.net/

A Dynamic Neighbourhood Discovery Protocol for Active Overlay Networks

Sylvain Martin and Guy Leduc

Research Unit in Networking, Université de Liège, 4000 Liège 1, Belgium
{martin, leduc}@run.montefiore.ulg.ac.be
www.run.montefiore.ulg.ac.be/

Abstract. *d-RADAR*[1] is a neighbourhood discovery protocol for overlay network environments designed for (but not limited to) active network overlays. The core of the algorithm is an expanding ring-search based on the IP routing table content augmented with traffic-based and dynamic refreshing techniques that allows it to react to virtual topology changes (nodes joining/leaving the overlay) as well as IP topology changes (broken and repaired link, route changes and moving nodes). This paper presents how the protocol detects overlay candidate nodes using probing capsules and the algorithms needed to select neighbours among the candidates. We also show how *d-RADAR* keeps the neighbouring table up to date and learns topology changes while keeping a low discovery and refresh overhead. A short summary of simulations carried out with our active network simulator illustrates how these algorithms actually behave.

1 Discovering Neighbours in an Overlay Network

1.1 Introducing the Problem

In several new network technologies like *ip multicast*, *IPv6* or *active networks*, we have to face the situation of a heterogenous network made of routers that understand the new protocol and *legacy IP routers* for which new packets are invalid. One solution to incrementally deploy a new routing protocol while keeping backward compatibility with the existing solution is to build *virtual links* or *tunnels* between routers that support the new technology (for instance using IP over IP encapsulation [11]).

The mesh obtained with these tunnels can then be considered as a regular network by the new routing protocol, and will be referred to as the *overlay network*. Experimental overlay networks have already been set up for the routing technologies cited above, respectively MBONE [6], 6BONE [7] and ABONE [4,5].

Several parameters distinguish overlay networks from 'real' networks, like the fact that link costs may change at any time (due to a change in the underlying topology), or the fact that there's usually no broadcast facility to discover peer routers.

---

[1] This work has been partially supported by the Walloon Region in the framework of the WDU programme (ARTHUR project), and by the Belgian Science Policy in the framework of the IAP programme (MOTION P5/11 project). This work has been partially supported by the Walloon Region in the framework of the WDU programme (ARTHUR project), and by the Belgian Science Policy in the framework of the IAP programme (MOTION P5/11 project). Sylvain Martin is a Research Fellow of the Belgian National Fund for Scientific Research (FNRS).

N. Wakamiya et al. (Eds.): IWAN 2003, LNCS 2982, pp. 151–162, 2004.
© IFIP International Federation for Information Processing 2004

If we consider the setup of a new router in a 'real' network, one of the first steps is to discover neighbour routers that are directly reachable through the router's interfaces. This discovery usually involves simple packets using a conventional ("all routers") IP destination address that are broadcast on the link/LAN to which the router is connected. In overlay networks, this technique can be used to maintain links once they're established, but not to setup the virtual links the router will use.

1.2   Approaches to Neighbourhood Discovery

In most existing frameworks, overlay networks use manually-provided lists of neighbours for their local domains and connect to a large scale backbone using a manually designated access router [4,5]. While this is affordable to interconnect small testbeds, it cannot reasonably be used to deploy a new technology in a large or frequently changing network.

Alternative solutions have been proposed, mainly based on the use of the local *DNS* server to locate candidate neighbours for a given protocol, or to locate database maintainers of these candidate neighbours. Once the DNS has been used as a rendez-vous point, the neighbourhood discovery is reduced to probe active[2] routers listed by the registry and select the most interesting ones. An algorithm like TAO [9], for instance, creates clusters of close nodes and selects a *leader* for each cluster, which is the sole router having virtual links to other clusters.

Even though DNS-based solutions may be useful in some circumstances, maintaining and updating DNS mapping usually requires human intervention which make them unappropriate for dynamic environments.

Other works expect active nodes to join a given multicast group used to advertise that they are active and listen for other nodes' messages. However, assuming that all the routers of a domain are multicast-enabled is a very restrictive hypothesis, and we can't assume that the active router is member of a multicast overlay, of course.

The approach we selected is completely distributed, and avoid the need for a single node which would register and list active routers. Candidate neighbours simply come from the IP routing table, which is used to feed an *expanding ring search* (we refer to this technique as *table-driven* discovery), and from *previous hop* information carried by traffic that uses the same execution environment (*traffic-based* discovery).

Our previous work on RADAR [10] has shown that this technique could be used to create an overlay network that guarantees that if node A is a neighbour of B on the overlay, no other node of the overlay receives the messages B sends to A.

Solutions developped for peer-to-peer overlays like *CAN*[16] or *Pastry*[15] are not well suited for building overlays of *routers*, but they could help *end-systems* to join an overlay built by *d-RADAR*.

1.3   Challenges in Neighbourhood Discovery

As a ring-based discovery combines the search for active routers and the check for neighbourhood in one single operation, special care must be taken to make sure the discovery is not flooding the network with scans.

---

[2] Without loss of generality, we'll restrict the discussion to overlays of active routers for the sake of readability.

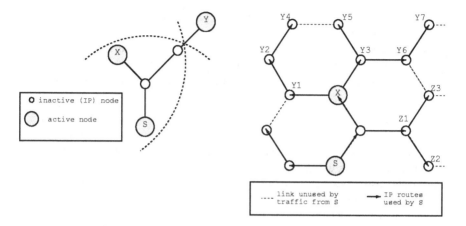

Fig. 1. (a) Stopping at the first discovered neighbour may isolate some nodes from the topology, (b) illustrating the problem of hidden targets.

- One neighbour per physical interface is usually not enough. If you look at fig. 1.a, you'll notice that stopping the search at the first neighbour discovered on an interface will result in the impossibility for both X and S to discover Y.
- Scanning targets in the whole domain will usually be too costly, but on the other side, it is not possible to tell *a priori* how far the scan should go. Depending on the density of active nodes in a domain, the distance needed to find N neighbours may change, as well as the amount of neighbours needed to keep routing efficient.

Note that registry-assisted discovery will suffer from the same kind of problem if the amount of active nodes in the domain becomes pretty large. As soon as a neighbour X is discovered by S, all the targets $Y_1 \ldots Y_n$ (see fig. 1.b) that require crossing X to be reached will actually be *hidden* by X, in the sense that as X will see any capsule sent to Y_i, the routing decision could have been deferred to X. Identifying hidden routers and avoiding to scan them as soon as possible will help reducing the unwanted discovery overhead.

Moreover, as soon as one considers *dynamic topologies* – i.e. networks where the subset of active nodes and the routes to targets may change frequently[3], *hidden* nodes become even more important as knowing the *hidden-by* relationship will help telling which previously discarded target need to be re-scanned due to a topology change.

It should also be taken into account that active routers may join or leave the overlay without a topology change at the IP level. Indeed, active routers may stop supporting a given execution environment due to administrative decision, while the router itself (at IP level) is still present in the network.

This means that a neighbourhood discovery technique that will be used to build active network overlays will *have* to check the state of the current neighbours periodically, even

---

[3] This will especially be the case in wireless networks, but may be extended to any network in which such a topology change is not considered as a exceptional event.

if no state change is announced by the IP layer, rather than waiting for an update of the IP table to learn that a neighbour is down.

Even though pro-active checking of the neighbours' state for non-active overlays is not mandatory, it may be an interesting property as it allows the overlay to recover situations (like selecting an alternative route) *quicker* than the underlying network.

1.4   Probing Targets

d-RADAR[4] uses *active probes*, known as *AYA*[5] capsules that it sends to neighbour candidates in order to check whether they're active or not. Compared to *ICMP echo* packets, *AYA* capsules also allow to check if the target is currently responding to specific execution environment's messages.

When no active router is met on the road to a non-active target X, the *AYA* capsule is lost when reaching X. But if any router on the road is active, it will intercept the *AYA* capsule and store its own address in it before sending it back to its source. This technique of allowing a capsule that has X as its IP destination to be intercepted by a node other than X - referred to as *capsule grabbing* - is detailed in *RADAR*[10].

While it isn't a usual behaviour for a non-active router, *grabbing* could also be implemented in non-active networks by means of techniques like IP router alert option [12]. However, router alerts usually slow down packets a lot on every node while a grabbable capsule is processed at top-speed by a legacy router.

2   Required Environment

d-RADAR has been implemented for the *ANTS* execution environment [1,2,3] which itself relies on NodeOS infrastructure [8]. Small modifications to the ANTS code are needed to implement our solution, mainly in order to allow emission and reception of *grabbable capsules* and to access the IP routing table. However, *d-RADAR* uses very lightweight capsules and could be easily adapted to overlays that use only passive packets.

d-RADAR expects the NodeOS to be able to deliver the network layer routing table for *table-driven discovery*, and it also requires a method to get notified of changes (added/removed entries and cost changes) to this table. It does not, however, make changes to the IP table and therefore its presence is transparent to legacy routing. The only system table alterred by *d-RADAR* is the *overlay's neighbourhood table* which may be used by active protocols that directly use neighbourhood information or an active routing protocol. Our discovery technique also expects that route table entries will at least contain the *route cost*, preferably expressed as a *hops count*, and an identifier of the interface used (for the purpose of grouping targets based on the interface they use).

It is important that the IP routing table holds enough information about the local domain. If some routers are not listed in that table, the only chance to detect them is by *grabbing* part of the traffic they send to other nodes. In particular, a *host* node is unlikely to discover any neighbour (but its default gateway) if it does not first start sending (or

---

[4] Dynamic Ring-based Adaptive Discovery of Active neighbour Routers

[5] For "Are You Active?".

receiving) traffic from another active node. To make this possible, the *overlay routing table* will always contain a "default" entry that will create direct tunnels to any IP destination on demand.

The routing protocol used to build the IP routing table has little significance, but *d-RADAR* may be made much more efficient if the table contains information about the *last router* crossed before a destination D is reached. With this information, we can retrieve the whole sink tree and deduce for some targets whether they can be reached or not without actually probing them. In the absence of such information, for instance if IP was running a distance vector or if we receive the *forwarding* table rather than the *routing* table, we can either try to get the information by sending *ICMP echo* packet that would have the *Route Record* option set, or simply assume that every target *must* be probed.

Finally, in order to support *traffic-based discovery*[6], it is mandatory that packets processed by the execution environment carry a *previous hop* information. While this is virtually true in every active network environment (as the previous hop is the node that will be asked for code download if the protocol of a packet is unknown by the current node), it's less direct in a IPv6 or multicast overlay, but the source address of the current tunnel should be a good candidate.

3   d-RADAR Approach

d-RADAR is mainly based on a ring-search discovery that adapts the maximum searching distance (a.k.a. the discovery *threshold*) to the density of neighbours. Targets are grouped by their cost[7] in *rings* and then probed by increasing ring cost. Everytime a new neighbour or a hidden target is found, the threshold is reduced multiplicatively by the α constant, and everytime a ring completes, the threshold is increased by the amount of remaining targets. In other words, if T_i is the threshold value after ring i discovery has been completed, we have

$$T_i = T_{i-1} \cdot \alpha^{a_i} + (n_i - a_i) \tag{1}$$

where a_i is the amount of positive replies (neighbours and hidden targets) for ring i and n_i is the total amount of targets on ring i. If there were enough replying targets on ring i, it may occur that $T_i < i$, which stops the discovery. Rather than excluding discovered neighbours that have a cost c such as $T_i < c < i$, we then use $max(i, T_i)$ as the effective threshold.

Our previous work on static topologies has shown that this approach offers good results, especially when $T_0 = 2$, $\alpha \in [0.5 \ldots 0.8]$ and that the exact value chosen for α has little significance on the overall mesh obtained[8]. One interesting property of this threshold computation technique is that, once a neighbour is found, the search will

---

[6] *traffic-based discovery* consists of selecting targets to probe by looking at the intercepted data capsules.

[7] Here comes the main reason why *hops count* costs are preferred: we need to ensure that a target on ring $i + 1$ can only be reached through a target on ring i.

[8] A higher α value will result in more neighbours per node, but it usually does not degenerate into a full mesh and α does not need to be fine-tuned for a particular network (see [10]).

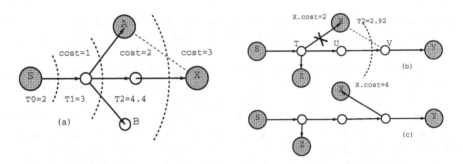

Fig. 2. Assuming $\alpha = 0.8$. (a) initial treshold after ring 2 detection is complete is $T_2 = 3 \cdot 0.8 + 2$, which is above 3 and allows S to scan X. If B now becomes active, we have $T_2 = 3 \cdot 0.64 + 1$, which excludes X from the neighbourhood of S. (b) if the link on default route to X is broken, X can no longer respond and is excluded from the neighbourhood of S. T_2 then raises to 4.4 which allows Y to join the neighbourhood. (c) when the IP routes are updated, X appears at level 4 and will come back to the neighbourhood.

stop quicker when the neighbour *hides* more targets (and thus potentially serves more destinations).

3.1   Neighbours Come and Go ...

The changes of the "activity" state of a router (i.e. an Execution Environment starts or stops) as well as routing updates that affect the cost of neighbours will be reflected on the set of neighbours a node can use. Not only because of trivial modifications – of course if X stops being an active node, X must be removed from the set of active neighbours – but also because it affects the global environment of the considered active router S. As explained in section 1.3 and illustrated in fig. 1.b, when a neighbour X leaves, a set of targets $\{Y_1 \ldots Y_n\}$ leaves the *hidden* state[9] and become potentially reachable. These new neighbour candidates must be re-scanned and the closest active ones have good chance to be included in the new set of neighbours.

The departure of X will also lower the active nodes density in S's surrounding and may require that S increases the maximum distance at which neighbours should be scanned (i.e. increasing the threshold in *d-RADAR*).

Similar changes may occur when an *inactive* (and not hidden) node with a cost that is lower than the actual threshold becomes active (see fig. 2.a) :

- some other inactive or neighbour nodes may become hidden.
- as a result of newly responding targets (the newly active one and nodes moving from *inactive* to *hidden* state), the threshold may be reduced, excluding some of the furthest neighbours from the new neighbourhood set.

The case of an IP route change (modification of the route's next hop or cost) is simply handled by removing every information we had about the route's destination and then re-inserting the new route as if it was a completely new target (see fig. 2.b and c).

---

[9] A node Y is *hidden* if *AYA* capsules sent to Y are intercepted and replied by another node X.

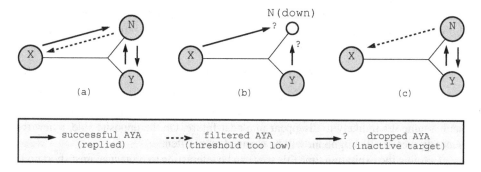

Fig. 3. A problematic scenario if down neighbours are not re-scanned periodically: (a) N is initially discovered by X which has a high threshold but X can't be discovered by N because it's out of its scope, (b) when N crashes, both X and Y notice it after their refresh *AYA* gets dropped, (c) after N recovered, only Y is able to detect it from N's boot-time scanning. X being out of scope, it believes N is still down.

d-RADAR stores, for each output interface, the *history* of the boot-time discovery as a list of (T_{i-1}, a_i, n_i) parameters that can be used to recompute the current threshold from T_k when a change occurs on n_{k+1} or a_{k+1}, by simply re-applying (1) on $T_k, T_{k+1}, \ldots$ until we reach $l : T_l \leq l$. As soon as the new threshold l is defined, its value is committed to the scanning processes that use this interface and will result in some probes being filtered out (if their cost is above the new threshold) or granted, and thus removing or reintegrating some active nodes in the neighbourhood set.

3.2   The Soft-State Refresh Mechanism

In order to maintain an up-to-date neighbourhood set, *d-RADAR* associates every entry X in the *neighbour* table with an *expiration date* E_X, which defines how long the entry will remain valid. Once the entry expires, it will trigger a *refreshing scan* of X, which may either confirm the current state of X or detect that X is no longer a responding neighbour, but that it has become a *down* target[10].

A similar timer is kept for every *down* target so that we can check whether an old neighbour has recovered or not.

To understand the role of *down* targets refresh, it is important to remember that a neighbourhood relationship may not be symmetric. Therefore, as figure 3 illustrates, it is possible that a target N, neighbour of X, will not send *AYA* capsules to X after it recovered from a crash, which could lead X to conclude that N is still down while it could actually be reintegrated in X's neighbourhood.

The duration of the *validity period*, i.e. the period between two refreshes for a given target, is not constant in *d-RADAR*. Instead, it depends on the *age* of the information. In

---

[10] A *down* target is a target that has been a neighbour earlier, but which no longer responds to *AYA* capsules. This state is different from the *inactive* node which never replied to any *AYA*.

other words, for a neighbour X, if T_X is the time at which X has entered the neighbourhood for the last time, and if C_X is the time at which the last refresh for X occurred, the current expiration for X will be E_X, given by (2).

$$E_X = C_X + k \cdot (C_X - T_X) \qquad (2)$$

Everytime a target moves between the *neighbour* and the *down* state, its last join/leave time T_X is reset. As a result, the more stable a neighbour is, the more we will *trust* it and assume it's unlikely to disappear in a near future. On the opposite side, a new (or recently recovered) neighbour will be scanned more often.

Defining the expiration time this way can be interesting to protect against short node failures. When a node stops responding, we first assume this is a temporary situation and that it is likely to respawn in a near future. As the time goes by, chances are that it was rather a permanent failure and refreshes will become more spaced. How fast a temporary situation will be considered as permanent will depend on the k value.

Another context in which this behaviour may be useful is the field of *ad hoc* networks where we could have a low refresh rate for permanent neighbours and keep a high refresh rate for more mobile neighbours.

In order to prevent the validity period from becoming too long in the case of very old entries and keep a useful failures detection time, a maximal refresh period (typically a few tenths of seconds) is enforced regardless of the age of the information.

3.3   Freshness Through Traffic Monitoring

In addition to the periodic neighbour state refresh controlled by E_X, it may be interesting to use traffic received from a neighbour X to monitor X's activity. As *d-RADAR* already catches every incoming capsules for the sake of *traffic-based discovery*, this additional monitoring would virtually come with no cost at all. A smart routing protocol that wishes to offer a low packet loss probability might compare those activity reports and select the route which goes through the most recently (or the most frequently) refreshed neighbour.

To help building such protocols, *d-RADAR* offers information about the last time a capsule has been received from neighbour X in the neighbourhood table (R_X) and maintains the average inter-arrival time $\overline{\Delta T_X}$ according to (3).

$$\overline{\Delta T_X} = \beta \cdot (now - R_X) + (1 - \beta) \cdot \overline{\Delta T_X} \qquad (3)$$

An active protocol that would like to ensure to be notified of node failures at last t seconds after the failure could check $now - R_X$ before sending a capsule to X and require X to send back an acknowledgement if $now - R_X > t$.

In classical networks, the incoming traffic on an interface can be used as a *replacement* of the heartbeat that maintains neighbourhood information up to date. If IP receives traffic from a link, the routing protocol can safely assume that the router at the end of that link is still up and running without even monitoring it. It can also decide to make heartbeats more frequent when there's not enough traffic to keep the information refreshed, as the monitoring traffic will *replace* the normal traffic without competing with it.

Even though information about incoming capsules from X provide a kind of *freshness* information about X, some neighbours in an overlay network cannot be monitored that way.

First, because our neighbourhood relationship isn't symmetric, we may receive no traffic from a neighbour X as well as we may receive traffic from a node Y that is not a neighbour. Indeed, when IP routes $N \rightarrow X$ and $X \rightarrow N$ are different, it is possible that an active node Y hides N from X while the messages sent by N directly reach X. We thus have to keep on sending *AYA* refreshes regardless of the amount of traffic we receive from our neighbours.

Moreover, on an overlay network, we should be very careful before we increase the *AYA* refresh rate. One should keep in mind that active capsules may represent only a small part of the traffic received from a given link and that other traffics like UDP, TCP or capsules from another execution environment could suffer from extra refreshes. Another possible problem comes from the fact that one single network interface card may be used to connect to a great number of neighbours $\{X_1 \ldots X_n\}$. A simultaneous increase of the probing traffic for those n neighbours could lead to an excessive scanning overhead on links close to the scanner.

Finally, *d-RADAR* lacks information about the requirements of the active data flows like minimal neighbour freshness or tolerated response time to a neighbour failure. All it could offer is a generic service which could be insufficient for some application and unneeded by other ones. We will thus defer the decision of whether a refresh is required or not to the active routing protocol (or to autonomous active transport protocols) which will base it on the statistics provided in the neighbourhood table, and possibly on other statistics gathered by the execution environment or the NodeOS.

4   Simulation Results

All the simulations have been run using our *Run Active Network Simulator*, which provides an ANTS platform for a generic network simulator (so far, both *SSFNet* [13] and *javasim* [14] are supported).

We have first run the *d-RADAR* on 4 series of 5 random networks, each consisting of 60 nodes, with a varying density of active nodes. Fig. 4 show how the network resource consumption evolves after every active node boot simultaneously, which is the worst possible situation. As one could expect, both the amount of AYA capsules sent by a node and the average travelled distance are higher when the density decrease. However, if we consider the global cost (summing the individual costs over all the active nodes), we can see on fig. 4b that dense networks consume more bandwidth than scarse ones.

Another interresting fact is that the *refreshing* traffic is quite independent from the considered density.

In addition, we ran a collection of proof-of-concept qualitative simulations to ensure that each of the possible topology change was identified by the protocol and that the proper updates were made to neighbourhood sets and discovery thresholds:

- stopping and resuming a neighbour's execution environment while keeping the IP layer of that neighbour up and running, including the case where the neighbour was hiding other active nodes (cf fig. 1.b),
- forcing active node X to be excluded from the neighbourhood set by activating other routers either on the path to X or not, but at a small enough distance to trigger threshold reduction (cf fig. 2.a),

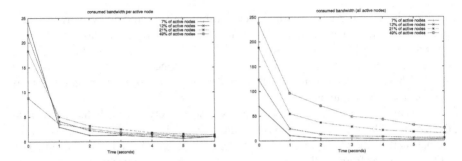

Fig. 4. Average bandwidth (in Kbps) consumed by AYA over all the links in random 60 nodes network. (leftmost) AYA traffic generated by one average active node, (rightmost) traffic generated by all the active nodes together.

- breaking and restoring links on the path to X, forcing *d-RADAR* to remove X from the neighbourhood until the IP routing table announces a new route with a different cost for X (cf fig. 2.b),
- making an active neighbour unreachable by breaking the sole path that reaches it or by stopping its IP layer.

In every situation that involved a change at IP level, *d-RADAR* has offered better response time due to its adaptive and pro-active behaviour (from 0.5 to 10 seconds to detect the loss of a neighbour X depending on the maximal value defined for D_X, respectively 5 to 25 seconds, compared to OSPF's 60 seconds heartbeat).

5   A Word about the Implementation

5.1   The Structure

We developped *d-RADAR* as an active application that runs on top of a slightly modified *ANTS* [1,3] framework. Special care has been taken to make the solution as modular as possible, mainly regarding to the dependence to *ANTS* and the NodeOS.

As fig. 5 shows, the core class NeighbourApplication, with its helper class IP-RouteTable, is the only component which depends on (and interfaces with) the execution environment. It will take care of sending capsules created by the scanners and dispatching capsules received to the appropriated scanner. The core also carries every communication between the other internal components it is connected to, which reduces the inter-components dependency to a small set of "pipes".

The protocol's policy is implemented in the Scanner classes, which decide when and to which target the *AYA* capsules should be sent. They are also responsible for modifying the threshold of their respective network interface appropriately when capsules come back or when timer for unreplied *AYA* expire. Decisions of the scanners are transmitted as new Target-based objects which will join the Neighbours hashtable.

This table receives clock ticks from the core and will send the expired objects back to the core for refresh, which will enqueue them to the appropriated scanner. the Neighbours table is the class where all the soft-state part of the algorithm takes place.

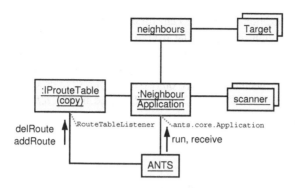

Fig. 5. Our software design.

5.2 Extensions Facilities

Unlike its former static version, *d-RADAR* can deal with several parallel scanners for the same interface, and share the same threshold result, which makes the encoding of the algorithms clearer and more straightforward. So far, only two types of scanners have been used (pro-active and refresh scanner), but the modular nature of the actual code allows *d-RADAR* to be easily extended by new types of scanners (such as a *reverse* scanner that would scan one far target from time to time when the "bottom up" ring expansion does not give good results), or even virtual scanners (forcing the state of some targets or reordering the search based on informations gathered from other neighbours).

This just requires a new extension of the *scanner* class to be written, overloading the behaviour of the periodic "time for scanning" and of the "capsule replied" events delivered by the core.

6   Conclusion and Future Work

We proposed a distributed algorithm that builds an overlay dynamically, adapting to the density of active routers in the network, and that can evolve to follow topology changes. This algorithm require no special support from non-active routers and its principles can be translated to overlays other than active networks.

The feature implemented by *d-RADAR* can be seen as a service that can be reused by several active routing protocols, decoupling the problem of neighbourhood discovery from the routing itself. Therefore, some of the routing-specific decisions, like adapting the refreshing rate to applicative flow requirements or filtering oscillating neighbours, are delegated to the routing protocol itself: *d-RADAR* simply includes required timing information into the neighbourhood table.

Simulations have been carried on our active networks simulator, which completes our previous results on static topologies ([10]) with response to events such as routing table updates, active node failure, etc. An appropriate refresh mechanism should also allow *d-RADAR* to keep track of mobile neighbours or handle ad hoc networks, even though no specific simulations have been performed in that area so far.

Several optimization techniques can still be envisioned, and the existing framework can host them without changing the overall code structure. For instance, the initial discovery cost could be reduced through the *reverse scanner* quickly introduced in section 5.2, or *d-RADAR* could be made more conservative on discovered neighbours by using an *hysteresis* mechanism based on two thresholds (T_{in} used by the *active scanner* to accept new neighbours and $T_{out} = \gamma \cdot T_{in}$ used by the *refresh scanner* to reject existing neighbours).

References

1. D. Wetherall, A. Whitaker : ANTS - an Active Node Transfer System. version 2.0.
2. D. Wetherall : Service Introduction in an Active Network. *http://www.cs.washington.edu/research/networking/ants/ants-thesis.ps.gz*
3. D. Wetherall, J. Guttag, D. Tennenhouse : ANTS - A Toolkit for Building and Dynamically Deploying Network Protocols. *IEEE OPENARCH'98*, April 1998
4. S. Berson, B. Braden : DANTE : Dynamic Topology Extension for the ABone. *ABone: Technical Specs - http://www.isi.edu/abone/DOCUMENTS/dante2.ps*
5. S. Berson, B. Braden, L. Ricciulli : Introduction to the ABone. *http://www.isi.edu/abone/DOCUMENTS/ABoneIntro.pdf*
6. H. Eriksson : MBONE : the multicast backbone, *Communications of the ACM, vol. 37 issue 8 pp. 54-60 (1994)*
7. I. Guardini, P. Fasano, G. Girardi : IPv6 Operational Experience within the 6bone. *http://www.isoc.org/inet2000/cdproceedings/1e/1e_1.htm*
8. L. Peterson (Editor) : NodeOS Interface Specification. *DARPA AN NodeOS Working Group Draft*, 1999.
9. A. Collins, R. Mahajan, and A. Whitaker : The TAO Algorithm for Virtual Network Management. *Unpublished work.* December 1999. *http://citeseer.nj.nec.com/collins99tao.html*
10. S. Martin, G. Leduc : RADAR: Ring-Based Adaptive Discovery of Active Neighbour Routers. *Lecture Notes in Computer Science 2546, "Active Networks", Springer, 2002 (IWAN 2002),* pp 62-73
11. D. Farinacci et al. : RFC 2784 - Generic Routing Encapsulation (GRE). *IETF, March 2000*
12. D. Katz (cisco Systems) : RFC 2113 - IP Router Alert Option, *IETF, February 1997*
13. SSFNet : Scalable Simulation Framework for modeling the Internet. *http://www.ssfnet.org*
14. Java-integrated, component based network simulation environment. *http://www.j-sim.org/*
15. M. Castro, P. Druschel, Y. C. Hu, and A. Rowstron: Topology-aware routing in structured peer-to-peer overlay networks, *Tech. Rep. MSR-TR-2002-82*
16. S. Ratnasamy et al.: A Scalable Content-Addressable Network, *Proceedings of ACM SIGCOMM 2001*

Chameleon: Realizing Automatic Service Composition for Extensible Active Routers

Matthias Bossardt, Roman Hoog Antink, Andreas Moser, and Bernhard Plattner

Computer Engineering and Networks Laboratory *
Swiss Federal Institute of Technology, ETH
Zürich, Switzerland
bossardt@tik.ee.ethz.ch

Abstract. Complex network services can be constructed by composing simpler service components in a well defined way. To benefit most from such an approach, service components should be reusable for different services. Furthermore the composition must be performed automatically and customized to the service execution platform.

In this paper, we focus on node local aspects of service composition. We contribute design and implementation details of Chameleon, a system targeted at automatic service composition. Our system is based on (1) service descriptors containing meta-information about service components and (2) a service creation engine composing and installing services in a platform specific and automatic way. Target platforms are modeled as active nodes featuring Execution Environments (EEs) to serve as runtime environments for service components.

To validate our concepts, we implemented an active node. It features two different EEs, an EE based on Click router technology, which is suitable for forwarding plane services, as well as a general purpose Java-based EE. A demonstration service, which performs traffic shaping, is briefly presented to illustrate the concepts and their applicability.

1 Introduction

Active nodes promise to be a very flexible platform for dynamic deployment of network services. A wide variety of active network nodes (ANN) have been developed so far. In the beginning, active packet-based approaches were predominant. Active packets contain code or a reference to code, which is executed in Execution Environments (EEs) of active nodes at packet arrival. More recently research has focused on component-based approaches. In contrast to active packets, component-based service models are based on code modules, which are usually deployed before arrival of packets to be mangled using a specific service deployment infrastructure. A detailed discussion of both approaches and their properties can be found in [7].

In the component-based approach, active nodes provide one or more EEs to run service components (SCs). Distinctive features of EEs are the abstractions (API) they

---

* This work is partly funded by ETH Zürich and Swiss Bundesamt für Bildung und Wissenschaft (BBW) under grant number 99.0533. A subset of it is part of ETH's contribution and work as a partner in the European project IST-FAIN (IST-1999-10561).

N. Wakamiya et al. (Eds.): IWAN 2003, LNCS 2982, pp. 163–177, 2004.
© IFIP International Federation for Information Processing 2004

provide to service components and the technology they are implemented in. We expect active nodes to feature two or more EEs. First, multiple EEs allow to separate transport, control and management plane of active nodes using different technologies and providing adequate APIs.[1] Second, it is possible to select SCs implemented in different technologies and optimize service composition.

In this paper we focus on service composition for a component-based service model. We provide a model that is generic enough to be implemented using a variety of EE technologies. Consequently, components in the fast path of a router (e.g. a forwarding table lookup) can be optimized for high performance, whereas control components (e.g. a routing algorithm) might be run in an EE optimized for control processes. Hence, the most appropriate technology can be selected for each service component, as long as the corresponding EE is available on the active node.

Components-based software and their composition have been studied in the context of distributed computing [2,1] or telecommunication networks [4]. They are based on middleware providing SCs with a homogeneous environment. Thus, a service can be implemented in the same way on different nodes. This approach results, however, in additional communication overhead among SCs at runtime, which is not acceptable for active networks where SCs must mangle packets at line speed.

In [8] we introduced Chameleon, a node-level service deployment architecture to cope with heterogeneity in active networks caused by active nodes featuring different sets of EEs. At the core of our architecture is the Service Creation Engine (SCE), which composes services by performing a node specific mapping of service descriptions to appropriate code modules. Furthermore, the SCE binds the code modules and configures both EEs and node operating system (nodeOS). As a result, we are able to describe services in the same way for all nodes, without introducing communication overhead at runtime. This comes at the cost of additional service deployment complexity, which is handled by the SCE.

Although this paper describes refinements of the Chameleon architecture, we focus on service composition facets of our system. We contribute the details of our approach to service description and composition. Moreover, we describe design and implementation of our prototype. A major requirement in the design and implementation of the SCE was to ensure that the same SCE can be used for many different active node designs/implementations. This paper presents how this is achieved by our design.

For our prototype implementation, we built two execution environments. One is based on Click router [10] and well suited to run transport plane service components. The second EE is based on a Java Virtual Machine (JVM) and useful for control plane service components. We implemented a traffic shaper service that uses both EEs and describe its deployment.

This paper is organized as follows. Section 2 describes our approach to service composition and the models involved. It further explains a formal language to describe the elements of our models. Section 3 discusses the design details of the service composition engine, while section 4 describes our prototype implementation. A sample service to

---

[1] The proper separation of forwarding (aka transport), control and management plane is a current concern of several major companies. More specifically, the IETF ForCES work group [9] intends to come up with a standardized protocol between transport and control components.

validate the implementation is briefly presented. Finally, we draw our conclusions in section 5.

2   Service Composition

Service composition allows building complex services from simpler *service components*. In that sense, service components take on the role as building blocks, similar to LEGO™ bricks to build toys. As a result service components can be reused to construct different services. For example a *packet classifier* may be used in a *diffServ* as well as in a *intServ* service implementation.

The adequate degree of granularity of service components has been discussed for a long time. High granularity (i.e. small service components) maximizes the reuse potential of service components, whereas low granularity (i.e. big service components) may allow for better performance optimizations and simpler design of components. As it is safe to assume that opinions on the appropriate degree of granularity continue to differ, our service model must not impose any constraints on granularity. Section 2.2 shows that we achieve this using a hierarchical composition mechanism.

A model of active services, as well as of platforms (active nodes) such services are executed on, is essential to define an appropriate description language for both, services and nodes. The description language is necessary to automatize service composition. This section presents service and node models, as well as their formal description.

2.1   Service Model

Our service model is based on *implementation service components (ISC)*, which are the entities of deployment. An ISC is a unit of code that performs a well-defined functionality (e.g. packet classification) when run in an execution environment (EE). A service is based on one or more connected service components.

Two ISCs running in the same EE communicate to each other via *ports* using EE-specific mechanisms. For example, in a JVM-based EE a component performs method calls on the other. A component may have zero or more ports.

Ports are defined by their name (optional) and type. There are two basic types of port semantics: *push*, and *pull* ports. A component's *egress* push port initiates the forwarding of data to an ingress push port of the *succeeding* service component. Using pull ports, however, it is the *ingress* pull port of a component that triggers the transfer of data from the *preceding* service component. Note that it is not allowed to bind a pull port to a push port, irrespective of the direction of data transfer.

An ISC may as well communicate with a component in a different EE, as long as the nodeOS provides adequate mechanisms. Such communications are completely transparent to ISCs. It is up to the node to provide adapters for the different EEs that render inter-EE communication transparent.

ISCs feature a configuration interface. Configurations can be passed to the component in the form of parameters.

2.2   Service Composition Model

While section 2.1 described our service model from a runtime perspective, this section focuses on composition of service components.

The composition model is based on two main abstractions, *implementation service components (ISCs)*, as explained in section 2.1, and *abstract service components (ASCs)*.[2] The purpose of *ASCs* is to model dependencies by grouping a number of service components and describing their interconnections. Hence, we are able to express that e.g. a (simplified) *diffServ* service consists of a *packet classifier* and a *priority scheduler* component, where data packets are first processed by the classifier and subsequently by the scheduler. In this example the *diffServ* component is an ASC, because it refers to other SCs in order to be implemented. *Packet classifier* and *priority scheduler* may be represented by ASCs or ISCs themselves. These ASCs, in turn, refer to other SCs, resulting in a tree structure of dependencies of arbitrary depth, with all leaves being ISCs. In this way, our model enables hierarchical service composition.

Two main advantages result from this model. First it is up to service implementors to decide which granularity of service components suits their requirements best. Second any service can be reused as a SC to construct a new service by defining a new ASC grouping and connecting it with other SCs.

The semantics of an SC is implicitly defined by its name. Different implementations with the same name may exist, as the same functionality can be implemented in several ways and technologies. As consequence it is possible to compose a service with a defined functionality in many different ways. It is up to standardization bodies to define the semantics assigned to an SC referred to by a specific name. This namespace may be organized in a hierarchical way to accommodate standardized *and* proprietary SCs.[3]

2.3   Service Description

To handle service composition automatically, a service description language formalizing the models is necessary. We propose a markup language based approach, which is implemented in XML to benefit from the wealth of available tools.

We require that each SC is described in an XML document that provides the necessary meta-information. Henceforth, we refer to these documents as *descriptors*. The following sections describe their content and structure. Henceforth, XML *elements* are graphically represented as ellipses, their *attributes* as boxes. Dashed ellipses stand for optional elements. Double ellipses signify one or more, or, if dashed, zero or more elements.

2.3.1   Elements of ISC Descriptions. Figure 1 presents the structure of an ISC descriptor, as indicated by the attribute `type=IMPLEMENTATION`. Hence, this descriptor contains meta-information about a piece of code that provides a defined functionality. As explained in section 2.2, the Element `servicename` encodes the semantics of the component. That is we assume that knowing the servicename of a component means

---

[2] We use the term *service component (SC)* for the generic case where both ISC *or* ASC apply.

[3] This is similar to the namespace of Management Information Bases (MIBs), where the name defines the semantics of a variable and proprietary extensions are possible.

knowing its functionality. Other elements define the type of runtime environment (EE and operating system) the component was implemented for. Thus it is possible to write ISCs providing the same functionality for different runtime environments. A list of ports, including their types, describe how the component can be connected to others. It is possible to define a set of default parameters for the component. Parameters are listed as name/value pairs. An optional element CODE_MODULE contains references to the files that contain the code module. The reference takes the format of an Uniform Resource Locator (URL) [6]. Omitting this element is only possible if a resource discovery system is in place that maps XML elements such as servicename, provider, etc. to URLs. Such a system, however, is out of scope of this paper.

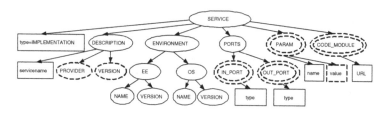

Fig. 1. Structure of ISC descriptor

2.3.2 Elements of ASCs Descriptions. In figure 2 the structure of an ASC descriptor is shown. The attribute type=ABSTRACT defines that the descriptor contains meta-information about an *abstract* service component. As for the ISC descriptor, the servicename defines the functionality of this component. There is a list of ports and their types to define how this component can be connected to others, as well as a list of default parameters in name/value notation.

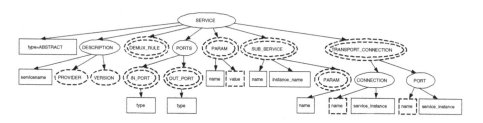

Fig. 2. Structure of ASC descriptor

An abstract service component descriptor has three distinctive elements: SUB_SERVICE, TRANSPORT_CONNECTION, and DEMUX_RULE. SUB_SERVICE is a list of references to service components the ASC depends on, which are identified by their servicename. Note that such references are ambiguous, as there exists probably more than one component with the same servicename. This ambiguity has been chosen deliberately to allow services to be composed in different ways. Section 3 discusses this issue

in detail. TRANSPORT_CONNECTION is a list of connections among sub-service components. In this way a topology of interconnected sub-service components is defined, which
results in the functionality assigned to the servicename of the ASC. DEMUX_RULE contains a list of rules that define which packets entering the active node must be dispatched
to the service component defined by the descriptor.

2.4 Active Node Model

Figure 3 shows the active node model our system is targeted at. The model is briefly
presented here to pave the way for section 2.4.1, which deals with the formal description
of an active node.

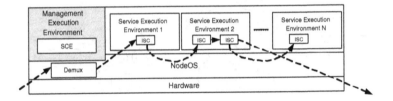

Fig. 3. Active Node Model

The node operating system (nodeOS) controls allocation of node resources (e.g.
memory, CPU, storage, communication ports) to different EEs. Furthermore, it contains
a demultiplexer, which forwards incoming packets to appropriate EEs.

There are two functionally different types of EEs on a node. First, there are *service
EEs*, in which ISCs are run, providing a defined service to end-users attached to the
network. Service EEs are often optimized for certain types of services components (e.g.
control plane or transport plane components). Therefore they are implemented in many
different technologies and provide different APIs to the service components. The set of
service EEs a node provides is not defined.[4] Second, there is a *management EE*, which
provides privileged access to the nodeOS to configure both, nodeOS and service EEs.
The service creation engine (SCE) configures the demultiplexer and the service EEs.

2.4.1 Active Node Description. Based on the node model from figure 3 many different
implementations of nodes are possible. To automate service composition, it is necessary
to formally describe the capabilities of a node. Figure 4 presents the structure and content
of a node descriptor.

The node descriptor contains an element describing the operating system of the
node (OS) including its name and version. More important for service composition are the elements listing available EEs (EE) and inter-EE communication facilities (EE_CONNECTION). EEs are identified by their name and version. They are further characterized by the types of ports they provide. A reference to the EE-specific

---

[4] Selecting the "best" set of EEs is left to node operators or manufacturers. The offered set of
EEs may serve as a means of differentiation among them.

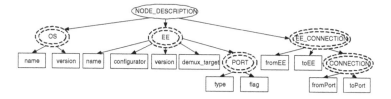

Fig. 4. Structure of active node descriptor

`configurator` is required by the SCE to load and configure the ISCs in the EE. Finally the `demux_target` defines the way an EE is attached to the demultiplexer. A node may provide facilities to allow communication among EEs. Such facilities are listed as `EE_CONNECTION`.

3   Automating Service Composition: The Service Creation Engine

This section presents the *service creation engine (SCE)*, a management subsystem that is able to interpret service and node descriptors. Based on these descriptors it performs automatic service composition. Hence, appropriate service components are selected according to node capabilities (e.g. types of EEs, communication facilities, etc.) and a mapping policy. The SCE performs for network services what compilers/linkers do for computer programs. While compilers produce executables for a specific computer architecture from source code, the SCE creates an executable service for a specific active node architecture from descriptors and code modules (so-called ISCs). Similar to cross-compilers, the SCE is capable of delivering different "executables" based on the target system being defined in the active node descriptor. Furthermore, the SCE provides means to load, bind and configure code components (ISCs).

3.1   SCE Overview

Figure 5 gives an overview of the SCE. The processing within the SCE involves two basic steps, which are carried out by the *composition engine* and the *deployment engine*, respectively. The composition engine is triggered by a service request issued by an authorized user of the node (e.g. the network operator). A service request has the format of an ASC descriptor. The composition engine interprets the request and – if necessary – retrieves SC descriptors of sub-components from a (possibly external) repository (descriptor server). Based on meta-information about the node, appropriate service components are selected. As a result we get a list of service components and information about their binding and configuration, which is passed to the deployment engine. The deployment engine parses the list and retrieves the necessary code modules from a (possibly external) repository (code server). Moreover, it interacts with EEs via EE-specific configurators to load, bind, and configure service components.

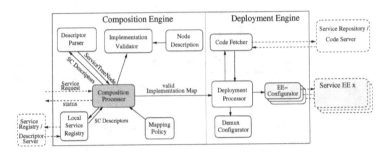

Fig. 5. SCE overview

3.2   Processing in the Composition Engine

As the core of the composition engine the composition processor coordinates the processing of descriptors and the composition of services. It utilizes several support modules to perform its task (see figure 5). This section discusses the processing within the composition engine chronologically.

3.2.1   Phase I: Dependency Resolution. The composition processor is triggered by a service request. Analyzing the initial ASC descriptor (included in the service request) with the help of the descriptor parser, one or more required sub-service components are identified. For each of those components one or more descriptors are fetched from the descriptor server. As a result we get a tree of all possible dependencies, which we call *service tree* because each node represents a service component. In the case of ASC descriptors other sub-service components are referenced and corresponding descriptors must be fetched. Hence more nodes are added to the tree. In the case of ISC descriptors, code modules are referenced and the resolution process stops for this branch. The service tree is finished when all leaves refer to ISCs.

It is important to note that each node may be represented by several SC descriptors. Hence the service tree may contain information about many possible combinations of ISCs that make up a service with the behavior defined in the service request. Further processing steps taken by the composition engine narrow down this set of combinations to one that is the most appropriate for the active node under consideration.

Parameter Handling. Any service component of the service tree (represented by tree nodes) may be configured by parameters. Two types of parameters are supported, which can be specified in the XML descriptors:

Required parameters only have a name without a value set in the considered node. They require the parent ASC to set the value. For a successful deployment it is necessary that an ASC passes the right number of required parameters to each of its children nodes. To do so, every service component sharing a common service name, has the same specific number of required parameters, which must be *"well-known"* (for example defined by a standardization body).

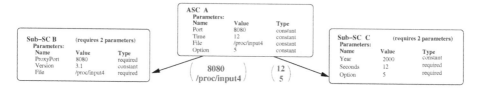

Fig. 6. Concept of parameter passing

Constant parameters have both name and value set in the considered node. The parent ASC does not need to deal with those parameters, but optionally overwrites their values.

ASCs are allowed to pass both required and constant parameters to their children nodes. For better illustration of this concept, figure 6 shows an example setting, where SCs B and C are children of ASC A. The

Handling Demultiplexing Rules. Similar to parameters *demultiplexing rules* are associated with SCs. They filter the packets being destined for a given SC. To take this decision, the deployment engine must configure the demultiplexer and therefore needs adequate rules. In contrast to the *parameters*, the composition engine can handle them in a simpler way: wherever demultiplexing rules appear in a SC descriptor they are passed to all its children and children's children.

3.2.2   Phase II: Service Tree Node Validation. Although an extensive service tree has been built with possibly many ways to deploy it, it can not be passed to the deployment engine yet. It is the task of the composition engine to carry out extensive checks and validation steps to ensure that the service is deployable on the node under consideration. The node validation includes checks for the following attributes: OS name, OS version, EE name, EE version, types of the in- and outports.

To do so the composition processor recursively analyzes the service tree and passes all ISCs to the implementation validator (see figure 5). This component checks whether the attributes associated with the analyzed ISC are supported on a given active node by comparing the ISC descriptor to the active node descriptor. Invalid ISCs are removed from the service tree. Please note that removal of an ISC may lead to parent ASCs becoming invalid as well.

3.2.3   Phase III: Port Mapping. In phase II each service component in the service tree has been validated separately, leaving aside any bindings among them. Bindings are defined through ports and connections. In the previous phase, it was already checked whether the specified types of ports are supported by the respective EE. This phase extends the previous checks by mapping ports to connections. First, all named connection end-points (i.e. end-points specifying a port name) are mapped to the respective ports of an SC. Second, non-named connection end-points are mapped to non-named ports in the order of appearance in the descriptor. Third, it is checked that all unconnected ports have the attribute *optional*. SCs that fail to pass these checks are removed from the tree.

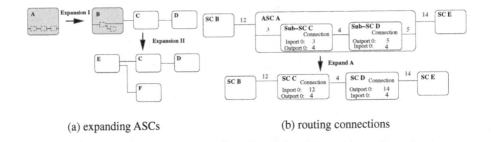

(a) expanding ASCs   (b) routing connections

Fig. 7. Flattening the service tree

3.2.4 Phase IV: Service Tree Flattening.

At this stage the service tree contains much information that is no longer relevant. Remember that the result of the processing in the composition engine is to be a list of ISCs including references to code modules and information about their configuration and binding. As a consequence, the hierarchical grouping of service components, which is achieved by ASCs, must be flattened. As several validation steps are carried out on the flattened data structure, we refer to it as *validation map*. All algorithms iterating the validation map consist of the same structure which is outlined in table 1.

Table 1. Validation map traversal

1	Go through all outports i
2	Go through all possibilities j of outport i
3	Trigger the logic of the algorithm in the successor node identified by (i,j)
4	Get the return of the successor triggered in 3
5	Execute the logic of the algorithm
6	Return the result of 5

To build the validation map all ASCs are expanded step by step (see figure 7(a)). In the beginning the validation map consists of nothing but the root ASC (*A*) of the service tree. In the first step this root node is expanded, which means that it is replaced by all its children nodes. The expand algorithm then expands all further ASCs until the validation map consists of (connected) ISCs only.

Figure 7(b) shows how connections are handled while expanding ASCs. Each connection between two SCs is identified by an unique ID. A port being attached to a given connection contains a reference to the connection ID. Let's now focus on the example in figure 7(b), where ASC *A* is to be expanded. Connections with ID 12, 3, 5, and 14 are affected by this operation. As a result of the previous port mapping operation, inport 0 of sub-SC *C* refers to connection 3, whereas outport 0 of sub-SC *D* refers to connection 5. To flatten the hierarchy, connections 12 and 3, respectively 5 and 14 must be merged. This is achieved by redefining the port mapping of ASC *A*'s child components to refer to the outside connections 12 and 14, respectively. Data structures related to ASC A, as well as connections 3 and 5 are no longer needed.

3.2.5 Phase V: Connection Validation.
At this stage the validation map consists of connected ISCs only. The objective of the next validation map traversal is to remove all transport connections between ISCs which cannot be deployed on the active node under consideration. This is done by analyzing for each connection EE name and EE version of the two ISCs attached to it, as well as the port types involved. This information is compared to the active node descriptor to check whether the connections are supported by the active node.

3.2.6 Phase VI: Evaluating Routes.
At this point validation is completed. The list of connected ISCs potentially yields a great number of possible installations of the requested service. The composition processor selects one of these and pass it to the deployment engine.

Therefore, the validation map is traversed to compute all possible routes. The list of routes can now be evaluated. To select one route a *mapping policy* is needed. This policy contains an algorithm the selection of components is based upon. Currently the mapping policy component of the SCE (see figure 5) enforces a policy to minimize the number of EE transitions. Given the modular design of the composition engine, other policies can be implemented and integrated easily with the SCE.

3.2.7 Phase VII: Creating the Implementation Map.
As seen in section 3.2.4 the validation map consists of nothing but linked ISCs. So does the implementation map. Therefore the translation from the selected route to an implementation map consists of a transformation of some data structures. The main difference between these data structures is the fact that those of the validation map allow multiple successors for one outport. This is not the case for the implementation map. Once the translation has been completed the valid implementation map is passed to the deployment engine.

3.3 Processing in the Deployment Engine

The deployment engine (see figure 5) has two main tasks: it downloads, installs and configures ISCs as defined in implementation maps, and it configures active node facilities, such as the demultiplexer and inter-EE communication channels, accordingly. Thus, the deployment engine may need to insert adapters between ISCs to allow for communications across EE boundaries, which is transparent to the involved ISCs. Further, EEs are configured by the deployment engine to allow for transparent communication between the demultiplexer and ISCs as well.

3.3.1 EE Configurators.
There is no standardized interface to configure EEs, neither now nor do we expect one for the future. We believe, however, that it is possible to agree on a common service model, like the one in section 2.1. For this reason, our architecture features EE-specific configurators, which translate the generic configuration commands

of the deployment engine, which depend on the service model only, into EE-specific ones.

For each EE on an active node, a corresponding configurator is registered with the SCE. In this way it is possible to cope with a wide variety of different EEs using the same SCE. Support for new EEs can be added to the SCE by simply updating the active node descriptor and installing an EE-specific configurator.

3.3.2   Demultiplexer Configurator. The demux configurator is kept simple. It gets a list of Netfilter style rules [3] and passes them to the demultiplexer. In our case no rule translation is necessary as demultiplexing is based on the Linux Netfilter subsystem [3].

4   Implementation

To validate our approach to automatic service composition, we implemented an active node prototype including our service composition system. Furthermore, a demonstration service was deployed on this node to serve as a proof-of-concept.

4.1   Service Creation Engine

The SCE is written in Java and (including EE-specific configurators) runs on its own JVM generally referred to as *management EE*. The configurators communicate with their respective service EE via Java Remote Method Invocation (RMI)[5]. RMI was selected for two reasons. First, it allows running the SCE in its own JVM, which results in a proper separation of the SCE from other node subsystems, such as service EEs and node OS. Second, it becomes simple to run the management EE, including SCE, on a physically distinct computer.Hence our implementation enables a physical separation of the management plane from forwarding/control planes. The overhead introduced by the RMI communication is not relevant in this context as only a limited amount of configuration information is exchanged.

We developed a common XML Schema [12] for service descriptors, which enables the SCE to check their syntactical correctness using a standard validating XML parser like Xerces [5].

4.2   Active Node Prototype

The prototype is based on a Linux 2.4.20 kernel. Its Netfilter [3] subsystem serves as the demultiplexer (demux). Each EE that is to receive packets from the demux has to provide an entry adapter element, as well as a target string. Adapter elements must be listed in the active node description and are inserted by the demux configurator into the implementation map.

To attach EEs to the demux a patch of the Netfilter subsystem of the kernel is necessary to provide a new target for data packets. Although this renders EE installation

---

[5] In the case of ClickEE, an RMI proxy was implemented to communicate with the proprietary *click installer.*

more complex, this solution was selected for performance reasons, as the entire demux is confined within the kernel space. The target string is required by SCE to compile Netfilter rules allowing to dispatch packets to proper service entry points.

Our node provides two service EEs: one, *ClickEE*, is based on the kernel internal Click router [10], whereas the other, *Chameleon Java EE (CJEE)*, runs on a Java Virtual Machine (JVM). Both support our component based service model, otherwise they are completely different. Click EE runs in kernel space, and implementations of the service components are compiled into the kernel. It needs a proprietary configuration file to be configured. This file is generated by the ClickEE specific configurator as a result of the deployment engines generic EE configuration commands. The CJEE on the other hand, runs in user space, and its service components may be retrieved from an external server. Its configuration interface implements the following methods: add service component, connect two components, start service thread, as well as a few others, which are not relevant here.

The node also provides inter-EE communication facilities. Our implementation supports the */proc file system (procfs)* and, to some extent, *Linux Netlink* for communication among service components in different EEs. Therefore we implemented communication adapters that allow both Click EE and CJEE service components to communicate with each other over the procfs and Linux Netlink.

4.3   Demonstration Service

To demonstrate the working of SCE and active node, we implemented a small service, which performs traffic shaping. The SCE deploys the service on our active node. Figure 8(a) shows a graphical representation of the implementation map resulting from the processing within the SCE's composition engine. Grey components are executed in the CJEE, whereas white ones run in the ClickEE. External components necessary for demonstration purposes are represented within dashed boxes. A simple GUI was implemented to set and modulate the *target value*, as well as to represent the temporal evolution of the *actual value* (see figure 8(b)).

The main goal of our system is to simplify service creation by providing means to compose services from components. Our experience with the demo service shows that this goal is achieved. To implement the service, we *reused* components provided by the developers of Click router and developed new ones for the CJEE. We had to write the descriptors for all the involved components. However, were such service descriptors to become a standard, we would expect the component developers to provide them as well. To glue components together, we wrote an ASC descriptor of our traffic shaping service, which is sent to the active node to trigger the deployment of the service.

The service was designed to demonstrate the major features of our system, which are *service composition, support for multiple EEs and inter-EE communication support*. This has been achieved. Figure 8(a) shows that the SCE composes the service from several service components, using different EEs. The composition algorithm selects, whenever possible, service components implemented in the faster EE (ClickEE). Communication adapters between *counter* and *emaRate*, inserted by the deployment engine, provide inter-EE communication support, which is transparent to the service components.

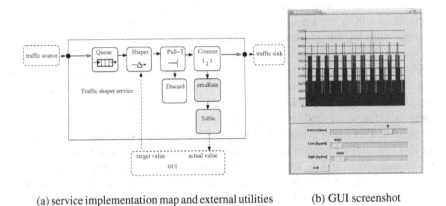

(a) service implementation map and external utilities   (b) GUI screenshot

Fig. 8. Demo service: a traffic shaper

To carry out measurements all subsystems of our architecture are run as separate processes on the same active node, which is based on a Pentium IV 2 GHz CPU with 512 MB RAM. Communication among processes uses the same protocols and mechanisms as in a distributed set-up. The measurements do not reflect any delay caused by a network while fetching descriptors and code. Total processing of the SCE to compose and deploy the traffic shaper service takes on average $2.98s$ on a just booted node. Only $0.85s$ thereof are used by the composition engine. $2.13s$ are spent by the deployment engine to fetch code, and to load and configure components in the different EEs.

5   Conclusions

In this paper we presented design and implementation details of Chameleon, a system for automatic service composition. Our central contribution is the design and implementation of the service creation engine (SCE), which maps a node independent service description to a node specific implementation by composing appropriate service components. The resulting mapping depends on node capabilities described in the node descriptor. Based on our service and composition models, we further contributed an XML-based service description language. The language is used to write descriptors containing meta-information about service components. Descriptors are processed by the SCE to automatically select, bind, load, and configure service components for a specific node.

Finally, we implemented an active node prototype, including two distinctive EEs. This platform was used to demonstrate an example service, which was deployed using the SCE. Configuring EEs as different as the Chameleon Java EE and the Click-based EE demonstrated the ability of our approach to deal with a wide range of EEs.

The versatility of the Chameleon approach has further been shown with other active node implementations: In the European IST-FAIN project a subset of our system was applied for node level service deployment [11]. Moreover Chameleon was used to deploy and configure services in the context of mobile networks [13].

Consequently, it is safe to state that our architecture consisting of description language and SCE provides the necessary means to cope with heterogeneity expected to be present in (partially) active networks.

References

1. Corba component model webpage. http://www.omg.org/.
2. Enterprise java beans webpage. http://java.sun.com/products/ejb/.
3. Netfilter webpage. http://www.netfilter.org.
4. Tina webpage. http://www.tinac.com.
5. Apache. Xerces2 webpage. http://xml.apache.org/xerces2-j/.
6. Tim Berners-Lee, Larry Masinter, and Mark McCahill. RFC 1738: Uniform resource locators (url), December 1994.
7. Matthias Bossardt, Takashi Egawa, Hideki Otsuki, and Bernhard Plattner. Integrated service deployment for active networks. In *Proceedings of the Fourth Annual International Working Conference on Active Networks IWAN*, number 2546 in Lecture Notes in Computer Science, Zurich, Switzerland, December 2002. Springer Verlag.
8. Matthias Bossardt, Lukas Ruf, Rolf Stadler, and Bernhard Plattner. A service deployment architecture for heterogeneous active network nodes. In *IFIP International Conference on Intelligence in Networks (SmartNet)*, Saariselka, Finnland, April 2002. Kluwer Academic Publishers.
9. IETF. Forces working group.
   http://www.ietf.org/html.charters/forces-charter.html.
10. Eddie Kohler, Robert Morris, Benjie Chen, John Jannotti, and M. Frans Kaashoek. The click modular router. *ACM Transactions on Computer Systems*, 18(3):263–297, August 2000.
11. Marcin Solarski, Matthias Bossardt, and Thomas Becker. Component-based deployment and management of services in active networks. In *Proceedings of the Fourth Annual International Working Conference on Active Networks IWAN*, number 2546 in Lecture Notes in Computer Science, Zurich, Switzerland, December 2002. Springer Verlag.
12. W3C. Xml-schema webpage. http://www.w3c.org/XML/Schema.
13. Qing Wei, Karoly Farkas, Paulo Mendes, Christian Prehofer, Bernhard Pattner, and Nima Nafisi. Context-aware handover based on active network technology. In *Proceedings of the Fifth Annual International Working Conference on Active Networks IWAN*, Lecture Notes in Computer Science, Kyoto, Japan, December 2003. Springer Verlag.

Multiple Language Family Support for Programmable Network Systems

Michael Conrad, Marcus Schöller, Thomas Fuhrmann,
Gerhard Bocksch, and Martina Zitterbart

Institut für Telematik
Universität Karlsruhe, Germany

Abstract. Various programmable networks have been designed and implemented during the last couple of years. Many of them are focused on a single programming language only. This limitation might—to a certain extend—hinder the productivity of service modules being programmed for such networks. Therefore, the concurrent support of service modules written in multiple programming languages was investigated within the FlexiNet project. Basically, support for three major programming paradigms was incorporated into FlexiNet: compiled programming languages like C, interpreted languages (e.g., Java), and hardware description languages such as VHDL. The key concept can be seen in an integral interface that is used by all three programming languages. This leads to a configuration scheme which is totally transparent to the programming languages used to develop the service. In order to get a better idea about the impact of the programming language used, some measurement experiments were conducted.

Keywords: Programmable Networks, Flexible Service Platforms, Execution Environment, Programming Language

1 Introduction

Active and programmable networks are a vital area of research that aims to improve existing networks, for example, with respect to the number and flexibility of services provided to customers or to network operators themselves. In order to achieve this, programmable networks introduce programmable nodes—a sort of middleboxes—that are incorporated into the network. These nodes provide services that are not available in the network itself. For example, routers at the edge of the network do not only forward packets but also provide some additional services, such as multicast support. These services can be provided on demand, i.e., they need not to be pre-installed when the router is put into operation in the network. As a result the number and flexibility of services being provided to customers can be largly increased without demanding the overall network infrastructure to be updated. Multicast serves as a good example, since the introduction of IP multicast into the network would require all routers to talk IP multicast and to provide suited routing protocols.

Although research in active and programmable networks is on-going since several years, few working frameworks exist only. The FlexiNet framework based on AMnodes discussed in this paper is considered as one of those frameworks. On the other hand,

N. Wakamiya et al. (Eds.): IWAN 2003, LNCS 2982, pp. 178–189, 2004.

an increased interest in these technologies can be observed recently, for example, from mobile network operators. With programmable nodes, mobility support can be easily integrated into a network. Performance enhancing proxies (e.g. [10]) can be named as an example. These proxies boost TCP performance in wireless scenarios. Furthermore, a high flexibility with respect to the network services needed is considered essential for next generation networks in general.

Up to now, most research projects concentrated on how to realise the packet mangling and manipulation, how to do resource management and overcome according limitations, or how to deploy such a system. From the customers point of view, services form the most critical part of networks. However, in the context of active and programmable networks a lack of readily available implemented services that can provide the targeted flexibility can be observed. On one hand this is due to the concentration of technical issues related to the design and implementation of such programmable nodes. On the other hand, many projects are restricted to individual programming languages and, mostly, just to a single programming language. Some projects have even developed their own service programming languages to achieve restrictions in their programming model or to ease tasks like resource control and management. This further limits the number of programmers that are motivated to implement new services. As a result, currently available services for programmable networks were mostly developed within related projects and, thus, are limited to few available services only. However, in order to attract customers a variety of widely interesting services needs to be readily available. To achieve this, the hurdle to implement new services should be as low as possible.

Enabling the development of services in a variety of well-known programming languages should help overcoming this problem and, thus, make programmable networks more attractive to customers and providers. Typically, programmers are used to a couple of programming languages they always select for network or service programming and can not be easily convienced to learn a new one. Their refusal further grows if that new language follows another programming paradigm. Programmers used to an object oriented programming language often refuse to use systems which only offer support for classical languages like C. Moreover, different programming languages have different fortes and bring along different sets of libraries. Some services may be easier implemented in Java whereas for other services C may be favourable. Therefore, the AMnet framework [4], currently part of the larger FlexiNet project, was extended to provide support for various programming languages.

In this framework service developers are no longer restricted to a single programming language. Support for different programming languages was first presented in [7] with special focus on resource control and limitations. This mechanism forms the basis for flexible usage of the programming language as long as the execution environment is run as a user space process. Any additional mechanism like a Java sandbox are usable but not necessarily needed to safely run the programmable node.

The reminder of the paper is structured as follows. Section 2 provides a brief overview of the FlexiNet framework for those readers that are not yet familiar with it. The concept of integrating different programming languages is discussed in detail in Section 3. As a usage example, an RTSP/RTP implementation with modules implemented in different languages is presented in section 4. Some measurement results on the integration of C and Java service modules complement the paper. A brief summary and outlook on future work concludes the paper.

1.1 Related Work

The basic concepts of programmable networks have been described in various publication, see, e.g., [2,3]. AMnet [5] which now provides the FlexiNet framework is an operational implementation of many of these fundamental ideas together with specific extensions and improvements [4]. Its concept is basically that of a Linux based software router. Similar approaches have been pursued by various other projects, e.g., the Click Modular Router project [8]. There, low-level extensions to the regular network protocol stack provide a router environment in which so-called *elements* perform the basic processing steps like packet classification and mangling. Compared to AMnet, which (mostly) runs in the user-space of an unmodified Linux installation, Click's direct hardware access trades security and programming ease against performance. Both projects' common objective, namely to benefit from existing operating system functionality, is also shared by SILK [1], in which a port of Scout [9] replaces the standard Linux protocol stack.

2 Brief Introduction into FlexiNet Framework

The FlexiNet framework provides a design and implementation for the paradigm of programmable networks. The design paradigm is based on the fact that programs (respecticely service modules) can be downloaded on demand in order to provide a service. This flexibility, however, is not expected to be provided on a per-packet bases but, in contrast, for dedicated end-to-end data flows. These service modules are available from so-called service module repositories. Installation and termination of services in the network takes place according to the demands of a service user. Thereby, a service can be constructed out of several so-called service modules. These service modules are arranged in a service module chain, i.e. different service modules are processed sequentially for a certain IP packet in order to provide it with the desired service.

The architecture of the programmable node (so-called AMnode) used in the FlexiNet framework basically consists of two major components: the framework and the execution environment (cf., Fig. 1). The framework itself provides all required system services, such as handling several execution environments as well as creation and setup of desired services. The execution environment acts as runtime system for a specified service, which consists of different service modules. For each service FlexiNet creates a separate execution environment and instantiates all modules that are needed to provide a certain service in this execution environment. Inside the framework several execution environments run separately and independent from each other. IP packets for a desired service will be forwarded to the corresponding execution environment and, then, can be processed accordingly by the chain of service modules.

Currently, FlexiNet provides support for the following programming languages: C, C++, Java and VHDL. They can be used concurrently, i.e., if a service is composed of different service modules, those modules can be written in different programming

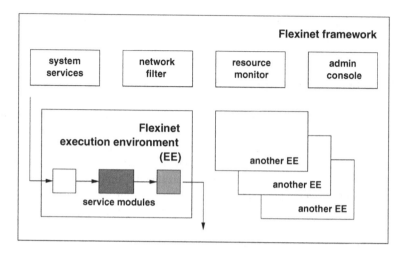

Fig. 1. Structure of FlexiNet framework and execution environment

languages. C and C++ were chosen since they are popular languages for network programming. Java brings additional support that is particular valuable for higher level services. The support of VHDL allows us to outsource processing intensive service modules on dedicated programmable hardware platforms.

In FlexiNet service modules are natively programmed in C and compiled to shared libraries which are dynamically loaded into the execution environment on demand. In [6] we introduced the concept of Happlets and gave an extensive overview on performance and interaction with other service modules. Happlets are an abstraction for various hardware programming languages, such as VHDL. With Happlets a so-called virtual service module is loaded into the execution environment which sets up and configures hardware like DSPs or FPGAs and redirects incoming packets to that hardware. The concept of Happlets itself will not be discussed further within this paper. Interested readers are referred to [6].

Furthermore, Java is integrated into FlexiNet as an example of an interpreted programming language. An advantage of integrating support for Java is its platform independence in contrast to object code which is compiled for a predefined system. This eases the deployment of modules in heterogeneous environments. Moreover, Java brings along a vast number of classes and packages which alleviate the design and programming of new services. Besides C Java is a popular network programming language. Many software developers are familiar with its principals and can implement modules very fast. Both facts are expected to help increase the number of FlexiNet service programmers considerably.

The decision to integrate the different programming languages as special FlexiNet modules gave us the freedom to develop them independently as long as the interface stays the same. Further on an execution environment only has to instantiate the language support for those languages which were used to program that service. In that way system resources can be saved but still any combination of service modules from various programming language is possible.

3   Integration of Multiple Language Support

This section focuses on the technical issues of integrating support for multiple languages in FlexiNet. It is our assumption that a service designer has broken up the problem in several subproblems. Each of these subproblems is realised in one service module. The module programmer can now freely choose from the programming languages supported by FlexiNet. The key concept can be seen in an integral interface that is used by all three programming languages. This leads to a configuration scheme which is totally transparent to the programming languages used to develop the service. An examples on how a service can be configured with service modules that are implemented in different programming languages is presented in section 3.

3.1   General Integration Concept

In the original design FlexiNet only supported shared object code. As a result, all service modules had to be implemented in C oder C++. For usage by the execution environment the modules must implement the following function prototypes (cf., Fig. 2).

```
1  #include "modules.h"
2
3  int module_init( struct module *module);
4  int module_shutdown( struct module *module);
5
6  int module_run( struct module *module, nl_packet_msg *nlPacketMsg,
7                  struct iphdr *ip);
8  
9  int getstatus( struct module *module);
```

Fig. 2. FlexiNet C module interface

The function module_init is called once after instantiation of the specified module. Accordingly the function module_shutdown is called once at termination of the module. The function module_run is called for all IP packets that are processed by the corresponding service modules. The parameters of the function provide some information about the module itself as well as the desired IP packet. Inside this function the module can create, delete or modify IP packets. For example, a service module may receive a single IP packet and provide multiple replicated IP packets at its output interface (e.g., in case of a multicast service). By setting special return codes the further processing of the IP packet can be guided.

3.2   Integration of Java-Based Service Modules

The interface for Java modules is analogous to the C interface:

```
1  package de.flexinet.modules;
2
3  public interface FlexinetModule {
4
5     public void moduleInit( Adapter a);
6     public void moduleShutdown();
7
8     public void moduleRun( IPPacket ip, NlPacketMsg nlPacketMsg)
9       throws FlexinetException;
10
11    public String status();
12 }
```

Fig. 3. FlexiNet Java module interface

To integrate support for Java-based service modules a programming interface for Java and a wrapper module was designed and implemented. The wrapper module is written in C and implements the classical FlexiNet module interface already described above. During module initialisation the Java Virtual Machine (JVM) is started and configured using the Java Native Interface (JNI). In addition some special memory is allocated which is used to pass IP packets from the wrapper to Java. Furthermore, within the JVM an adapter class is started which functions as a counterpart to the wrapper module is started. As a result, service modules written in Java only must implement the interface FlexinetModule (cf., Fig. 3).

To process an IP packet the wrapper copies the IP packet into the allocated memory and calls the function moduleRun of the adapter which only calls the corresponding function within the Java module. After packet processing within the JVM the wrapper passes the packet to the next service module or back into the IP layer if that was the last module of the service module chain.

3.3   Startup Script for FlexiNet Modules

The FlexiNet configuration scheme is transparent to the programming language used to implement service modules. All startup scripts contain two parts: the first one configures the modules used to realise the desired service, the second one defines filter rules to select packets to which the service is applied to.

The module configuration section contains all information, required for correct instantiation and setup of a specified module. The following example (cf. Fig. 4) shows the module configuration section of a C and a Java module.

```
1  loadmodule nop_c {              1  loadmodule nop_java {
2    file "libnop.so";            2    file "libjmod.so";
3                                  3    className = "Nop";
4    myparameter = "some string"; 4    myparameter = "some string";
5  };                             5  };
```

Fig. 4. Module configuration section of FlexiNet execution environment script (C and Java)

The left side of figure 4 presents the configuration section for the NOP module written in C. The right side shows the configuration section for the equivalent module written in Java. Both start with the `loadmodule` command in line 1. In line 2 the C example loads the shared library `libnop.so`, which contains the NOP module written in C. In the same line the Java example loads the library `libjmod.so`, which contains the wrapper for Java modules. This wrapper creates a virtual machine and loads the desired service module. Information about that module is taken from the parameter `className` which is shown in line 3. In this case the class Nop should be loaded. Both module configuration sections contain the setting of a paramenter called `myparameter` in line 4.

In addition to the module configuration section each startup script must contain a network configuration section. This network configuration section is independent of the module implementation language. The section holds information about the network traffic that should be processed by the module. With the following configuration it is indicated, that the packets for all TCP connections from server `www.some-server.net` port 80 should be processed by the service module. The command `nfhook` in line 3 specifies the Netfilter hook of the Linux kernel, that applies to the service module. In the example the module selects hook `PREROUTING`. As a result, the processing of the IP traffic by this service module takes place before the routing lookup takes place.

```
1  listen {
2    protocol "tcp";
3    nfhook PREROUTING;
4
5    source {
6      name "www.some-server.net";
7      port 80;
8    };
9  };
```

Fig. 5. Network configuration section of FlexiNet execution environment script

3.4   Structuring the Service Modules

Only very few services can be implemented within one module. Most services are composed of several different modules each of those providing a single task. The next section shows an example service which consists of three modules.

The easiest way to connect modules is to build a single chain where packets get processed by each module consecutively. This is the standard behavior of the FlexiNet execution environment. However the service programmer can influence the order of modules. The FlexiNet execution environment supports the dynamic creation of multiple in-ports. One optional parameter of a filter entry is the module name of that module which should start the packet processing. This mechanismen was used in the following example as shown figure 6 where RTSP packets are handled diffrently from RTP packets. A second way to alter the order of modules is by building conditional branches or loops. Within each module the programmer can set the next module by a simple call to the execution environment. Furthermore it is possible to abort the packet processing any time by either deleting the packet or by returning it to the IP layer. All thoses possiblities can be used in C and Java.

Finally an effective way to pass parameters from one module to another must be provided to realise real cooperation of modules. The FlexiNet execution environment provides to mechanisms for that. The first way is to set configuration parameters of one module by a simple call the the execution environment by another module. This provides a easy interface of module interaction. The second way is to use a stack which is provided by the FlexiNet execution environment. Any module can push data onto that stack where it will remain until a module pops it from there. The access to the stack from within Java is realised by JNI functions.

4   Cooperation among Heterogeneous Service Modules

To demonstrate the cooperation of service modules programmed with different programming languages (so-called heterogeneous service modules) we chose to realise an RTSP/RTP application level multicast service. The decision was driven by the goal to provide relevant services to emerging applications. RTSP/RTP has proven to be such a service. For example, web radio applications often use RTP to deliver audio data to the end system after the RTSP protocol negotiated several communication parameters. Many times, multiple end users will request the same audio stream from RTP servers. In such cases, programmable nodes, such as the once developed within the FlexiNet project, can help to reduce the server load and the bandwidth utilisation if multiple receivers of the same audio stream are located behind the same programmable network node. Therefore, the service placed at the programmable node acts as both, an audio stream client as well as an audio server. The client role is dedicated to the sender of the stream, i.e., the programmable nodes acts as one client receiving the audio stream. Locally, the programmable node replicates the audio stream and forwards it to all clients in its subnet. Thus it owns the server role with respect to these clients.

In order to implement the above scenario, various service modules are required, as depicted in figure 6.

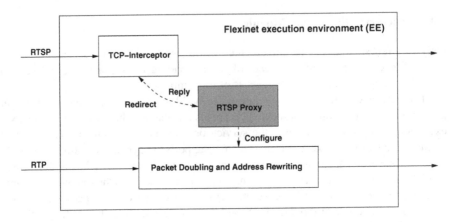

Fig. 6. A RTSP/RTP application level multicast service

The TCP interceptor module redirects incoming packets from any client to the local machine. As a result, the RTSP proxy module receives the data and parses the RTSP message accordingly. RTSP messages are text based similar to HTTP messages. If the received RTSP message is the first request for a stream, the RTSP proxy initiates a new RTSP client connection to the requested server and forwards the server information to the client. If already an earlier request for that stream was received, the RTSP proxy retransmits the corresponding cached RTSP messages to the client. Any client is added to a list of receivers for that particular audio stream. The Packet Doubling and Address Setting module reads this list of clients and replicates as required. Furthermore, the addresses are set appropriately.

The above described RTSP/RTP scenario is currently being implemented in the FlexiNet project. For the implementation it turned out to be very convenient to use different programming languages for the service modules. Since text parsing can be very easily implemented in Java—regular expression were added in version 1.4 of Java—we decided to implement that module in Java. The TCP interceptor was already implemented for other services in C. The packet duplication and address setting is a simple task that has to be applied to lots of packets. Therefore, we decided to implement this module in C. Due to the integration concept of service modules written in different languages, the described modules can interact seamlessly.

5   Some Performance Considerations

In order to get a feeling for the overhead associated with service modules written in different programming languages, we conducted a number of measurement experiments. For example, the overhead introduced by using Java was of some interest. The experiments were performed on a Pentium III 800MHz Linux (2.4.19) Router with 256MB memory. Client and server were both directly connected to this router via a 100Mbit Ethernet network.

5.1   Overhead of Java Service Modules

To measure the overhead introduced by Java several experiments were conducted. First measurements were taken on a router that was not running a FlexiNet execution environment at all. Then, first a C module and second a Java module was added to that router. Both service modules simply decremented the IP TTL field. We used the `ping` program to measure the round trip time of packets. Every test was run with 100000 packets. The results are summarized in table 1.

Table 1. Overhead measurements

Module	Min/ms	Avg/ms	Max/ms
no module	0.083	0.085	0.177
C NOP module	0.101	0.106	2.259
Java NOP module	0.111	0.118	2.776
Java NOP module (cold)	0.111	0.120	14.801

As table 1 shows, a small overhead can be noticed by the Java service module compared to the C module. Mainly, the additional copy operation of the IP packet from the wrapper to the Jave service module is responsible for that.

The last line of table 1 reflects the effect of just-in-time compilation. The Java service module is compiled at its initial execution. As a result, the maximum value is drastically higher than all other measured times for the Java service module were just-in-time compilation did not take place.

5.2   Initial Performance Tests

For the performance measurements reported here, the network tool `iperf` with packet size of 1470 byte and UDP as transport protocol was used. The test setup consisted of 3 machines. One machine acts as client, one as server and the other as a programmable node between both. The network traffic generated by the client was varied from 10Mbit/s up to the theoretical maximum of the network (100Mbit/s) and the incoming bandwidth at the server was measured.

The measurement results are summarized in figure 7. The practical achievable throughput was measured without any processing of IP packets inside the FlexiNet execution environment. Further measurements were conducted with simple service modules, that implement UDP `checksum` calculation in C and Java.

As long as the programmable node can keep up with the received load, no packet loss and, thus, no performance degradation can be observed. As soon as the node is overloaded packets must be dropped and, as a result, the bandwidth of the incoming data stream at the server degrades accordingly as shown in figure 7. Alltogether, the experiments show that the performance of the Java service modules is lower than the one of the service modules written in C. This, however, is not surprising. Furthermore, the Java modules consume more resources since they require JVM to be installed.

Relating the measurements to the above described example of an RTSP/RTP implementation with heterogeneous service modules, it can be stated that the application of Java for text parsing makes sense. This service module is part of the control plane and, thus, is not as performance critical as those modules of the data plane. Using Java to implement such a service module is perfectly suitable. On the other side, it is also advisable to write performance critical service modules, for example, in C.

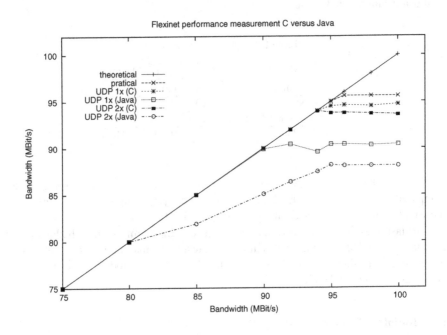

Fig. 7. Performance measurements

6   Summary

Programmable networks still lack readily available services. Among many issues that are responsible for that situation, an important aspect can be seen in the possibility of using service modules that are written in different implementation languages, dependent on the implementers preference. On the one hand service designers and programmers have varying experience in different programming paradigms or even programming languages. On the other hand programming languages have different fortes. The support of multiple programming languages eases the work of service module designing and programming and may very well raise the productivity with respect to service module implementations.

Motivated by this idea, FlexiNet was enhanced in order to simultaneously support multiple programming languages even for service modules being part of the same service module chain.

The integration of C, Java, and Happlets in FlexiNet is seamless and transparent in view to programming interfaces and configuration. In order to get a close idea on the overheads involved in the different programming languages, particularly C and Java, various measurement experiments were conducted. The higher overhead of Java could be clearly seen. However, the performance is by far good enough to apply Java service modules, for example, in the control plane as demonstrated in the RTSP/RTP example.

References

1. Andy Bavier, Thiemo Voigt, Mike Wawrzoniak, Larry Peterson, and Per Gunningberg. SILK: Scout paths in the Linux kernel. Technical Report 2002-009, Uppsala Universitet, February 2002.
2. Kenneth L. Calvert, Samrat Bhattacharjee, Ellen Zegura, and James Sterbenz. Directions in active networks. *IEEE Communications Magazine*, 36(10):72–78, October 1998.
3. Andrew T. Campbell, Herman G. De Meer, Michael E. Kounavis, Kazuho Miki, John B. Vicente, and Daniel Villela. A survey of programmable networks. *ACM SIGCOMM Computer Communication Review*, 29(2), April 1999.
4. Thomas Fuhrmann, Till Harbaum, Panos Kassianidis, Marcus Schöller, and Martina Zitterbart. Results on the practical feasibility of programmable network services. In *2nd International Workshop on Active Network Technologies and Applications (ANTA 2003)*, 2003.
5. Thomas Fuhrmann, Till Harbaum, Marcus Schöller, and Martina Zitterbart. AMnet 3.0 source code distribution. Available from http://www.flexinet.de.
6. Till Harbaum, Anke Speer, Ralph Wittmann, and Martina Zitterbart. Providing Heterogeneous Multicast Services with AMnet. *Journal of Communications and Networks*, 3(1), March 2001.
7. A. Hess, M. Schöller, G. Schäfer, A. Wolisz, and M. Zitterbart. A dynamic and flexible access control and resource monitoring mechanism for active nodes. In *Proceedings of the 5th International Conference on Open Architectures and Network Programming (OPENARCH) (Short Paper Session)*, 2002.
8. Eddie Kohler, Robert Morris, Benjie Chen, John Jannotti, and M. Frans Kaashoek. The click modular router. *ACM Transactions on Computer Systems*, 18(3):263–297, August 2000.
9. David Mosberger. *Scout: A Path-based Operating System*. PhD thesis, Department of Computer Science, University of Arizona, July 1997.
10. M. Schlaeger, B. Rathke, S. Bodenstein, and A. Wolisz, editors. *Advocating a Remote Socket Architecture for Internet Access using Wireless LANs*, volume 6 no. 1 pp. 23-42. Mobile Networks and Applications (Special Issue on Wireless Internet and Intranet Access), January 2001.

Dynamic Deployment and Configuration of Differentiated Services Using Active Networks

Toshiaki Suzuki[1], Chiho Kitahara[2], Spyros Denazis[3], Lawrence Cheng[4],
Walter Eaves[4], Alex Galis[4], Thomas Becker[5], Dusan Gabrijelcic[6],
Antonis Lazanakis[7], and George Karetsos[7]

[1] Hitachi, Ltd., Central Research Laboratory, Japan
toshiaki@crl.hitachi.co.jp, Tel:+81-42-323-1111, Fax:+81-42-327-7868
[2] Hitachi, Ltd., Systems Development Laboratory, Japan
kitahara@sdl.hitachi.co.jp, Tel:+81-44-959-0266, Fax:+81-44-959-0853
[3] Hitachi Europe Ltd., Hitachi Sophia Antipolis, France
spyros.denazis@hitachi-eu.com, Tel:+33-4-89-87-41-72,
Fax:+33-4-89-87-41-51
[4] University College London, United Kingdom
{l.cheng, w.eaves, a.galis}@ee.ucl.ac.uk, Tel:+44-20-7419-3946,
Fax:+44-20-7387-4350
[5] Fraunhofer Institute for Open Communication Systems FOKUS, Germany
becker@fokus.fhg.de, Tel:+49-30-3463-7393, Fax:+49-30-3463-8393
[6] Jozef Stefan Institute, Laboratory for Open Systems and Networks, Slovenia
dusan@e5.ijs.si, Tel:+386-1-4773-757, Fax:+386-1-4232-118
[7] National Technical University of Athens, Greece
laz@telecom.ntua.gr, karetsos@cs.ntua.gr, Tel:+30-210-7721511,
Fax:+30-210-7722534

Abstract. This paper presents the detailed components of the Future Active IP Networks (FAIN) [1] [2] [3] active node framework based on the novel Virtual Environment (VE) concept. It also presents the dynamic and autonomic deployment of differentiated services and the configuration capabilities thereof enabled. The FAIN node supports the dynamic deployment and instantiation of multiple active VEs, each one of them capable of hosting multiple Execution Environments (EE) and supporting communication among different EEs in the same node. The EEs may, in turn, be deployed and instantiated on demand thereby introducing new features and functionality in the node according to new requirements and arising needs. We tested the FAIN active network by developing and dynamically deploying a control EE, which was designed and tested for the QoS configuration of the Diffserv-enabled pan-European FAIN testbed [4]. The work presented in this paper was performed in the European Union research and development project under the Information Society Technologies programme.

Keywords: FAIN, Active Node, Virtual Environment, Execution Environment

1 Introduction

In the world of network architectures, we are experiencing a significant paradigm shift resulting in new technologies and approaches. The motivation behind this shift is

N. Wakamiya et al. (Eds.): IWAN 2003, LNCS 2982, pp. 190–201, 2004.

the still elusive goal of rapid and autonomous service creation, deployment, activation and management, resulting from new and ever changing customer and application requirements. Research activity in this area has clearly focused on the synergy of a number of concepts: programmable networks and services, managed networks, network virtualisation, open interfaces and platforms, application level programming and increasing degrees of intelligence inside the network. Next generation networks must be capable of supporting a multitude of service providers that exploit an environment in which services are dynamically deployed and quickly adapted over a common heterogeneous physical infrastructure, according to varying and sometimes conflicting customer requirements.

Programmable and Active Networks have been proposed as a solution for the fast, flexible and dynamic deployment of new network services. These networks aim at providing easy introduction of new network services by adding dynamic programmability to network devices such as routers, switches and applications servers. The basic idea is to enable third parties (end users, operators, and service providers) to inject application-specific services (in the form of code) into the network. Applications are thus able to utilize the required network capabilities in terms of optimised network resources and as such they are becoming network-aware. Programmable networks allow dynamic injection and deployment of code as a promising way of realising application-specific service logic, or performing dynamic service provision on demand. The viable architectures for programmable networks have to be carefully engineered to achieve suitable trade-offs between flexibility, performance, resilience, security and manageability.

In this paper we present the detailed components of the FAIN active node, and the dynamic deployment of differentiated services and the configuration thereof enabled by a novel active and programmable node architecture. More specifically, in section 2 we describe the FAIN active node architecture and its major components. The focus is on the deployment and instantiation of VEs and EEs as host environments for the introduction of new functionality. In Section 3 we present the design and implementation of a secure control EE that is based on the SNMP [11] and hosts a control protocol. In Section 4 we demonstrate the uses of the deployed control EE for the dynamic configuration of a Diffserv network in order to provide the required levels of QoS. Finally conclusions and future work are presented in section 5.

2 FAIN Active Node

Figure 1 depicts the major components of the FAIN programmable node and its interaction with the management node, which includes at both network and element levels an Active Service Provisioning (ASP) and a Policy Based Network Management System (PBNM) components [9]. When the FAIN node boots up a Privileged VE is automatically instantiated and a new component is installed, namely the VE manager, which implements the VE management framework. This component offers access to a number of node services that are deemed necessary to configure and setup the node. It is used for instantiating new VEs together with appropriate EEs and to install components therein which potentially offer new control interfaces that allow services inside VEs to customise resources according to application-specific requirements.

The VE manager is complemented with the security component (SEC) that offers a set of security services and enforces node policies, the resource control component (RCF) responsible for implementing the FAIN resource control framework and the demultiplexing/multiplexing component (De/MUX) which delivers packets to the right VE and EE. In the subsequent sections we describe each one of these components in detail.

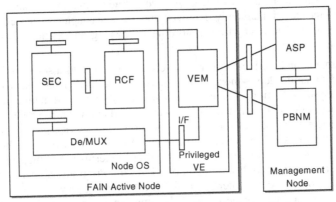

Fig. 1. Initial Components of the FAIN Active Node

In our architecture, multiple EEs can be executed in one VE since the unit for management is VE not EE. Therefore interaction between EEs is allowed. On the other hand, the conventional works for active networks are mainly contributed to make new possibilities in one EE. Therefore interaction between EEs looks out of scope in the past researches. In this sense, the concept of VE is the most crucial idea. Another benefit of VE is related to the accounting. The real VE is composed of multiple resources. Therefore it provides easy accounting based on the resource consumption.

2.1 Virtual Environment Management

As we have mentioned before, services are installed in VEs and eventually instantiated and executed inside the associated EEs. In FAIN, services are described according to a component-based approach. As such a service is defined as a graph of service components, which in turn can be developed and deployed independently as and when needed [3][5]. It is an advantage when the hosting environments for services, i.e. the execution environments are also component-based. This allows to move aspects such as lifecycle management, dynamic configuration, access control, monitoring, etc. to a supporting framework and avoid re-implementation inside the service code. The implementation of the VE management is an example for this.

During the boot procedure of the FAIN active node, the privileged virtual environment is started together with a default execution environment. Any subsequently created virtual environment will need some basic resources in order to support service installation and component instantiation. For this reason various resource managers are installed inside the privileged virtual environment during the boot procedure as it is shown in figure 2.

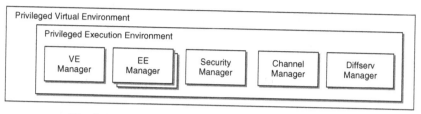

Fig. 2. Initial manager components of FAIN active node

The privileged execution environment runs in the context of the privileged virtual environment. Inside the privileged execution environment there exist the resource managers for the basic services. They will be used to create resources for other virtual environments. These basic resource managers comprise the following:

A Virtual Environment Manager is used for the creation of new virtual environments. This manager will examine the resource profile submitted as part of a VE creation policy and try to create any referenced resource using other basic managers. The resulting resource components will be inherited by the new virtual environment. A number of Execution Environment Managers are used for the creation of specific execution environments. Since running instances of services can exist only inside execution environments, there has to be at least one execution environment attached to any virtual environment. A Security Manager is a core component of the security architecture that exports a minimal set of interfaces to other node subsystems. A Channel Manager is used for creating channels to receive and send packets from and to the network. A Diffserv Manager is used for creating Diffserv controllers to control particular packet flows based on priorities.

2.2 Demultiplexer and Multiplexer: De/MUX

Our framework supports multiple VEs and multiple EEs running in VEs and as such the packets are delivered to the right entity inside a node. To this end packets must carry all the necessary information based on which the De/MUX component may forward the packet to its destination inside the node. In this case, we need to specify both environments, the VE and EE, to execute real processing to active packet data. We have adopted the Active Network Encapsulation Protocol (ANEP) [7] for the FAIN active packet data and extended its definition by introducing two new options: one for the VE identifier and one for the EE identifier.

	0			31
N	4N+ 0 byte	4N+ 1 byte	4N+ 2 byte	4N+ 3 byte
0	FLG	option type		option length
1	VE-ID or EE-ID (32bit)			

Fig. 3. VE/EE identifier

The formats for two new options are the same as shown in figure 3. The FLG indicates how to handle the option data. The owner of the option defines the value of the

FLG. The option type indicates a type of option. The value of the option type for VE and EE identifiers are 101 and 102 which were defined for the FAIN VE environment. The option length specifies the size of option field in 32 bit words. The value of the option length for the VE-ID or EE-ID is 2 in 32 bit words. The VE-ID or EE-ID indicates an identifier to transmit active packets to a proper VE/EE.

In figure 4, we present the block diagram of packet data delivery.

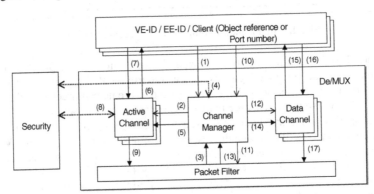

Fig. 4. Block diagram of packet delivery

Active (ANEP) packet data delivery. (1) A client requests a Channel Manager to create a new Active Channel for receiving ANEP packet data by registering a VE-ID, an EE-ID and an object reference of itself or a socket port number. (2) The Channel Manager creates the Active Channel by registering an active consumer object, which includes the VE-ID, the EE-ID and the reference or the socket port number, into an internal table for active packets. (3) The packet filter transmits the received ANEP packet to the Channel Manager since the manager sets conditions to intercept ANEP packets at the booting process. The filter could be implemented by the Netfiler [8]. (4) The Channel Manager calls a security function for checking the ANEP packet before sending it to a proper client. (5, 6) After executing the security check, the Channel Manager sends the ANEP packet data to the proper client through an appropriate Active Channel by getting a target from the internal table. The table includes the relation between VE-ID/EE-ID and the target receiver. (7) If there is an ANEP packet to be sent to another node, the client sends the ANEP packet to the proper Active Channel. (8) The Active Channel inserts the security information into the ANEP packet by interacting with the security component before sending it to the outside network. (9) After that, the Active Channel transmits the ANEP packet to the outside network.

Data (Non-active) packet data delivery. (10) A client requests the Channel Manager to create a new Data Channel for receiving non-active packet by registering flow conditions and object reference of itself or a socket port number. (11) The Channel Manager sets the filter conditions such as a source IP address and so forth. (12) The Channel Manager creates the Data Channel object, which includes the flow conditions and the reference or the socket port number. (13) The filter transmits data packet to the Channel Manager. (14, 15) The Channel Manager sends data packet to a proper client through an appropriate Data Channel. (16) If there are some packet data to be sent to another node, the client sends them to the proper Data Channel. (17) The Data Channel transmits data packet to the outside network.

2.3 Resource Control Framework

RCF (Resource Control Framework) has been designed by taking strongly into consideration and exploiting the capabilities of the component model that has been introduced in the VE management framework that was previously described. The part of RCF that is responsible for the management of the resources is actually part of the VE Management framework while the run-time control of the resources is done by other lower level RCF components. RCF can be defined as the aggregation of all the FAIN active node components that operate and interact in order to control and manage resources. As it is depicted in figure 5, there are the component families of the RCF.

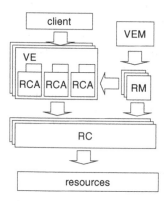

Fig. 5. RCF Architecture

Resource Controller (RC). RC is the responsible entity for the runtime control of a resource inside the active node. RC can be a component running in the Kernel Space of the node for a software router or can be a specific device of a hardware router. It can be the Traffic Control framework of the Linux. Every RC has an interface that allows its runtime configuration, which includes the allocation and monitoring of the resources.

Resource Manager (RM). For every RC, an RM exists in the user space. It is responsible for the configuration of the corresponding RC in order to enforce the resource partitioning among the various VEs. Moreover, the RMs are responsible for the RCAs creation, configuration and management. Among others the RMs are responsible for the Admission Control of the incoming requests for new allocations and for the realization of the allocation by configuring the corresponding RCs.

Resource Controller Abstraction (RCA). For every resource capacity that is allocated to a VE, an RCA of that resource is created. For every VE, a resource controller abstraction (RCA) exists that represents part of the RC functionality to the VE client: the part of the resource that has been allocated to the VE. The RCAs export interfaces and accept requests by VE owners and/or users for resource access. Resource access includes requests for resource consumption and management. RCAs check those requests against resource status and the requested entities' privileges and enforce the valid requests by configuring the corresponding RCs accordingly.

In FAIN we adopted a two-phase approach for admission control, namely, the creation phase and the activation phase. We note here that the creation and activation of a VE is part of a larger activity, which results in the creation, and activation of a virtual network across the entire active network. During the creation phase, the client requests the creation of a new VE. The VEM passes these requirements to the corresponding RMs. Every RM decides if the requested allocation can be carried out or not. When the VEM has collected all the replies from the RMs, it decides if the new VE may be admitted or not. If any of the RMs is unable to provide the requested resource capacity, the admission of the VE is aborted while the VEM informs all RMs that they have to release any pre-allocated resources.

When all the replies from the RMs are positive, the VEM replies positively as well. But even then, the VEM does not activate the newly created VE and the resources remain preallocated. If the creation of all VEs across the entire active network nodes has succeeded, only then the newly created VEs are activated. The activation request arrives at the VEM from the Network management station, which collects and checks all the responses from the VEMs of the nodes across the active network. In this case, the VEM gets in contact with all the involved RMs in order to activate the RCAs, configure the RCs accordingly, and enforce the appropriate resource allocations.

We have implemented two types of resource controller. The one is a bandwidth controller of a software router based on Linux. The other is a controller of the Diffserv functions of a hardware router. In this paper, the Diffserv control and management are presented as an example of the RCF implementation. The Diffserv controller and the hardware router are regarded as the RCA and the RC respectively.

2.4 FAIN Security Architecture

We propose high level security architecture as shown in the figure 6. Basic security services are positioned in the privilege VE because of the following reasons: we want to treat all possible technologies and their implementations, implementing VE and services in the one and only one manner, reducing the risk of multiple implementations, and the services offered in the pVE are protected again with the same services and mechanisms. This doesn't preclude VEs or services from implementing their own security services or mechanisms when it is reasonable to do so.

The FAIN security architecture was designed as a complete security solution for programmable and active node. It provides two level communication security, authorization and policy enforcement on the node, static and dynamic code verification, system integrity and accountability through audit service and logging. Only the first three aspects will be briefly described.

Two level communication security is provided for active packets with hop-by-hop protection in between two neighbor nodes based on symmetric cryptography and end-to-end authentication of data origin of the static parts of the active packets based on asymmetric cryptography. Two ANEP options were designed to support two level protection: hop-by-hop option, with security association identifier, replay protection field and keyed hash, and credential option with credential filed, type and location, optional timestamp and target and digital signature field. Multiple credential options can be in the packet related to different users, which digital signatures cover static parts of the packet. Communication security is supported with a protocol for automatic establishment of security association between nodes and protocol for exchanging user credentials between nodes in a hop manner. For efficient operation credentials are cached on nodes. Management sessions to nodes use CORBA over SSL and credential used (X.509v3 certificates with extended attributes) were handled in the same manner as user credentials supplied in the active packet.

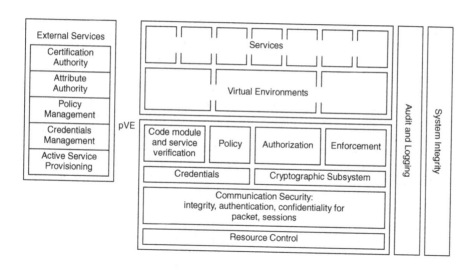

Fig. 6. High level security architecture

Authorization and policy enforcement on the nodes is provided by transparent enforcement layer, based on CORBA interceptors, components/packets security context and two level policy. Security context is build from user supplied credentials either in active packet or exchanged during SSL session negotiation. Low level policy is mandatory and it is enforced based on VE and service/EE identifiers, while high level policy allows fine grain discretional control. Multiple types of security policies can be supported by the system; we have implemented a simple one based on user roles like VE manager, manager, observer, user etc. Enforcement layer enables us to control access to the level of component interface or port while component run time instance can be a thread or a process. Static Code verification is based on digital signature mechanism while dynamic verification, like in SNAP case, see section 3., was enabled with separation of variable data (SNAP packet) and its static part, data origin authentication, same as used for communication security, and code verification performed by ASPE, see section 3.2.

3   A Secure Control EE (Active SNMP-EE)

The Active SNMP-EE is the control EE in FAIN. This EE is realized with the Safe and Nimble Active Packets (SNAP) interpreter [6][10][12]. The Active SNMP-EE consists of two components: a) SNAP Activator that generates SNAP packet programs with various SNMP commands; b) ANEP-SNAP Packet Engine (ASPE) that provides ANEP encapsulation and security provisioning for SNAP active packets across nodes. In the Active SNMP-EE, the active extensions were realized by using an extensible SNMP [11] agent. The Active SNMP-EE is able to execute SNMP primitives. The SNAP Activator generates SNAP packet programs that carry SNMP commands. SNAP packet programs are encapsulated into ANEP for the purpose of integration and interoperability. Further details of the SNAP Activator can be found at [1]. Noted that SNAP is a light-weight protocol, it has no facility for authentication at all. The ASPE works together with the Security Manager to provide the necessary security facilities to protect the end-to-end and hop-by-hop authenticity of SNAP packet programs generated by the Active SNMP-EE.

In active networks, hop-by-hop authentication should be included as well as end-to-end authentication. Principle authentication must be performed at an intermediate node since the traversing active packet will be modified. In order to enforce both end-to-end and hop-by-hop authenticity of active packets, we determine the static data of SNAP packet programs, and then encapsulate these data into ANEP separately from the SNAP dynamic data. We define the SNMP commands that are carried in the SNAP packet programs to be the static data; whereas the dynamic data is the SNAP packet itself (SNAP consists of a heap and a stack which are used to carry variable data) [13]. The eventual goal is to merge the ASPE with the SNAP Activator so that ANEP encapsulation can be performed whilst SNAP packets are being generated. Our current implementation fingerprints the SNAP packet (which contains both static and dynamic contents) before enforcing hop-by-hop protection. This static field will be digitally signed by the principle's private key (the digitally signing is performed at SEC), and the signature will be verified by each of the intermediate modifying nodes. The SNAP packet program is encapsulated entirely into Option-5. When an ANEP-SNAP packet arrives at a hop node, the SNAP packet will be extracted from Option-5, subjected to integrity and authenticity check by SEC. We use symmetric cryptographic techniques. Under this arrangement, neighboring hops would have established a trusted relationship among themselves i.e. by creating a negotiated security association (SA). With a SA, neighboring nodes can achieve peer authentication plus inter-node integrity and confidentiality protection of active packets.

3.1   Packet Flow in the ASPE

In figure 7, a block diagram of the ASPE is depicted. (1) The SNAP Activator generates a SNAP packet. (2) The SNAP Analyser determines the VE-ID, EE-ID, destination IP address, the SNAP Packet ID and the SNAP static command from the SNAP packet. (3) The Communication Manager uses the SNAP Packet ID as a reference to extract the corresponding Security ID (SID) in the Option-4 of this SNAP packet from its database, if no SID is found then this SNAP packet will be treated as a fresh packet. (4) The Digester provides additional internal integrity check for the SNAP packet. (5) The SNAP Encapsulator encapsulates the SNAP packet and the SNAP static command into ANEP Option-5 and the Payload field respectively. The SNAP Encapsulator then assigns the VE-ID, EE-ID, destination address and the SID of this SNAP packet to Option 1 to 4 respectively. (6) After that the ANEP-SNAP packet is transmitted to a local SEC for security provisioning before being forwarded to its next hop. (7) When an ANEP-SNAP packet arrives at its next hop, the De/MUX dispatches the packet to the SNAP De-Encapsulator after successful security checks performed at SEC. (8) The SNAP De-Encapsulator extracts the SNAP packet Option-5. (9) The Digester performs internal security checks for Option-5. (10) If the destination of the ANEP-SNAP packet is not local then the SNAP Analyser will extract the SNAP packet ID and the Security ID from the SNAP packet and Option 4 respectively, (11) The Communication Manager keeps this SNAP packet ID-SID pair in its database. The ID pair is needed by the SNAP Encapsulator for future ANEP-SNAP encapsulation. (12) The SNAP De-Encapsulator passes the SNAP packet to SNAP Activator for service control purposes. The same process is repeated at every traversing node.

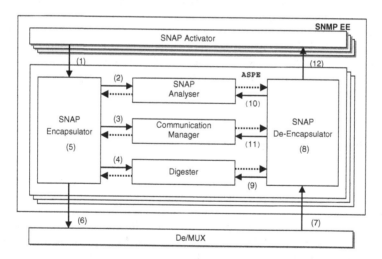

Fig. 7. Block diagram for ANEP-SNAP packet flow

4 Dynamic Diffserv QoS Configuration and Consideration

To test our architecture, we executed dynamic Diffserv QoS configuration. With regard to QoS management by active networking, the management has been reported[14]. However our main objective is not executing QoS management. The point is execution of application in the VE/EE.

In this test, a video flow was transmitted from Cambridge test-bed to Berlin test-bed. A user tries to execute Diffserv transmission. The user connects Cambridge and Berlin through hybrid active network nodes (Hardware router and Active Proxy (VE with Diffserv controller)). The hardware router is just a box for transmission of packet based on priorities. The Active Proxy provides an environment to instantiate a Diffserv controller. Then the user assigns DSCP-0 to a video flow from the Cambridge test-bed and DSCP-8 is assigned to a jam flow in Berlin test-bed in the beginning. In this case, the jam traffic has a high priority. Therefore if the jam traffic fully consumes available bandwidth for an output port of the hardware router, the video flow will suffer service degradation. To avoid this, SNAP active packet is injected from SNAP sender at Berlin to the video sender at Cambridge and the DSCP value of the video flow is changed from DSCP-0 to DSCP-56 at Cambridge. In this case, the video flow acquires higher priority than that of the jam flow. Therefore the video flow is transmitted unaffected by the jam flow.

To realize the function, the VEM creates a new VE and basic components such as the De/MUX, the SEC and the RCF components including the Diffserv Controller in the Java-EE. In addition, the ACTIVE SNMP-EE is also created. To configure the active nodes, the ACTIVE SNMP-EE injects a SNAP packet and the De/MUX intercepts it. Integrity of the ANEP-SNAP packet is guaranteed by the SEC function and the RCF component assigns QoS to a specific flow dynamically. Through this test, the FAIN network provides a secure and dynamic network configuration. In addition, users can create their Diffserv controller in their VE and configure them independently. Besides, we have realized communication between the Java-EE and the ACTIVE SNMP-EE. Usual active network framework is constructed based on one EE. However, our framework is constructed based on resources. The users can create multiple EEs in VE. Therefore it supports communication between EEs. In this sense, our architecture has high flexibility.

5   Conclusions and Future Work

In this paper, we have described the detailed components of the FAIN active node framework based on the novel Virtual Environment (VE) concept. The VE framework provides the natural coexistence of multiple EEs in each VE and it is supporting interactions between EEs. It has been validated by the communication between two types of Execution Environments: Java-EE and Active SNMP-EE. In addition, we have provided a secure control framework by the active packet. It has been guaranteed by the hop-by-hop and end-to-end authenticity and integrity checking of the active packet. Further more, we have controlled the Diffserv functions. In the near future, we will extend our framework to other resources and to other cases of autonomic deployment of services bringing just the right services to the customer at just the right context.

Acknowledgement. This paper describes work undertaken in the context of the FAIN – Information Society Technologies (IST) 10561 project. The IST program is partially funded by the Commission of the European Union.

References

1. FAIN Project WWW Server (FAIN Deliverable) - http://www.ist-fain.org
2. A. Galis, S. Denazis, C. Klein, C. Brou (eds.), book: "Programmable Networks and their Management", Artech House Books (www.artechhouse.com) , ISBN: 1-58053-745-6 (to be published 4th Quarter 2003)
3. S. Denazis, T. Suzuki, C. Kitahara, T. Becker, D. Gabrielcic, A. Lazanakis, W. Eaves, L. Cheng et al., "Final Active Node Architecture and Design", FAIN Deliverable 7, May 2003
4. P. Flury, E Boschi, T. Suzuki, C. Kitahara, D. Gabrielcic et al., "Evaluation Results and Recommendations", FAIN Deliverable 9, May 2003
5. S. Denazis, S. Karnouskos, T. Suzuki, S. Yoshizawa, "Component-based Execution Environments of Network Elements and a Protocol for their Configuration", IEEE - Transactions on Systems, Man and Cybernetics, Special Issue on Technologies that promote computational intelligence, openness and programmability in networks and Internet services, 2003 (to appear).
6. SNAP (Safe and Nimble Active Packets) - http://www.cis.upenn.edu/~dsl/SNAP/
7. D. Alexander, B. Braden, C. Gunter, A. Jackson, A. Keromytis, G. Minden, D Wetherall, "Active Network Encapsulation Protocol (ANEP)", Intrenet Draft - http://www.cis.upenn.edu/~switchware/ANEP/docs/ANEP.txt
8. Netfilter - http://www.netfilter.org/
9. C. Brou, C. Kitahara, C. Tsarouchis, J. Vivero et al, "Final Specification of Case Study Systems", FAIN Deliverable 8, May 2003
10. J. Moore, M.Hicks, S. Nettles, S., "Practical Programmable Packets", Proceedings IEEE INFOCOM 2001. Conference on Computer Communications. Twentieth Annual Joint Conference of the IEEE Computer and Communications Society.
11. D. Harrington, "An Architecture for Describing Simple Network Management Protocol (SNMP) Management Frameworks", RFC3411, December 2002, IETF.
12. W. Eaves, L. Cheng, A. Galis, "SNAP Based Resource Control for Active Networks", GLOBECOM 2002.
13. L. Cheng, W. Eaves, A. Galis, "Strong Authentication for Active Networks", accepted for presentation at and to appear in the proceedings of IEEE-Softcom 2003.
14. S. Vrontis, I. Sygkouna, M. Chantzawa, E. Sykas, "Enabling Distributed QoS Management utilizing Active Network Technology", 2003 IFIP-IEEE International Conference on Network Control and Engineering, 11-15.10, 2003, Muscat, Oman.

A Globally-Applied Component Model for Programmable Networking

Jó Ueyama[1], Geoff Coulson[1], Gordon S. Blair[1], Stefan Schmid[1],
Antônio T. Gomes[2], Ackbar Joolia[1], and Kevin Lee[1]

[1] Computing Department
Lancaster University
LA1 4YR Lancaster, UK
{ueyama, geoff, gordon, schmid, joolia, leek}@comp.lancs.ac.uk
[2] Departamento de Informática,
PUC-Rio
R. Marquês de São Vicente, 225 –Gávea – 22453-900, Rio de Janeiro, RJ, Brasil
{atagomes}@telemidia.puc-rio.br

Abstract. We argue that currently developed software frameworks for
active and programmable networking do not provide a truly generic approach
to the development, deployment, and management of services.
Furthermore, current systems are typically targeted at a particular level
of the programmable networking design space (e.g. at low-level, in-band,
packet forwarding; or at high-level signaling) and/or at a particular hardware
platform. In addition, most existing approaches, while they may address
the initial *configuration* of systems, neglect dynamic *reconfiguration*
of running systems. In this paper we present a reflective component-based
approach that addresses these limitations. We show how our approach
is applicable at all system levels, can be applied in heterogeneous hardware
environments (specifically, commodity PC-based routers and network
processor-based routers), and supports both initial configuration
and dynamic reconfiguration. We especially address the latter point; we
show the viability of our approach in (re)configuring services on an Intel
IXP1200 network processor-based router.

1 Introduction

Although significant progress has been made in programmable networking, numerous
research challenges remain. In particular, there remain important issues
clustered around *configurability* and *heterogeneity*. Programmable networking
systems must be highly configurable and, moreover, run-time reconfigurable, to
meet requirements for dynamic fine-grained deployment, 24x7 operation, managed
software evolution, dynamic quality of service (QoS) and resource management,
and configurable security [19]. Similarly, these systems must be easily
deployable in complex, multi-programming language, multi-operating system,
and multi-hardware platform environments, and offer transparency and portability
without sacrificing performance.

N. Wakamiya et al. (Eds.): IWAN 2003, LNCS 2982, pp. 202–214, 2004.
© IFIP International Federation for Information Processing 2004

In recent years significant progress has been made in the design and implementation of generic *component-based* systems-building methodologies (e.g. [THINK [11], OpenCOM [10], Knit [18]]) which, because of their emphasis on fine-grained configurability, reconfigurability, and system heterogeneity, have interesting implications, we believe, for programmable networking research. Based on these observations, we have initiated a project that is attempting to apply component-based principles to programmable networking environments.

Deriving from this project, this paper presents the design and implementation of a component-based architecture for programmable networking systems, which provides an integrated means of developing, deploying and managing such systems. The proposed architecture consists of i) a generic, reflective, component model that, we argue, can be uniformly applied at *all levels* of the programmable network design space (i.e., from fine-grained, low-level, in-band packet processing to high-level signaling and coordination), and ii) an extensible architecture of component frameworks that are built in terms of the generic component model and support plug-in functionality in diverse areas of the programmable network design space. The claimed benefits of the proposed architecture are detailed in section 3.

The paper is structured as follows. First, section 2 provides background to our approach: it presents the basics of our reflective component model, introduces the concept of component frameworks, and provides a brief overview of the network processor-based router environment in which we are primarily working. Section 3 then presents our "globally applied" approach to network programmability, and section 4 discusses our results and implementation efforts so far. Subsequently, section 5 presents an application scenario that illustrates our approach. Finally, section 6 surveys and analyses related work; and section 7 offers conclusions.

2   Background

2.1   OpenCOM

Lancaster's OpenCOM [7] is a lightweight, efficient, flexible, and language-independent component model that was originally developed as part of previous research on configurable middleware [10]. OpenCOM is fine-grained in that its scope is intra-capsule (see below for definition of "capsule") and it imposes minimal overhead on cross-component invocation. It is currently implemented on top of a subset of Mozilla's XPCOM platform [16].

OpenCOM relies on five fundamental concepts:

Capsules: a capsule is a logical "component container" that may encompass multiple address spaces (although capsules do not cross machine boundaries). For example, a capsule could encapsulate multiple Linux processes, or different hardware domains on a network processor-based router. Encapsulating multiple address spaces offers a powerful means of abstracting over tightly-coupled but heterogeneous hardware (e.g. the PC, StrongARM and micro-engines of an Intel IXP1200 router platform; see section 2.3 and figure 1).

Components: components serve as programming language-independent units of deployable functionality. One builds systems by loading components into capsules, and then composing these with other components (by binding their interfaces and receptacles; see below).

Interfaces: interfaces of components are expressed in a language independent interface definition language and express a unit of service provision; multiple interfaces can be supported per component.

Receptacles: define a unit of service requirement on a component and are used to make explicit the dependency of one component on others.

Bindings: are associations between receptacles and interfaces in the same capsule: a binding represents a communication path between one receptacle and one interface. Bindings in the original OpenCOM implementation [10] were exclusively implemented in terms of vtables [3] (a vtable is essentially a table containing pointers to virtual functions). Currently, however, we are extending OpenCOM to support bindings implemented in a variety of ways (see section 4).

Importantly, OpenCOM also supports a range of built-in *reflective meta-models* which form the basis of configuration and reconfiguration in our approach. In particular, it supports an *architecture* meta-model that represents compositions of components as a graph, and allows the programmer to manipulate this graph to effect corresponding changes on the underlying systems (e.g. in terms of inserting/ deleting components and making/ breaking bindings). It also supports an *interception* meta-model that enables the insertion of arbitrary code within bindings that is executed when a call is made across the binding; and an *interface* meta-model that allows the programmer to introspect on available interface and receptacle types on a component. There is also a *resources* meta-model that represents types and quantities of resources dedicated to various components or sets of components. More details on the reflective meta-models are given in [10].

OpenCOM deploys a singleton per-capsule runtime, which manages a repository of component types and provides interfaces for the creation and deletion of components and for binding/ unbinding. All create/delete/bind/unbind requests are reflected in the above-mentioned architecture meta-model.

A crucial aspect of OpenCOM that is heavily exploited in our programmable networking research is its support for *plug-in loaders* and *plug-in binders*. Essentially, loading and binding are viewed as components frameworks (see below) in the OpenCOM architecture, and it is possible to extend the architecture with many and various implementations on loading and binding. We return to this topic in section 4 below.

2.2 Component Frameworks

Although necessary, the component model's explicit representation of dependencies and its reflective meta-models are not in themselves sufficient for the management of reconfiguration. In particular, their genericity precludes *specific* competencies in imposing and policing domain-imposed constraints on reconfiguration. For example, they cannot prevent the nonsensical replacement of an H.263 encoder with an MPEG encoder, or mandate that a packet scheduler must always receive its input from a packet classifier. Such semantic constraints are essential if we are to ensure meaningful configuration and reconfiguration, and therefore the system must provide support for their expression and enforcement.

To add the necessary dimension of specificity and constraint, we apply the notion of *component frameworks*. These were originally defined by Szyperski [22] as "collections of rules and interfaces that govern the interaction of a set of components 'plugged into' them" (see figure 4). More concretely, component frameworks (hereafter, CFs) are targeted at a specific domain and embody 'rules and interfaces' that make sense in that domain. For example, a packet-forwarding CF might accept packet-scheduler components as plug-ins; or a media-stream filtering CF might accept various media codecs as plug-ins [10]. (In the rest of the paper we use the shorthand "plug-in" to refer to a component that is plugged into a CF.)

Essentially, CFs serve as "life-support environments" for components in a particular domain of application. They contain arbitrary CF-specific state, embody shared services for plug-ins, and actively police their plug-ins to ensure that they conform to their domain-specific rules and interfaces (e.g. interfaces can be inspected at run-time using the interface meta-model). CFs can support multiple instances of multiple types of plug-in, and plug-ins can either be independent of each other or can be bound together in arbitrary configurations (as long as these conform to the rules imposed by the host CF).

Overall, our component-based approach is strongly predicated on the benefits of reflection and CFs: reflection provides an open and flexible architecture by supporting the inspection, adaptation and extension of underlying component topologies, while CFs provide runtime structure for domain-specific configurations of components and encapsulate domain-specific rules and constraints.

In our programmable networking research we have designed a generic "Router CF" on top of OpenCOM that enables the flexible configuration and reconfiguration of software routers. This is described in detail in [9]. The use of the Router CF is illustrated in section 5.

2.3   The Radisys Intel IXP1200-Based Router

The Radisys Development Platform, on which we are basing the bulk of our router implementation work, is based on the Intel IXP1200 network processor. This is an Intel-proprietary architecture that conforms to the Intel IXA architecture [12]. It is attached to a host PC and combines a StrongARM processor (running Linux) with six independent 32-bit RISC processors called microengines, which have hardware multithread support, and are used for fast-path processing. There are also various types of memories, buses, and specialised hardware assists available on the processor. The outline architecture is illustrated in 1.

Programming support on the router is very primitive, especially in the microengine environment. This environment does not run an operating system and all

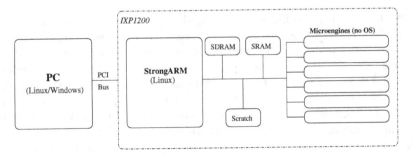

Fig. 1. Testbed–PC and IXP1200 router

resource allocation and inter-process communication has to be manually managed. The current Intel-provided programming environment has no support for dynamic reconfiguration.

3   Our Approach to Building Programmable Networking Software

3.1   The Design-Space of Programmable Networking

We conceptually partition the global design space of programmable networking [9] into four layers or *strata*. We use the term "stratum" rather than "layer" to avoid confusion with layered protocol architectures. The four strata are illustrated in figure 2.

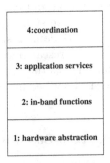

Fig. 2. Stratification of the Programmable Networking Design Space

The *hardware abstraction* stratum contains necessary hardware and operating system functionality such as threads, memory, I/O, and library loading. Services in this stratum are often implemented as wrappers around underlying native facilities in order to support heterogeneous platforms. The *in-band functions* stratum consists of packet processing functions like packet filters, checksum validators, classifiers, diffserv schedulers, and traffic shapers. Given that these are low-level, in-band and fine-grained (and therefore highly performance critical) performance is a key concern in this stratum. The *application services* stratum encompasses coarser-grained functions (in the active networking execution environment sense [1]). These are less performance critical as they act on pre-selected packet flows in application specific ways (e.g. per-flow media filters). Finally, the *coordination* stratum supports out-of-band signalling protocols which carry out distributed coordination, including configuration and reconfiguration of the lower strata. It includes, for example, routing protocols, signalling protocols such as RSVP, or architectures that allow resource allocation in dynamic private virtual networks (e.g. Genesis [4], Draco [13], or Darwin [6]).

3.2   Benefits of a Globally-Applied Component-Based Approach

We argue that our proposed approach of uniformly applying the same component model, supported by the notions of reflection and CFs, yields the following potential benefits:

- *a simple and uniform model* (based on OpenCOM)–we provide a simple and uniform programming model for thecreation of services in all strata, and also a uniform run-time environment for deployment, and (re)configuration; a key aspect here is the separation of concerns between building systems (using the basic component model) and managing/ reconfiguring them (using a combination of reflective meta-models and CFs).
- *enables bespoke software configurations*–according to the composition of CFs in each stratum, desired functionality can be achieved while minimising memory footprint; trade-offs will vary for different system types (e.g. embedded, wireless devices; large-scale core routers);
- *facilitates ad-hoc interaction*–e.g. application or transport layer components can directly access (subject to access policies) "layer-violating" information from, e.g., the link layer; this kind of "layer-breaking" is of growing interest in the research community [2].

We are applying our approach in PC-based routers as well as the Intel IXP1200 environment discussed above. This heterogeneity is fundamental to validate our claim of a generic model. We also strive to implement this model without compromising performance so that we can reasonably apply the approach in the lower as well as the higher strata (see section 4).

4   Implementation

To pursue the approach, we are extending OpenCOM to enable highly configurable *loading* and *binding* of components in all strata of the programmable networking design space. As mentioned in section 2.1, the core architecture supports these two functions, loading and binding, as CFs.

The API for loading and binding is as follows (*capsule_id* specifies the capsule where the component will be loaded or already resides–see figure 3; *Component_guid*, *interface_guid* and *receptacle_guid* are globally unique IDs for components, interfaces and receptacles respectively):

- `load(capsule_id, component_guid);`
- `unload(capsule_id, component_guid);`
- `bind(receptacle_guid, interface_guid);`
- `unbind(receptacle_guid, interface_guid);`

These API calls are IDL-specified for language independence, and the CFs underlying them are system-independent. However, underlying these CFs are system-dependent plug-in loader and binder components which are dynamically installed/ removed by means of a meta-interface on the CFs. As explained below, the ability to transparently access this system-dependent functionality from a system-independent API is key to the power and generality of our design.

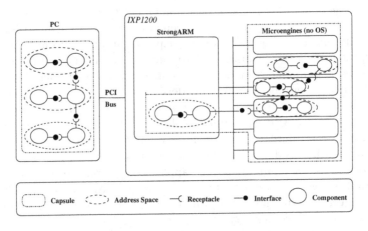

Fig. 3. Multi-address-space capsules

We have implemented plug-in loader components (or *loaders*) that load components into Windows address spaces, Linux address spaces, and IXP1200 microengines. In the general case, the programmer may either select a specific loader manually, or (more commonly) elect for transparency and let the CF make the choice. In the former case, the programmer would use the architecture meta-model to make the alternatives visible, and then interact with a specific loader. In the latter case, the selection is made on the basis of attributes attached to both components and loaders (e.g. a "*CPU-type*" or "*OS-type*" attribute). Loaders themselves may espouse a further level of choice (which may also be attribute driven) of which address space to load into. For example, a microengine loader might make a choice of which microengine to use for a particular load request by taking into account factors such as resource usage, QoS, and security/ safety constraints. Furthermore, it is possible, using a "placement" meta-model supported by the loader, to manually control this placement if desired.

In addition, we have implemented the following set of plug-in binding components (or *binders*):

- *vtable-based* – This binder was implemented as part of the original OpenCOM platform. It operates only in the Linux environment (on the host PC or StrongARM) and enables the binding of any component generated by a compiler whose binaries employ the vtable function-call convention.
- *shared memory* – We have developed a microengine-specific binder that uses shared memory (i.e., scratch memory, static and dynamic RAM - SRAM and SDRAM; see figure 1), to bind components that reside in different microengines. We also have a shared memory binder that binds a microengine-based component to a Linux-based component; and another that binds two components running in different Linux processes.
- *branch instruction* – This binder enables bindings between components on the same microengine. Essentially, a component is bound to another (cf. Netbind [5]) by rewriting a branch instruction so that execution jumps to the desired target.

As with the loader CF, the programmer may either select a binder manually, or elect for transparency and let the binder CF make the choice on the basis of attributes and heuristics.

Importantly, it is not necessary in our architecture to execute the OpenCOM runtime on the microengines (which would, in any case, be infeasible). Instead, the pluggable loader/ binder frameworks running in a Linux process on the StrongARM control processor subsume all the microengine specifics. These are then encapsulated within specific plug-in loaders/ binders. The end result is that the programmer has the benefit of full transparency while retaining the full generality of the programming model regardless of which environment his/her code is running in.

We have not yet carried out a comprehensive performance evaluation of the IXP1200-specific loaders and binders. We observe, however, that the overhead of establishing and reconfiguring bindings is entirely "out-of-band" and does not impact data flowing between components. The major factor impacting the overhead of in-band inter-component communication is the choice of binding mechanism involved. As we are using essentially the same mechanisms as other well-evaluated systems (i.e. Netbind and MicroACE [12]) there is no reason to expect that performance should suffer. The one OpenCOM-specific feature that might significantly impact performance is the *number* of inter-component bindings involved – which is a function of the granularity of components. Again, based on evaluations of previous fine-grained systems such as Click [15] we have no a-priori reason to believe that fine-grained componentisation is necessarily problematic.

5   Application Scenario

To demonstrate our approach, we present a configuration of our recently-implemented Router CF (that was mentioned in 2.1) which covers strata 2, 3, and 4 (the OpenCOM runtime itself deals with statum 1 by wrapping the underlying OS with CFs for thread management, buffer pool management etc.). The below scenario demonstrates how OpenCOM's (re)configuration capabilities can be used to extend the network services on a router at run-time. In addition, the scenario emphasizes the benefits of a single, uniformly-applied, component model, which allows configuration and reconfiguration of service components across several strata of the programmable network design space and across different hardware environments (i.e., a PC and an IXP1200-based router). It also shows how reconfiguration can be carried out in dimensions that have not been foreseen when the system was designed.

The Router CF configuration illustrated in Figure 4 (minus the dotted box) is a typical configuration for IP forwarding. It consists of several low-level, in-band components (stratum 2) on the "fast-path" of the router, namely a classifier and a forwarder, as well as scheduling components, an application service-level component (stratum 3) for the processing of IP options on the "slow-path", and a "routing protocol" CF in the control plane of the router (stratum 4).

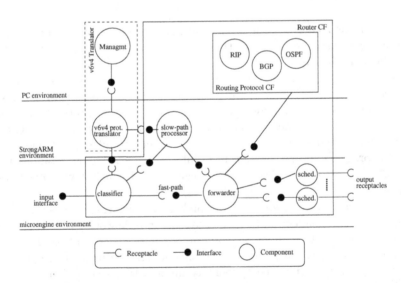

Fig. 4. IPv6v4 translator application scenario

To best exploit the capabilities of the different hardware elements of the IXP1200, we target the above functions at the hardware best suited to them. Thus, we deploy the "fast-path" components on the microengines, the IP options component on the StrongARM, and the routing protocol CF on the PC. Note that we can additionally exploit the multi-address-space capsule feature of OpenCOM to address security/ safety issues. For example, we can load un-trusted components into separate address spaces (within the same capsule) so that they cannot maliciously or accidentally disrupt or crash the whole system.

To illustrate run-time reconfigurability, we dynamically install IPv6-to-IPv4 protocol translation functionality (collectively called a "translator"), into the ini-tial configuration (note that, like the Router CF itself, the translator is spread across different layers of the router architecture: while the actual protocol trans-lation takes place on the StrongARM, management is performed on the PC). Such dynamic extensibility might be required to adapt to a network environ-ment providing IPv6 support without needing to restart the network device. For example, if our system was running on a mobile PDA, we would only require IPv6 functionality when we become attached to a fixed network. When oper-ating in a wireless network environment, we can save memory by omitting this functionality.

To integrate the translator we first attempt to load its two consituent compo-nents into the appropriate address spaces. This is achieved transparently (based on a "CPU-type" attribute attached to the components) by the loader CF. Fur-thermore, the CF checks that the components being loaded conform to its rules (e.g. the interface meta-model is used to ensure that they support appropriate interfaces/ receptacles). We then obtain a new receptacle on the classifier, and, by manipulating the architecture meta-model, arrange for this to be bound to the translator. An appropriate binder is selected transparently (by the binding CF). We could also use the resources meta-model to ensure that the translator has adequate resources (e.g. in terms of its thread priorities, and buffer pool availability) to perform with a required level of QoS. And, we could additionally add an interceptor to the binding to count the number of IPv6 packets actually forwarded. Note that none of these steps need to have been foreseen when the initial configuration was defined, and that they are entirely decoupled from the basic functionality of the components involved.

6   Related Work

The various NodeOS implementations (e.g. the Scout-based implementation re-ported in [17]) address generic system support for active and programmable networking. However, they do not focus primarily on building programmability in terms of componentisation – rather they are targeted at the support of coarse-grained execution environments (mainly strata 2 and 3) which themselves may or may not internally support componentisation.

Recent work at FOKUS, Berlin [21] discusses a flexible component-based architecture for programmable routers. Like our work, this aims at language in-dependence and system heterogeneity. However, the initial implementation work has been in a Java environment which has to date precluded applying the ap-proach in the fast-path, and in network processor-based routers. In addition, the work focuses of the managment of dynamic deployment rather than unplanned reconfiguration.

VERA [14] is a strata 2 and 3 extensible router architecture that explicitly supports adding new components, such as packet forwarders, to routers. VERA is also deployed on network processor-based routers (specifically, Intel IXP1200-based). However, VERA's architecture is limited in its flexibility: extensions can only be added at pre-defined "hooks" provided by the system. In addition, key elements of the architecture itself (e.g. the router and hardware abstractions, as well as the distributed router OS) can not be removed or changed. Furthermore, VERA's component model does not address the provision of services belonging to all strata of the networking design space.

NetBind [5] proposes an approach to construct in-band packet-forwarding paths on a network processor-based router (again, based on the IXP1200), and to reconfigure forwarding paths dynamically. Low latency in these paths, despite the possibility of changing them at run-time, is one of the outstanding features of NetBind. This is achieved by patching branch instructions at the machine code level which involves minimal overhead (we borrow this technique from Netbind; see section 4). Nevertheless, NetBind is not a generic framework for adding new services on network processor-based routers; e.g., it does not address strata 3 or 4. Instead, it aims to tackle solely the construction of dynamic data paths. In addition, like VERA, there are many parts of the architecture which can neither be configured at deploy-time, nor reconfigured at run-time.

Click [15] is an extensible component-based router targeted at PC-based environments. A Click router is constructed by selecting from a library of components called "elements" that carry out fine-grained tasks, and which are aggregated into a graph structure. Click offers extensibility by providing a straightforward and flexible means of defining new configurations; but, crucially, it does not support dynamic reconfiguration. Although Click was not initially deployed on network processor based routers, NP-Click [20] is a recent implementation for such environments (but this still suffers from the same lack of dynamic reconfiguration).

Villazón [23] introduces the use of reflection to support flexible configuration in active networks, but this work only addresses an architecture in which active nodes use reflection better to structure services. Essentially, the work defines a reflective architecture for configuration rather than (re-)configuration.

Overall, while there has been substantial research addressing the need for configurability in active and programmable networks, few approaches address both configuration and reconfiguration in a fully general and comprehensive manner. For example, some systems, like VERA, support reconfiguration, but only in pre-determined ways. Furthermore, most of these systems are *partial*, addressing either high-level concerns (e.g. the Villazón work) or low-level concerns (e.g. Netbind). None of them proposes an integrated architecture allowing configuration and reconfiguration of services running in all strata.

7 Conclusions

In this paper we have proposed a generic component-based model for programmable networking systems that enables (re)configuration of systems using reflective techniques and CFs. A key strength of this model is that it is based on a platform and language-independent approach, which can be applied across different network processing hardware. Furthermore, we argue that the proposed framework can be applied to configure and reconfigure component-based services on all levels (strata) of the design space of a programmable network system.

We believe that such a globally-applied component model has the potential to greatly facilitate the (re)configuration of services, as a single, unified programming model is used to compose and adapt services across the different strata of the design space.

Furthermore, we expect our framework to considerably facilitate the programmability and reconfigurability of network processor-based systems. These architectures are widely acknowledged to be very difficult to program [8] and, as a consequence, reconfiguration is hardly considered on these "primitive" platforms. However, the provision of an OpenCOM-based programming model for these architectures gives the programmer a friendly interface (abstraction) with which to orchestrate low-level functions in a uniform manner, and also facilitates the imposition, via the CF concept, of domain-specific constraints on these routers.

Acknowledgements. Jó Ueyama would like to thank the National Council for Scientific and Technological Development (CNPq - Brazil) for sponsoring his scholarship at Lancaster University (Ref. 200214/01-2). We would also like to thank Intel Corp for their generous donation of equipament, and the UK EPSRC for funding the bulk of our research.

References

1. ANTS. The ants toolkit. `http://www.cs.utah.edu/flux/janos/ants.html`, 2002.
2. R. Braden, T. Faber, and M. Handley. From Protocol Stack to Protocol Heap — Role-Based Architecture. In *ACM SIGCOMM Computer Communication Review*, volume 33, No 1, January 2003.
3. K. Brown. Building a Lightweight COM Interception Framework Part 1: The Universal Delegator. *Microsoft Systems Journal*, January 1999.
4. A. Campbell, Meer G., M. Kounavis, K. Miki, J. Vicente, and D. Villela. The Genesis Kernel: A virtual network operating system for spawning network architectures. In *OPENARCH'99 - Open Architecture and Networking Programming*, New York, USA, March 1999.
5. A.T. Campbell, M.E. Kounavis, D.A. Villela, J.B. Vicente, H.G. de Meer, K. Miki, and K.S. Kalaichelvan. NetBind: A Binding Tool for Constructing Data Paths in Network Processor-based Routers. In *5th IEEE International Conference on Open Architectures and Network Programming (OPENARCH'02)*, June 2002.

6. P. Chandra, A. Fisher, C. Kosak, T.S.E. Ng, P. Steenkiste, E. Takahashi, and H. Zhang. Darwin: Customizable Resource Management for Value-added Network Services. In *6th IEEE Intl. Conf. on Network Protocols (ICNP 98)*, Austin, Texas, USA, October 1998.

7. M. Clarke, G.S. Blair, G. Coulson, and N. Parlavantzas. An Efficient Component Model for the Construction of Adaptive Middleware. In *Proceedings of the IFIP/ACM Middleware 2001*, Heidelberg, November 2001.

8. D. Comer. *Network Systems Design using Network Processors*. Prentice Hall, 2003.

9. G. Coulson, G. Blair, T. Gomes, A. Joolia, K. Lee, J. Ueyama, and Y. Ye. Position paper: A Reflective Middleware-based Approach to Programmable Networking. In *ACM/IFIP/USENIX International Middleware Conference*, Rio de Janeiro, Brazil, June 2003.

10. G. Coulson, Blair G.S., M. Clarke, and N. Parlavantzas. The Design of a Highly Configurable and Reconfigurable Middleware Platform. *ACM Distributed Computing Journal*, 15(2):109–126, April 2002.

11. J.P. Fassino, J.B. Stefani, J. Lawall, and G. Muller. THINK: A Software Framework for Component-based Operating System Kernels. In *USENIX 2002 Annual Conference*, June 2002.

12. Intel. Intel IXP1200. http://www.intel.com/IXA, 2002.

13. R. Isaacs and I. Leslie. Support for Resource-Assured and Dynamic Virtual Private Networks. In *JSAC Special Issue on Active and Programmable Networks*, 2001.

14. S. Karlin and L. Peterson. VERA: An Extensible Router Architecture. In *4th International Conference on Open Architectures and Network Programming (OPENARCH)*, April 2001.

15. R. Morris, Kohler E., J. Jannoti, and M. Kaashoek. The Click Modular Router. In *17th ACM Symposium on Operating Systems Principles (SOSP'99)*, Charleston, SC, USA, December 1999.

16. Mozilla Organization. XPCOM Project.
http://www.mozilla.org/projects/xpcom, 2001.

17. L. Peterson, Y. Gottlieb, M. Hibler, P. Tullmann, J. Lepreau, S. Schwab, H. Dandelkar, A. Purtell, and J. Hartman. An OS Interface for Active Routers. *IEEE Journal on Selected Areas in Communications*, 19(3):473–487, March 2001.

18. A. Reid, M. Flatt, L Stoller, J. Lepreau, and E. Eide. Knit: Component Composition for Systems Software. In *Proc. of the 4th Operating Systems Design and Implementation (OSDI)*, pages 347–360, October 2000.

19. S. Schmid, T. Chart, M. Sifalakis, and A Scott. Flexible, Dynamic, and Scalable Service Composition for Active Routers. In *IWAN 2002 IFIP-TC6 4th International Working Conference*, volume 2546, pages 253–266, Zurich, Switzerland, December 2002.

20. N. Shah, W. Plishker, and K. Keutzer. NP-Click: A Programming Model for the Intel IXP1200. In *2nd Workshop on Network Processors (NP-2) at the 9th International Symposium on High Performance Computer Architecture (HPCA-9)*, Anaheim, CA, February 2003.

21. M. Solarski, M. Bossardt, and T. Becker. Component-based Deployment and Management of Services in Active Networks. In *Proceedings of the Fourth Annual International Working Conference on Active Networks IWAN*, Zurich, Switzerland, December 2002.

22. C. Szyperski. *Component Software: Beyond Object-Oriented Programming*. Addison-Wesley, second edition, 2002.

23. A. Villazón. A Reflective Active Network Node. In *IWAN*, pages 87–101, 2000.

Active Routers in Action:
Evaluation of the LARA++ Active Router Architecture in a Real-Life Network[1]

Tim Chart, Stefan Schmid, Manolis Sifalakis, and Andrew C. Scott

Distributed Multimedia Research Group, Computing Department,
Lancaster University, Lancaster, LA1 4YR
{chart, sschmid, mjs, acs}@comp.lancs.ac.uk

Abstract. The paper reports on lessons learned from developing, deploying and operating LARA++ based active routers [1] along with a number of active services used daily in a real-life network environment. We evaluate how LARA++, which claims to be a truly generic and flexible active router architecture, performs when deployed in an operational network. The architecture is assessed whilst providing a range of diverse active services from well-known network services like NAT and firewalls to novel types of services such as Mobile IPv6 handoff optimisation. A particular challenge we consider is the transparent and concurrent introduction of new services by different end users and network administrators.

Besides a qualitative evaluation of the LARA++ architecture, the paper provides a number of quantitative results that show the performance of LARA++ whilst providing the different services. The results indicate that LARA++ not only supports highly generic programmability by independent users, but also provides sufficient performance for today's edge networks.

1   Introduction

Active and programmable network technologies were conceived to allow the introduction of new, value added services inside the network. This is particularly the case for edge networks, close to the end-user, where the demand for such services is highest. This trend is seen in today's networks, where most sophisticated functionality remains within the access or edge networks (for example, firewalls, NATs and v4/v6 transitioning mechanisms), while the core evolves into a 'simple' high-speed routing/switching network.

To be successful in edge networks, active and programmable network architectures must be sufficiently flexible and generic to accommodate not only a diverse range of current services, but also future services that have not yet been conceived. Moreover, the fact that routers are shared resources, which have to provide network services for end-users with different application and service requirements at the same time, further emphasises the importance of flexible and generic programmability.

---

[1] This research is funded by the EPSRC (grant number GR/R31461/01)

N. Wakamiya et al. (Eds.): IWAN 2003, LNCS 2982, pp. 215–227, 2004.

Most current active router platforms fall at this first hurdle. Some are built with only a specific range of services in mind (for example, network management [2,3], signalling [4], and multicast [5,6]), while others fail to provide the necessary flexibility or extensibility to dynamically deploy new types of services, which have not been considered by the developers (for example, Scout [7], Click [8] and RouterPlugins [9]). Yet, the most neglected requirement in today's active router architectures is support for service composition enabling the installation and management of diverse services by independent users who may be unaware of each other.

In this paper we analyse the experiences gained from deploying active routers in real edge networks where several network services such as network address translation, firewall and mobile handoff optimisation are needed. We have learned that any active router platform that aspires to be genuinely useful in such an environment must exhibit a number of properties. It must be generic and flexible enough to support a diverse range of active services. It must also allow multiple services to co-exist and, where necessary, overlap so that a suitable service composite is generated. And finally, the service composition framework orchestrating multiple services on an active router must allow independent users (for example, network administrators and end users) to integrate active services in a meaningful and structured manner. The main aim of this paper is to relate our experience of deploying actual services on a real active router platform exhibiting these properties.

The rest of this paper is structured as follows: Section 2 recaps the main elements of the LARA++ architecture that are relevant to this paper. In section 3, we describe three LARA++ active components that have been developed, deployed and tested in a real-life edge network. Section 4 relates LARA++ to other active and programmable network solutions. Finally, we conclude in section 5 with some lessons learnt from our experiences with LARA++.

2   LARA++ Architecture

LARA++ [1] is a software augmentation designed for router and commodity operating systems; implementations currently exist for Microsoft Windows XP, Server 2003 and also Windows CE. LARA++ embodies a framework that exposes a programmable interface, which allows active programs, referred to as *active components*, to provide network services on LARA++ active nodes, and will operate on any packet or frame-based network.

LARA++ installs "hooks" directly into the host OS in order to allow the transparent interception of packets passing through the node. Packets are re-injected back into the host OS subsequent to processing. The placement of these hooks is crucial to the interoperation of LARA++ active components with the conventional network services of the router. Since packets are intercepted and re-injected in such a way that they still pass though the host-provided routing and delivery engine, LARA++ can extend the functionality of the router's conventional network services. Although this is not a required behaviour, as packets can also be fully processed and directly forwarded by LARA++ components, it enables lightweight augmentation of network services and allows for gradual replacement of conventional router functions.

LARA++ treats a router as a resource shared by all of its users. The extent to which it is programmable by individual users is configurable by the router administrator. By means of node-local policies, the administrator can restrict access to packets that pass through the router and the resources of the router. In addition to the security provided by resource and access control, users are protected from each other's actions by a safety model that gives each component a sandbox called a *processing environment* (PE). LARA++ also allows users that trust each other and all of the components of a user to execute inside the same PE. Because this safety is provided at the operating system level, LARA++ does not need to restrict programmability using language safety features like dynamic type checking or by enforcing the use of type-safe languages such as Java or Caml [10].

LARA++ uses a sophisticated model for service composition [11] enabling components from many sources, including users and applications, to be merged into a single composite service. Each component that is to become part of the service composite installs *packet filters* into the nodes of an extensible directed graph, referred to as the *classification graph*. The classification graph defines the structure and semantics for binding active components together in a meaningful way; in other words, providing the 'glue' for the composition of the overall service.

Packet filters inserted by components into the nodes of the classification graph specify the kind of packets a component wishes to process. Each filter consists of a number of rules that LARA++ uses to determine whether packets match the filter. While these *component filters* hook the functionality or service provided by a component into the desired position on the forwarding path, other filters, referred to as *graph-filters,* are used to form the arcs between nodes in the classification graph. Figure 1 illustrates this in more detail and illustrates how conditional branches in the graph allow packets to be reclassified as they traverse the graph.

This model of service composition offers several major advantages over other active router classification systems. The use of a dynamically configurable and extensible classification graph allows LARA++ to process packets on any type of packet-based network from standard IP networks, through networks with ANEP-based active packet encapsulation [12], to bespoke signalling networks. LARA++ is simply configured with an appropriate classification graph by the node administrator.

In order to make use of the graph, users must know its basic structure. For that reason, we define a well-known structure for general processing of packets in IP and IPv6-based networks. This structure, called the *classification graph table* (CGT), may be customized with finer-grained classification where appropriate.

The filter-based packet interception and the classification graph make LARA++ a platform on which active components with overlapping interests, in terms of the packets they wish to handle, can operate without disrupting each other. For example, if one component installs a filter to express an interest in all packets containing a specific IP option, and another expresses an interest in all TCP SYN packets, the classification graph delivers packets that match both filters to both components in the order defined by the graph. Therefore, service composition on a LARA++ active router is defined implicitly by the classification graph, and it can be exploited as a medium to manage both co-operation and competition between active components.

As packets traverse the classification graph, they are redirected to components with matching filters, where they are processed. Once the component has released the packet, the process of classifying the packet is resumed in the classification graph. Both explicit and implicit ordering of processing can be achieved by placing filters at different points in the graph, and through the structure of the graph, components can co-operate and compete safely.

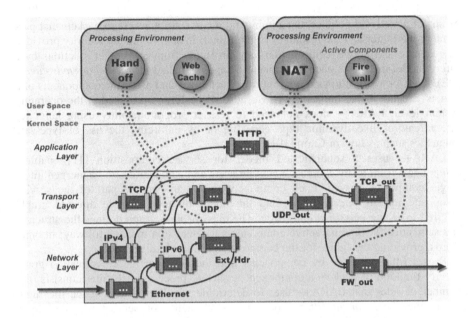

Fig. 1. Classification Graph, showing how components express interest in classes of packet.

Packet filters are extremely flexible from the component writer's viewpoint as they can limit component processing to specific packet flows. Packets can be identified using a powerful bit pattern recognition mechanism and by performing calculations and comparisons on the information in the packet. Once a packet is matched, the filter defines how to direct packets around the classification graph and send packets up to components for processing. The whole system of the classification graph and packet filters is protected from misuse by a permission-based security scheme.

LARA++ filters are easily specified and installed by active components using an XML-based mark-up language supporting the complex nature of filters, which have to be flexible enough to give components the power to identify classes of packets based upon non-trivial features and characteristics. The filter description language provides a similar degree of flexibility to that provided by the Berkeley Packet Filter [13], but with a higher level of representation. The function of filters specified using this mark-up is easily discernable, but in contrast to other high-level languages such as ANQL [14], our filter mark-up language does not depend upon a pre-defined or standardised naming scheme for packet fields. Figure 2 illustrates a filter that intercepts HTTP requests over IPv4.

LARA++ does not restrict the way in which code is loaded onto active routers. Any component with the authority to instantiate other components may do so. This flexibility allows code to be instantiated in various ways, namely from a local copy of the component already held on the active router, by explicit out-of-band code loading techniques, or using in-band code directly from packets traversing the node. As part of the LARA++ project, we have developed a generic active service discovery and deployment protocol (ASDP) [15], which is an open "pluggable" protocol to support user-definable out-of-band code loading mechanisms.

```
<Filter Name="HTTP-FILTER" InstallationNode="TCP">
    <Rule>
        <Requirement Name="IP-Protocol" Type="Pattern"
         Length="1" BitField="40" BitMask="f0"
         Offset="Focus{IP}"/>
        <Requirement Name="HTTP-Port" Type="Pattern"
         Length="2" BitField="00 50" BitMask="ff ff"
         Offset="This + 2"/>
        <MatchingRule Rule="IP-Protocol && HTTP-Port"/>
    </Rule>
    <Processing Operation=<FilterId> AccessMode="rw"/>
</Filter>
```

Fig. 2. Filter mark-up to intercept HTTP requests carried by an IPv4 transport.

As a result of the LARA++ safety model, which restricts the execution of untrusted code to isolated processing environments, LARA++ does not impose any restrictions in terms of programming languages. As a consequence, active components can be implemented in the developer's favourite programming language (for example, C, C++, C# or Java). All that is needed to support yet another programming language is an implementation of the compact LARA++ programming API as a library acceptable to the target language development tools. This feature also allows component developers to utilise existing language and platform debugging tools (for example, Microsoft Visual Studio.Net) to debug components running live on top of LARA++ as packets flow through them. Due to the often complicated nature of network software, and particularly the semantic leap from conventional to active networks, we believe that this is an invaluable feature.

3   Experimentation with Real-Life Active Network Services

In order to demonstrate the ease with which LARA++ active components can be developed and deployed, we have implemented a number of active components with tasks ranging from remote packet capture (i.e. a "tcpdump" for remote routers) to complex packet routing components. In this section, we detail the development and operation of some of these components.

3.1   Fast Handoff for Mobile-IPv6

Mobile-IPv6 [16] is a technology, recently approved for RFC, which allows network hosts (mobile nodes) to move between subnets whilst remaining addressable via their permanent address (home address). The main functionality is based on the existence of an agent node (home agent) at the mobile node's home network that is responsible for intercepting all traffic destined to the mobile node and relaying it (using tunnels) to the mobile's current network address (care-of address) in the visiting network.

As a routing optimisation, the communication peer (correspondent node) can be informed of the mobile node's care-of address (using a message called a binding update), which allows it to send packets directly to the mobile's actual network location rather than through the home agent. While this optimization is necessary to prevent scalability issues and improve efficiency, it leads to an awkward situation when the mobile node migrates to a new subnet. Upon configuring its new address, the mobile node will send a binding update to the correspondent node informing it of its new care-of address. Since the correspondent cannot address packets to the new care-of address until the binding update has arrived, packets will still be arriving on the subnet of the old care-of address for at least one round-trip time between the mobile node and the correspondent. These packets would be lost unless the mobile node still had an interface configured on that subnet, which is typically not the case.

Using LARA++ active routers on our mobile access network, we can circumvent this deficiency by augmenting the handoff process using an active component installed at a router close to the handoff. The active component performs "re-routing" of traffic destined to the mobile node's old care-of address to the new care-of address.[2] This simple optimisation reduces the delay between the mobile node sending the binding update and packets being received at the new care-of address to almost nothing, and more importantly greatly reduces the packet loss during handoff procedure. The basic idea of this mechanism along with more details concerning its operation has been previously published by the authors [17].

This Mobile-IPv6 handoff optimisation can be deployed in two ways on an active router: pre-emptively or on-demand. In the pre-emptive scenario, a network administrator or service provider might roll out a component onto strategically chosen active routers as a service to network users. The component would listen for binding updates from all machines on the subnets, and perform the routing optimisation when it detects a mobile node handing off. In the on-demand scenario, the mobile node would dynamically instantiate a component to redirect packets on a convenient active router after it had detected it had moved, or before it moved if it had advance warning (for example, from layer 2 drivers). LARA++ can support both approaches.

Implementing the Mobile-IPv6 handoff optimisation as a LARA++ active component is conceptually quite simple. Essentially, our implementation uses the pre-emptive approach and installs one packet filter to intercept all home address options that pass through the node. A typical LARA++ configuration would not allow just anybody to install such a wide-ranging filter, so that is why this approach is only suitable for a network administrator. Untrusted users should only have permission to install filters on their own flows of packets.

Some implementations of Mobile-IPv6 allow a different care-of address to be used for the same home address when talking to different correspondents. This is useful for multi-homed devices where the routing mechanism decides that the most efficient route to two different correspondents may be via two different interfaces, but it adds additional complexity to the handoff optimisation component. It requires the component to keep track of each correspondent node and mobile node pair. This scalability issue could be a reason why active router administrators may prefer individual users to install the component for their own flows rather than to provide the handoff optimisation service to all users.

Once a home address option is intercepted, the active component can keep a record of the home address binding for that correspondent. If, at some point, it sees a new

---

[2] This route optimisation is only performed during the transition period, between the mobile node handing-off and the correspondent node adopting the new address for traffic.

care-of address is being used for the correspondent address - home address pair (i.e. a handoff took place), the handoff optimisation component dynamically inserts a short-lived filter for the reverse route which intercepts all packet from the correspondent to the mobile node's old care-of address. For the lifetime of the filter, packets that are intercepted can be re-routed to the correct (new) care-of address thus avoiding packet loss caused by the latency of the round-trip.

```
if (LInsertClassificFilter(ACID,BINDING_UPDATE_PACKET))
    // error handling
while (component_active) {
    if (! LGetPackets(ACID, &Packets, &PacketCount))
        // error handling
    for (Packet=Packets; Packet; Packet=Packet->Next){
        if (Packet->Filter == BINDING_UPDATE_PACKET)
            // Process Home Address Option
        else if (Packet->Filter == PACKET_TO_REDIRECT)
            // Redirect Packet
    }
    if (! LReturnPackets(ACID, Packets))
        // error handling
}
```

Fig. 3. Source code fragment showing the processing loop of the fast handoff component

The source code fragment in figure 3 shows the packet processing loop of the handoff optimisation component. It illustrates the ease with which packets can be intercepted (filtered) and transparently processed by means of LARA++ components.

Figure 4 presents the measurements taken on one of our test LARA++ routers[3] while running the handoff optimisation service. The graph shows the number of packets that would have been lost without the handoff optimisation component (or in other words the number of packets that our component had re-directed and hence saved from being lost) for a range of different media streams (for example, GSM, PCM audio, DivX, MPEG1). The results indicate that the number of packets lost due to the propagation delay of the binding update is proportional to the round trip delay between the active router at the edge of the mobile node's network and its correspondent node. Providing this service in a mobile access network, where the majority of handoffs are localised, can therefore greatly improve handoff performance for mobile devices communicating with distant (in terms of delay) nodes.

This example shows LARA++ is an ideal platform on which to roll out such services as it allows components to operate transparently to the users of the network. In can vary depending on the needs of the network users and the types of traffic flowing through addition, it allows new services to be instantiated dynamically and operate flexibly so the overall service composite the network.

Other ways of addressing the packet loss caused by the end-to-end latency on mobile devices and their correspondents during network handoffs commonly rely upon middle boxes that must be pre-configured to act in a specific way. For example, Hierarchical Mobile-IPv6 [18] uses a "MAP" node to localise handoffs and thus reduce the end-to-end delay of the binding updates, and Fast Handovers for Mobile

[3] A LARA++ active router running on a Windows XP based PC with a 1.7 GHz Pentium 4 processor, 384 MB RAM and three Fast Ethernet Interface Cards.

IPv6 [19] uses extra infrastructure in the network to initiate handovers and establish routing tunnels to the new location of the mobile node. Indeed, had our fast Mobile IPv6 handoff component not been implemented as an active service, it too would have required a dedicated, pre-configured middle box to host the service. A key strength of LARA++ is that it can be used as a basis for the implementation of any of these three mobility solutions and even allows them all to co-exist on the same LARA++ box. Moreover, it enables the dynamic roll-out of all of these services as they are released.

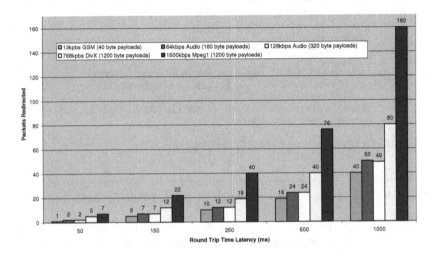

Fig. 4. Measurements of packet loss during Mobile-IPv6 handoff in various network latency and traffic load conditions.

3.2 Network Address Translation

Network Address Translation [20] allows hosts on a non-routable IP network to communicate with other hosts on the Internet via a transparent middle box that translates the private addresses to public addresses for outgoing packets, and vice versa for incoming packets. We implemented NAT as a LARA++ active component in order to further demonstrate the flexibility and range of applicability of LARA++.

The implementation installs packet filters to intercept all inbound IP traffic from the "inside" network of the router (i.e. on each interface on the private network). Upon intercepting every packet using this filter, the active component looks for an existing association between the private address and port, and the correspondent address and port. If no such association for the connection exists, the component creates a new association and assigns it a valid global address and port from a pool. For new connections, the active component then installs another filter for the reverse path from the correspondent address and port to the global address and port for inbound traffic to the "outside" interface. These filters, although numerous, exploit LARA++'s scalable flow filters [11], enabling many thousand of such filters to be installed without adversely affecting the performance. The component is also able to insert a filter so that it can intercept and respond to ARP requests for any addresses from the address pool that the router uses for NAT.

From then on, the NAT component simply intercepts incoming packets on both the inside and outside interfaces (before they reach the standard TCP/IP stack). This allows the active component to co-operate with the standard TCP/IP stack in order to route the packets. Packets intercepted on the inside interface have their source address and port replaced with the global address for the connection, and packets intercepted on the outside interface have their destination address and port swapped for the private address for the connection. After the IP, TCP and UDP checksums have been adjusted to accommodate the change packets are released by the component and then reach the standard TCP/IP stack, which then routes the packets as normal.

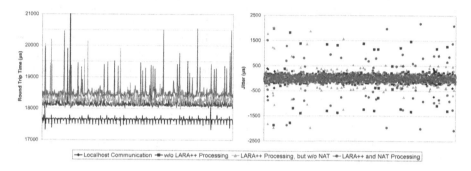

Fig. 5. Performance measurements of packet RTT (left) and jitter (right) of a UDP/IP stream across a LARA++ router with our NAT component instantiated and three other control cases.

We measured the latency and jitter introduced by LARA++ and the NAT component using a UDP-based ping application. The application measured the round-trip delay while sending approximately 60 echo requests per second (see figure 5 – "LARA++ and NAT Processing"). In order to compare the results, we also measured three other configurations: (i) where the LARA++ subsystem was running without the NAT component, (ii) where LARA++ was not running and no NAT was performed, and finally (iii) where UDP communication took place solely on the local host[4].

Of the total 18.5 ms average RTT latency, 17.7 ms is caused by the protocol stacks and the test application at each end of the connection. On average a further 0.4 ms is added by the latency of the actual network. The LARA++ active node OS adds another 0.2 ms to the RTT, and finally the NAT component is responsible for the remaining 0.2 ms. Considering that these latencies can be halved for uni-directional traffic, we can conclude that LARA++ and the NAT component have only a minimal effect on the overall latency.

It is also interesting to compare the jitter on the different experiments. As figure 3 shows, packets to be processed by LARA++ components are more likely to experience additional queuing delays. Consequently, we would expect streams that are processed by LARA++ to have more variance in the packet latencies. However, figure 5 shows that while jitter is increased slightly by LARA++, it remains marginal. For example, while 92.4% of packets have less than 250 μs jitter under normal conditions, with LARA++ and NAT processing this value only drops to 89.7%.

---

[4] This last control scenario shows the majority of the RTT latency (around 17.7 ms) is caused by the conventional protocol stack and test application, and not by LARA++ or the network.

In order to test the throughput of our test router described in section 3.1, we ran the NAT component on its own with increasing traffic throughput. With 1KByte UDP packets the router was able to sustain approximately 82 Mbps. This compares favourably with a maximum throughput of just over 83 Mbps without LARA++.

3.3 Firewall

Relating back to the previous two examples of active components, while users might legitimately want to install an active component to perform a routing optimization for mobile handoffs on their own flows of packets, there are some applications that could be harmful to the network if end users were able to install them. For example, an application such as NAT installed for a specific user may frustrate the network administrator's attempts to limit access to other networks using conventional means. For example, NAT could be used to bypass security provided by a non-routable network, or some simple variant could be used to bypass port blocking.

This problem is characteristic of a number arising as we deploy active networks. Thus an important lesson highlighted by LARA++ is the need to consider threats to the router by active applications when configuring the router. Just as in conventional routers, configuration of active networks must either systematically prevent undesirable behaviour by active applications or be based upon a well tested "safe" configuration, which is modified only with care.

Users could be prevented from using an active router to circumvent security, as in the case of the flow-specific NAT and port-blocking avoidance examples, by means of a firewall designed to handle such threats. With this in mind, we have implemented a firewall active component designed to be installed and configured in a way that it is tamper-proof to other active components. Much of the difference between this and a conventional firewall is not in the way the component is implemented but rather the way in which it is installed and configured in the classification graph.

It is imperative that unprivileged users have no access to packets, not even their "own" streams, until after a firewall has eliminated packets it regards as undesirable. One way to achieve this is to augment the standard CGT-defined graph with a new classification node that accepts packets immediately prior to the node that processes network layer headers. Also, the classification graph can be configured so ordinary users have access permission only for certain types of packet and no others.

Another consideration is that it is no longer just the network that is the untrusted domain. Filtering out undesirable packets as they are received by the router is no longer a guarantee that all packets forwarded by the router will be desirable. Therefore, a "well-behaved" active router configuration that prevents undesirable behaviour on its networks should also enforce filtering on packets leaving the router.

4   Related Work

The main goal behind LARA++ was to build a highly generic and flexible active router architecture. While we have successfully demonstrated this with a range of very different active services (in section 3), we have not been able to find many related evaluations of active routers in real world deployments. As a consequence, we focus more on a comparison of LARA++ with other active network approaches.

A common objective of most active network approaches is to expedite network evolution through solutions that enable extensibility of network functionality by way of dynamically loaded code. Many active network approaches, such as RouterPlugins [9], Click [8] and the configurable operating system Scout [7] accomplish this through software modules or plug-ins. However, as it has been shown by Hicks and Nettles [21], these approaches all use a fixed "underlying" data structure or program that defines the "glue" for the service composition on the active node. The fact that these composition structures are defined at compile time of the kernel limits extensibility to predefined "slots". LARA++, by comparison, allows the dynamic extension of the classification graph (i.e. allows the creation of new nodes at run-time) and also overcomes the limitation that only one plug-in can be incorporated per slot (i.e. many components can hook packet filters into a classification node).

CANEs/Bowman [22], in contrast, extends the plug-in based approach by a packet filter mechanism that allows the selection of an underlying program, which composes active services provided by the code plug-ins. This flexible classification approach allows Bowman to dynamically deploy new protocols at run-time like LARA++. However, Bowman restricts the selection to a single underlying program; i.e., once an appropriate underlying program has been identified, the service composite is fixed and only dependent on the plug-ins. Furthermore, the literature on CANEs/Bowman implies that only one copy of the packet can be sent to each logical input channel which prevents implicit active program co-operation.

Similarly, VERA [23] appears to be limited in that it allows only one forwarder to be chosen for each packet that is classified. And even if packets could be classified several times, VERA would still lack a method for the chosen forwarders to compose an overall service in a cooperative and deterministic way.

5   Conclusion

The experiences described in this paper have led us to a number of conclusions about LARA++ and about the deployment of active routers in general. LARA++ is a maturing technology suitable for deployment in current IP and IPv6-based networks. It has been designed and built from the ground up with particular focus on interoperability and co-operability with conventional network services on routers, as well as the ease of the development process for network programmers.

We have attempted to demonstrate the flexibility of LARA++ by example. For this reason we developed, deployed and tested three distinct active services through which we have shown that the LARA++ service composition model is sufficiently generic and flexible to provide the different types of services, and allows independent users (role-players) to program the shared network device in a collaborative manner. The measurement results have also indicated that our prototype implementation of LARA++ is suitable in performance for typical edge networks, where value added services and network functionality is often of greater value than only high-speed data forwarding (for example, the fast handoff functionality improves a mobile user's service in a way that clearly outperforms any a high-speed forwarding engine).

However, it is important to note that the range of applications for LARA++ is by no means limited to those mentioned in section 3. The service composition approach based on the classification graph model allows almost any imaginable active network application, such as media transcoding, protocol experimentation and deployment, routing optimisation, access control, intelligent proxies, and many more.

The most important conclusion we have reached is that LARA++ works! We have successfully deployed LARA++ in real-world situations one would find in today's conventional networks. The service composition model allows multiple applications to co-exists, despite overlapping interests, and contribute towards the overall service composite of the active router. Our implementation of LARA++ has also allowed us to take advantage of existing OS-provided network functionality and interoperate with it. We regard this as essential in allowing a smooth transition from conventional networking towards active networking. This approach leaves open the option of retaining conventional router functionality where the overhead of active solutions cannot be justified by the increase in flexibility.

Our experience developing active components has convinced us that for an active router to be successful, it must offer a very user-friendly interface for developers. This broad requirement encompasses the ability to write active components in many different programming languages, and in particular, the ease of debugging these components. LARA++ does not impose the use of a particular user-space language or development environment, putting active component developers at ease with a familiar development process. LARA++'s filter mark-up language also adheres to this principal with a clean and extensible syntax, making the design of new filters trivial.

Our experiences of deploying LARA++ have taught us a great deal about the trade-off between performance and flexibility. The line speeds we have been able to sustain, whilst good, are far short of those appropriate for core networks, but are acceptable within typical edge networks. Also, we have come to the conclusion that the majority of active network applications are ideally provided at the edge of the network, as this is where the services are required to have the desired effect. For example, the fast Mobile IPv6 handoff component relies on being deployed close to the point of path aggregation between the old and new care-of addresses. So long as handoffs are between topologically close networks, this is almost always at an edge router. Similarly, the NAT component must be installed at the edge of a private network.

Indeed, most active applications are best suited to deployment in edge networks, and in edge networks the flexibility to deploy such functionality is more important than optimal performance. Thus, we see edge routers as the most suitable candidates for augmentation with LARA++ functionality.

Finally, we have also noted that as new network capabilities are deployed, new threats to the network arise. Conventional solutions such as port blocking and firewalling may not completely close the avenues of attack. A secure system of permissions and trust is helpful, but is no substitute for careful and systematic configuration with regard to the new potential threats.

References

1. S. Schmid, J. Finney, A.C. Scott, W.D. Shepherd, "Component-based Active Network Architecture", IEEE Symposium on Computers and Communications, July 2001.
2. B. Schwartz et al., "Smart Packets: Applying Active Networks to Network Management". ACM Transactions on Computer Systems, volume 18(1), pp 67-88, 2000.
3. G. Goldszmidt and Y. Yemini, "Delegated Agents for Network Management". IEEE Communications, volume 36(3), pp 66-70, March 1998.

4. B. Braden et al., "Introduction to the ASP Execution Environment 1.5". Technical report, http://www.isi.edu/active-signal/ARP/DOCUMENTS/ASP_EE.ps, November 2001.
5. T. Harbaum, A. Speer, R. Wittmann and M. Zitterbart, "Providing Heterogeneous Multicast Services with AMNET". Communications and Networks, 3(1), March 2001.
6. R. Keller et al., "An Active Router Architecture for Multicast Video Distribution". In Proc. of IEEE INFOCOM (3), pp 1137-1146, 2000.
7. A. Montz et Al., "Scout: A Communications-Oriented Operating System", In Operating Systems Design and Implementation, page 200, 1994.
8. R. Morris, E. Kohler, J. Jannotti, M Kaashoek, "The Click Modular Router", In Proc. of ACM Symposium on Operating Systems Principles, pages 217-231, December 1999.
9. D. Decasper, Z. Dittia, G. Parulkar, B. Plattner, "Router Plug-ins: A Software Architecture for Next Generation Routers", In Proc. of SIGCOMM, pp 229-240, September 1998.
10. The Caml Language. Online Reference, INRIA, http://caml.inria.fr/.
11. S. Schmid, T. Chart, M. Sifalakis, A. C. Scott, "Flexible, Dynamic and Scalable Service Composition for Active Routers", In Proc. of IWAN 2002, pp 253-266, December 2002.
12. D.S. Alexander et al., "Active Network Encapsulation Protocol (ANEP)", July 1997.
13. S. McCann and V. Jacobson, "The BSD Packet Filter: A New Architecture for User-level Packet Capture". In Proc. of USENIX Conference, Berkeley, 1993.
14. C. M. Rogers, "ANQL – An Active Networks Query Language". In Proc. of IWAN 2002, Zurich, pp 99-110, December 2002.
15. M. Sifalakis, S. Schmid, T. Chart, D. Hutchison, "A Generic Active Service Deployment Protocol". In Proc. of ANTA 2003, pp 100-111, Osaka, May 2003.
16. D. Johnson, C. Perkins, J. Arkko, "Mobility Support in IPv6", Internet Draft draft-ietf-mobileip-ipv6-24.txt, June 2003. WORK IN PROGRESS.
17. S. Schmid, J. Finney, A. C. Scott, W. D. Shepherd, "Active Component Driven Network Handoff for Mobile Multimedia Systems". In Proc. of IDMS 2000 (pp 266-278), University of Twente, Enschede, The Netherlands, October 2000.
18. H. Soliman, C. Castelluccia, K. El-Malki, L. Bellier, "Hierarchical Mobile IPv6 Mobility Management", Internet Draft draft-ietf-mobileip-hmipv6-08.txt, June 2003.
19. R. Koodli, "Fast Handovers for Mobile IPv6", Internet Draft draft-ietf-mobileip-fast-mipv6-07.txt, September 2003. WORK IN PROGRESS.
20. K. Egevang et al., "The IP Network Address Translator (NAT)", RFC 1631, May 1994.
21. M.W. Hicks and S. Nettles, "Active Networking Means Evolution (or Enhanced Extensibility Required)", In Proc. of IWAN 2000, October 2000.
22. S. Merugu et al., "Bowman and CANEs: Implementation of an Active Network", In Proc. of 37th Conference on Communication, Control and Computing, September 1999.
23. S. Karlin, L. Peterson, "VERA: An Extensible Router Architecture". In Journal "Computer Networks (Amsterdam, Netherlands, 1999)" 38(3), pp 277-293, 2002.

A Proactive Management Framework in Active Clusters

Eunmi Choi[1] and Dugki Min[2]

[1] School of Computer Science and Electronic Engineering, Handong Global University, Heunghae-eub, Puk-ku, Pohang, Kyungbuk, 791-708, Korea
emchoi@handong.edu
[2] School of Computer Science and Engineering, Konkuk University, Hwayang-dong, Kwangjin-gu, Seoul, 133-701, Korea
dkmin@konkuk.ac.kr

Abstract. An active Web cluster system is an active network that has a collection of locally distributed servers that are interconnected by active switches, providing a Web application service. In this paper, we introduce the ALBM (Adaptive Load Balancing and Management) active cluster system that provides proactive management. The architecture of the ALBM active cluster and its underlying components are presented. We focus on system-level and service-level management of the active cluster system by presenting the corresponding proactive ALBM framework. The system-level framework considers performance counters of resource state dynamics; the service-level framework concerns service quality and proactive actions based on event occurrences. The experimental results on adaptive load balancing are presented in terms of system-level proactive management. In addition, a proactive event message service tool is introduced for providing effective services and management in terms of service-level proactive management.

1 Introduction

An active network contains network nodes that perform customized processing of packets [15,16,17]. An active Web cluster system is an active network that has a collection of locally distributed servers interconnected by active switches[5,18], providing a Web application service. It is shown as a single transparent cluster system to the user with one site name and one virtual IP address [1,2,3]. Due to their characteristics of cost-effectiveness, high scalability, and high availability, active Web cluster systems have become a typical solution to the next generation Internet services[4].

Various active Web cluster architectures have been developed in many forms. The most popular form is based on hardware L4 active switches [5,6,7]. The H/W switch-based cluster systems are easy to deploy only by connecting server nodes to the active switch box. The employed H/W L4 active switches act as traffic managers that would direct IP traffics to the highly appropriate healthy server in a cluster, performing network address translation on messages flowing through

N. Wakamiya et al. (Eds.): IWAN 2003, LNCS 2982, pp. 228–239, 2004.

them. Since these systems are based on H/W switches, it is impossible to add any customizing schedules or new management services that contain capability to automatically recover the system from partial failures. Recently, some cluster systems are constructed on top of the Linux Virtual Server (LVS) [8,9,10,11]. The LVS is a software load balancer that directs network connections to multiple servers, so that servers can share their workload. As a S/W active switch, the LVS supports most of connection scheduling algorithms that are provided by the H/W active switches. Moreover, since the LVS is an open software, it can be customized to collaborate with other software tools or extended to add more improved scheduling algorithms for reflecting the system state of each node. Several variations of LVS[11,12,13] have been introduced to make the LVS be more adaptive.

In this paper, we introduce the ALBM (Adaptive Load Balancing and Management) active cluster that has a hybrid cluster architecture, which employs S/W active switches as well as middleware agents on server nodes. The ALBM cluster has proactive management framework that could provide both adaptive load balancing and proactive event-driven management. For adaptive load balancing, its active switch, called Traffic Manager, provides network-level server load balancing that changes the scheduling adaptively according to node state information by means of node agents. In order to analyze the dynamics of server performance due to workload, we perform several experiments with performance counters. We compare the performance results of adaptive scheduling algorithms to those of non-adaptive ones on various kinds of workload. For proactive management, the ALBM proactive framework includes service-level and server-level monitoring mechanisms for collecting performance counters. It also contains the rule-based event processing engine, and has direct and indirect event notification mechanisms for collecting and processing events.

This paper is organized as follows. Section 2 presents the ALBM active cluster system architecture and its components. Section 3 introduces the proactive ALBM management framework. In Section 4, we show experimental results on the performance of ALBM active cluster for various adaptive load balancing algorithms. In Section 5, we introduce a proactive event message service tool. We summarize in Section 6.

2   The ALBM Active Cluster Architecture

In this section, we introduce the architecture of ALBM (Adaptive Load Balancing and Management) active cluster system with its underlying components. As shown in Figure 1, the ALBM cluster system is composed of active switches, application servers, and the management station. Although the cluster consists of tens of application servers, called nodes, it is published with one site name and one virtual IP address that are assigned to one or more active switches, called Traffic Managers(TMs).

The Traffic Manager(TM)s interface the rest of cluster nodes with the Internet, making the distributed nature of the architecture transparent to Internet

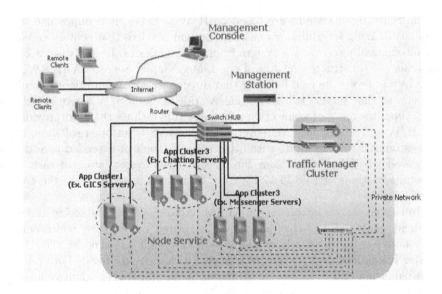

Fig. 1. Architecture of the ALBM Active Cluster System

clients. The TM is an active switch that performs customized processings on incoming and outgoging packets. When client traffic arrives, the TM routes the client packet to one of the servers according to its load balancing algorithm and policy, performing network address translation on the packets flowing through them. In order to decide traffic routing adaptively, it collects the status information of collaborated servers periodically and schedules servers in a specific order according to employing load balancing algorithm. After translating to a proper address, it routes a packet to the assigned server on the OSI Layer 4 level. Our TM provides several load scheduling algorithmss, such as Round-Robin, Least-Connected, Weighted, Response-time basis, and adaptive algorithms. Currently, our TM supports two types of L4 switching mechanisms: Direct Routing (DR) and Network Address Translation (NAT). Compared to other typical L4 switches, our TM considers current nodes states to manage the load-balancing mechanism. The TM receives information of real servers on the fly, such as state of workloads, dead node, and cluster configurations. To have the system highly fault-tolerant and scalable, two or more TMs can be organized as a cluster of TMs. In this case, each of TMs executes the Traffic Manager Node (TM-Node) Service. The TM-Node services perform membership management in an efficient way to be prepared with possible combinations of active or stand-by TM. The TM is implemented in C to achieve a high performance and take a small portion of memory.

On each of application servers, a middleware service, called Node Agent (NA), is running. The NA is a system-level service that is remotely and dynamically deployed and initiated by our middleware deployment service. The NAs are indicated by Circle As on the bottom of each node in Figure 1. The NA makes the underlying server be a member node of the ALBM system. The NA takes two types of agent roles. First, it works as an agent for managing the managed node. It monitors and controls the system elements or the application service of the node, and collects the state and performance information on its local management information basis. It interacts with the M-Station, giving the local information and receiving administrative commands for management purposes. Second, it works as an agent for clustering. Regarding membership management, it sends heartbeat messages to one another. When there is any change in membership, the membership convergence mechanism is initiated by the master node. The master node is dynamically elected by members whenever there is no master node or there exists inconsistent master information among members. Besides, the NA provides L7 APIs to application services running on the node.

The management station, called M-Station, is a management center of the entire ALBM cluster system, working together with the management console through Web-based GUIs. All administrators commands are received into and executed through the M-Station. By interacting with the master node of a cluster, the M-Station collects the dynamic state or performance information of the cluster system resources and application services. Also, the M-Station checks the system state in the service-level, and carries out some actions when values monitored from service-level quality are significantly far behind the service-level QoS objectives. According to the management strategies and policies determined by the human administrator, the M-Station takes proper management actions, such as alarming events or removing failed nodes. The M-Station is implemented in Java.

All the components in the ALBM system are interconnected with public and private networks. The public network is used to provide public services to Internet clients, while the private network is used for secure and fast internal communications among components on management purpose.

2.1   Adaptive Load Balancing Mechanism

The adaptive scheduling algorithms in the ALBM active cluster system adjust their schedules, taking into accounts of dynamic state information of servers and applications collected from servers. The ALBM algorithm is as follows. By collecting appropriate information of server states, the NAs customize and store the data depending on the application architecture, machine types, and expectation of a system manager. Each NA decides if the current state is overloaded or underloaded by using upper or lower thresholds of resource utilization determined by system configuration and load balancing policies of cluster management. Each cluster has a coordinator that is in charge of any centralized task in the cluster. We call the coordinator a Master NA, and only the Master NA communicates with TM as the representative in order to control the incoming TMs traffic. After collecting state data of all NAs in a cluster, the Master NA reports the state changes to the TM. Thus, real-time performance data are transferred to the M-Station, and the state data of servers are reported to the TM. By using the state information reported by Master NAs, the TM adjusts traffics of incoming requests properly to balanced server allocation. The TM does not allocate requests to overloaded servers, until the overloaded server state is back to a normal state. The scheduling algorithms are applied to the TM through the control of M-Station.

3   Proactive ALBM Framework

This section presents the proactive management framework on the ALBM active cluster system. This framework provides a management environment to adaptively control the system according to the system dynamics. For short-term management, it detects faults, failures, or overload states and reacts automatically to recover the system from the fault or performance degradation situation. It also accumulates the states of system and the state changes, such as events, into databases. Information stored in these databases is used for mid-term and long-term management, such as performance analysis, root cause analysis, and capacity planning.

In our proactive management framework, three types of dynamic system information are collected. One type is performance counters of resource states in a server node. Theses counters are retrieved directly from the server node in the system level. Typical examples of resource state counters are available memory in Kbytes, processor time, and NIC total bytes. The next type of system information is performance counters of service quality that are measured in the service level, i.e., collecting service counters outside the service cluster. Typical examples of service quality counters are the average response time per request and the average throughput per second. These types of system information represent the system state in different views. The third type is events that occur while serving applications and managing the system. The system listens and stores events in terms of management, since events represent the state changes of the system that might affect the performance or availability of the system.

The this section, we describe the architecture of our proactive management framework in two views: one shows the structure of how to collect the performance counters of resource states and service quality, and the other shows the structure of how to collect the events.

3.1   Architecture for Collecting Performance Counters

Figure 2 shows the architecture of modules that are related to performance counters collection and process. Performance counters of resource states are collected by the Resource Monitor in our framework. The Resource Monitor is implemented as a separate process that is independent of the NA process in a server node, since the Resource Monitor includes operations that could wait for failed resources. The Resource Monitor checks the resource status by accessing OS APIs and sends the measured information to the Resource State Collector of the NA. The Resource State Collector collects resource states from a number of resources periodically. Resource states collected by the Resource State Collector are passed to the Node State Evaluator. The Node State Evaluator evaluates the status of the server node based on the pre-defined node policies and makes the Event Delegator generate an event if necessary.

Another way to measure performances of server nodes is to monitor the service quality in service level. The Service Level (SL) Monitor checks the service quality of each node in the service level, by measuring service availability, response time, and recovery time. As a separate process, the SL Monitor can be deployed on any machine, which may locate outside of the service cluster or run on the same machine where the M-Station locates. By considering the objectives, the SL manager generates events and notifies them to the M-Station with the corresponding measured QoS information.

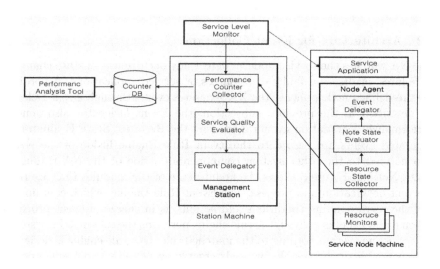

Fig. 2. Architecture of Performance Counter Collection

The resource state counters and the SL quality counters are collected by the Performance Counter Collector in the M-Station. The M-Station stores the performance counters into the Counter DB. This Counter DB is retrieved by the Performance Analysis Tool to trace system resource states and service quality states. Meanwhile, resource state counters and SL quality counters are passed to the Service Quality Evaluator for evaluating the system states and service level. If it is necessary to generate an event, the Event Delegator generates and sends the events to the appropriate system components.

The TMs interface the rest of cluster nodes, making the distributed nature of the architecture transparent to Internet clients. All inbound packets to the system are received and forwarded to application servers through the TMs. It provides network-level traffic distribution services by keeping on balancing the servers loads. On each of application servers, a middleware service, called Node

Agent (NA), is deployed. The NA is in charge of management and operation of the ALBM cluster, such as cluster formation, membership management, and adaptive management and load balancing. The management station, called M-Station, is a management center of the entire ALBM cluster system. All administrators commands typed through management console are received and delivered to the M-Station. Communicating with NAs, the M-Station performs cluster management operations, such as cluster creation/removal and node join/leave. The M-Station also collects current states and configurations of the entire system, and provides them to other authenticated components in the system. Using the server state information provided by NAs, it performs proactive management actions according to the predefined policies. Besides, the M-Station checks the state of the system in service-level, and carries on some actions when the monitored service-level quality value is significantly far behind with the service-level QoS objectives.

3.2   Architecture for Event Collection

The NA watches the service node to detect any occurrences of state change due to failures, errors, and faults of resources or service applications. According to the pre-defined node policies, the NA generates events through Event Delegator. As described in the previous subsection, the Event Delegator also generates performance degradation events guided by the Resource State Evaluator. The generated events are passed to the Event Rule Engine inside of the NA and also notified to the other system components outside of the NA through the Event Notifier. Figure 3 shows the architecture of the modules that are related to event notification and process. The Event Rule Engine, which contains rules and the corresponding conditions and actions, is in charge of event processing. When a new event is arrived, the rule engine performs the rule-matching step and processes the event according to the matched rule. Our rule engine is designed to be expandable or changeable for newly created event types and event processing conditions or actions; it can generate action or condition classes during run time from a XML rule definition schema. Some actions are performed and activated by the Event Rule Engine, but other actions are delegated to the Managed Agent.

Events are delivered toward the outside of the NA through the Event Notifier. The Event Notifier provides a direct event notification environment between two remote applications or components. As a separate service process, the Event Notifier can be shared by several applications running on the same server. Whenever a distributed component has changed its state, the component uses the Event Notifier to notify a state-change event to other related distributed components. The target where to disseminate an event is determined by the dissemination information that is dynamically updated according to the event rule definition as well as the system state and configuration. For outgoing or incoming events, simple event processing actions, such as filtering or formatting, can be applied according to the event rule definition.

In our proactive framework, if an event is so urgent that an automatic action should be performed immediately, the urgent events are directly passed to the

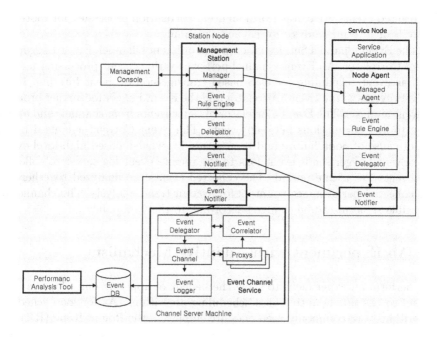

Fig. 3. Architecture of Event Collection

M-Station through the Event Notifier. The Event Delegator of M-Station collects all directly transmitted events from NAs. The Event Rule Engine of M-Station determines if the proper action should be performed after looking at the collected events. The Event Rule Engine contains a rule engine where rule matching and executing process is performed when a new event is arrived. In our rule engine system, a rule is activated by a number of correlated events that satisfy a given condition, and then an activated rule executes a predefined action. Thus, a rule is defined by a combination of a number of correlated events, called Event Token, a rule condition, a rule action, as well as by its properties, such as a rule name and a priority. The rule priority determines the order of applying rules when there are two or more rules compete. The event token name follows a format of domain-name:event-type-name. The condition and action codes are written in Java. The Manager of M-Station carries out the action to the associated managed agents. The process and result are reported to the Management Console.

The Event Notifier also sends all the events including the urgent events to the Event Channel Service that provides the indirect event communication service. The Event Channel Service provides indirect event transmission service that decouples event consumers from event producers. For each event customer or producer group, the Event Channel Service provides different quality of services or different event transmission mechanisms (push or pull mode). Also, the Event Channel Service is used as an event collection center where all the events are collected from NAs and various event producers in the cluster system. Using the aggregated events, we can perform an event correlation processing for root-cause analysis or a trend analysis for capacity planning.

The Event Channel Service is composed of Event Channel, Event Logger, and Event Correlator. An Event Channel performs various event-processing services, such as event scheduling for QoS-based transmission or event filtering. It also delivers events to the Event Correlator and the Event Logger for further processes of event analysis. The Event Correlator obtains events from channels and applies rules to find correlations between events. The Event Correlator is used to find a root-cause of node failure and to generate knowledge-based high-level events. The Event Logger sends event logs to the remote event log server to collect all the events for a time period. The collected events are analyzed together with the collected performance counters for system trend analysis. The channel has a flexible structure to be changed according to the QoS policy.

4   An Experiment with Adaptive Mechanism

We perform an experiment to show the benefit of applying our adaptive mechanism to the non-adaptive load scheduling algorithms. As for load scheduling algorithms, two commonly used ones are employed: the Round-Robin(RR) algorithm that is a popular static algorithm, and the Least Connection (LC) algorithm that is a popular dynamic algorithm. The adaptive version of RR and LC are called ARR and ALC, respectively. In our adaptive mechanism, the cost of adaptive operation is negligible since reporting the state information of servers to the TM is not a periodic processing and it occurs only when the state changes. It is very few compared to the amount and frequency of incoming requests.

We make a realistic workload that is heavy-tailed. In literature, many researchers have concluded that general Internet traffics follow heavy tail distributions [8,9,10]. In order to make heavy-tailed e-commerce traffic, we mix an e-commerce traffic provided by Web Bench tool[7] and a memory-intensive traffic at the rate of 80% and 20%, respectively. The e-commerce traffic contains mixed requests of text pages, image files, and CGI requests. The memory-intensive traffic contains memory requests of random size and random duration. The random size and duration are randomly selected between 5MB to 15MB and between 0 to 20 seconds, respectively.

The workload requests are generated by tens of client machines, which are interconnected with a cluster of server nodes in the same network segment. Each server has PIII-900MHz dual CPU and 512 MB memory. Each client has PIV 1.4GHz CPU and 256MB memory. The network bandwidth is 100MB. The number of connections per client thread is 4. The total running time is 2 minutes, think time between requests in a client is 10 seconds, and ramp-up time is 20 seconds.

Figure 4 shows the experimental result; adaptive ARR and ALC algorithms achieve about 10% better performances than non-adaptive ones. The best performance is achieved with the ALC algorithm. Due to the active characteristic of traffic manager (i.e. network switch), the adaptive mechanism could achieve better throughput by adjusting the load scheduling dynamically. According to the feature of Web Bench Tool, the next request is generated after the response of the previous request has received. That is, Web Bench Tool slows down sending requests when the server responds late. Due to this feature, all scheduling algorithms reduce their throughputs after reaching their maximum performances. This makes results after the peak points meaningless.

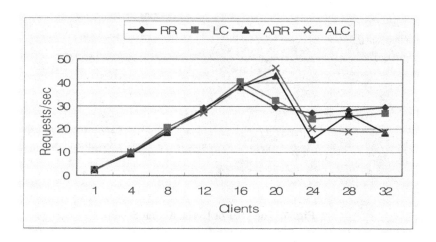

Fig. 4. Experimental Comparison

5   Proactive Event Messaging Service Tool

In addition to adaptive load balancing, the dynamic state information is used in the M-Station for proactive management. The M-Station provides proactive actions in two levels: system level and service level. In system level, the M-Station receives system state transition events from NAs and takes actions according to the rules managed by an event rule-engine. Events are transmitted to the M-Station through underlying event notification and channel services. In service level, a service-level (SL) monitor takes the similar role as NAs. The SL monitor checks the service quality of the ALBM cluster in service level, such as availability, response time, and recovery time. By considering the QoS objectives, the SL monitor generates events and notifies them to the M-Station with the corresponding measured QoS information. The SL monitor can be deployed on any place and computer in Internet.

In this section, we present a proactive event messaging service is implemented on top of the proactive management framework. The proactive event messaging service sends a message to the system manager according to the predefined event rules when an event occurs. Figure 5 shows the GUI to set up actions according to the event type. When an event occurs, the setting action is triggered and performed as desired. It is possible to send an e-mail to a human administrator, an

MSN message passing, or an SMS cellular phone message delivery. The message can be delivered to one person or a collection of people with a specific role.

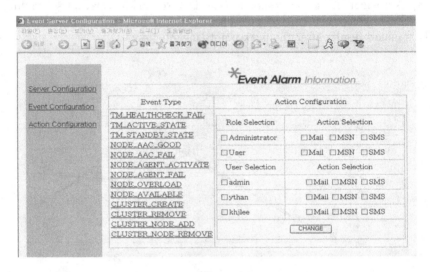

Fig. 5. The GUI of Event Action Set-up

6   Conclusion

In this paper, we introduced the ALBM active cluster system that provides proactive management. The architecture of the ALBM active cluster and its underlying components are presented. As an active switch, the TM is in charge of routing the client packet to one of the servers according to its scheduling algorithm and policy, performing network address translation on the packets flowing through them. In order to applying system-level and service-level management to the active cluster system, a proactive ALBM framework is introduced. It collects system information and processes them according to system state changes. The system-level framework considers performance counters of resource states by probing, processing, making a decision, and performing an action based on state changes of resource utilization. The experimental results on adaptive load balancing are presented in terms of system-level proactive management. Adaptive scheduling algorithms result in a good performance compared to the non-adaptive ones for a realistic heavy-tailed workload. Besides, a proactive event message service tool is introduced for providing effective services and management.

References

1. Gregory F Pfister: In Search of Clusters, 2nd Ed. Prentice Hall PTR (1998)
2. Daniel A. Menasce: Trade-offs in Designing Web Cluster. IEEE Internet Computing, Volume:6 Issue:5 Sep/Oct (2002) 76 ?80
3. Ana-Maria Cretu, Voicu Groza, Abdul Al-Dhaher, Rami Abielmona: Performance Evaluation of a Software Cluster. IEEE Information and Measurement Technology Conference May (2002) 1543-1548
4. Jeffray S. Chase: Server switching: yesterday and tomorrow. Internet Applications (2001) 114-123
5. Valeria Cardellini, Emiliano Casaliccho, Michele Colajanni, Philip S. Yu: The State of the Art in Locally Distributed Web-server Systems. IBM Research Report, RC22209(W0110-048) October (2001) 1-54
6. Ronald P. Doyle, Jeffrey S, Chase, Syam Gadde, Amin M Vahdat: The trickle-down effect: Web caching and server request distribution. In Proceedings of the Sixth International Workshop of Web Caching and Content Distribution, 2001
7. Lee Breslan, Pei Cao, Li Fan Graham Phillips, Scott Shenker: Web Caching and Zipf-like distributions: Evidence and implications. In Proceedings of IEEE infocom Mar (1999)
8. TurboLinux: Turbo Linux Cluster Server 6 user guide. http://www.tubolinux.com, (2002)
9. LVS documents, http://www.linuxvirtualserver.org/Documents.html
10. Wensong Zhang, Shiyao Jin, Quanyuan Wu: Scaling Internet Service by LinuxDirector. High Performance Computing in the Asia-Pacific Region, 2000. Proceedings. The Fourth International Conference/Exhibition, Volume: 1, (2000) 176-183
11. Wensong Zhang: Linux Virtual Server for Scalable Network Services. Linux Symposium 2000, July (2000)
12. M. Wangsmo: White paper: Piranha ? load-balanced web and ftp clusters. http://www.redhat.com/support/wpapers/piranha (1999)
13. J. Trocki: mon: Service monitoring daemon. http://www.kernel.org/software/mon
14. Eunmi Choi: Performance Test and Analysis for an Adaptive Load Balancing Mechanism on Distributed Server Cluster Systems. 2004 Future Generation Computer Systems, Elsevier Science, Vol. 20. No. 1, (2004, will be appeared)
15. M. Brunner: A Service Management Toolkit for Active Networks, IEEE Network Operations and Management Symposium(NOMS) April (2000) 265-278
16. Marcus Brunner: Active Networks and its Management, IEEE Universal Multiservice Networks (ECUMN) Oct (2000) 414-424
17. Marcus Brunner, Rolf Stadler: Service Management in Multiparty Active Networks, IEEE Communications Magazine, Vol:38 Issue:3, March (2000) 144-151
18. Jiani Guo, Fang Chen, Laxmi Bhuyan, and Raj Kumar: A Cluster-Based Active Router Architecture Supporting Video/Audio Stream Transcoding Service, IEEE Proceedings of International Parallel and Distributed Symposium (IPDPS) (2003) 44

A Policy-Based Management Architecture for Flexible Service Deployment in Active Networks

Yiannis Nikolakis[1], Edgar Magaña[2], Marcin Solarski[3], Alvin Tan[4],
Epifanio Salamanca[2], Joan Serrat[2], Celestin Brou[3], and Alex Galis[4]

[1] National Technical University of Athens
Heroon Polytechniou 9, 15773 Athens, Greece
`ynikol@telecom.ntua.gr`
[2] Universitat Politècnica de Catalunya
Dept T.S.C. Campus Nord D4 c. Jordi Girona, 1-3 c.p. 08034 - Barcelona, Spain
`{emagana, epi}@nmg.upc.es, serrat@tsc.upc.es`
[3] Fraunhofer Institute FOKUS
Kaiserin-Augusta-Allee 31, 10589 - Berlin, Germany
`{solarski, brou}@fokus.fraunhofer.de`
[4] University College London
Dept of Electronic & Electrical Engineering, Torrington Place, London WC1E7JE,
United Kingdom
`{atan, a.galis}@ee.ucl.ac.uk`

Abstract. This paper describes a dynamic, scalable and extensible policy-based network management (PBNM) system that is fully integrated with a service provisioning architectures for active networks. The key result is network customisation according to the needs of the different service providers and its end users. Our component-based service provisioning architecture enables us to render service- and user-specific requirements, across single/multiple administrative domains, at deployment time and to dynamically map service components onto the network using the corresponding management policies. The architecture presented in this paper describes the approach undertaken by the IST-FAIN research project as well as the main issues that we encounter in developing and integrating the PBNM with the service provisioning mechanism.

1 Introduction

Active and programmable networking technology introduces innovative approaches for enabling the user to set up the network configuration and its corresponding services dynamically, according to specific requirements. The dynamic nature of active networks and its continuously emerging new services, calls for efficient management mechanisms to configure the network according to the needs of the service providers and the services themselves, as well as to dynamically extend the management functionalities to adapt to the requirements set by new services.

N. Wakamiya et al. (Eds.): IWAN 2003, LNCS 2982, pp. 240–251, 2004.
© IFIP International Federation for Information Processing 2004

The FAIN project [1], [2] is aimed at developing a fully managed, multi-EE prototype active node to support deployment and provisioning of component-oriented services. The FAIN programmable node is described in [3]. The FAIN network management architecture consists of the Policy-Based Network Management (PBNM) [4] and the Active Service Provisioning (ASP) [5] systems, which provide higher-level management and service deployment mechanisms built on top of an active network infrastructure.

In this paper we describe the final implementation of both the PBNM and ASP systems as well as the intercommunication mechanism developed in order to offer a flexible service deployment on active networks. We further introduce new PBNM components at the network-level that were developed to address the management aspects of end-to-end service creation and deployment, i.e., Resource Manager (RM), Service Manager (SM) and the Inter Domain Manager (IDM). For these purposes, the network-level ASP was developed, which enhances our node-level ASP [5] work. We also consider the case when the network management system is requested to deploy a service in a target node outside of its domain. The FAIN services and their needs are described using technology-independent (i.e., achieved via XML implementation) service descriptors and abstractions from the actual implementation details. The service requirements are used to create a Virtual Active Network (VAN), which is dedicated to provide the service with appropriate computational and communicational resources. The paper is structured as follows: Section 2 provides an overview of the FAIN PBNM with emphasis on the component functionality; Section 3 presents the details of the ASP framework; Section 4 gives an explanation of the architecture and interaction use cases between the PBNM and the ASP frameworks; Section 5 illustrates an example scenario that successfully demonstrates our expected functionalities, while Section 6 gives a brief review of related work. Finally, Section 7 concludes the paper.

2   Policy-Based Network Management (PBNM) Architecture

The FAIN PBNM management architecture is designed as a hierarchically distributed architecture. It consists of two levels: the network management level (NMS) and the element management level (EMS). The NMS is the entry point to the management architecture. It is the recipient of policies, resulting from the ANSP's management decisions or service level agreements (SLA) between various categories of users. The enforcement of these SLAs requires reconfiguration of the network, which is automated by means of policies sent to the NMS. Network-level policies are processed by the NMS Policy Decision Points (PDPs), which decide when policies can be enforced. When enforced, they are delivered to the NMS Policy Enforcement Points (PEPs) that map them to element level policies, which are, in turn, sent to the EMSs. EMS PDPs follow a similar procedure at the element level. Finally, the active node PEPs execute the enforcement actions on the managed network nodes [6].

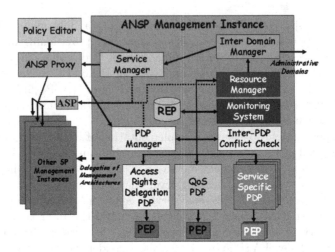

Fig. 1. FAIN management instances and their components

The defined policies are categorised according to the semantics of management operations, which may range from basic configuration and fault management operations to service-specific operations. Policies that belong to a specific category are processed by dedicated PDPs and PEPs. The three main actors of the FAIN Enterprise Model, the ANSP, SP, and the Customer, may request their own (virtual) management architecture through which they are able to manage the resources allocated to the Virtual Environments (VE) of their virtual network. The VE is an abstraction used only for the purpose of partitioning the resources of the active node so that different communities of users can stay isolated from each other.

This allows each actor to select and deploy his own management architecture freely, in order to manage its allocated resources, which can be policy or non-policy based. This model corresponds to a 'management instance' associated with the particular service provider.

The main components of the FAIN PBNM are illustrated in the Figure 1. Service Manager, Resource Manager and the Inter Domain Manager (IDM), are summarised in the table below. They have been developed in order to support service deployment, decision- making with regards to resources control, and inter-domain communication respectively. A detailed description of all components is given in [7].

3   Active Service Provisioning (ASP) Architecture

One of the key results of the FAIN project is an architecture for service provisioning called Active Service Provisioning (ASP). Like the PBNM, it is a two-layered system that comprises the network level and node level. An overview of its architecture is depicted in Figure 2 and has been described in [6] in detail. The network level functionality is responsible for finding the target nodes for deploy-

Table 1. Description of FAIN PBNM components as depicted in Figure 1

PBNM Component	Description
Service Manager	This component is responsible for setting up a VAN in response to a service request. It receives, as an input, the SLA that has been agreed between this domain and the one that requests it. It uses this information together with the topological requirements imposed by a service, which it retrieves from the ASP, to generate the relevant policies for the service. When a VAN is successfully created, the service manager instructs the ASP to trigger the deployment of the requested service.
Resource Manager	The Resource Manager maintains information about the nodes and links of the system and can compute possible end-to-end routes for a given service, based on the network topology and resource information obtained by the Monitoring System. It co-operates with the ASP system, in order to address service-specific requirements.
Inter-Domain Manager	It is in charge of implementing end-to-end negotiation of service deployment into separate active nodes that belong to different administrative domains, managed by different organisations.

ing a service by matching the network level service requirements against the actual network capabilities, coordination of the deployment process at the node level (i.e., Network ASP Manager), and providing a service code retrieval infrastructure (i.e., Service Registry where the service descriptors are kept and Service Repository where the code modules are kept). At the node level, the ASP identifies necessary service components by resolving node-level component dependencies and coordinates component installation, activation and pre-configuration in the execution environments located on the node. Active services that can be deployed using the ASP system have to conform to the FAIN service model presented in [5]. The work described in this paper extends the one presented in [6] by discussing the network-level deployment process. In this section, the deployment requirements are categorized taking into account their scope (network and node level) as well their lifetime characteristic (static and dynamic requirements).

3.1 Service Description

The FAIN service model used is component-based [5]. It allows structuring services using self-contained software units of deployment, management and computation, called service components. A service component may be associated with a code module that can be downloaded from the service repository and installed on an active node in an execution environment. This code module is executable in a particular execution environment and may have a number of dependencies/requirements on the resources needed for its execution.

The principal composition pattern is a component hierarchy, where service components may be recursively composed of sub-components. An example service conforming to the FAIN model is depicted in Figure 3.

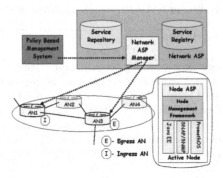

Fig. 2. The ASP overall architecture and relations to other FAIN components

From the deployment perspective, an active service, composed of a set of components, can be divided into a number of co-located component groups, each of which is to be deployed on a single host. Thus, deploying a compound active service means identifying groups of co-located components and deploying each of such groups on a node matching the deployment requirements of the component group. The deployment requirements of a service can be divided into two categories:

- the network level deployment requirements describing the requirements shared by all subcomponents of a top component; and
- the node level deployment requirements of each component within the group. These requirements include the execution environment and node resources needed for execution and they are specified with the help of node level service descriptor as described in [5].

A FAIN active service is described with a network-level service descriptor that specifies the 'top' service components which are abstract components (in the sense they do not have any code directly associated) grouping all service components to be deployed on the same node. Deploying a service on a network level means finding a mapping of the service top components onto the available active node in the network so that the network level deployment requirements are fulfilled by the selected nodes. The network level descriptor specifies the following items:

- the top service components, including references to node level descriptors of the subcomponents; and
- the static topological constraints of every top service component, which include partial information on the requested node location. In the current implementation, we differentiate node roles (ingress, intermediate and egress with respect to domain borders and the main service packet flow) and locations relative to other nodes, whose location is determined otherwise, for instance.

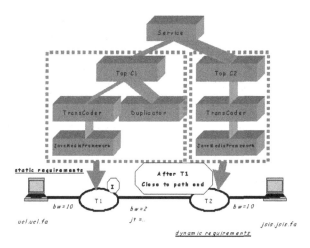

Fig. 3. Example description of a distributed FAIN service - component topology and its network deployment requirements

The network level requirements specified above are of static nature and do not change whenever the service is deployed. However, they are specified so that a number of physical network topologies may address them and thus do not allow fully determining the mapping of top components onto the physical network. To complete this mapping, additional requirements are specified. They can usually be determined only at deployment time and are called dynamic requirements because of this. It is the service deployer that specifies them when requesting a service deployment. These additional deployment requirements include QoS of the virtual links, for instance, the jitter or the bandwidth as well as the edge constraints on the mapping of the logical service topology onto the real network, like physical nodes/networks on which or close to which given top components have to be placed.

4   Integrated System Operation

Having designed and developed the PBNM and the ASP systems as individual entities, we further seek to obtain synergistic benefits by integrating both systems to establish a seamless, fully managed service provisioning mechanism.
Once an SLA between ANSP and SP has been agreed upon, the following steps are carried out when providing a service. Firstly, the SP (or a service itself) requests for a service to be provided with the given edge constraints and the PBNM, with the support of the ASP, computes a mapping of service components to the nodes of the active network. It considers the SP's constraints, the deployment requirements of the service and the actual resources in the active

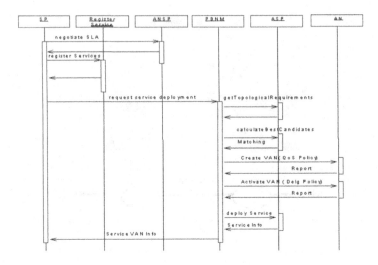

Fig. 4. System operation process

network. Secondly, once the PBNM has obtained the target nodes that make up the VAN, our management system creates a VAN that meets the service requirements. Thirdly, the PBNM requests the ASP to deploy the service in the activated VAN. Figure 4, shows the phases mentioned before, while details of these steps are described in the following subsections.

4.1   Service Requirements Matching

One of the core activities of our system is mapping the components of a given service to the available nodes in the network. The Network ASP Manager decodes the service topological requirements from the service network-level service descriptor, and the edge constraints from the service deployer. The RM receives the topological requirements and checks the resource availability along the possible routes between the two given service endpoints. Resources for a particular VAN are allocated in a 'hard' manner, so that the full requested amount of computational and communication resources must be available on all nodes and links of a route. If multiple paths satisfy the resource requirements, the RM submits the list of the candidate mappings, along with resource information to the Network ASP Manager.

The network-level ASP performs the requirements matching process on the node-level. It validates the deployability of the service according to each of the candidate mappings one after another, by checking that every service component can be installed on a pertinent node ASP for each identified node in a candidate VAN. The node-level determines whether a node-level deployment is successful by resolving the technological requirements of the service components. This includes checking the availability of the execution environment type and computational resources needed by the service components. As a result of this mapping, the Network ASP returns a selected candidate VAN with service components assigned to the nodes that belong to this VAN.

We have adopted this two-phase process, in order to maintain a clear separation of tasks and responsibilities between the management and the service provisioning frameworks. An alternative solution would be to place all the necessary functionality in only one component, namely the Resource Manager, which would be able to consider both resource and service-specific requirements in one pass. In this way, however, the Resource Manager should also be able to access and interpret service-related information, required for the mapping of service components. Effectively, this would result into duplicating parts of the service provisioning functionality inside the management system and mixing up the scope of the two separate frameworks. The drawback in our approach is that for each candidate path, the corresponding resource information must be transmitted from the Resource Manager to Network ASP.

4.2   Virtual Active Network Creation

A VAN is specified by three sets of requirements: the QoS parameters (e.g., the required bandwidth), the computational parameters (e.g., the amount of memory) and the specific service requirements (e.g., the VE types).

The VAN creation process is started when an SP triggers the deployment of a service. The SP uses the corresponding GUI offered by the Policy Editor or by directly contacting the Service Manager (SM). The network-level management system (via the SM) receives the request and translates it into a set of policies, a network-level QoS policy that creates a VAN by allocating resources to it and a network-level Delegation policy that activates the VAN and delegates management of the allocated resources through the creation of a new management instance for this particular SP.

Service Resources Reservation. The determination of the VAN topology is done through the process described in section 4.1. The information about the new VAN is sent to the QoS PDP that integrates this information with other VAN requirements in a structure that is forwarded to the QoS PEP. Next, the QoS PDP forwards the decision to its corresponding PEP. The QoS PEP transforms the request into a set of appropriate element-level QoS policies (one policy for each of the active nodes that constitute the VAN) and it sends the policy to the EMS of the established nodes. Once the QoS policy is enforced, the EMS calls the reservation method within the active node, thus ending the reservation process. The internal active node interactions that guarantee the reservation of resources, are not within the scope of this paper, but can be found in more detail in [3].

Service Resources Activation. After the enforcement of the QoS policies has successfully terminated in all nodes, the PDP Manager starts processing the delegation policies by forwarding them to the delegation PDP to be evaluated. A network level policy is translated into two element level delegation policies: one for assigning access rights to the VE and activating it (i.e., VE activation), and the other for creating the management instance (MI) inside the EMS so that the SP can manage its resources (i.e., MI creation).

A policy set is created and submitted to the respective EMSs. The policies are forwarded to the appropriate management instance, where they are processed sequentially. The first delegation policy causes the assignment of a security profile to the created VE, to be afterwards used for its activation. Since this policy must be enforced immediately, it is forwarded to the delegation PEP running inside the privileged VE in the active node. The delegation PEP enforces the policy that activates the new VE using the API offered by the active node.

Service Deployment. When the SM is made known of the correct activation of the network resources, it will ask the NetASP to perform the corresponding service deployment, indicating the kind of service required and the VAN identifier for the related customer. The network-level ASP iterates through the nodes of the final VAN and contacts the node level ASP on each of these nodes. The node ASP may perform the installation and configuration of the service components identified during the mapping process. To perform the actual installation, the ASP makes use of the node management framework, which provides a unified CORBA-based platform for different types of execution-environment. Through this interface, it is possible to access the EE capabilities and isolate the deployment and management code. The deployment process ends after all service components have been deployed on the target nodes.

4.3   Inter-domain Management

The role of the inter-domain manager (IDM) comes in when ANSPs need to propagate their SPs' traffic across each other's administrative domain. A successful negotiation will lead to a request to create a VAN between the two domains. As such, ANSPs need to derive contracts with other ANSPs to encompass the geographical spread of their targeted client base. For example, in Figure 5, the administrator in Domain 1 needs to establish a relationship with Domain 2 in order to reach its customers.

When the network management system is requested to deploy a service that involves installation of the code in a target node outside of its domain the IDM contacts a corresponding IDM of the other domain in order to negotiate the service deployment in one or more of their active nodes and lets the SP of the first domain to use them. The role of this component is highlighted for reservation of computational and communicational resources for service deployment, particularly as requests occur between different administrative entities.

In our design we have established a repository that maps a destination address to an IDM, i.e., a 'many-to-one' relationship. As such, an ANSP must register a list of destination addresses within its domain on a repository that has well-

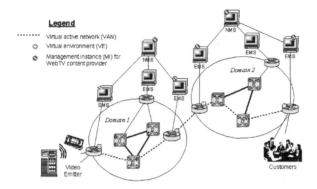

Fig. 5. A view of multiple domains, using the WebTV scenario as an example

known address, so that this repository can provide a discovery mechanism for mapping destination addresses to their respective IDM.

5   Example Scenario

A demonstration of the overall architecture has been carried out over the distributed FAIN testbed, which interconnects several different sites across Europe, using IP tunnels over the public Internet.

According to the demo scenario, an SP is offering a WebTV service, emitting a video stream in MPEG format. Two customers subscribe to the service. The first one uses a device with limited bandwidth, which is not in position to receive the video stream as it is emitted by the WebTV application and requires a H323 format as input. For this reason a transcoder service will have to be installed in the active node placed closest to the customer, to convert the video stream to a format understandable to the receiver. The second customer connecting to the WebTV service does not have the limitations of the first one. However the service is not using a multicast protocol and thus a duplicator service will have to be installed after the video source, which will replicate the multimedia data into a new flow, targeted to the second client.

As mentioned before, the first client has bandwidth limitation and for this reason, it is necessary that the PBNM knows the QoS parameters of the user by QoS policies. As the customers are not expert users, they are classified in three QoS categories, i.e., Gold, Silver and Bronze. These categories involve several QoS parameters:"if User_Category = Silver then Priority = 5 and Bandwidth = 50 end" , etc.

When the PBNM decides which QoS parameters apply, it transforms the high-level policies into element-level policies; the new policies are distributed to the targeted active nodes (where the service will be installed) and the VAN is created. After that, the delegation phase willbe executed and the VAN is prepared to receive service components. For this reason the management system requests the ASP to deploy servicecomponents, as we have explained in the earlier section. Finally the customers have a service-integrated VAN, which supports the transcoderand duplicator services in order to receive the corresponding video stream from WebTV server. The complete WebTV service scenario is explained in [8].

6   Related Work

The VAN [9] framework introduces the concept of the Virtual Active Network, which can be established on-demand for a particular customer, offering a separate service management interface. Our architecture can be seen as an extension of this work.

The Tempest [10] project provides a programmable network infrastructure, with inherent support for virtual private networks. However Tempest is restricted to the partition of resources and lacks service deployment capabilities.

The Darwin [11] project uses the notion of virtual meshes to describe the virtual networks that encompass the network and computational resources allocated and managed to meet the needs of service providers or applications, providing strong resource control mechanisms. In our approach we have also adopted the use of a component-based service model, which provides greater flexibility in the deployment of new services.

The autonomic service deployment in programmable networks [12] allows deploying component-based services in large-scale networks. The deployment process is executed in two phases, corresponding to the network and node level deployment in our approach. Unlike our approach, the interactions between deployment and management frameworks are not considered.

7   Conclusions

In this paper we have described the approach adopted by the FAIN project for the flexible support of service provisioning, according to the customer-specific requirements. In our view, network management and service deployment are closely related and the corresponding support systems should interoperate when deploying a service. As such, we integrated these two aspects by means of incorporating the PBNM and the ASP systems. The management system is responsible for setting up a suitable network topology and reserving the resources required for the smooth operation of a service, also considering an interdomain situation. The service provisioning system deals with the service-specific requirements and is involved in the process of mapping the service to the network, while it also deploys the appropriate service components to the selected target nodes. The architecture presented has been developed and tested in the framework of the FAIN project. The future work will focus on providing improved support for service reconfigurability. Deployment algorithms and more optimised target environment selection algorithms will also be investigated.

Acknowledgements. This paper describes work undertaken and in progress in the context of the FAIN - IST 10561, a 3-year project from 2000 to 2003, which is partially funded by the Commission of the European Union. The authors would like to acknowledge all FAIN partners for the fruitful discussions that have taken place within this project.

References

1. Galis, A., B. Plattner, J.M. Smith, S. Denazis, E. Moeller, H. Guo, C. Klein, J. Serrat, J. Laarhuis, G.T. Karetsos, C. Todd: "A Flexible IP Active Networks Architecture" International Working Conference on Active Networks (IWAN2000), 16-18 October 2000, Tokyo, Japan
2. FAIN Project WWW Server http://www.ist-fain.org.
3. FAIN Deliverable D7 "Final Active Node Architecture and Design" May 2003 - http://www.ist-fain.org
4. Salamanca, E., E. Magaña, J. Vivero, A. Galis, B. Mathieu, Y. Carlinet, O. Koufopavlou, C. Tsarouchis, C. Kitahara, S Denazis and J. L. Mañas: "A Policy-Based Management Architecture for Active and Programmable Networks" IEEE Network Magazine, Special issue on Network Management of Multiservice Multimedia IP-Based Networks, May 2003, Vol. 17 No.3
5. Solarski, M., M. Bossardt, T. Becker: "Component-based Deployment and Management of Services in Active Networks" IWAN 2002, Zürich, CH, Dec. 2002
6. FAIN Deliverable D8 "Final Specification of Case Study Systems" May 2003 - http://www.ist-fain.org
7. Galis, A., S. Denazis, C. Klein, C. Brou (eds.): "Programmable Networks and their Management" Artech House Books (www.artechhouse.com), ISBN: 1-58053-745-6 (commission for publication in 4th Quarter 2003)
8. FAIN Deliverable D9 "Final Specification of FAIN Scenarios" May 2003 - http://www.ist-fain.org
9. Brunner, M., R. Stadler: "Service Management in Multi-Party Active Networks" IEEE Communications Magazine, Vol. 38(3), 2000
10. van der Merwe, J.E., S. Rooney, I.M. Leslie, S.A. Crosby: "The Tempest - A Practical Framework for Network Programmability" IEEE Network, Vol 12, Number 3, 1998
11. Gao, J., P. Steenkiste, E. Takahashi, and A. Fisher: "A Programmable Router Architecture Supporting Control Plane Extensibility" IEEE Communications Magazine, March 2000
12. Haas, R., P. Droz, B. Stiller: "Autonomic service deployment in networks" IBM Systems Journal, Vol. 42, No. 1, 2003

Adaptation Planning for Active Networks

Alexey Rudenko and Peter Reiher

UCLA, Computer Science Department
{arudenko, reiher}@cs.ucla.edu

Abstract. Active networks and adaptive middleware can improve network service through data adaptation and data rerouting. Automated distribution of adapters is desirable, because choosing proper adapters (from a large set) to handle arbitrary network conditions is complex. The paper presents an automated planning system that helps an active network system choose adapters and their locations. The paper describes the design and implementation of this system and provides performance data on its costs and benefits.

Keywords: active networks, planning, heuristic search, real-time adaptation.

1 Introduction

Modern networks vary considerably in bandwidth, latency, jitter, reliability, etc. Wireless LANS, telephone lines, cellular telephony, and new devices lead to a wide variety of network conditions. One approach to handling such heterogeneity is to adapt data streams. If the sending and consuming applications can handle different forms of data, they can adapt transmissions to current conditions. However, while many applications have some flexibility about the type of data they consume, few are capable of negotiating proper versions of data streams with their providers.

An alternate solution is to use middleware to perform such adaptations. A simple form of such middleware is a proxy server that adapts data sent over wireless. More powerful alternatives like active networks allow adaptation at multiple points.

The adapters used by such middleware handle network problems using different methods to adapt user data. Some adapters handle limited bandwidth, e.g. compressors that run lossless compression algorithms or distillers that drop inessential portions of the data. Encryption adapters handle untrustworthy links. Caches and prefetchers can store user data at middleware adaptation sites. Wireless interface schedulers save power by frequently turning off their radios. Unreliable links can be improved by applying forward-error-correction (FEC) adaptation to user data.

Open network architectures (ONA) combine adapters to address multiple network problems, handling dynamic adapter deployment. This paper discusses planning in active networks, but the results can be applied to other ONA systems.

Choosing adapters and their locations is complex. The right adapters must be chosen in the right order, since misordered adapters can be counterproductive. For example, applying encryption before compression renders compression ineffective. If

N. Wakamiya et al. (Eds.): IWAN 2003, LNCS 2982, pp. 252-265, 2004.

multiple active network nodes are available, choosing which of them to host adapters is also difficult. Some choices will provide better efficiency and latency than others.

These problems are solved by creating a *plan* describing which adapters to run, in what order, and where. The problem is too complex for users, and too dynamic to be preprogrammed. This paper presents the design, implementation, and measured performance of an automated planning system that serves unicast connections by applying distributed adaptation to adaptation-unaware real-time applications.

2   The Planning Problem

Consider a user viewing confidential large images over several links. A wireless link is low bandwidth, insecure, and unreliable. An Internet link is insecure. The connection will benefit if compression, prioritization, encryption, and packet-level FEC [15] are applied to the wireless link and encryption applied to the Internet link.

Compression, encryption, and FEC have paired adapters. The first adapter adapts the data; the second adapter returns the data to its original state. In this example, someone must order and distribute nine adapters on three connection nodes. Exhaustive search of possible plans requires two seconds on a Dell Inspiron 333 MHz computer to examine 9600 plans, too long for many real-time applications.

In another example, field archeologists collect graphical images, video clips, and teleconferencing materials at an excavation area and exchange this data with remote colleagues [1]. Video data is sent via wireless to a nearby base station, connected to the Internet via DSL. This communication requires teleconferencing QoS. Confidentiality is important. Thus, the wireless link requires compression, encryption, and packet level FEC. The DSL link has lower bandwidth, requiring distilling and compression. The archeologists sacrifice video stream quality for teleconferencing real-time guarantees. The Internet link requires encryption. In this example, we must order and distribute eleven adapters across four nodes. Checking all of the hundreds of thousands of possible plans requires tens of minutes, an unacceptable latency.

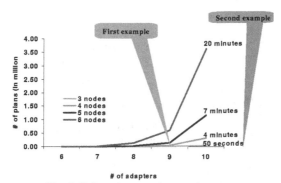

Fig. 1. Exhaustive search on a plan space

Figure 1 shows the size of plan spaces for differing numbers of connection nodes and adapters. Adapters are deployed in order, i.e. compressor upstream, decompressor downstream, etc. The plan space grows exponentially with the number of nodes and adapters, making exhaustive search infeasible, even for realistic examples. With the growth of ad hoc networking, the number of nodes in a connection will grow (and with it, presumably the number of available ONA nodes), making exhaustive search planning even less suitable. The number of minutes shows the latency of exhaustive search for connections with 10 adapters.

One planning method is to use a small number of precalculated plan templates containing ordered dummy adapters assigned to virtual nodes. Real adapters and actual nodes are substituted at connection establishment. The planner chooses an appropriate plan template for current conditions, adds real adapters, and adjusts the template to the connection.

A simpler version puts all adapters on nodes adjacent to the problem links. The resulting plan may inefficiently use an adaptation multiple times. In Figure 2, compression is inefficiently applied twice on adjacent low-bandwidth links. Another simplification is to put all adapters on the end nodes of a connection (Figure 3). Two adjacent links require compression and encryption. The end nodes should run both adaptations, but those nodes lack the resources to do so. Thus, the plan calculated with this method is unusable.

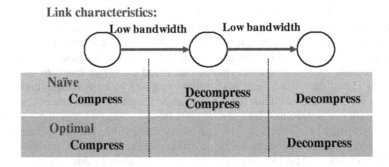

Fig. 2. Example 1 of simple template planning

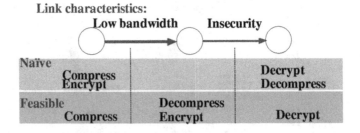

Fig. 3. Example 2 of simple template planning

Full-scale template planning is not flexible enough to handle the entire problem. The more templates the planner has, the more flexible a plan, but harder it gets to find it. Assume N links in a connection and P problems on the connection links. Then 2^{NP} possible link situations can occur in a connection. Either an exponential number of templates must be provided, or some possible situations will not be handled properly. The number of possible adapter locations adds complexity. Node resource constraints may make a template unusable. The more complexities added, the less advantage one gets from the supposed simplicity of template planning.

This paper presents another approach that avoids the combinatoric explosion of the planning problem. In this approach, the planner calculates a plan online during the connection establishment using a heuristic search in the plan space.

3 The Planner Design

Our planner had to meet several requirements. It had to be fast, to serve real-time applications. Its plans had to use adapters consistently so that no adapter inhibits the work of another adapter or destroys the semantics of user data. The planning system had to be extensible, allowing later addition of new adapters.

The planner uses *adapter descriptions*, which contain the following data:

Problem ID. Network problems are described with unique problem identifications, e.g. low bandwidth, insecurity, etc. Problem ID is used to match observed problems to suitable adapters.

Method of resolution. A given problem can be solved in more than one way. For example, the low-bandwidth problem can be solved by compression, distilling, prioritization, etc.

Adaptation effect. The properties of applying an adapter, such as estimated efficiency of adaptation. The planner uses this adapter efficiency attribute to choose between two adapters that solve the same problem. The data size impact describes the adapter's effect on data throughput, and whether it is lossy. A compressor reduces the amount of data sent, while FEC increases it. The planner extends the effect of the adapters that reduce data volume over more connection links. The planner prefers lossless adaptation to lossy adapter.

Adaptation cost. Adapters have costs: CPU, memory, etc. Adapters use can also have monetary or deployment latency costs. The planner will try to minimize these costs.

Preconditions of adapter use. Some adapters require that certain pre-conditions be satisfied, such as data must be in a particular format. Once a Lempel Ziv compressor or encryption is applied, another Lempel Ziv compression becomes useless. We use various compressabilities as preconditions that characterize whether a particular compressor can be applied to user data.

Postconditions of adapter use. Adapter postconditions describe the properties of the data after adapter application, allowing them to be matched to the next adapter's pre-conditions.

The planner requires some information to calculate a plan. Planning data consists of stream characteristics, stream requirements, user preferences, link conditions, and node resources.

Stream characteristics. These describe the user data stream, such as format of data and whether the data is compressed or encrypted by the user application that generated the stream.

Stream requirements. These show the minimal useful throughput of the stream, confidentiality requirements, etc.

User preferences. Users can optionally choose a particular problem solution (e.g., dropping video stream resolution instead of color), or require the use of a particular adapter.

Link conditions. Link conditions affect the data transfer. The planner compares stream conditions, stream requirements, and link conditions to detect problems and select remedies. Link conditions include bandwidth, jitter, latency, reliability, security, etc. Small fluctuations in a link attribute can be handled by choosing adapters able to handle a wide range of conditions.

Node resources. A plan's use of node resources must be verified as feasible during plan calculation. An ONA node's policy on resource sharing (priority, client quotas, purchased levels of service) affects feasibility, preventing one connection from hogging all node resources. Node resources consist of CPU, hard drive, memory, associated costs, etc.

The planner uses heuristic search in the plan space to calculate a plan, executing three consecutively executed processes: *adapter selection*, *adapter ordering*, and *plan optimization*.

Adapter selection allows the planner to verify plan feasibility at any point, since it is working with real adapters. But if the wrong adapter is selected, it will affect all the following planning steps, and changing the adapter requires starting the entire process over again.

Adapter ordering uses precalculated templates. These are used exclusively to determine acceptable ordering of adapters, avoiding the earlier-mentioned problems of template planning.

After adapters are selected and ordered, the plan is optimized.

Dividing planning into these steps reduces the search space. Some early choices affect further steps, which could prevent finding the best plan. The planner does not guarantee optimality. The selection of effective heuristics is the key issue for the heuristic search. We verify our heuristic choices through comparison with exhaustive search.

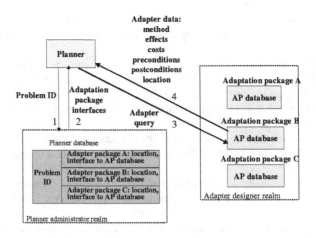

Fig. 4. Adapter selection

Adapter selection. Adapter selection is the first step of planning (Figure 4). The planner analyzes stream characteristics, stream requirements, and link resources to detect problems, and uses problem IDs to select the adapters. The planner searches its database by problem ID, step 1. Adaptation package records (APRs) are associated with a problem ID, which also contains the package's location and an interface to the package's own database. More than one APR can be returned to the planner for a single problem ID, step 2. The planner uses various techniques to choose adaptation packages, such as self-learning or always choosing a preferred package.

The planner uses the chosen APR's interface to query the adaptation package database, which returns the real adapter data step 3 and 4. The adaptation package database is provided by the adapter designer. This two-level access to adapter data allows the planner and adaptation designers to work independently, relying on the interface to reconcile their requirements. This process produces an unordered set of adapters associated with nodes adjacent to the problematic links.

Adapter ordering. Partial-order plan templates are calculated off-line. The adapters in the templates are represented by adapter methods that define proper adapter order (e.g., Figure 5). Some adapters are arranged sequentially, such as distilling, compression, encryption, and FEC. Other adapters are arranged in parallel, such as format conversion, data storage, and filtering; their order is determined later, as described below. A format converter can be applied to data before or after distilling, as long as the data format is recognizable. Caching should be applied before FEC, to avoid wasting caching resources. Format-insensitive filtering is not limited by order.

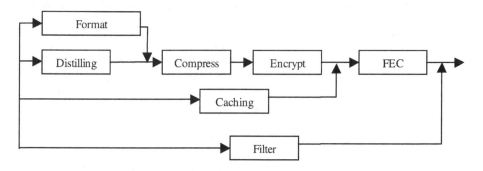

Fig. 5. An example of partial-order template plan for adapter ordering

The planner then replaces adapter methods with real adapters. Parallel orderings are resolved using additional constraints of the real environment, such as application requirements, adapter pre- and postconditions, and network conditions.

Adapter conflicts are detected by analyzing their pre- and postconditions. The planner resolves conflicts by changing the adapter order if possible, or it adds a format conversion adapter to resolve the conflict. If a conflict cannot be resolved, the planning process must restart with adapter selection.

Adapter selection and ordering produces a chain of local plans where every adapter is selected, ordered, and located in the nodes adjacent to the link with the problem. Figure 6 shows an example from the archeology scenario. This plan can be used, but it may be inefficient. It may include redundant adapters (see Section II). Or link resources can be wasted when compression is applied to one link and not to others.

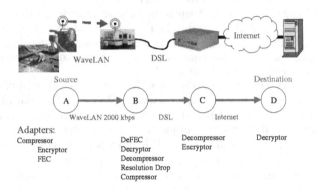

Adapters:

Compressor	DeFEC	Decompressor	Decryptor
Encryptor	Decryptor	Encryptor	
FEC	Decompressor		
	Resolution Drop		
	Compressor		

Fig. 6. The result of adapter selection and ordering: the chain of local plans

Plan optimization. Plan optimization uses a variant of a recursive best-first search algorithm. The initial point is the chain of local plans described above. The optimization algorithm applies transformations to the current point, evaluating each transformation's value and feasibility. If a transformation produces a better value of the evaluation function and the new plan is feasible, the plan is recorded as a potential solution. The goal is to find the minimum of the evaluation function. The transformations are based on merging neighboring plans, preserving the order of adapters from both plans. Merging two plans involves three nodes: the node common to both plans (the median point) and two other end nodes. Merging moves adapters from the median point to the end nodes. After all adapters are moved, redundant adapters are dropped, resulting in a new plan to be merged with its neighboring plan. The goal is to merge as many plans as possible–ideally all plans of the connection.

Plan merging can be interrupted for various reasons, including a worse evaluation function value, insufficient node resources, or unrecoverable adapter conflict. If merging is interrupted in one place, it can be resumed in another place in the chain of plans. If time runs out, the merging process stops and the best plan found so far is chosen. An example of creating an optimal plan by merging for our archeological scenario is presented in Figures 7 and 8. First the plans on links AB and BC are merged, then the resulting merged plan is merged with the CD link plan.

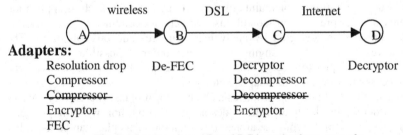

Fig. 7. Merging plans AB and BC in archeology example

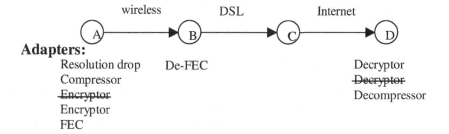

Adapters:

Resolution drop	De-FEC		Decryptor
Compressor			~~Decryptor~~
~~Encryptor~~			Decompressor
Encryptor			
FEC			

Fig. 8. Merging plans AC and CD in archeology example

We use an evaluation function to drive the optimization process:

$$f = \sum^{links}\sum_{k}^{resources} \alpha_k lr_k + \sum^{nodes}\sum_{m}^{resources} \beta_m nr_m,$$

where *lr* and *nr* are link and node resources, and α and β are normalizing weight coefficients. We optimize the plan by minimizing the link and node resources used by the connection. Although the function does not contain latency explicitly, dropping the redundant adapters reduces adaptation latency.

Feasibility verification involves comparing the resources required by the adapters to available node resources at the locations where these adapters must be executed.

Thus, the planning algorithm contains the following steps:

1. Detect network problems by analyzing the application stream characteristics and requirements and available link resources.
2. Select adapters that solve any detected problems.
3. Order the chosen adapters on the nodes adjacent to problematic links using the partial-order plan template.
4. Merge the first two plans from the resulting chain of plans.
5. Evaluate the result with the evaluation function.
6. Verify the consistency of adapters.
7. Verify the feasibility of the resulting plan.
8. If the plan is better according to the optimization function, if the adaptations are consistent, and if the plan is feasible, record it.
9. Merge the plan that is the result of the previous merging with the next-neighbor plan. If all plans are merged, return the last recorded plan and stop.
10. Go to step 5.

The result of adapter selection and ordering is a plan that can be used as a solution. The transformations change the state of one potential solution to another potential solution. The minimization of the evaluation function helps to find the best solution, but it may only find a local minimum. The optimization produces a best-effort plan.

During the merging process we preserve the original order of adapters. However, the consistency of adapters may be violated. Thus, we must verify adapter consistency during plan merging. If it is violated, it must be restored using the techniques described earlier. If adapter consistency cannot be restored, plan merging fails.

With *p* adapters and *n* nodes, the total merging complexity is $O(pn)$. Each optimization step has complexity $O(n)$. Hence, the total complexity is $O(pn^2)$.

4   The Planner Implementation

The planner was implemented in the Panda active network middleware [5]. Panda uses active network technology to serve adaptation-unaware applications. Panda intercepts normal data packets set to a destination and converts them into active packets, which are stored on the source node until a plan is calculated and deployed. Panda collects the planning data, invokes plan calculation using the planner described in Section III, and deploys the plan. The source node then sends the active version of the application packets to the destination. They are intercepted at any Panda nodes along the path that have had adapters deployed for this connection.

This planner can calculate a local plan for a particular connection link or a whole-connection centralized plan for all links. In this implementation, local plans are calculated as a fast, but often subotimal, solution to start data transfer quickly. Local plan calculation involves only adapter selection and ordering. A whole connection plan is simultaneously calculated and ultimately replaces the local plan.

If Panda detects that the network conditions change sufficiently during a connection that the existing plan cannot satisfy the connection requirements, Panda replans, substituting a newer, more suitable plan for the old obsolete plan. The unused adapters are garbage collected by Panda nodes later.

5   Performance

In this section we present some performance measurements of the planner and the Panda planning implementation described above; more results are presented in [16].

We tested a Java implementation of the planner on 333 MHz Dell Inspiron laptops. Connections were generated in a randomized fashion. The links between the nodes were randomly assigned bandwidths of 10 Mbps, 2 Mbps, or 100 Kbps. Moving data over a 10-Mbps link required no adaptation. Moving it over a 2-Mbps link required Lempel-Ziv compression. Moving it over a 100-Kbps link required both lossy filtering and LZ compression. Each link was designated secure or insecure, requiring no adaptation or encryption and decryption, respectively. We generated a resource availability for each node, expressed as the number of adapters the node could run.

Figure 9 shows the latency ratio between heuristic and exhaustive search for differing numbers of connection nodes and adapters. For small cases (e.g., three nodes, 4 adapters), exhaustive search is better, but the planning latency is less than 10 milliseconds here. For larger cases, heuristic search was better, and had larger latencies. Exhaustive search becomes infeasible as the number of nodes and adapters grows. A hybrid approach could use exhaustive search for small numbers of nodes and adapters, but the relatively low cost of heuristic search in such cases might make the extra complexity of supporting both styles of search unnecessary.

Figures 10 and 11 show that the latency of heuristic planning is below 90 milliseconds for 6 nodes with 14 adapters, and below 160 milliseconds for 12 nodes with 9 adapters. Exhaustive search would require many hours or days in these cases. Heuristic search failed to find the optimal plan for a four-node connection in only one case of 1000 tests, and in only three of 1000 tests for a five node connection. In 1 percent of the cases for six-node connection that were tested, an optimal plan was not found. Thus, in 99+ percent of realistic cases, the heuristic search planner found the optimal plan. The cases where it was not found by heuristic search occur when the majority of connection nodes are able to run a very limited numbers of adapters.

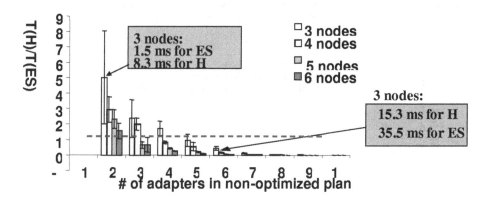

Fig. 9. Heuristic/exhaustive search latency ratio

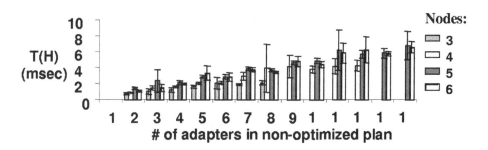

Fig. 10. Heuristic planning latency with respect to number of adapters and nodes

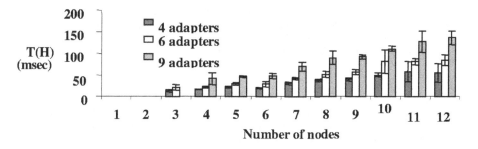

Fig. 11. Heuristic planning latency with respect to number of nodes and adapters

The Panda planning system was tested on true real-time applications. A video stream was generated by the WaveVideo multimedia package [3] and sent to a destination using a connection of HP 500 MHz machines running Panda. The efficiency of the transmission is measured in dB of PSNR (peak signal-to-noise ratio). The graph in Figure 12 demonstrates the advantages of adapting video streams in low-bandwidth, often-insecure network links. The darkest bars represent a connection not using Panda. This connection's PSNR is 10dB lower than the Panda-adapted connections on low-bandwidth (150, 800 kbps) links. Even when Panda adds other benefits (encryption), the PSNR is still significantly better than not using Panda.

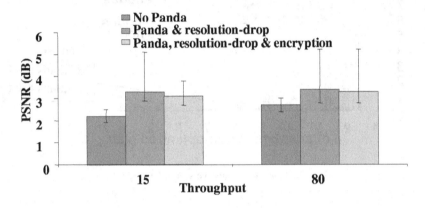

Fig. 12. PSNR (luminance) of adapted and unadapted (no Panda) video streams.

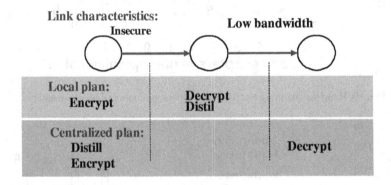

Fig. 13. Centralized versus local planning

Figure 13 shows the advantages of centralized planning. One link has insufficient bandwidth, another is insecure. If the first link needs encryption and the second needs filtering, then the incremental plan puts an encryptor on the source node and a decryptor and a filter on the next node. This is worse than the optimized plan that puts the filter and encryptor on the source node and the decryptor on the next node. In the latter case, encryption and decryption are applied to fewer packets. This difference is measurable (Figure 14). Centralized planning displays better PSNR than local planning, and adaptation shows better PSNR than no adaptation.

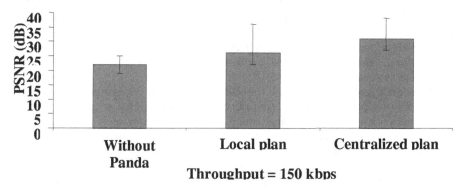

Fig. 14. PSNR of non-adapted, local planning, and centralized planning video streams.

6   Related Work

Many ONA technologies require applications to do their own planning, including ANTS [19] and SwitchWare [8], and the Rover tool kit [10]. Providing benefits to ONA-unaware programs usually require explicit user or system administrator configuration. In the Berkley proxy system [4], Protocol Boosters [13], and Odyssey [14], the services are typically simple and must be prelocated.

Choi [2] uses automated planning route through the network. Their planning problem has the same complexity as the graph shortest-path problem. MediaNet [9] uses stream characteristics, user preferences, and templates to build a simple plan based on resource scheduling to improve performance and utilization. Conductor [20] is able to plug in a variety of plan formulation algorithms, but so far uses a relatively cheap and simple planning algorithm. The Panda planning approach is consistent with Conductor's planning model. CANS [6] plans based on high-level specifications of component behavior and network routing characteristics. The CANS algorithm complexity is $O(p^3n^3)$, while our algorithm has a lower complexity of $O(pn^2)$.

Planning is well studied in artificial intelligence and operational research [17]. Approaches include partial order planning in a solution space [18], recursive best-first search [12], and genetic algorithms [11].

7   Conclusions

This paper has demonstrated that it is possible to build a quick, effective, extensible automated planning system to bring the benefits of active networks to applications not written to use them. This system out-performs alternatives such as exhaustive search or treating the problems of each link separately. The system can be thousands of times faster than exhaustive search, and can handle problems too large for exhaustive search. Our system produced plans up to 100% better than incremental planning. The system can significantly improve the observable performance of real-world applications. Our Panda-based automated planner provided more than 10 dB PSNR improvement over an unadapted data stream. These measurements also show the value of a sophisticated planning algorithm. The central plan produced by our complete algorithm provided around a 7 dB improvement over unsophisticated per-link planning. This planner could be used in a wide variety of open network architecture systems.

This planner is of particular value for peer systems. Such systems are likely to face multiple network problems on several different links, since each peer might be using a wireless network, a modem, or other problematic link. Peer systems often belong to unsophisticated users, and are unlikely to have good means of handling dynamic problems. Automated planning of adaptations avoids many such shortcomings.

Automated planning might assist design of distributed component systems, especially when they face unpredictable and dynamic conditions. For example, automated planning may support roaming services with drastically changing conditions . Our experience suggests that leveraging specifics of the problem space is vital to achieve success. While the planner outlined here is directly usable, the ideas and techniques used to create this planner may prove more even widely applicable.

References

1. M. Ancona, G. Dodero, C. Fierro, V. Gianuzzi, V. Tine, A. Traverso, "Mobile Computing for Real Time Support in Archaeological Excavations," *Proceedings of Computer Applications in Archaeology*, University of Birmingham, UK, April 1997.
2. Sumi Choi, J. Turner, and T. Wolf, "Configuring sessions in programmable networks," *Proceedings IEEE INFOCOM 2001*, vol. 1, pp. 60-67, April 2001,.
3. G. Fankhauser at al., "WaveVideo — An Integrated Approach to Adaptive Wireless Video," *Mobile Networks and Applications*, 4(4): 255-271, December 1999.
4. A. Fox, S. Griddle, E.. Brewer, and E. Amir, "Adapting to Network and Client Variations Using Infrastructural Proxies: Lessons and Perspectives," *IEEE Personal Communications*, September 1998, 5(4), pp. 10-19.
5. V. Ferreria, A. Rudenko, K. Eustice, R. Guy, V. Ramakrishna, and P. Reiher, "Panda: Middleware to Provide the Benefits of Active Networks to Legacy Applications," *DANCE 02*, January 2002.
6. X. Fu, W. Shi, A. Akkerman, and V. Karancheti, "CANS: Composable, Adaptive Network Services Infrastructure", USITS, March 2001.
7. John S. Gero and Vladimir A. Kazakov, "Evolving Design Genes in Space Layout Planning Problems," *Artificial Intelligence in Engineering*, vol. 12, 1998, pp. 163-176.
8. Michael Hicks and A. D. Keromytis, "A Secure Plan. Active Networks," *First International Working Conference, IWONA'99 Proceedings*, Springer-Verlag, 1999. pp.307-314.
9. Mickael Hicks, Adithya Nagarajan, and Robert van Renesse, "User-specified Adaptive Scheduling in a Streaming Media Network," IEEE OPENARCH'03, April 2003.
10. A. Joseph, A. deLespinasse, J. Tauber, D.. Giffort, and M. Frans Kaashoek, "Rover: A Toolkit for Mobile Information Access," *Mobicom '96*, November 1996.
11. F. B. Kelly, "Routing in circuit-switched networks: optimization, shadow prices and decentralization ," *Advances in Applied Probability*, vol. 20, 1988, 112-144.

12. R. Korf, "Linear-Space Best-First Search," Artificial Intelligence, 62, 1993, pp. 41-78.
13. A. Mallet, J. Chung, and J. Smith, "Operating System Support for Protocol Boosters," HIPPARCH Workshop, June 1997.
14. B. Noble, D. Narayan, J. Tilton, J. Flinn, K. Walker, "Agile Application-Aware Adaptation for Mobility," *Proceedings of the 16ᵗʰ ACM Symposium on Operating Principles*, 1997.
15. L. Rizzo "Effective erasure codes for reliable computer communication protocols", Computer Communication Review, 27 (2), April 1997, p 24-36
16. Rudenko Alexey and Peter Reiher, "Experience with automated planning for Panda," Tech Report CSD-TR 010041, Computer Science Department, UCLA, 2001.
17. S. Russel and P. Norvig, *Artificial Intelligence*, Prentice Hall, 1995.
18. D. Weld, "An Introduction to Least Commitment Planning," *AI Magazine*,.15(4), 1994.
19. D. Wetherall, J. Guttag, and D. Tennenhouse, "ANTS: a toolkit for building and dynamically deploying network protocols," *IEEE Open Architectures and Network Programming*, Apr. 1998.
20. Mark Yarvis, Peter Reiher, and Gerald J. Popek, "Conductor: A Framework for Distributed Adaptation," *HotOS VII*, Rio Rico, AZ, March 1999.

Risky Business: Motivations for Markets in Programmable Networks

Ian Wakeman, David Ellis, Tim Owen, Julian Rathke, and Des Watson

University of Sussex

Abstract. We believe that the problems of safety, security and resource usage combine to make it unlikely that programmable networks will ever be viable without mechanisms to transfer risk from the platform provider to the user and the programmer. However, we have well established mechanisms for managing risk - markets. In this paper we argue for the establishment of markets to manage the risk in running a piece of software and to ensure that the risk is reflected on all the stakeholders.
We describe a strawman architecture for third party computation in the programmable network. Within this architecture, we identify two major novel features:- Dynamic price setting, and a reputation service. We investigate the feasibility of these features and provide evidence that a practical system can indeed be built.
Our contributions are in the argument for markets providing a risk management mechanism for programmable networks, the development of an economic model showing incentives for developing better software, and in the first analysis of a real transaction graph for reputation systems from an Internet commerce site.

1 Introduction

The core problem being tackled in active networking is the same as for any mobile code approach - how can we allow computation to take place on behalf of some third party, yet be sure with high probability that the outcome of the computation will not be harmful to the local machine or environment? There have been attempts to use technologies from the programming language design community, such as safe typing [1,2] and namespace protection [3,4], to design safe programming languages for active networks and service. Systems have been built to control the execution environment of third party programs using and extending the techniques from operating systems for controlling scheduling, memory usage and general access control [5,6,7]. Yet another approach for component based programs is to check a priori that the program composition graph is acceptable [8,9].

Yet despite this panoply of technical solutions, there is no widespread deployment of platforms supporting third party computation for networks or anything else[1]. We would argue that this situation exists because there is no benefit to the

---

[1] One could argue that PlanetLab is a distributed programming platform, yet the users have to pay by providing computers to use the system. This is therefore evidence that the market has to be involved.

N. Wakamiya et al. (Eds.): IWAN 2003, LNCS 2982, pp. 266–279, 2004.

manager of any platform in supporting third party computation, and further, that there is no way for the manager to reflect the risk undertaken by hosting the platform.

The risks to the platform from running software on behalf of someone else are that the software, whether through malice or accident, will deny resources to other users, potentially leading to crashes of their programs and the platform. This will result in the platform being perceived as *unsafe* by the affected users, and they will become reluctant to run software on the platform again. In the worst case, the software may open up the platform owner to liability for loss and damage caused to other users. Despite the increasing reliability and safety of operating systems, there remains a probability that software can deny resources to other users.

Instead we propose that the manager of the computing platform has to be appropriately reimbursed for the risk they are taking in hosting the third party computation, and that the amount of reimbursement should be decided through market mechanisms. The remainder of this paper provides an overview of market based scheduling of programs, and outline a strawman architecture for using markets to calculate the riskiness of running a given program. We then demonstrate the feasibility of two novel aspects of this strawman architecture; the spreading of risk through market mechanisms and the use of a distributed reputation system. We conclude with a discussion of the possibilities for future work.

2   Market Based Computational Systems

Market mechanisms for scheduling computation are not novel. There have been systems designed for the grid and other systems, such as Condor [10], Spawn [11], the Java Market [12] and Nimrod-G [13]. Surveys and taxonomies of the various approaches can be found in [14] and [15]. Market mechanisms appear in many other places, most notably for controlling congestion [16,17,18].

Negotiating which buyers buy from which sellers is a fundamental choice in the design of any market-based system. Given that our motivation for a market based system is for sellers to set prices to guard against the various risks of the different buyers, we consider mechanisms which allow sellers to set prices. A more commonly adopted approach is to use a tender/contract approach, where buyers issue a tender for contract, to which sellers respond with a bid based upon their estimate of their costs and the value of their service to the seller. Buyers can then set a buyer-specific price, resulting in different buyers receiving different prices for the same product.

It is a well-established economic principle that differential pricing with large fixed costs can be very efficient [19]. By selling each unit at the highest price each individual is willing to pay, the producer maximises profit and increases the number of consumers who are able to buy the product. Telecommunications and airlines are good examples of real markets where this happens. There are two main arguments against differential pricing in reality:

1. How can sellers get enough information to set prices appropriately?
2. What happens if buyers resell the product?

If differential pricing is to be effective, it behooves the infrastructure designers to ensure that there is sufficient information for sellers to match prices to
customers' perceived value. We propose the use of a distributed database containing the outcomes of each transaction, which can then be used to determine
the reputation of each seller, customer and program. The reputation of the seller
and program can be used to adjust prices to account not only for the expected
resource usage, but also for the lost opportunity cost if the program misbehaves
and affects other customers.

We would argue that reselling is not necessarily a bad thing. In our current
design, when the contract between the seller and buyer is made, the right to
process uses a cryptographic ticket tied to the identities of the seller, buyer and
program. To transfer a ticket, the buyer has to chain the identity of the new
ticket owner onto the ticket by re-signing the ticket to confirm the ticket has
been transferred. The outcomes of running the program are then inserted into
the reputation system under both the original buyer and the rebuyer. Any future
price setting will use these outcomes to set price, so that if the reseller wishes to
continue trading, they have to ensure that their customers don't adversely affect
their reputation. By allowing trade in tickets bearing a right to process, the
market can be made more efficient, since the brokers can accept the responsibility
of matching prices to buyers, and the processor owners need only worry about
the reputations of the resellers.

3   The Risk Compensation Architecture for Third Party Computation

To explore the design space for building an infrastructure to support risk com-
pensated third party compensation, we produced a strawman architecture, based
on rapid prototyping of the various system components. We assume that there
are a small number of platforms at each locality which can have the necessary
capabilities to run software on behalf of a set of customers. The software can
run for a short duration, e.g. in providing rerouting of critical services during
a Denial of Service attack, or of long duration, such as offering a game server.
We assume that the service location problem is solved elsewhere. The customer
either directly interacts with the system, or a software agent [20] acts on the
customer's behalf.

The sequence of interactions is illustrated in Figure 1.

1. The customer makes a request for a price to run an identified piece of software. The customer and software are named through a self-certifying naming
   system, e.g. by the software using a tree of hashes [21] and identifying the
   customer through a hash of their public key.
2. The processors look up the customer's entries in the reputation service
   database. All relevant records are returned.

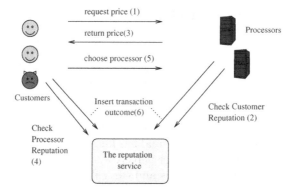

request price (1)

return price(3)

choose processor (5)

Processors

Customers

Insert transaction
outcome(6)

Check Customer
Reputation (2)

Check
Processor
Reputation
(4)

The reputation
service

Fig. 1. The Strawman Risk Compensation Architecture for Third Party Computation

3. The processor calculates and returns a price to the customer, using the entries from the reputation service.

4. The customers check the processors' reputations.

5. The customers make a judgment on which is the best processor for their job and request execution.

6. After execution, the processor and customer sign an xml certificate describing the memory and processor cycles used, and whether the jobs generated uncaught signals or exceptions. They insert the certificate into the reputation service.

Many of the pieces of this architecture have been built and used together before, e.g. in the systems surveyed in [14,15]. Cryptographic requests and tickets are easily built from standard security protocols and digital signatures [22]. Mobile code systems have been shown to work in many projects, such as in our previous work on SafetyNet [23].

The novel features of the strawman design are in calculating an offer price based upon the reputation of the customer, and in the use of a reputation service. In our initial prototype, the setting of an offer price would often lead to wild fluctuations in the offered price. To understand this behaviour further and to develop more stable pricing systems, we built further simulations described in Section 4.1. Our initial implementation of the reputation service was based upon a single mysql database. If the reputation service is to be practical, then it must scale in the number of entries and the number of users, be resistant to manipulation by malevolent users, and provide appropriate information to the users of the service. We undertook studies of existing reputation systems, and show how the results of these studies should guide the design of future reputation services.

4   A Simple Market Model

We base our model firmly in the microeconomic theory of oligopolies. We assume that each location has a small number of processors available, and that there are a set of customers who wish to use these machines. For each processor, there are zero marginal costs for supplying customers - there is purely a fixed cost for maintaining and running the processor. Each processor can set a customer specific price for the customer to run their software. Each processor is aware of the funds available to each customer, and has knowledge of the utility function of each customer - i.e. how the customer perceives *value*. Each customer is aware of the other customers' utility functions and can calculate the expected *load* upon each processor.

We model each processor as a simple M/M/1 queuing system. Thus for each customer i there is a load λ_{ij} placed upon the processor j. Each processor has a capacity μ_j. The total waiting and service time, T_j, from the processor is therefore:

$$T_j = \frac{1}{\mu_j - \sum^i \lambda_{ij}}$$

The customer cares about the response time from the processor (larger is worse), their own load placed upon the processor (larger is better) and the cost of using the processor (less is better). We follow a conventional economic approach and model the customer's utility function as:

$$u_i = \sum^j T_j^\alpha \lambda_{ij}^\beta (p_{ij}\lambda_{ij})^\gamma$$

If we set $\alpha = -1, \beta = 2$ and $\gamma = -1$, then we obtain[2]:

$$u_i = \sum^j \frac{\lambda_{ij}(\mu_j - \sum^k \lambda_{kj})}{p_{ij}}$$

where p_{ij} is the price offered by processor j to customer i per unit of service. We model the load setting game as follows: For each customer, the customer searches for the load vector to load on each processor that would maximise the customer's utility, subject to the constraint that their expenditure mustn't exceed their income I_i:

$$p_i.\lambda_i \leq I_i$$

This set of loads is their *best response* to the loads set by the other processors. This game is repeated until no processor can increase its income by adjusting its price vector. This is the *Nash Equilibrium* point of the of the customer utilities for a given price matrix by definition. It should be noted that the Nash equilibrium is guaranteed to exist since the utility function is continuous and concave in the the Euclidean space defined by the feasible set of loads [24]. We describe this theory more in the accompanying technical report [25].

---

[2] These values are chosen arbitrarily

We assume that the processors set prices, as in the oligopoly theory of Bertrand [26]. Processors will set prices so as to maximise their income. The income received by each processor π_j is simply the sum of the price offered to each customer multiplied by the load offered by that processor over all customers.

$$\pi_j = \sum^i p_{ij}\lambda_{ij}$$

We model risk by assuming that there is a failure rate associated with the software run by each customer, f_i. Our simulation runs through a set of discrete rounds, where the prices and associated loads are calculated for each round. The perceived failure rate of a processor is then the weighted sum of the failure rates of the software run upon the processors, weighted by how much load each customer places upon the processor. We modify the utility function of the customers to use the last seen failure rate in their utility calculation.

$$u_i = \sum^j \frac{\lambda_{ij}(\mu_j - \sum^k \lambda_{kj})}{p_{ij}f_j^2}$$

The analytic solution of the load setting game for the customers is derived in the Appendix.

In our model, the processors take turns setting prices that maximise their revenues from the loads which the customers have maximised. This game is repeated until no processor would increase its revenues by changing its prices. This is again a Nash equilibrium. In calculating the expected revenue, the processors not only maximise the revenue for the current round, but the expected future revenue based upon how their perceived failure rate will be modified.

We built a Matlab simulation of the above model and ran it through many different sets of experiments. As we discuss in the appendix, the discounting of future income will generally result in a complex equation to predict future income, and the price setting game is not guaranteed to converge on a single optimum point. Instead, we have found that the price setting may develop a *limit cycle* in which there are a cycle of best responses to each of the other processors' prices. We are attempting to develop the theory further to show that the game will either converge to a single point in the pricing space, or will develop a limit cycle and will never diverge. We have not discovered any combinations of settings where the prices diverge. To deal with this eventuality, our simulation terminates a round either when the price setting converges to a stable set of prices, or a limit cycle is detected over a number of iterations.

4.1   Case Studies and Simulations

We illustrate two of the more interesting cases below. In each of the scenarios, the processors discount 2 rounds into the future, calculating their expected income as a weighted sum of income, assuming that perceived failure rates change based on the expected customer load, and using the same price vector in the future. The customer and processor tournaments carry on until the change per round is less than a given small amount.

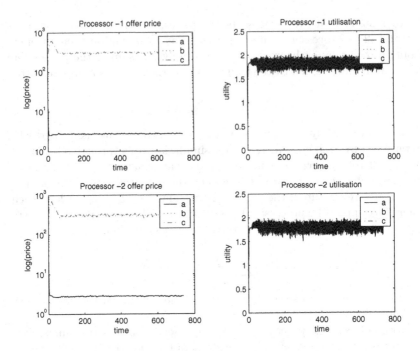

Fig. 2. Offered price for bad software

Bad *Software*. In this scenario, there are 3 customers wishing to run software on either of 2 equal processors. Customers 1 and 2 are *good* customers whose software doesn't crash the processor with income of 10 units each. Customer 3 has *bad* software which crashes the processor, disrupting the other jobs and a relatively low income of 1 unit. In Figure 2, notice how the price offered to customer 3 by either of the processors becomes so high that customer 3 cannot afford to offer very much load. Even with a relatively simplistic optimisation game, there are emergent behaviours which penalise bad software due to their detrimental effects on the reputation of the processors.

Bad *Software and Risk-Taking Processors*. In this scenario, there are 3 customers wishing to run software on 3 processors. Customers *a* and *b* run good software with a failure rate of 0.1 units, whilst customer *c* has bad software with a failure rate of 1 unit. Each of the customers has 10 units of income. Processors 1 and 2 have capacity of 10 units, whilst processor 3 has a capacity of 1 unit. In Figure 3, the processors serve two different market segments. Processors 1 and 2 become low failure rate processors mainly servicing the good customers, whilst the other processor becomes a relatively failure prone machine thus getting a large part of customer *c*'s income. This illustrates that differential pricing can create niche markets.

We believe that a major advantage of using software reputation in setting the price for running a program will be in creating incentives for better software.

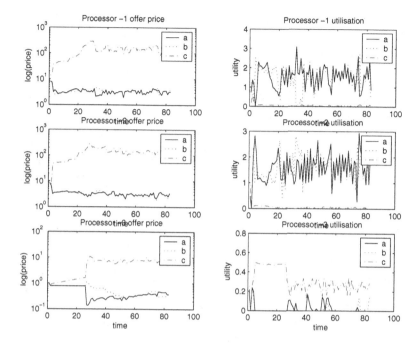

Fig. 3. The emergence of risk taking processors

If software has a lot of bugs, then its reputation will decrease and the price to run it will rise. Customers will then have an incentive to pressure the software developers for better software, either through economic pressure by reducing sales, or through exerting social pressure to reduce the number of bugs.

As program developers will feel more direct pressure to produce better software, then developers will have incentives to adopt technology which increases the safety of their programs. In this way software technology, such as type safe languages have better chance to compete in the market.

Segmentation of the market will provide separate resources for production code and for testing code. Free and best effort platforms may emerge, whose reputation and load will provide indicators as to whether they should be trusted.

Although our simulation modes indicate that differential pricing provides many good features, more work needs to be done yet. Our model only uses one approach to negotiating a price. There are many other possible mechanisms for negotiating prices, and the emerging area of mechanism design for the Internet and computational systems may provide better technology [27].

5 The Feasibility of a Distributed Reputation System

In our initial implementation of a reputation service, we had no data upon which to base our design. To ensure that our future work was tested upon real data, we analysed an existing reputation system in which products and services were bought by real people with real money. The Amazon.co.uk website provides a variety of commerce activities through its "Marketplace" and "Z-Shops". Each user of these services chooses a unique user id and receives an associated tag from Amazon. After each transaction, feedback is entered where the recommender gives a rating of between 0 and 5 to each recommendee. These recommendations can be inspected for each user.

The data was collected by using the web services available from Amazon.co.uk. We set up an initial set of seeds by collecting names through searching for a set of disparate items. The graph of recommendations was then followed to collect the set of links and entities. In all we collected 405,661 different nicknames, or *nodes*.

Each node has one or more *recommendations* going from it to other nodes, or one or more recommendations pointing at itself. Each recommendation consists of a numeric rating of the transaction, from 0 to 5, the date of the rating and a comment. We did not collect the comments.

From this collected data, we determined the proportion of nodes which have k neighbours, $P(k)$. We excluded multiple recommendations between the same nodes, and self-recommendations. These are plotted in the log/log graphs of Figures 4 and 5. We show the residuals from the fitted curves, which indicate that both the outbound and inbound $P(k)$ functions are better fitted by polynomials of degree 2 in the log/log curves, ie that the relationship between $P(k)$ and k can be modeled by:

$$P(k) \propto k^{f(k)}$$

If we examine the undirected graph formed by the recommendations, we find the graph to be connected, and the diameter of the graph i.e. the largest shortest path between two nodes, is measured to be 21 hops. The average shortest path between two nodes is 8.1.

5.1   Analysis of Reputation Services

As expected, the transaction graph exhibits the properties of a power law graph. Following Barabasi [28] the transaction graph will grow in the number of nodes and each node will exhibit preferential attachment. If we classify nodes as either predominantly buyers or sellers, then a buyer will tend to buy from existing sellers with established reputations, whilst incoming sellers will be used predominantly by existing buyers who are already well-connected. The low connectivity of the directed graph can be explained by the clustering of buyers and sellers around particular types of item, such as videos or books.

In the following discussion, we assume that the characteristics of the transaction graph described above can be generalised to other transactional based systems, such as the execution of a third party piece of software. In the absence of any other data, it is valid to criticise design approaches to reputation systems assuming that their transaction graph will show similar characteristics.

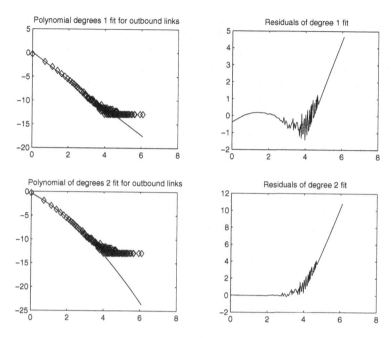

Fig. 4. Log/log plot of relative frequency of outbound links per node of the undirected graph

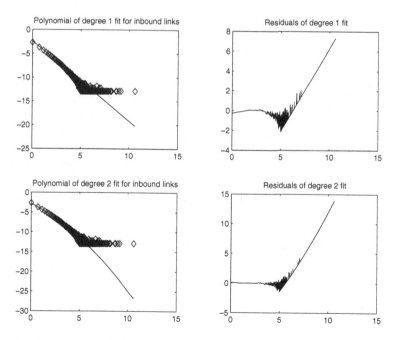

Fig. 5. Log/log plot of relative frequency of inbound links per node of the undirected graph

There are a number of peer to peer reputation systems which rely on polling trusted neighbours to find the reputation of the target system, hoping that they will have had some direct interaction with the target system such as [29,30]. The P2PRep system [30] is designed to operate in Gnutella file sharing systems and is typical of such an approach. To check the reputation of a server, the requesting node polls other local servents to get certificates detailing their interactions with the servers. If this technique is reused where the transaction graph is a power law graph, then there are many nodes which will have had few interactions with other nodes, and thus will be unlikely to receive any certificates. However, the localised nature of the cliques will mean that this technique is effective for highly connected nodes.

The Eigentrust system [31] is based on the distributed computation of the principal left eigenvector over a normalised version of the transaction graph, using a similar approach to the pagerank algorithm of Google. In the secure version discussed by the paper, a node's "trust" value is computed by a set of score managers. In each iteration, the score manager's collect the current trust value from each of the neighbours of the node, and return the results after calculating using the local column of the transaction graph matrix. If the transaction graph is a power law graph, this may result in local hot spots, and a high number of messages for some nodes, slowing down the computation. Since each change in the reputation graph may trigger a recomputation of reputation, the load may become unacceptable.

In making an assessment of a node in the transaction graph, it is necessary to both have the directly relevant information, and ways of assessing the reliability of the direct information. If this is not provided, then the direct information is susceptible to *sybil* based attacks, where the attacker inserts multiple entries into the database. We propose a multi-metric, multi-type approach, in which each transaction entry is accorded a type, so that users can check entries of relevant type, and the use of metrics to assess the reliability of each transaction entry.

Since the graph is a power law graph, it becomes feasible to search through the graph in a distributed fashion, since power law graphs are amenable to efficient distributed searching [32,33]. We are currently investigating and comparing distributed path finding techniques starting from trusted nodes as alternatives to metrics such as EigenTrust.

Any system should have high availability. The most effective solution may be to have a dedicated set of high availability servers, running either a DBMS, or a distributed storage system such as a distributed hash table e.g. Pastry [34]. The tendency to hot spots in the graph may make the DHT approach vulnerable to hot spots.

6   Future Work

We are currently building a distributed reputation system, providing a multimetric view of the transaction graph, using a distributed hash table as the underlying storage. We will be using the collected data as the basis for analysing performance.

We are working towards incorporating information about resource usage in the next generation of the SafetyNet language, and its associated runtime. We are hoping to incorporate both endogenous information from static analysis of the program and exogenous information from the transaction certificates. We will be looking to port the runtime to the XenoServer environment[35].

7 Conclusion

In this paper we have argued that the difficulty of managing risk is one of the major reasons that active networks and other third party computational infrastructures have not achieved widespread deployment. If risk is to be managed, programs must be priced according to the potential lost revenue from running a program which deters other customers from using the platform. We have described simulations which indicate that pricing according to risk produces a stable environment which provides market niches for different platforms, and incentives for good software. Finally, we have presented the first analysis of the transaction graphs of an ecommerce site, and used this to motivate the design principles required for a distributed reputation service. The results reported here indicate that it is feasible to develop a third party computational infrastructure.

References

1. Beverly Schwartz, Alden W. Jackson, W. Timothy Strayer, Wenyi Zhou, R. Dennis Rockwell, and Craig Partbridge. Smart packets: applying active networks to network management. *ACM Transactions on Computer Systems*, 18(1):67–88, 2000.
2. Dennis Volpano and Geoffrey Smith. Language issues in mobile program security. *Lecture Notes in Computer Science*, 1419, 1998.
3. D. Alexander. *Alien: A Generalized Computing Model of Active Networks*. PhD thesis, University of Pennsylvania, 1998.
4. Pankaj Kakkar, Michael Hicks, Jonathan T. Moore, and Carl A. Gunter. Specifying the PLAN networking programming language. In *Higher Order Operational Techniques in Semantics*, volume 26 of *Electronic Notes in Theoretical Computer Science*. Elsevier, September 1999.
5. Paul Menage. RCANE: A Resource Controlled Framework for Active Network Services. In *Proceedings of the First International Working Conference on Active Networks (IWAN '99)*, volume 1653, pages 25–36. Springer-Verlag, 1999.
6. Grzegorz Czajkowski and Thorsten von Eicken. JRes: A resource accounting interface for Java. In *Proceedings of OOPSLA '98*, pages 21–35.
7. Ian M. Leslie, Derek McAuley, Richard Black, Timothy Roscoe, Paul T. Barham, David Evers, Robin Fairbairns, and Eoin Hyden. The design and implementation of an operating system to support distributed multimedia applications. *IEEE Journal of Selected Areas in Communications*, 14(7):1280–1297, 1996.
8. Robert Morris, Eddie Kohler, John Jannotti, and M. Frans Kaashoek. The click modular router. In *ACM Symposium on Operating Systems Principles*, pages 217 – 231, Charleston, South Carolina, 1999. ACM Press.

9. Stefan Schmid, Tim Chart, Manolis Sifalakis, and Andrew Scott. Flexible, dynamic and scalable service composition for active routers. In *Proceedings of the 4th International Working Conference on Active Networks (IWAN'02)*, December 2002.

10. M. Litzkow, M. Livny, and M. Mutka. Condor — a hunter of idle workstations. In *Proceedings of the Eighth Conference on Distributed Computing Systems*, San Jose, California, June 1988.

11. Carl A. Waldspurger, Tad Hogg, Bernardo A. Huberman, Jeffrey O. Kephart, and W. Scott Stornetta. Spawn: A distributed computational economy. *Software Engineering*, 18(2):103–117, 1992.

12. Yair Amir, Baruch Awerbuch, and Ryan S. Borgstrom. The java market: Transforming the internet into a metacomputer. Technical Report Technical Report CNDS-98-1, Johns Hopkins University, 1998.

13. R. Buyya, D. Abramson, and J. Giddy. Nimrod/g: An architecture for a resource management and scheduling system in a global computational grid. In *Proceedings of the 4th International Conference on High Performance Computing in the Asia Pacific Region*, May 2000.

14. R. Buyya, D. Abramson, J. Giddy, and H. Stockinger. Economic models for resource management and scheduling in grid computing. *The Journal of Concurrency and Computation: Practice and Experience (CCPE)*, May 2002.

15. D. Ferguson, C. Nikolaou, J. Sairamesh, and Y. Yemini. *Market-Based Control: A Paradigm for Distributed Resource Allocation*, chapter Economic models for allocating resources in computer systems. World Scientific, 1996.

16. R. J. Gibbens and F. P. Kelly. Resource pricing and the evolution of congestion control. *Automatica*, 35:1969–1985, 1999.

17. Ron Cocchi, Scott Shenker, Deborah Estrin, and Lixia Zhang. Pricing in computer networks: Motivation, formulation, and example. *IEEE/ACM Transactions on Networking*, 1, December 1993.

18. Xi-Ren Cao, Hongxia Shen, Rodolfo Milito, and Patrica Wirth. Internet pricing with a game theoretical approach: Concepts and examples. *IEEE/ACM Transactions on Networking*, 10:208–216, 2002.

19. Hal Varian. Differential pricing and efficiency. *First Monday*, 1(2), August 1996.

20. Michael Wooldridge. *Introduction to MultiAgent Systems*. John Wiley & Sons, 2002.

21. Kevin Fu, M. Frans Kaashoek, and David Mazières. Fast and secure distributed read-only file system. *Computer Systems*, 20(1):1–24, 2002.

22. Bruce Schneier. *Applied Cryptography: Protocols, Algorithms*. John Wiley & Sons, second edition, 1995.

23. Ian Wakeman, Alan Jeffrey, Tim Owen, and Damyan Pepper. Safetynet: A language-based approach to programmable networks. *Computer Networks and ISDN Systems*, 36,1, June 2001.

24. Drew Fudenberg and Jean Tirole. *Game Theory*. MIT Press, 1991.

25. Ian Wakeman, David Ellis, Tim Owen, Julian Rathke, and Des Watson. Risky business: Motivations for markets in programmable networks. Computer science technical report, University of Sussex, 2003.

26. H. Gravelle and R Rees. *Microeconomics*. Longman, 1992.

27. Joan Feigenbaum and Scott Shenker. Distributed algorithmic mechanism design: Recent results and future directions. In *Proceedings of the 6th International Workshop on Discrete Algorithms and Methods for Mobile Computing and Communications*, pages 1–13, New York, 2002.

28. Barabasi, Albert, and Jeong. Mean-field theory for scale-free random networks. *Physica A*, 2272:173–187, 199.

29. Giorgos Zacharia, Alexandros Moukas, and Pattie Maes. Collaborative reputation systems in electronic marketplaces. In *Proceedings of the 32nd Hawaii International Conference on System Sciences*, 1999.

30. F. Cornelli, E. Damiani, S. De Capitani di Vimercati, S. Paraboschi, and P. Samarati. Choosing reputable servents in a p2p network. In *Proc. of the Eleventh International World Wide Web Conference*, Honolulu, Hawaii, May 2002.

31. Sepandar D. Kamvar, Mario T. Schlosser, and Hector Garcia-Molina. The eigentrust algorithm for reputation management in p2p networks. In *Proceedings of the Twelfth International World Wide Web Conference*, 2003.

32. L. Adamic, R. M. Lukose, A. R. Puniyani, and B. A. Huberman. Search in power-law networks. *Phys. Rev. E*, 64, 2001.

33. Beom Jun Kim, Chang No Yoon, Seung Kee Han, and Hawoong Jeong. Path finding strategies in scale-free networks. *Physical Review E*, 65(027103), 2002.

34. A. Rowstron and P. Druschel. Pastry: Scalable, distributed object location and routing for large-scale peer-to-peer systems. In *IFIP/ACM International Conference on Distributed Systems Platforms (Middleware)*, pages 329–350, Heidelberg, Germany, November 2001.

35. Dickon Reed, Ian Pratt, Paul Menage, Stephen Early, and Neil Stratford. Xenoservers; accounted execution of untrusted code. In *IEEE Hot Topics in Operating Systems (HotOS) VII*, March 1999.

Context-Aware Handover Based on Active Network Technology

Qing Wei[1], Károly Farkas[2], Paolo Mendes[1], Christian Prehofer[1], Bernhard Plattner[2], and Nima Nafisi[1*]

[1] DoCoMo Communications Laboratoires Europe
Landsberger Str. 308-312, 80687 Munich, Germany
{ wei, mendes, prehofer, nafisi }@docomolab-euro.com
[2] Computer Engineering and Networks Laboratory, ETH Zürich
Gloriastr. 35 8092 Zürich, Switzerland,
{ farkas, plattner }@tik.ee.ethz.ch

Abstract. Context-aware computing can play a major role to improve the services of mobile networking systems. In this paper, we focus on optimizing handover decisions based not only on the signal quality, but also on the knowledge about the context of mobile devices and networks. Since context information and context processing evolves fast, we propose a flexible, integrated approach for context management, which can adapt in several ways. Our architecture encompasses active platforms in network nodes and mobile devices, distributed context management components on these platforms, and service deployment for network services. This flexible architecture is able to actively deploy different handover services. It can manage different kinds of context information and allow mobile devices to be always connected to the most suitable access network. Our architecture is validated in a prototype implementation.

1 Introduction

With mobile networks rolling out in our daily life, offering better support for wireless services becomes an important topic. To optimize the services in this heterogeneous environment and fulfil the user needs, context-aware computing is essential. Context-aware computing is defined as a pattern where the application uses knowledge related to a set of environment states to determine and change the application behaviour.

In this paper, we focus on *Handover* (HO) decisions based on context information. The concept of context-aware HO can be defined as follows: a HO procedure that selects a target *Access Point* (AP), based not only on the signal quality or explicit advertisements sent by the AP, but also on the knowledge of the context information of the *Mobile Node* (MN) and the network, in order to take intelligent and better decisions. However, implementing context-aware HOs poses some problems, namely because context information is diverse, dynamic and distributed among network nodes and MNs. Besides this, fragile and/or low-bandwidth wireless links constrain the exchange of context information.

---

* Currently at King's College London, nima.nafisi@kcl.ac.uk

N. Wakamiya et al. (Eds.): IWAN 2003, LNCS 2982, pp. 280–291, 2004.

Therefore, it is required to ensure that the correct context information is available at the right place and at the right time. For this, the context information should be provided proactively to the MN, i.e., before the HO takes place and when the MN has good radio connectivity. Moreover, the type of context information may change over time, and new services emerging continuously. This requires the use of new algorithms to collect and process the context information.

This paper describes a flexible architecture which is able to satisfy the described requirements in order to provide efficient context-aware HOs. The proposed architecture actively deploys different HO support modules, which are able to manage different context information, allowing the MN to be always connected to the most suitable access network.

The proposed architecture includes a framework to manage diverse, dynamic and distributed context information to support context-aware services. This framework is built upon the active infrastructure. It consists of two parts: active platforms installed in network nodes and MNs which allow the flexible installation and use of software modules; second, a service deployment framework capable of deploying different software modules implementing context-aware handover services.

The main contribution of this paper is an integrated architecture for context-aware HO and its evaluation. It uses two layers for flexibility and performance. First, customized modules for efficient context exchange and context-aware decisions are used for context-aware handover. Secondly, the service deployment framework supports the flexible update of the customized modules on the active nodes, when needed. Furthermore, we show practical evaluation results by a prototype including the above three parts of the architecture (i.e., active platform, service deployment framework and context management framework). The evaluation of the proposed architecture is based on a prototype scenario that considers the context information of location of MNs and the traffic load of access networks except for the signal strength.

The remainder of the paper is organized as follows. Section 2 provides an analysis of the requirements of flexible active context-aware architectures. In Section 3, we describe the proposed context-aware HO architecture based on active network technology. The functionality of the proposed architecture is illustrated and evaluated in Section 4. In Section 5, we take a look at research issues and prior work related to context-aware services and service deployment, and Section 6 concludes the paper.

2   Requirements of Context-Aware Handover Service

Our goal is that the mobile node behaves in an optimal way depending on the context. This requires a mechanism to efficiently collect and manage the context information and an appropriate platform to use the context information for an optimal decision.

Context information may be classified as static or dynamic, depending on the frequency and cause of changes, and based on the location where such information is maintained. Table 1 explains our classification of context information. It is just a snapshot, as novel kinds of context information may appear. For instance, in future networks, new kinds of context information like user groups may be relevant. Some items, such as the user profile, appear twice, as the information is often spread over the user device, the operator and possibly several service providers. As an example, the user profile may include subscribed services and service preferences, e.g. which services have to be downgraded or dropped if sufficient resources are not available.

Table 1. Context Information Classification

	Context information on mobile device	Context information on network side
Static	User settings and profile Application settings	User profile and history Network location Network capabilities and services Charging models
Static within a cell	Reachable APs	Potential next AP
Dynamic	Type of application Application requirements Device status (battery, interface status, etc)	Location information and location prediction Network status Network load

However, context information is not readily available to the involved entities in a HO for several reasons. Firstly, context information is distributed. For instance, some pieces of context information may be available in user's home network, some may be available in the visiting network and some resides on the terminal. Secondly, dynamic context information may change frequently or lose accuracy over time. For instance, it is tempting to convey information about the current AP loads, yet its relevance decreases quickly over time. Thirdly, what is relevant about context information and the methods to interpret it may evolve over time. Hence algorithms for interpreting the context data need to be adapted to new requirements.

Therefore, we need a context management framework which assures that the right information is available just in time. Still, information exchange between network and MNs should be minimized to save wireless resources. Furthermore, a context-aware handover requires an appropriate execution platform which is flexible enough to adapt to the changing requirements of this service. It should be able to cope with continuously changing context and automatically alter the handover decision policy or algorithm in use. It should support continuously the context exchange between the nodes involved in the handover service in an efficient way. It should also enable the mobility management of the mobile node to take the right handover decision.

3   An Integrated Approach for Context Management

This section introduces an approach which integrates a context management framework, an active platform and a service deployment scheme to provide the functionalities needed for context-aware HO. The context management framework is in charge of collecting the relevant context information for different services and managing the context information. The active platform is used to exchange and process the context information. The service deployment scheme is used to synchronize and manage the working of involved active nodes. In our architecture shown in Fig. 1 context information is stored in context information repositories (e.g.,

Location Information Server (LIS), *Network Traffic Monitor* (NTM), user profile repository, etc).

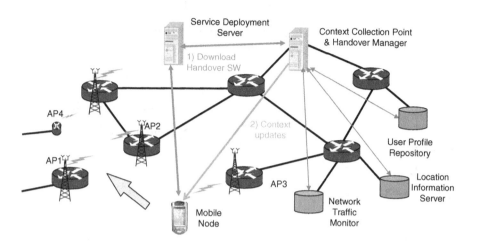

Fig. 1. Architecture for Context-aware HO Using AN Technology

The LIS is responsible to track the position of each mobile device in the provider's network and has the knowledge of nearby APs, while the user profile repository stores the user profiles as seen by the network service providers. We introduce a *Handover Manager* (HM), which controls the handovers carried out in some part of an access network. The HM is responsible for filtering and processing HO-related context information. Finally, a *Service Deployment Server* (SDS) is used to manage and install the service modules needed in the network nodes and mobile nodes.

The realization of this service can be divided into three steps, which are explained in the message sequence diagram shown in Fig. 2. Step one (phase A,B,C in Fig. 2) is service deployment, which includes fetching the right service components for a required service, installing them on the appropriate network node and confirm the successful installation of all the components for this service. Step two (phase D in Fig. 2) collects relevant context information. In step three (phase E in Fig. 2) the context information is evaluated and the HO decision is made.

Fig. 3 shows the execution platforms of the nodes used in our scenario (see Section 4), which is the execution environment where active modules are installed. For example, to realize a context-aware HO service, we need to install a context exchange protocol - HO support module (HSM) and a HO decision mechanism - HO decision module (HDM) in the related nodes. More specifically, here we need to install appropriate versions of both the HSM and the HDM in the active platform of the MN and the HM. This is realized by the service deployment in Phase A, B and C. The signalling used by the HDM to request the needed context information is detailed in phase D. After the HDM made the decision on AP based on the collected context information, the decision is sent to the *mobility management component* of the mobile node to execute the handover (phase E); in our approach, mobility management is done with Mobile IP.

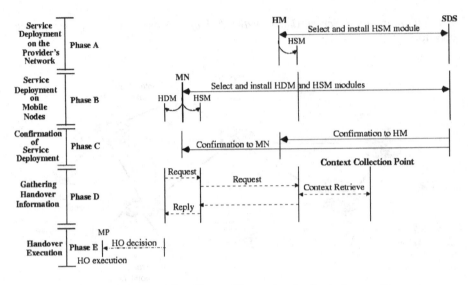

Fig. 2. Sequence of Signalling and Processing for Context-aware Hos

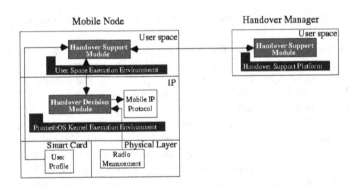

Fig. 3. Active Modules for Context-aware HO

Context Management Framework

Our context management framework is in charge of context collection, compiling, exchanging and evaluation. Details of this framework can be found in [10]. It defines the following main entities:

- The *context collection point* on the network side, which collects and compiles the relevant context information from different sources. In our scenario, the context collection point is placed in the HM shown in Fig. 1.
- The *HO decision point* decides which AP is to be selected for the handover. In our scenario, the HO decision point is placed in the MN, as shown in Fig. 1.

The HO decision point uses simple algorithms (e.g., rule-based logic) for interpreting the data delivered by the context management framework. It is the task of the service deployment service to assure that both the HO decision point and the context collection point are proactively supplied with the appropriate algorithms.

The algorithms need to be altered if there are structural changes of the context information, e.g., when the context format, user profile or context processing algorithm changes. Notice that software updates can be applied in different ways. For instance, each time the user profile changes, e.g. when entering a car new software modules are installed. The context information will be exchanged when needed using context exchange protocol. In this way, up to date context information is used for HO decision. The detailed steps for context-aware HO are:

1. Prepare a software module at the context collection point with the algorithm and the collected context data needed at the handover decision point.
2. Download the software module proactively to the HO decision point before HO.
3. Exchange context when needed.
4. The software module is invoked at the HO time. It makes the decision on AP with the input of the dynamic terminal context (e.g., reachable access points, application requests and sessions), and transferred dynamic context from the network.

In the architecture described in section 3, the HO decision algorithm is implemented as HDM which is installed in MN, and the context exchange protocol is implemented as HSM which is installed in both MN and HM.

Active Node Platform and Service Deployment

In the following, we describe the node platform for our architecture. We use active networking technology to meet the requirements in section 2. Since the decision algorithms for optimal AP are context-dependent, the network elements and the mobile end systems involved in this process need to be programmable. Active networking technology is a good candidate to fulfil this requirement. Our active node consists of the basic processing hardware, a node operating system and several execution environments, in which active applications will execute the handover algorithms. The node has to support the dynamic installation of a handover decision module at run-time, without interrupting the node's proper working. The active node architecture and implementation we use for our system is PromethOS [8]. It is a generic platform for running active applications in a Linux environment, allowing for on-demand installation of user- or kernel-space modules.

While PromethOS provides a basic active node platform, our application scenario also calls for a framework capable of handling the selection, installation, configuration, and management of the service components. The Chameleon service deployment framework [7] can accomplish these functions. However, Chameleon, in its current implementation, only provides node level service deployment functions. We therefore extended it with a simple, centralized network-level service deployment framework called Octopus. In the rest of this section, we first give a brief overview about our use of Chameleon and the new Octopus framework.

Chameleon, a Node Level Service Deployment Framework

Node-local service deployment comprises selecting, downloading and installing implementations of service components on an active node, such that these components jointly provide the specified service. Chameleon uses a service specification – to be generated by the network-level service deployment – and a description of the intrinsic properties of the active node to determine which implementations of service components need to be installed on the active node. The service specification is given as an XML document, which follows an XML document type definition; the latter defines the structure and format of service specifications. Chameleon resolves the service specification against the description of the node properties, thereby creating a tree-like structure representing all possible implementations of a service. In our application of Chameleon, such service specifications are generated by Octopus, our network-level service deployment scheme supporting context-aware handovers.

Octopus, a Network Level Service Deployment Scheme

The core of Octopus is a central management entity, called SDS, as illustrated in Fig. 4. The SDS contains a *Service Deployment Manager* (SDM) module which controls the network-wide signalling and all related synchronization functions needed during service deployment. Moreover, it contains a *Service Server* (SS) which stores the descriptors of the services known to the system and a *Code Server* (CS), which stores the implementations (code modules) of the service components available in the provider's network. These servers are managed by the SDM; they can be located anywhere in the network.

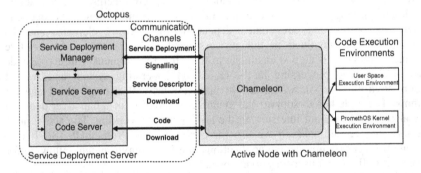

Fig. 4. Communication between the SDS and a Chameleon Node

Fig.4. shows how Octopus and Chameleon communicate. Three signalling channels are used: (1) Service deployment signalling for requesting and/or sending the proper service specification to the Chameleon instance on the active node, (2) Service descriptor download signalling for retrieving service descriptions, to which the service specification (1) refers; the download is initiated by Chameleon while the service specification is resolved; and (3) Code download signalling, which is used by Chameleon to retrieve the implementation modules needed from the Code server for execution of the service; this retrieval, again, is initiated by Chameleon.

The specific operation of Octopus varies depending on where Chameleon is executed.

- If the node is a network node such as HM in our context-aware HO service, then the SDM module of SDS establishes a connection to the node's Chameleon on the signalling channel and requests the installation of the given service. Subsequently, the Chameleon instance on the HM autonomously resolves the service specification and installs the component implementations.
- If the node is an end user node as the MN in our context-aware HO service, then this node's Chameleon initiates the service deployment by requesting a list of available services and selecting a service from this list; the SDM then sends the requested service specification and Chameleon proceeds as in the previous case.

Service deployment can be either provider-initiated or user-initiated. In the former case, the service is deployed in the network proactively, before the arrival of any service user. While in the latter case, service deployment is on demand. The arrival of the first service user initiates the installation of the service. The extended Chameleon with Octopus can cope with both policies and the active nodes can act either as network node or end user node by setting the parameter of Chameleon.

4   Prototype and Evaluation

In this section, we evaluate the proposed architecture by using a prototype that illustrates a scenario, in which a provider has three access points, and a user is driving or traveling by train along a trajectory leading through an area where all three networks intersect. Without context aware HO mechanisms, the selection of a new access network during a handover would be driven by Mobile IP version 6 (MIPv6) [16] route advertisements. In this case, the mobile device may register with any of the possible destination networks. However, if active networking is used, the user's MN can request the utilization of a HO service based on context information.

To illustrate the behaviour of the proposed architecture, two types of context information are considered: the user's location, speed and trajectory, which depends on how the user moves, and the *Quality of Service* (QoS) required by the application. Considering the user's location-context, the HO may be made to a network that has a better coverage along a train track or to a network with small range, but high QoS if the user is walking. Additional criteria could be the network traffic load, which normally would have an effect on the QoS perceived by the user.

Prototype and Scenarios

The used prototype, illustrated in Fig. 5, encompasses one HM that controls the three access networks. To reduce the complexity of the prototype, the behaviour of the LIS and NTM is simulated with static information, and only one type of wireless interface is used. We make the distinction between overloaded and non-overloaded networks, by generating more traffic to specific networks, using the MGEN tool-set [17].

Four scenarios are used in the prototype. Scenario one is based on MIPv6 HO. The remaining three scenarios aim to show the advantages of using context information and active networking to choose a right AP, while the hypothetical user travels in a train. Scenario two uses a service based on the user's location-context. Scenario three

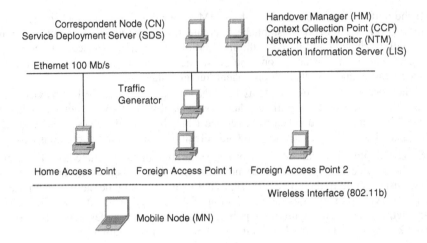

Fig. 5. Prototype for Context-aware HO

also considers the user's location-context, but in this case the user is receiving a streamed video sent by the CN. In the fourth scenario, the user is also receiving a streamed video, but we also consider the QoS requirements of this application. For scenarios three and four, *Foreign Access Point* (FAP1) is first unloaded and then is heavily loaded, while in any scenario the *Home Access Point* (HAP) and FAP2 are always unloaded. In each scenario, a context-specific HSM and HDM, able to process information about the user's location-context and/or QoS-context are downloaded, installed and used by the HM and MN.

Experimentation and Evaluation

The goal of this analysis is twofold: first, to exemplify the behaviour of the proposed architecture, as a proof of concept. The second goal is to evaluate the signalling overhead of the proposed architecture and to understand how much time it requires to deploy context-aware services and to collect customized HO data.

In what concerns the behaviour of the proposed architecture, scenarios one and two show that with context information MNs have higher control over their HOs. In scenario one, the MN registers with the FAP from which it gets the first route advertisement. However, in scenario two, the MN registers with FAP1, independently of the order of received router advertisements. This corresponds to the assumption that the MN is in a train and that FAP1 has the best coverage along the train track.

The results of the experiments done with scenarios three and four, illustrated in Fig. 6 demonstrate the importance of using the appropriate modules.

In scenario three, the MN registers with FAP1, at second 70, since this is the network with wider coverage near the train track. This ends up in the deterioration of the perceived video quality since FAP1 is loaded and the used context-aware modules do not consider the load of networks. In scenario 3 the video remains with low quality, since the MN is only aware of the user's location, which does not change.

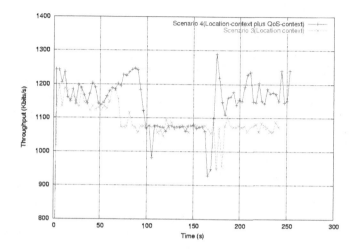

Fig. 6. Throughput of the Video Stream on Scenarios Three and Four

In scenario 4, the MN also registers with FAP1, because FAP1 and FAP2 are both unloaded in the beginning, and so the HO decision is only dependent on the location context. Starting at second 90, FAP1 is loaded to show that with location-context plus QoS-context modules the MN can react properly to significant changes in the load of networks. As shown in Fig. 6, the MN registers with FAP2 at second 170, after receiving and processing the new context information, and the perceived video quality increases again. The throughput oscillations shown in Fig. 6 are mainly due to the instability on the wireless link.

In the current prototype, the service deployment takes about 850ms in the HM and up to 9.3s in the MN. This long time required to deploy a service in the MN is mainly due to the fact that in the current prototype, the user is allowed to select the service to be installed in the MN based on the list received from the SDS. Concerning the exchange of context information, our measurements show that it takes 1.8 ms.

We also conducted an analysis about the communication overhead involved in collecting context information. The length of the packet sent by the MN to request context information is 64 bytes: 60 bytes of TCP/IPv6 headers and four bytes to indicate the current user's context. As a reply, the HM sends to the MN information about each access network. With location-context-aware modules, such information occupies 20 bytes per access network: 16 bytes for the IPv6 address of the AP and four bytes indicating the priority of the network. With location-context plus QoS-context modules, four bytes corresponding to the load of the network are added to the information send to the MN. Considering a scenario with 1000 access networks, in which the user is requesting location-context plus QoS-context modules, and the *Maximum Transfer Unit* (MTU) is 1500 bytes, the control information is of 24.4 KB. Considering a worst-case situation where the load of any AP changes every 1s, and the HM is configured to check the load of the networks also every 1s, the control information overhead is of 199.7 kb/s.

5   Related Work

In [12][13], sophisticated handover procedures have been considered. However, the parameters, which have been considered for the handover decision, are confined to the type of the radio access technology plus the signal strength. In [14], different handover policies for heterogeneous networks are used, considering as handover parameters mainly the air-interface type and the available bandwidth at the access router. There are several approaches aiming at a more intelligent handover in heterogeneous access network (e.g., [15]). Yet none of them presents a general framework for a handover mechanism that will benefit of the various contexts the mobile node might be confronted with.

In the area of active service deployment several proposals have been made, but often these are restricted to the needs of a specific platform (e.g., the Active Networks Daemon [2] of ABone [3]). Some of them have the potential to be used as a generic service deployment scheme (e.g., ASCP [4]). Recent publications discuss approaches, which are explicitly targeted towards a generic solution for service deployment, e.g. ASDP [5] or pattern based service deployment [6] with Chameleon [7].

6   Conclusions

This paper describes an architecture that aims at optimizing mobile network services based on context information. This means to gather information from different network elements and to use this information in mobile nodes for local context-aware and better decisions. Our proposed architecture allows for a flexible use of different protocols to exchange different types of context information, as well as a flexible use of different context-aware decision algorithms in mobile nodes. Our solution ensures that the correct context information is available at the right place at the right time, and handles diverse, dynamic and distributed context information.

Our solution integrates three main parts: first, we use an active platform installed in network nodes and mobile nodes. Second, we integrated a framework capable of performing network-wide and node-local deployment of various context-aware services on these platforms. Third, use an efficient and flexible context management to handle diverse, dynamic and distributed context information.

The active platform and our service deployment framework are not specific to the context-aware hand-over service but it is more generic and can be used in case of other network services. The deployment framework is scalable in two dimensions, concerning the number of services and the size of network (number of involved nodes in a service).

Our evaluation of the proposed architecture, based on a prototype, has shown the feasibility and utility of our approach. Specifically, we show that context awareness increases the efficiency of hand-overs. We also show that the deployment of active modules is fast in the network and discuss the problems of service deployment to mobile nodes over the wireless link. The evaluation results show that customized exchange of context information is quick and that it does not have a significant communication overhead. Only if the context processing or exchange formats change, the modules have to be updated.

References

[1]   Jamalipour, S. Tekinay (eds.): IEEE Personal Communications Magazine, *Special issue on Fourth Generation Wireless networks and Interconnecting Standards*. October 2001.

[2]   *Anetd: Active Networks Daemon*. ACTIVE project, ISI & SRI, http://www.sdl.sri.com/projects/activate/anetd/

[3]   Branden, L. Ricciulli: *PA Plan for a Scalable ABone – A modest proposal*. Technical Report, USC – Information Science Institute, January 1999.

[4]   E. Amir, S. McCanne, R. Katz: *An active service frame-work and its application to real-time multimedia transcoding*. ACM SIGCOMM'98, Canada, 1998.

[5]   M. Sifalakis, S. Schmid, T. Chart, D. Hutchison: *A Generic Active Service Deployment Protocol*. In proceedings of the Second International Workshop on Active Network Technologies and Applications, ANTA, Osaka, Japan, May 2003.

[6]   M. Bossardt, A. Mühlemann, R. Zürcher, B. Plattner: *Pattern Based Service Deployment for Active Networks*. In proceedings of the Second International Workshop on Active Network Technologies and Applications, ANTA, Osaka, Japan, May 2003.

[7]   M. Bossardt, L. Ruf, R. Stadler, B. Plattner: *A Service Deployment Architecture for Heterogeneous Active Network Nodes*. Kluwer Academic Publishers, 7th Conference on Intelligence in Networks (IFIP SmartNet 2002), Saariselkä, Finland, April 2002.

[8]   R. Keller, L. Ruf, A. Guindehi, B. Plattner, PromethOS: *A Dynamically Extensible Router Architecture Supporting Explicit Routing*, IWAN 2002, Dec. 2002, Springer-Verlag

[9]   Matthias Bossardt, et al. *Integrated service deployment for active networks*. In International Working Conference on Active Networks(IWAN2002), Zurich, Switzerland

[10] Christian Prehofer, Nima Nafisi, and Qing Wei. A framework for context-aware handover decisions.In *IEEE International Symposium on Personal, Indoor and Mobile Radio Communications*,Beijing, China, September 2003

[11] Christian Prehofer and Qing Wei. *Active networks for 4G mobile communication: Motivation, architecture and application scenarios*. IWAN 2002, Zurich, Switzerland

[12] M. Stemm and R. Katz, *Vertical handoffs in wireless overlay networks*, ACM Journal on Mobile Networks and Applications, Vol. 3, No. 4, 1998.

[13] K. Pahlavan, et al, *Handoff in hybrid mobile data networks*, IEEE Communication Magazine, April 2000.

[14] Helen J. Wang, Randy H. Katz, and Jochen Giese. *Policy-Enabled Handoffs across Heterogeneous Wireless Networks*, In WMCSA 99, IEEE, Feb.1999

[15] Michael E. Kounavis, et al, *Design, Implementation and Evaluation of Programmable Handoff in Mobile Networks*, ACM Journal on Mobile Networks and Applications (MONET), September 2001

[16] Johnson, C. Perkins, and J. Arkko, *Mobility Support in IPv6*, IETF Internet-Draft, June 2003, Work in Progress.

[17] MGEN: The Multi-Generator Toolset, http://manimac.itd.nrl.navy.mil/MGEN/

Implementation of Adaptive Control for P2P Overlays

Theofrastos Koulouris[1], Robert Henjes[2], Kurt Tutschku[2], and Hermann de Meer[1,3]

[1] Department of Electronic and Electrical Engineering, University College London,
Torrington Place, London, WC1E 7JE, United Kingdom,
t.koulouris@ee.ucl.ac.uk
[2] Institute of Computer Science, University of Würzburg,
Am Hubland, 97074, Würzburg, Germany,
{henjes|tutschku}@informatik.uni-wuerzburg.de
[3] Faculty of Mathematics and Informatics, University of Passau,
Innstr. 33, 94032, Passau, Germany,
demeer@fmi.uni-passau.de

Abstract. Peer-to-peer networking enjoys euphoric support and fierce resistance simultaneously, and for the same reasons. It presents a model where decentralization and lack of structure, hierarchy and control are promoted. Although significant research is carried out to tackle individual issues arising from that paradigm, there has been no obvious approach for evening out differences on a more general basis. In this paper we introduce a framework and provide implementation techniques for such an approach. The framework aims at integrating partial techniques that solve individual problems and has been designed for flexibility. The integrated approach we are proposing includes forming and maintaining of peer-to-peer overlays, controlling the underlying topology being formed, limiting the signaling traffic being generated and optimizing the payload traffic.

1 Introduction

Peer-to-peer (P2P) applications are close to become the dominating application of the Internet: P2P cooperation appears highly attractive to an increasing number of users due to appealing "free" resource sharing and easy use. P2P services can be loosely defined as being about *networked cooperation of equals*. Three main characteristics of P2P services can be emphasized: sharing of pooled and exchangeable resources, all nodes having similar roles, and all nodes being highly autonomous. That contrasts sharply with other distributed architectures such as Client/Server where asymmetric roles are typical. While loss of a primary component, i.e. the breakdown of a server, in an asymmetric architecture may result in a major disruption, any peer in a peer-to-peer architecture can be moved without resulting in a loss of service.

P2P systems are often referred to as being self-organizing where a coherent behavior emerges spontaneously without external coercion or control. Pure P2P architectures, such as early the Gnutella service, however turned out to be non-scalable. As a response, the need to introduce structure and limited control has been recognized, cf. [19]. In order to introduce heterogeneity into unstructured, pure P2P services, various mechanisms have been proposed. The suggestions range from "ultrapeers" and "superpeers", as in Gnutella [9] and Kazaa [18] respectively, to distributed mediation

N. Wakamiya et al. (Eds.): IWAN 2003, LNCS 2982, pp. 292–306, 2004.

servers and peer caches as in eDonkey2000 [20]. These approaches comprise only partial solutions to a more complex control problem. In particular, variability in service demand or load patterns can only be dealt with in a limited way. The demand for services may form hot spots which may shift within an overlay from one location to another one over time. P2P applications may therefore require a more flexible and dynamic method of control and management [3]. In particular, different control methods should be in place when and where needed, should be flexibly usable in combination with each other, and should be extensible in an evolutionary manner. More generally, it is our goal to introduce and to implement control and structure into peer-to-peer applications on demand.

In this paper we introduce a framework which facilitates a flexible and highly adaptive mode of P2P service management and P2P overlay management. The framework provides means for supporting self-organization, e.g. by mechanism to restructure an overlay topology. We present in detail the implementation of our scheme for an adaptive control of peer-to-peer overlays. The approach is based on the introduction of the concept of virtual nodes, called Active Virtual Peers (AVP). The proposed approach based on AVPs includes for example a *dynamic* forming and maintaining of peer-to-peer overlays or an adaptive routing of signaling and download traffic. The approach is also extensible to enforce security or ownership rights and to include mechanisms of charging. These additional features, however, are beyond the scope of this paper.

This paper is organized as follows: Section 2 discusses the objectives and requirements of control for P2P overlays. Section 3 presents the Active Virtual Peer concept. Next, in section 4, a prototype implementation of an AVP for optimizing Gnutella is described. Section 5 presents a discussion of the performance features of the AVP concept. A related work section is following in Section 6. Finally, Section 7 summarizes and concludes the paper.

2 Objectives and Requirements on Control for P2P Overlays

P2P services are effective in providing solutions in a large area of applications because of their distributed nature and focus they give to the resources found on the edges of the network. However, it has become evident over the past few years that some form of control is necessary to tackle issues such as the use of the service, the separation between the P2P overlay and the network layer, the short and unpredictable lifecycles of peer relations and the high signaling traffic generated, as we examine in [3]. We believe that there exist four areas where the enforcement of control will be beneficiary for such applications.

The first is *access control*. Participants of P2P overlays are typically granted access to all resources offered by the peers. These resources are valuable. Thus, the resource provider, either content provider or network provider, need to identify and regulate the admission to the overlay. In particular for P2P file sharing applications, access control should block off P2P applications or enable controlled content sharing.

The second area is *resource management*. The resources of individual peers have to be treated with care, e.g. low-bandwidth connected peers should not be overloaded with download requests and exploited equally. For P2P file sharing applications, for example, content caching capabilities will improve the performance while reducing the stress imposed on the network.

A third area of interest is *overlay load control*. Overlay load control copes with traffic flows inside the overlay. Its goal is to balance the traffic and load in order to maintain sufficient throughput inside the overlay while also protecting other network services by mapping this load in an optimum way onto the underlying network infrastructure

Finally, the forth area of command is adaptive *topology control*. Overlay connections may be established or destroyed arbitrarily by the peers since they can join or leave the virtual network at any time. Topology control may enforce redundant connections, thus increasing the reliability of the service. In addition, topology control may force the structure of the virtual network to be more efficient and faster in locating resources when using broadcast protocols.

The last two areas support the aim of having adaptive and application-suited, management strategies for P2P services. The outlined control objectives might violate the populist concept of unlimited access to free resources in P2P services, but control mechanisms governed by these objectives do increase the stability of P2P services based on overlays. It is necessary to find the proper trade-off between regulation and autonomy in P2P overlays.

Having identified the objectives of control for a P2P overlay, it is important to examine how adaptive and un-supervised control mechanisms need to be implemented, without diminishing the virtues of the P2P model or introducing further complexity and overhead to the network. We believe that it is vital to preserve the autonomy of the peers inside a P2P network. Additional control loops, which adapt to the behavior of a P2P overlay, must not interfere with the autonomous nature of any P2P application. To achieve this goal, we suggest implementing control through an additional *support infrastructure*. This infrastructure will provide all the necessary tools and interfaces to implement the desired forms of control and at the same time protect a P2P application. In addition, it is able to combine different algorithms in order to obtain optimally suited control structures. Finally, the mechanisms in this infrastructure permit self-organization or constraint-based self-organization, with the ultimate aim of flexibility and adaptivity. The support infrastructure will be formed of self-organized, interworking modules that may resemble a P2P network on their own.

3   The Active Virtual Peer Concept

The main element of the support infrastructure suggested in this paper is the Active Virtual Peer (AVP). As its name implies, an AVP is a virtual entity which interacts with other peers inside a P2P network. An AVP is a representative of a community of peers. Its purpose is to enhance, control and make the P2P relation more efficient inside that community. AVPs enable flexibility and adaptivity by the use of self-organization. An AVP consists of various distributed and coordinated components that facilitate different forms of control. By combining these components based on network conditions or administrative policies, we can create AVPs of different functionality.

The AVP performs certain functions, not expected by an ordinary peer. These AVP functions are arranged in horizontal layers as well as in vertical planes, see Figure 1.

The horizontal layers correspond to the layers on which an AVP imposes control. The vertical separation describes the functional planes of AVPs. These architectural planes have been examined in detail in [3,4].

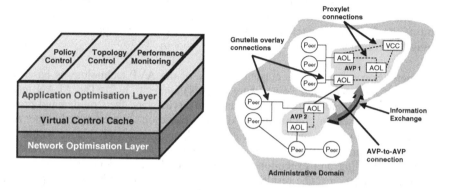

Fig. 1. The AVP architectural layers.   **Fig. 2.** The AVP realm.

The upper horizontal layer of an AVP is called the "Application Optimization Layer (AOL)". It controls and optimizes the peer-to-peer relation on the application level. The AOL may apply application-specific routing in conjunction with *access policies*. The routing performed by the AOL is based on metrics such as the state of the peers ("virtual peer state") or the state of the links between peers ("virtual overlay link state") thus changing the peer load and overlay link characteristics such as packet drop rate, throughput, or delay. In addition, the AOL allows for active overlay topology control, which is accomplished in two ways. The Active Virtual Peer may initiate, accept or terminate overlay connections based on access restriction or topology features. Topology characteristics such as the number of overlay connections or characteristic path length can be enforced or may govern the overlay structure. Furthermore, the AOL layer makes also use of the ALAN control mechanisms, examined below, for implementing its self-organization features. The AOL can instantiate modules implementing AOL functions whenever and wherever needed. These features enable the AOL to adapt the virtual overlay structure to varying demand, traffic patterns and connectivity requirements by launching new overlay connections and new virtual peers. These self-organization features make the AOL a very flexible architecture.

The middle layer of the AVP is denoted as the "Virtual Control Cache (VCC)". The VCC provides content caching on the application-level similar to conventional proxies. By maintaining often-requested content in close proximity, for instance inside an ISP's domain, large economies in resources and performance gains can be achieved. In addition, the VCC may offer control flow aggregation functions.

The lower layer of AVPs is denoted as the "Network Optimization Layer (NOL)". Its main task is the implementation of dynamic traffic engineering capabilities that map the P2P traffic onto the network layer in an optimized way. The mapping is performed with respect to the performance control capabilities of the applied transport technology. The AVP architecture may apply traffic engineering for standard IP routing protocols [7] as well as for explicit QoS enabled mechanisms like MPLS [8].

Figure 2, above, depicts a scenario where two AVPs, AVP 1 and AVP 2, are located within a single administrative domain. AVP 1 consists of three AOL modules and one VCC component, while AVP 2 comprises of two AOL modules. Multiple ordinary peers, denoted by "Peer", maintain connections to them. The two AVPs maintain overlay connections to each other. The AOL modules of the AVPs are in command of the overlay connections. This way, the AVPs can impose control on the overlay connection.

Implementation support. The current instance of the AVP technology is based on the *Application Level Active Networking* (ALAN) concept [1, 2]. The ALAN infrastructure allows a rapid deployment of network services and their on-demand provision to specified users or communities. ALAN is based on an overlay technique: Active nodes, which operate on the application level, are strategically placed within the network. These nodes, called *Execution Environments for Proxylets* (EEPs), enable the dynamic loading and execution of active code elements, denoted as *proxylets*, from designated servers. The resulting services may interfere with data transport and control. ALAN provides mechanisms for EEP discovery, application specific routing, and service creation by deploying a web of proxylets across the physical infrastructure. The Self Organizing Application-level Routing (SOAR) protocol [1], which is a key component of ALAN, enables clustering and grouping of proxylets. This way, ALAN facilitates the creation of an application-specific connectivity mesh and the dynamic forming of topology regions. Finally, ALAN provides the basic administrative mechanisms necessary for managing such an architecture.

The AVP layer modules are implemented by single or multiple interconnected proxylets. This allows the implementation of the layered AVP architecture in separate components. For instance, a proxylet may execute the AOL functions whereas an additional proxylet may materialize the Virtual Control Cache or the Network Optimization Layer. This approach facilitates better flexibility and efficiency in the constantly changing conditions of a Peer-to-Peer overlay. Different configurations of AVPs can be deployed in parts of the network that experience different characteristics, or even in the same network at different times of the day when conditions have changed. In addition, it is possible that different proxylets exist which implement the same layer functions differently. This gives further choice over the functionality of the AVP.

How an AVP imposes control. Having earlier identified the objectives for control of a P2P overlay, it is time to see how the AVP facilitates these control issues. Deployed AVPs create a realm wherein they constantly exchange information. Each AVP consists of multiple AOL and VCC proxylets which communicate and collaborate. The exchange of information allows for coordinated control of the overlay. A realm of AVPs is more suitable to evaluate the conditions inside a particular part of a P2P overlay than a single entity and this knowledge is distributed in order to achieve better results. Again, this capability promotes the flexibility and adaptivity of the AVP approach. Continuing, an AVP imposes control by providing effectors on connection level. The effectors comprise so far the *Router module* and the *Connection Manager module*. The Connection Manager enforces control by manipulating the connections peers maintain with each other. That is a significant difference compared to most P2P applications where the way peers connect to each other is random. By applying connection management, the AVP can enforce different control schemes.

The *Router module* governs the relaying of messages on application–level according to local or federated constraints, e.g. access restriction or virtual peer state information. The *Sensor module* provides state information for the distributed and collaborative control scheme. In the remainder of the paper, we discuss in detail how the suggested effectors are implemented.

4 Implementation of the AVP

The AVP concept is not based on any particular P2P application and does not require any specific P2P components in order to operate. Furthermore, the AVP does not address issues found only on P2P file-sharing applications but provides a generic performance management framework suitable for any type of P2P application that uses overlays. Nevertheless, for evaluating our prototype implementation, we use the Gnutella P2P file-sharing protocol as a vehicle and test environment. We chose Gnutella because it is a well-tested, open source, fully distributed P2P network with thousands of users; therefore ideal for realistic experiments. Furthermore, through Gnutella we are able to illustrate several realistic showcases where the AVP technology can provide solutions, many of them presented below. The showcases presented in the next section are all representative of experiments carried out at the University of Wuerzburg and University College London. We focus on the Gnutella protocol version 0.6 [5] to join the Gnutella network (GNet).

Access control. One of the core capabilities of the AVP is access control. The AOL component can create areas of control inside a P2P overlay, where all communications between the controlled domain and the global Gnutella network are managed by the AOL. Its goal is to control who can access the peers and their resources inside the domain. An AOL proxylet imposes access control by blocking and modifying Gnutella packets communicated between the controlled domain and the global Gnutella network. The result is that peers inside the controlled domain see only each other and become invisible to any peer outside that domain that is not granted access. At the same time, the AOL proxylet becomes the single point of contact between the controlled domain and the global network.

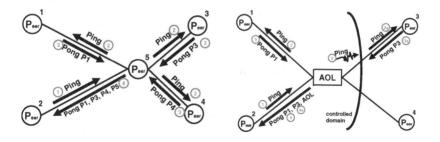

Fig. 3a. Gnutella conventional forwarding   **Fig. 3b.** New routing by AOL proxylet

The access control as implemented by an AOL proxylet can be better illustrated by the following scenario, depicted in Figures 3a and 3b, and examined more extensively in [26]. In Figure 3a, Peers 1 to 5 reside inside the global Gnutella overlay. Peer 2 sends out a Gnutella "Ping" message in order to discover other peers. Under the Gnutella protocol, a Ping has to be forwarded by the receiving peer, i.e. Peer 5, to any peer in its vicinity, who in turn has to respond with a "Pong" message. Thus, Peer 2 receives "Pongs" from Peers 1, 3, 4, and 5.

In the access controlled scenario, see Figure 3b, an AVP forms a *controlled domain* (CD) for Peers 1 and 2. In order to facilitate the access control, the AOL proxylet establishes connections with all peers. When Peer 2 sends out a "Ping" to discover other peers, the AOL proxylet intercepts the "Ping" message and forwards it unmodified to Peer 1 which is part of the CD. In addition, it modifies that Ping so it seems like it was initiated by the proxylet and relays it to the outside world. Peer 2 receives "Pongs" by Peer 1 and the AOL proxylet and concludes that only these two peers comprise its neighborhood. The AOL proxylet captures all messages originating from the global Gnutella network, modifies them if necessary, and forwards them inside the controlled domain.

Routing Control and Load Balancing. The AOL router represents the core mechanism for application of control. One of its main features is the ability to handle multiple protocols at the same time. To facilitate these different protocols in an effective and expandable way, the implementation of the router is divided into multiple, partly autonomous elements. In the current version of the AOL proxylet, two different mechanisms and protocols have been implemented: the Gnutella protocol version 0.6 [5] and an AOL intercommunication protocol, denoted as the *AOL-to-AOL protocol*. A major feature of the AOL-to-AOL protocol is the tunneling of other protocol messages between AOL proxylets, in our example the Gnutella packets. The current version of the AOL has the following routing capabilities:

- Routing of Gnutella packets
- Routing of AOL-to-AOL packets
- Routing between local Gnutella and AVP networks

The routing of Gnutella packets follows the specification of Gnutella version 0.6 but is significantly enhanced. The major enhancement lays in the "Probabilistic Routing" module, which drops broadcasted packets, e.g. Query messages, Ping messages, etc., based on a random value compared to a given threshold per connection. If the random value for a packet is larger then the configured threshold the packet is discarded. As a result, certain links become less loaded than others. Since the Gnutella protocol is based on event-triggered responses, discarding of a limited amount of packets doesn't sacrifice the file locating capability of the system when sufficient responses are still available, e.g. by receiving responses on multiple paths and from multiple sources. An example of probabilistic routing is depicted in Figure 4.

In this example four Peers (1, 2, 3, 4) are directly connected to an AOL proxylet. The proxylet has configured different threshold values for the links to Peer 2 (threshold is 0.3), Peer 3 (threshold is 0.6) and Peer 4 (threshold is 0.0). Peer 1 sends a message, e.g. a Query[1], to the AOL proxylet. The proxylet determines a random value of

---

[1] Query: Gnutella protocol message containing search criteria, used to search the P2P network for files [5].

0.5 for this packet[2]. Since the random value is smaller than the threshold value on the link to Peer 3, the AOL proxylet drops the packet along this connection whereas it keeps the packet on the links Peers 2 and 4.

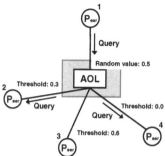

Fig. 4. Operation of the "Probabilistic Routing" feature of the AOL.

The AOL monitors and evaluates constantly the condition of the overlay, e.g. it measures and analyses the virtual link state or the virtual peer state. If these states degrade, the AOL may adjust the thresholds on the different proxylets and overlay connections. Through adaptive probabilistic routing, the AOL performs dynamic load control. Finally, by distinguishing messages between *implied events* (i.e. responses like Pongs and QueryHits) and *initial events* (i.e. requests like Pings and Queries), the probabilistic routing module makes sure superfluous traffic is not generated.

Topology Control. As mentioned earlier, topology control as enabled by the AVP enforces optimal P2P relations inside an overlay, based on a variety of metrics such as virtual peer state and virtual link state. The AOL proxylet achieves topology control by selectively setting up or closing connections to other AVPs and ordinary peers. By shaping the way peers are connected and communicate inside the overlay, an AVP can give it certain characteristics like better performance or greater stability.

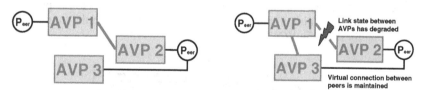

Fig. 5a. Dynamic overlay topology control (before)   **Fig. 5b.** Dynamic overlay topology control (after)

Based on the virtual peer state, the AOL can initiate or terminate overlay connections between AOL proxylets in order to maintain good connection characteristics inside the overlay, e.g. more durable overlay connections. The virtual peer state can be monitored using parameters like the number of overlay connections maintained, routing capability of the peers, processing load etc. Let's examine the following scenario,

---

[2] Without the loss of generality, the random value is equally distributed in the interval form [0, 1].

as depicted in Figures 5a and 5b. Figure 5a shows three AVPs and two peers existing in that part of the overlay. The link between AVP 1 and AVP 2 is significantly degraded, affecting the stability and performance of the information exchange between the two peers.

AVP 1 discovers that the virtual link is degraded and decides to re-structure the overlay topology in order to maintain good overlay characteristics. Therefore, AVP 1 establishes a link with AVP 3 which is in proximity, cf. Figure 6b, and shuts down the overlay connection to AVP 2. This way, AVP 1 manages to maintain the connection between the two peers in the desired levels of connectivity and quality without any knowledge or action taken from their part.

This scenario shows how the AOL proxylets create and terminate overlay connections in order to enable dynamic topology management of the overlay by means of self-organization. It has to be noted that similar schemes where certain peers have some influence on the way the overlay is formed have been proposed elsewhere, like the Gnutella "Ultrapeer" concept, see Section 5. However, an AVP achieves improved adaptivity and flexibility due to its self-organization features and the coordination between multiple AVPs or multiple AOL proxylets.

Resource Management and Caching using the VCC. An AVP may contain a VCC (Virtual Control Cache) proxylet. Its task is to provide content caching on the application-level by maintaining often-requested content in close proximity. This feature is illustrated in Figure 6.

An AVP that has spawned and configured a VCC, controls a domain of peers by applying routing and access controls as shown previously. Each time a query is made by the peers inside the domain, it is only visible by other peers in the domain and the VCC. Moreover, the AOL does not forward the Query message outside the domain but modifies it accordingly, so that peers outside the domain see the AOL as the actual initiator of the query. This way, the peers inside the domain receive QueryHit replies only by other peers in the domain and by the VCC. If the content is available locally, a direct download connection may be established. Otherwise, the AOL upon receiving a QueryHit from outside the domain downloads the content on behalf of the VCC where it is ultimately stored. Then, the AOL sends a QueryHit to the peer that demanded the content pointing to the VCC. If the file is requested in the future it can be retrieved directly from the VCC.

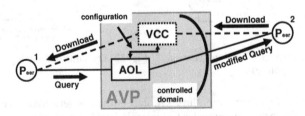

Fig. 6. Caching by the VCC proxylet.

Implementation details. AOL-to-AOL communication is achieved via TCP connections, although UDP may be used for shorter types of communications in order to decrease bandwidth use and other overheads. Table 1 below, lists all types of connections an AVP may currently implement.

The AOL protocol, used for AOL-to-AOL communications, allows the exchange of information vital for the communication and self-organization of the AVPs. This protocol was designed to be independent from existing protocols and realizes a simple and flexible way to communicate between AOL proxylets. An AOL protocol packet contains the following fields: *Source connection attributes* (AOL ID, IP address, Port number), *Destination connection attributes* (AOL ID, IP address, Port number, alternative route), *Type of payload*, *Payload* and *Priority*.

Table1. AOL-implemented types of connections.

Connection	Connection details
AOL-to-AOL	TCP/IP UDP for short information exchange planned
Gnutella-to-AOL	TCP/IP (Gnutella Protocol v0.6)
AOL-to-Gnutella	TCP/IP (Gnutella Protocol v0.6) UDP Ping for Availability Test
Telnet-to-AOL (Statistics interface)	Configuration / Statistic View
EEP-to-AOL	ALAN proxylet technology

Because of the "Type of payload" and "Payload" fields, AOL protocol packets allow the exchange of various types of data. Route advertisement and topology information are the most important for topology control. However, the payload may be an encapsulated Gnutella packet that will be tunneled through the AOL overlay.

All elements within this version of the AOL proxylet are connected via a modular design. So it is possible to include custom needs at different positions within the code. The main parts of the AOL proxylet are:

- Connection Manager (manages all connections, outgoing and incoming)
- Router (tree like connected modules, see Figure 8)
- Protocol (packet interfaces, protocol specific implementations)
- Configuration (create specific configurations for included modules)

Different connections can be added to the connection manager. The connection manager will manage all connection listeners as well as all active connections. If a connection is shut down, either by a user, due to a network error, or by the topology control mechanism, the connection manager will "clean up" this connection. Besides that, the connection manager provides information about all active connections, in order to support control loops. There are values like connection type, destination, simple statistics, errors logs kept within this module etc.

The router is the central module of an AOL proxylet. It is itself internally organized in a modular way. As illustrated in the Figure 7 below, the *root element* is the entry node of the entire router. Every connection module delivers the received packets to the root element of the router, where all active connections are added as possible routes. All elements after the root element process the packets according to their specific capabilities, e.g. Gnutella protocol routing or AOL protocol routing. Every element decides on its own whether it should handle a packet or not. The different elements are grouped according to their purpose (Gnutella Router, AOL proxylet

Router). At the end of each path the *send element* is found. The send element is either forwarding the packet to another peer or is able to relay the packet via tunnel to another AOL proxylet.

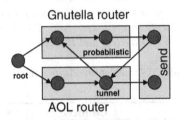

Fig. 7. Information flow in the router module of the AOL proxylet.

An AOL-specific module is the configuration module, which allows the transmission of commands via a telnet console from an administrator over the network. It will also contain in future versions an interface to receive configuration data through other AOL proxylets from the same AVP. This way, it will be possible for the AOL proxylet to establish a connection to another AOL proxylet or peer to support self-organization mechanisms.

5 Performance of AVP Concept

The performance of the AVP concept has to be characterized within the context of three areas: *a)* the overhead introduced by the AVP concept in relaying P2P protocol messages, *b)* the impact of the new routing strategies implemented by the AVP on network load, and *c)* the change of the overall performance of the P2P application, e.g. the boost of stability in the P2P overlay by using the AVP.

Overhead: For the intra-AVP and inter-AVP communication, cf. Section 4, the following protocol overhead is introduced due to packet encapsulation. Each relayed packet, i.e. Gnutella packet in the case of this prototype, will be extended by an additional 40 bytes header. The overhead introduced by the encapsulation is considerable but permits the distinct handling of messages without holding state information as for tunnels needed.

Impact of AVP Routing Strategies on Network Load: If necessary, the network load can be reduced immediately and locally by the AVP concept. If an intra-AVP or inter-AVP connection is overloaded, i.e. an AVP experiences reduced packet throughput on that connection, the AOL component of an AVP has two choices as examined in Section 4 ("Routing Control and Load Balancing" and "Topology Control"): It may alter the path, e.g. set up a new virtual connection to another AOL which can relay the messages more appropriately, or it may drop distinct signalling packets randomly on a path. The latter mechanism can be applied in Gnutella without severe degradation of the service since Gnutella applies multi-path broadcasting instead of unicast communication.

P2P Service Performance and Overlay Stability: Previous studies have revealed a high variability of the original Gnutella overlay [3]. For example, the observed average overlay connection holding time in this study was 405 sec with a 90% interval of approximately 10^-1 sec and 10^3 sec, cf. Figure 8. This average is very short compared with typical overlay architectures such as VPNs (Virtual Private Networks). The high variability is, of course, a result of the key P2P characteristic that a peer may leave or join the network arbitrarily, a feature which should be maintained. The AVP concept is capable of decoupling the peer behaviour from the AVP behaviour and the AVP overlay behaviour in particular. The connection holding time of the intra- and inter-AVP connections is can be chosen to be much larger than that of ordinary peers. This way, the AVP concept offers always stable overlay connectivity for peers. The increased the stability of the AVP overlay, in turn, boosts the stability of the Gnutella service.

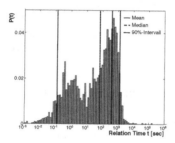

Fig. 8. Observed Gnutella Overlay Connection Holding Time Distribution [3].

In addition, an AVP is composed of multiple nodes, holding redundant information in an effective way. So it is possible that an AVP can leave the structure only with loosing a minimum of information, for example about routing or alternative available nodes. This way, the AVP concept may permit a more failsafe overlay and increases the resilience performance feature on P2P systems.

Finally, the performance and scalability of other P2P services was significantly boosted with the introduction of self-organizing hierarchy. Gnutella is the most famous example. With serious scalability problems and inefficient use of the resources in its first versions, it experienced serious performance gains upon the introduction of the "ultrapeers". Similarly, Kazaa became the leading P2P file-sharing application because of the efficient use of network resources, that the users viewed as better performance, enabled by the use of the "superpeer" concept. The AVP allows amongst other things the creation of a two-level or even multi-level hierarchy, so we anticipate significant performance gains offered to P2P applications.

6   Related Work

Earlier work on the virtualization of resources and group management of has been investigated by Birman et al. [17] in the ISIS toolkit. While appearing similar in architecture that approach provides limited support for autonomous node operation and self-organization.

The inability of Gnutella and most other P2P applications to maintain topology and membership information in an efficient manner has been partly acknowledged by Limewire, developers of Gnutella client software, who proposed the concept of Gnutella "ultrapeers" [9]. This concept suggests the creation of a two-level node hierarchy inside the GNet, where the "ultrapeers", i.e. nodes possessing better networking capabilities and processing power, take charge of much of the load from the slower peers by maintaining more overlay connections. The decreased number of nodes responsible for message handling and routing, reduces the signaling traffic significantly, as well as it makes the Gnutella network more scalable. The concept of AVPs is similar to the "ultrapeers" since both apply a peer hierarchy and reduce signaling traffic. AVPs differ from "ultrapeers", however, because of their overlay load control capability and adaptivity to the underlying network structure. The well-known Kazaa P2P filesharing service [18] applies a concept similar to "ultrapeers". In Kazaa these distinct nodes are denoted as "superpeers".

The Gnutella2 framework [10] extends the "original" Gnutella protocol beyond file sharing. The Gnutella2 architecture promotes "leaf mode" node operation, supports reliable UDP communication, enables bandwidth management schemes, and aims to create an efficient, self-organized P2P network. However the access control features in Gnutella2 are limited.

In [23], the authors suggest the use of dedicated P2P application "boosters" at the ingress/egress links of administrative domains with the aim of improving scalability and reducing signaling traffic of P2P file-sharing services. While they envisage multiple scattered boosters to create a two-level hierarchy achieving the aforementioned goal, their concept dramatically lacks flexibility. The formation of sets (groups) of nodes, based on application level and network level information, is examined in [24]. The authors describe many possible uses of that service, with P2P networking one of them. While in areas such as reliable multicast such a service may be beneficial, we argue that it is very demanding in terms of underlying network infrastructure (it assumes Ephemeral State Processing capabilities) and considerably inflexible when applied to P2P. Both approaches, [22] and [23], however, are limited in their capability to adapt toward varying network load condition in contrast to features of the AVP concept.

The OverQoS architecture [25] aims to provide QoS services for overlay networks. Dedicated OverQoS routers are placed at fixed points inside an ISP's (Internet Service Provider) network and connected through overlay links. The aggregation of flows into controlled flows of an overlay enables this architecture to adapt to varying capacities of the IP network and ensure a statistical guarantee to loss rates. This OverQoS approach complements and extends the limited load control provided so far in the AOL proxylet. However, it lacks any adaptivity to the varying network topology as addressed by the AVP.

Resilient overlay networks (RONs) [24] provide considerable control and choice on end hosts and applications on how data can be transmitted, with the aim of improving end-to-end reliability and performance. However, RONs are mostly restricted within single administrative domains..

Finally, the characterization and quantification of the connectivity topology characteristics is widely investigated. Power-law type or small-world topologies are widely identified with P2P systems [11,12] and are extensively examined as part of the AVP concept. Distributed Hash Tables have recently been widely introduced for search of information in P2P systems [13]. Examples include Pastry of Microsoft Research

[14], Chord from UC Berkeley and MIT [15] or CAN (Content Addressable Networks) form ICSI at UC Berkeley [16]. Measurement of duration and size of P2P connectivity in Gnutella overlays as well as topology control have been investigated in [3]. Understanding of P2P traffic volume and connectivity behavior is essential for network planning, traffic regulations, security assurance, performance guarantees and, possibly, revenue generation.

7 Conclusions

We have presented a new framework and an implementation technique for a flexible management of peer-to-peer overlays. The framework provides means for self-organization to yield an enhanced flexibility in instantiating control architectures in dynamic environments, which is regarded as being essential for P2P services.

Application level active networking (ALAN) was chosen as a natural vehicle to enable evolutionary adaptation on the application layer. P2P services can be predominately viewed as overlay networks which lend themselves to application level management and control in order to maintain their beneficial characteristics. In particular, the incorporation of ALAN maintains the decoupling of network and application layers while providing operational support at the same time. Furthermore, the ALAN infrastructure enables the AVP to respond to changing network conditions on the time scales that match network scales as well as native P2P application behavior by decoupling the P2P behavior from the AVP behavior.

The proposed concept relies on Active Virtual Peers as the main building block. The presented AVPs for Gnutella implement means for overlay control with respect to access, routing, topology forming, and application layer resource management. The AVP concept not only allows the combination of algorithms and techniques with proven merit that address only individual issues but allows them to operate over a flexible and adaptive framework. The significance of this approach lies with the expandability and adaptivity of the system as P2P services evolve.

In order to facilitate a more complete control, additional AVP features will be implemented in future work such as mechanisms that allow monitoring of overlay traffic and strategies for topology self-organization.

References

1. A. Ghosh, M. Fry, J. Crowcroft: "An architecture for application layer routing", Active Networks, LNCS 1942, H. Yasuda, Ed 2000, pp 71-86 Springer.
2. M. Fry, A. Ghosh: "Application level active networking", Computer Networks, 31 (7), 1999, pp. 655-667.
3. H. De Meer, K. Tutschku, P. Tran-Gia: ``Dynamic Operation in Peer-to-Peer Overlay Networks'', Praxis der Informationsverarbeitung und Kommunikation, (PIK Journal), Special Issue on Peer-to-Peer Systems, Volume 26 No 2, pp 65-73, June 2003.
4. H. De Meer, K. Tutschku, "Dynamic Operation in Peer-to-Peer Overlays", poster session, proceedings of 4th Annual International Working Conference on Active Networks, ETH Zurich, Switzerland, 4-6 Dec 2002

5. T. Klingberg, R. Manfredi, "The Gnutella protocol version 0.6 draft", Gnutella developer forum (http://groups.yahoo.com/group/the_gdf/files/Development/), 2002
6. Anonymous, "Gnut: console Gnutella client for Linux and Windows", http://www.gnutelliums.com/linux_unix/gnut/, 2001
7. B. Fortz, M. Thorup, "Internet traffic engineering by optimising OSPF weights", Proceeding of IEEE INFOCOM 2002, pp 519-528, 2000
8. X. Xiao, A. Hannah, B. Bailey, S.Carter, L.M. Ni, "Traffic engineering with MPLS in the Internet", IEEE Network Magazine, vol. 14, no. 1, pp 28-33, 2000
9. A. Singla, C. Rohrs, "Ultrapeers; another step towards Gnutella scalability", Gnutella developer forum (http://groups.yahoo.com/group/the_gdf/files/Proposals/Ultrapeer/ Ultrapeers_1.0_ clean.html), 2002
10. M. Stokes, "Gnutella2 specification document – first draft", Gnutella2 website (http://www.gnutella2.com/gnutella2_draft.htm), 2003
11. A.L. Barabasi, R. Albert: "Emergence of Scaling in Random Networks", Science Vol. 286, 1999.
12. E. Cohen, S. Shenker: "Replication Structures in Unstructured Peer-to-Peer Networks", ACM SIGCOMM, Pittsburg 2002.
13. H. Balakrishnan, M.F. Kaashoek, D. Karger, R. Morris, I. Stoica: "Looking up Data in P2P Systems", Communications of the ACM, Vol 43, No. 2, February 2003.
14. M. Castro, P. Druschel, A.M. Kermarrec, A. Rowstrom: "One ring to rule them all: Service discovery and binding in structured peer-to-peer overlay networks", SIGOPS, France, September 2002.
15. I. Stoica, R. Morris, D. Karger, M.F. Kaashoek, H. Balakrishnan: "Chord: A Scalable Peer-to-Peer Lookup Service for Internet Applications", ACM SIGCOMM`01, San Diego, September 2001.
16. S. Ratnasami: "A Scalable Content-Addressable Network", PhD Thesis, UC Berkeley, October 2002.
17. K. P. Birman et al, Isis – A Distributed Programming Environment: User's Guide and Reference Manual Verion 2.1, Dept. Computer Science, Cornell Univ., Ithaca, N.Y., Sept. 1990.
18. Kazaa Media Desktop http://www.kazaa.com.
19. Q. Lv, S. Ratnasamy, S. Shenker: "Can Heterogeneity Make Gnutella Scalable?", Proceedings for the 1st International Workshop on Peer-to-Peer Systems (IPTPS '02), Cambridge, MA, USA, March 2002.
20. MetaMachine Inc. http://www.edonkey2000.com
21. I. Clarke, S. Miller, T. Hong, O. Sandberg, B. Wiley: "Protecting Free Expression Online with Freenet" IEEE Internet Computing, Vol. 6, No. 1, pages 40-49, January/February 2002.
22. S. Rooney, D. Bauer, P. Scotton, "Efficient Programmable Middleboxes for Scaling Large Distributed Applications", IEEE OpenArch 2003, 2003
23. A. Sehgal, K.l. Calvert, J. Griffioen, "A Generic Set-Formation Service", IEEE OpenArch 2003, 2003
24. D.G. Andersen, H. Balakrishnan, M.F. Kaashoek, R. Morris, "Resilient Overlay Networks", Proc. 18th ACM Symposium on Operating Systems Principles, 2001.
25. L. Subramanian, I. Stoica, H. Balakrishnan, R. Katz: "OverQoS: Offering Internet QoS Using Overlays", Proc. of 1st HotNets Workshop, October 2002.
26. A. Galis, S. Denazis, C. Klein, C. Brou, "Programmable Networks and their Management", Artech House, 2004

Author Index